David Dufty is a historian and researcher. He is the author of *The Secret Code Breakers of Central Bureau*, winner of the 2017 Nib Military History Prize, and of *Radio Girl*, the story of a pioneering engineer and wartime legend.

NABBING NED KELLY

The extraordinary true story of the men who
brought Australia's notorious outlaw to justice

DAVID DUFTY

ALLEN&UNWIN
SYDNEY•MELBOURNE•AUCKLAND•LONDON

Allen & Unwin
83 Alexander Street
Crows Nest NSW 2065
Australia
Phone: (61 2) 8425 0100
Email: info@allenandunwin.com
Web: www.allenandunwin.com

 A catalogue record for this book is available from the National Library of Australia

ISBN 978 1 761067 34 1

Internal design by Midland Typesetters, Australia
Set in 12/17 pt Adobe Garamond Pro by Midland Typesetters, Australia
Printed in Australia by McPherson's Printing Group

10 9 8 7 6 5 4 3 2 1

The paper in this book is FSC® certified. FSC® promotes environmentally responsible, socially beneficial and economically viable management of the world's forests.

They laughed and lark'd at what they'd done as from the town they turn'd,
They rode away like brigands bold—the Kellys, Hart, and Byrne.
They chatter now about police, and say they're not effective,
But the fear of God is in their hearts of Michael Ward, detective.

Corowa Free Press, 13 June 1879

Contents

Seeking the Kelly Brothers

After Stringybark

Euroa

Jerilderie

Agents

Glenrowan

Epilogue: Two mysteries and their possible solutions

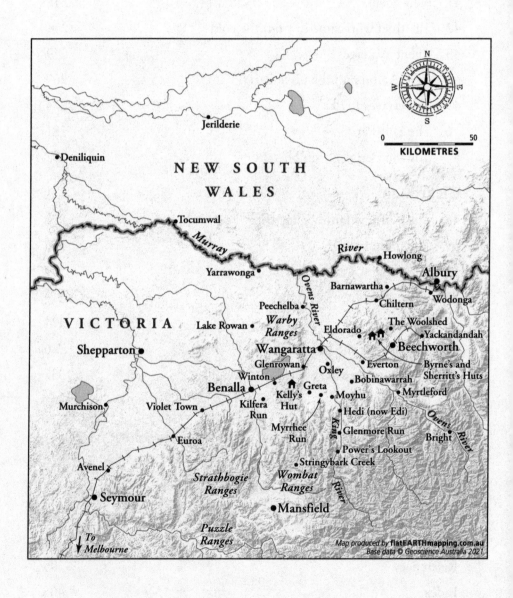

Introduction

Ned Kelly was tall, strong, good-looking, charismatic and a formidable hand-to-hand brawler. But he was no hero. A compulsive liar, he was also paranoid and delusional.

Ned was good at crime. He was the architect of a large inter-colonial criminal syndicate at a time when police were unaccustomed to dealing with organised crime. He stole cattle, horses, guns and gold. He robbed banks. He murdered. And in the end, he was undone by an insane plan to commit an act of mass murder.

I'm sure you've heard the legends about him. That he was an Australian Robin Hood. That the murders he committed were in self-defence. That the bank robberies and kidnappings were merely ploys to raise awareness of police injustice. That the common people supported him because he opposed greedy, rich landholders. But none of those things are true, nor are many other things said about him.

The original idea for this book was to tell the story of the Kelly Gang from the police point of view. It seemed like an intriguing, exciting and overlooked angle on a popular topic. The end result—the book you're holding now—is still broadly in line with that vision, but it has evolved into a wider investigation of myths and lies. That wasn't the plan, but the deeper I dug, the more it became an imperative.

There was already so much written and said about Kelly; it was overwhelming. How could one person possibly read it all? There have been dozens of books, as well as songs, plays, poems, documentaries, websites and movies. But then came the realisation: all those books,

1

movies, documentaries and so on used the same original source material, so why not start with that? So I initially skipped past all the other books about the Kelly Gang and went right back to basics, studying the original police reports, news coverage and the proceedings of the 1881 Police Royal Commission.

Only after immersing myself in the archival sources, and through them forming my own view of events, did I explore the work of others. That approach—of rebuilding the story from its foundations—has led me to question almost everything about the standard historical narrative about the Kelly Gang, and to counter much of what is considered to be fact. The version of events you're about to read here is at odds with most versions you're likely to find elsewhere.

The 'Kelly outbreak', as it was called at the time, was a cataclysmic event. There was saturation news coverage of everything Kelly-related for more than two years, from the Stringybark Creek murders in 1878 to sometime after Kelly's execution in November 1880. The news articles retained by the National Library of Australia are a goldmine of contemporary—and sometimes primary—sources. The public records are a wealth of data too: while many aspects of colonial life were rudimentary, Victoria was ahead of other colonies in record-keeping, and consequently there are thousands of pages of official documents, ranging from detective reports to witness affidavits to internal memos, all in the Victorian Public Record Office.

During his reign of terror, Kelly made accusations of police persecution which gained widespread media coverage. In 1881 the Victorian government established a Royal Commission to investigate the causes of the Kelly outbreak and the police response. The Commissioners found no evidence that Kelly or his family were persecuted. Likewise, in searching the various archives 140 years later, I didn't find any evidence of it either. The Royal Commission cross-examined more than 60 witnesses, and the transcripts of those cross-examinations provide fascinating firsthand accounts of events.

Those stories form the backbone of this book, providing a rich cast of characters from every rung of the ladder. At the top is the police commissioner, Captain Standish, a colourful, deeply flawed character with enough redeeming features to make him likeable; vain and inept senior officers; drunk inspectors; taciturn sergeants; and constables who ranged from cowardly to courageous. And in the midst of it all is the Irish-born Detective Michael Ward, unjustly portrayed as a minor villain in Kelly mythology, who was Kelly's most dogged and tenacious adversary.

When I eventually delved into the subgenre known as Kellyana, I discovered that modern retellings of the Ned Kelly story don't much resemble the narrative that emerges from the archival documents. In some cases, it appears that historians have wilfully distorted the historical picture. Most astonishing was my discovery that Ned Kelly himself has been used as a primary historical source.

For example, most versions of the Kelly story feature Kelly's step-father, George King, as his partner in crime for a string of robberies. That's what Ned claimed. Yet there is no mention of George King in any newspaper of the day or in archival records, other than a mention of his marriage to Ned's mother, Ellen, in 1874. The local police had not even heard of him. He seems to have just disappeared, if he existed at all. George King does not feature in this book.

In one of his famous *Ned Kelly Series* paintings, Sidney Nolan depicted Constable Fitzpatrick with his arm seductively around Ned's sister Kate, with Ned's figure seen outside through the window. Nolan commented on the historical basis of the artwork, saying, 'The action looks a little comic but it began the real trouble.' Since he was an artist rather than a historian, Nolan can be forgiven for believing that falsehood. There are varying accounts of the young policeman's seduction of Kate, but they're all wrong. Not only is there no evidence for it, Ned Kelly himself denied that it happened.

Fitzpatrick is a much-maligned figure in the fantasy world inhabited by Kelly mythologists. Many claim that when Constable Fitzpatrick came to arrest Ned's brother Dan, he was drunk. There is no evidence for that, other than that he had a single drink earlier in the day, midway on his two-hour journey. It is also said that Fitzpatrick was an alcoholic, and that he died of cirrhosis of the liver, but he wasn't, and he didn't.

Ned Kelly claimed that he murdered three police at Stringybark Creek in self-defence, but the forensic evidence, and the testimony of the only police survivor of the massacre, comprehensively refuted that version of events. Yet Ned's version is routinely treated as historical fact.

It is said that the courts had it in for him, yet the opposite was true. Browsing court reports in old newspapers, I discovered that district magistrates, either through corruption or fear, went easy on crime, using any paltry excuse to acquit. Prosecutors struggled to produce witnesses, who failed to appear, or changed their testimony on the stand, or simply vanished before they had a chance to testify.

There are plenty more myths. Many arise either from strange and unreliable source material, such as interviews with the children or grandchildren of people who were there, or second- or third-hand memoirs that amount to nothing more than rumour and hearsay. Others arise from cherrypicked or misinterpreted quotes from the proceedings of the Royal Commission. It's appalling.

I am not the first to discover the hollow heart of the Ned Kelly myth. Others have challenged the lies, but their voices have been drowned beneath the chorus of adulation for a manipulative, violent psychopath.

But this is not Ned Kelly's story.

This is the story of the men who tried to bring him to justice.

The Days of Harry Power

I

Magistrate McBean's heirloom watch

Robert McBean was a squatter and magistrate from north-eastern Victoria. He owned Kilfera, a large sheep station (called a 'run'), near the township of Benalla. He was doing reasonably well, although Kilfera's soil wasn't as fertile as that of nearby runs. He had also lost some of his land, which had been sold off by the government in small parcels known as 'selections', under recent land reform laws.

While patrolling his property on horseback on a pleasant afternoon in March 1870, he noticed two horsemen. The older of the two, a bushranger known as Harry Power, approached McBean. The younger man held back and turned away, as if concerned that McBean would recognise him. And indeed, McBean believed he did recognise him as Ned Kelly, a young man he had seen in court a time or two.

Harry Power ordered McBean to dismount. When McBean refused, Power drew a revolver, pointed it at him, and asked a second time. McBean dismounted.

Power wanted cash, but McBean had none—after all, he was just riding around his own property. However, he was carrying a watch. That would do. Power told him to tie the watch to the horse's bridle, then, after he did so, Power led the horse away.

The gold watch was a cherished family heirloom and worth more than the horse.[1]

McBean was particularly aggrieved by the robbery because he believed that as a magistrate he had cultivated a tacit understanding with the local criminals through leniency and generosity. The judiciary would go easy on well-connected organised criminals, and in turn would either get a quiet bonus, or would not be targeted for crime. Their stock would not be stolen, nor would their haystacks catch fire overnight.[2]

Harry Power, whose real name was Henry Johnson, had escaped from Pentridge Prison a year earlier in February 1869. He had been serving time with hard labour for shooting a policeman and horse theft. He was also suspected of two murders, never proven.

One day, while working in the prison labour gang he lay down in a grassy hollow and waited for nightfall. When the guards escorted the other prisoners back inside the prison walls, he fled. By the time they realised he was gone it was too late.

He had scars on his right cheek, forehead and arms, and the third finger on his left hand was deformed. His feet were so diseased with bunions that he had trouble walking and needed oversized boots.[3]

Despite being easily recognised and hobbled by disease, he wasn't caught. Power headed to north-eastern Victoria, to the hills and mining towns of the Ovens and Murray River catchments, where he took refuge with old mates and resumed his life of crime. Over the next year, he robbed rich and poor alike, appearing with his shotgun and shouting the infamous bushranging cry, 'Bail up!'. He bailed up stagecoaches, farmhouses, liquor stores, lonely travellers and itinerant workers. He set fire to a store in Gundagai, savagely beat a Chinese miner who refused to obey him, and stole a little boy's comforter at gunpoint. He boasted that he loved targeting farmhouses after the husband had gone to work and the wife was home alone. He criss-crossed the colony, sometimes committing robberies more than a hundred miles distant in the space of a day.[4]

There were reports that he had a young accomplice who was initially known only by the name 'Lake'. The identity of his accomplice had now been established by McBean as Ned Kelly, a lad who

lived with his mother and several siblings on a small property near
Greta, east of Benalla.[5]

Some months before he was robbed, McBean had gone to court
after two of his employees had stolen and killed two of his sheep. There
he had encountered Ned Kelly. One of the thieves, Alex Gunn, was
Ned Kelly's brother-in-law. The teenaged Kelly appeared as a witness
for the defence, claiming he had sold Gunn the sheep. When asked
what brands the sheep had, Kelly said there were no brands. Keeping
a straight face, he explained it was because they were pets.[6]

Gunn was issued with a £10 fine, a slap on the wrist for a crime
that attracted serious prison time.

Edward Kelly, better known as Ned Kelly, was probably born in
June 1855, in the colony of Victoria. His parents were both Irish.
His father, John 'Red' Kelly, had been transported to a prison in Van
Diemen's Land as a convict, gained freedom and tried to make a new
life in Victoria. But he was a heavy drinker and died of alcohol-related
illness when Ned was still a boy.[7]

Ned's mother Ellen had come to Victoria in 1841 as a child with
her parents and many siblings, as free settlers. Her father, James Quinn
senior, was a hard worker and a prudent saver who had hoped his children
would have a better life in Victoria than the impoverished existence they
had left behind in Ireland. But it turned out that Ellen's brothers cared
only for drinking and stealing cattle. It was generally said that James
was an honest man, although the land he purchased—the Glenmore
Run—was on the stock-smuggling route through the King Valley.[8]

After Red died, Ellen had other lovers and more children. Ned fell
under the influence of his criminal uncles, then took up bushranging
with the notorious Harry Power. Meanwhile, a plan to end Power
and Kelly's crime spree was born over drinks at an exclusive club in
Melbourne.

2

The Melbourne Club

The Melbourne Club on Collins Street looks much the same today as it did in 1870. The lampposts at the entry, the three-storey brick-and-stucco walls, the bay windows, the basement windows below street level that peer onto the mossy servants' alley. Inside, there is still a labyrinth of hallways, entryways, bedrooms, sitting rooms and dining rooms. Of course, there aren't stables anymore—those are long gone—along with the servants living in the basement. But it's largely unchanged from a century and a half ago. And furthermore, it's still an exclusive men's club, restricted to men of status and wealth in Melbourne society.

It was founded in 1838 by a group of 23 'gentlemen', most of whom were wealthy farmers who wanted the club to provide a comfortable place for them to stay when visiting Melbourne. The membership soon expanded to include lawyers, bureaucrats, military officers, merchants and other respectable professions. Nobody pays attention to the Melbourne Club these days. It's a historical curiosity, a quiet feature of the city that somehow resisted the sweep of progress. It has no influence and, for the most part, attracts little ire.[1]

Not like then. Not like the days when a new governor's first social engagement, after stepping ashore from England, would be to dine as guest of honour at the Club; when most parliamentarians were Club members; or when a Victorian premier attacked 'the clique or cabal who aspire through the Melbourne Club to rule the colony . . .'[2]

9

But even then, its political power was exaggerated. Its membership included politicians of all political stripes, not just reactionaries, and even included that bane of squatters, Premier James McCulloch. And the Club, perhaps sensitive to such criticisms, went to lengths to quash any hint of political activity behind its austere walls. Activism, including the circulating of petitions, was forbidden. Private discussions over a cigar and brandy were acceptable.

Which brings us to March 1870, to a private conversation over brandy between two club members. One of them was Robert McBean. The other was Captain Frederick Standish, the chief commissioner of police. McBean was telling Standish about his recent experience on his farm.[3]

In their conversation McBean complained bitterly that Harry Power had been terrorising the north-eastern towns near the Ovens River for more than a year, and the police had done nothing. Why?

Well, he and Standish both knew the answer to that. The police force was a shambles.

Frederick Standish had been born into a wealthy upper-class English family, had mixed with royalty, and had held the rank of captain in the British army. But he was a man of pleasure, and amassed such a colossal gambling debt that he had fled Britain for Victoria under the pseudonym F.C. Selwyn, without a penny to his name. He became a miner in Ballarat in 1852, experiencing firsthand the tyranny of the goldfields police and bureaucrats prior to the Eureka rebellion. Eventually, desperate for income, he dropped the pseudonym and entered the public service. He ascended quickly. The following year he was appointed to the role of 'Chinese Protector,' a position created in response to ethnic tensions on the goldfields. Standish took to it with gusto, using his position to champion the interests of the Chinese community. On one occasion, an inter-racial couple—a Chinese man and a Caucasian woman—came to him for help, complaining that the local clergy had refused to conduct their wedding. Standish conducted the ceremony himself, pronounced them man and wife, then forged the name of the town's Anglican priest on the registration document.[4] In 1858, he was appointed as chief commissioner of police, and became responsible for reforming a dysfunctional service.[5]

In the earliest days of the colony, police had been recruited primarily from ex-convicts, and although that hiring practice had now ceased, many were still either former convicts or former convict guards. There had been no entry requirements until 1853—not even the ability to read and write—and no training. Alcoholism was rampant. The force had come under public and political scrutiny after the Eureka rebellion on the Ballarat goldfields. A reformer, Standish managed the evolution of the force into a functional, respectable institution.[6]

But old habits returned. With his generous salary, he resumed gambling and drinking. His parties and all-night card games were legendary.

Standish's love of pleasure was his greatest weakness, and led to his greatest failing as chief commissioner. He was fond of his drinking and gambling friends, and officers who aspired to higher ranks discovered an easy pathway to promotion. Standish played favourites, and in this, his judgement was clouded. He had only partial control over promotions, which were ultimately decided by the politicians, but to the extent that he did, he did not always choose well.

The Melbourne Club became a second home to him, and indeed in 1872, two years after the conversation with McBean, he moved in permanently, conducting the business of running the Victorian police force from its cloistered private rooms.

As the evening wore on at the Melbourne Club, a waiter dressed in blue-and-red livery with gilt buttons kept up the flow of drinks while

McBean and Standish talked over the Harry Power problem. Power must be getting local assistance, and McBean had an idea how he might discover who had been helping him. Power had served time in Pentridge with a local thief named Jack Lloyd, who had since been released. The Lloyd family were notorious criminals, and Jack Lloyd himself was married to a Quinn, which made him Ned Kelly's uncle. Lloyd probably knew who was harbouring Power.

Standish proposed that Jack Lloyd could be recruited as a 'fiz-gig'—a paid informer who would share in the reward then being offered for information leading to Harry Power's capture. He proposed a plan to McBean, one that bypassed the incompetent local police. McBean was sceptical, but he really wanted his watch back.[7]

3

The fiz-gig

Under Standish's instructions, a warrant was issued for Jack Lloyd's arrest, and he was arrested on 9 April 1870 by two Melbourne detectives. The warrant was bogus; they arrested him for an armed hold-up near Seymour that they knew had been committed by Power. The local police were cut completely out of the loop. The next day he was transported to Seymour lock-up, awaiting a hearing. He was a captive audience for Robert McBean's proposal. McBean told Lloyd about his watch, stolen by Power, and said he wanted it back. If Lloyd was willing, he could meet McBean at Kilfera Station for further discussions. It seems he was willing, because when he appeared in Seymour court, all charges were either dropped or dismissed.[1]

The second part of Standish's plan was to increase the reward money for the capture of Power, to make it worth Lloyd's while. Standish made the case to the chief secretary, who increased the reward to £500.[2]

In early May, Standish visited the police depot at the Melbourne suburb of Richmond, where he had a quiet chat with Superintendent Frank Hare. He explained the set-up he had arranged with McBean and Lloyd to catch Harry Power, and asked (or rather ordered) Hare to run the operation. The chief secretary, James McCulloch, had directed him to place Frank Hare in charge.[3]

As Lloyd's visit to Kilfera Station was imminent, Standish told Hare to get on his way as soon as possible. He promised him that if he succeeded, he would be promoted at the next opportunity. Before parting, he gave Hare complete latitude: 'I leave you to make your own arrangements, and take with you whoever you please.'⁴

Frank Hare was a large, tough man. He had been born in South Africa in 1830, the youngest of twenty children. He arrived in Victoria to join the gold rush in 1852. He went from Ballarat to Beechworth and then to Bright, striking luck occasionally, but mostly striking dirt. He lived rough and poor, and had several run-ins with the police before throwing in his shovel and moving to Sydney, where he struggled to find work.

A well-connected relative, a distant cousin named Colonel Butterworth who was the governor of Singapore, looked him up when visiting Sydney. Butterworth pitied his sad, down-at-heel relative, so he pulled some strings and got Hare a job as a constable in the Victorian police. That was the extent of Hare's connections: he knew someone who knew someone who knew Captain Standish. He would never be a member of the Melbourne Club, enjoying port and cigars with Standish and his circle of judges and politicians. But it was enough to get a start. His experience on the goldfields helped.

Whenever gold was found in a creek or river, there was a 'new rush'. A city would grow and spread across river plains and mountain valleys like weeds, with winding mazes of tents, makeshift huts, and mine shafts. The muddy roads, carved by boots and wagon wheels, were lined with hawker carts, makeshift theatres and grog shops. Women mostly avoided these places; but male fortune-seekers, scoundrels and dreamers flocked to them. Theft, assault and murder were common. Riots sometimes broke out. The police were often simply engaged in crowd control. A big, burly police officer like Hare, who had been a miner himself, was ideally suited for the job.

At 40, he was putting on weight and slowing down, but was still fit and strong enough for a bushranger hunt.

As Hare prepared his horse and buggy, Superintendent Charles Nicolson came to Richmond depot. He told Hare that he knew about the mission and asked if he could come along. Head of the police district at Kyneton in the Macedon Ranges, Nicolson was currently in Melbourne on extended sick leave due to migraines and inflamed eyes.

Nicolson was Scottish, 41 years old, and had come to Victoria in 1852, the same year as Hare. But he had joined the police force a year earlier than Hare, which technically made him the senior officer of the two, a fact he liked to mention.

Nicolson would have been right at home in the Melbourne Club with Captain Standish, but he was not a brandy-and-cigar type. His wife, Helen, was the daughter of John Thomas Smith, a long-serving, prominent member of parliament and also one of Victoria's highest-ranking Freemasons. Nicolson's life was comfortable from start to finish. He had never lived in desperate poverty as Frank Hare (or Captain Standish, for that matter) had done. But many years earlier, as a young policeman, he had been responsible for a stunning act of bravery.

In his first year as a police cadet, he had been engaged with a small party of police in a search for some bushrangers and had come under fire. Nicolson tore up his own shirt to make a tourniquet for a colleague's wound, saving his life, then he and his superior galloped off in pursuit and engaged the bushrangers in another gunfight. Nicolson was shot in the face. The wound left a permanent scar and gave him migraines for the rest of his life.[5]

Nicolson had an excellent work ethic but a dour and condescending manner, perhaps exacerbated by chronic pain. He was also a snob. Standish referred to him behind his back as 'the cranky Scotchman'.

Around 10 May, they rode together in Hare's horse and buggy to Kilfera, where Robert McBean was expecting them. Jack Lloyd arrived. Hare spoke to Lloyd in private, then returned to tell the others the deal was off. Hare didn't trust Lloyd, and Lloyd didn't trust Hare.[6]

Nervously McBean said, 'If that be the case, what risk do I run now? Having trusted and arranged with this man to take the reward!'

It showed the power of the local criminal gangs, that a police magistrate was worried about being a police snitch.

Nicolson offered to try to win Lloyd over. He and Lloyd moved away and spoke privately; then when they returned, Nicolson announced that the deal was back on, with the proviso that Lloyd received all the reward money. Nicolson wrote him a memo, promising him the entire £500 if he helped to catch Power. The four arranged to meet again once Lloyd had made some inquiries.

Only days earlier, the local police had received a tip-off that Harry Power and Ned Kelly were at Kelly's mother's shanty, having ridden overnight after committing a distant robbery. At daybreak on 4 May, four police surrounded the Kelly shanty and moved in. They were led by District Superintendent Nicolas and also included Sergeant James Whelan, Constable Mullane and Constable Arthur. Harry Power was gone, but young Ned was home, so they brought him in.[7]

A crowd gathered in Benalla to see the arrested bushranger. Kelly was in a cheerful mood, smiling and nodding at familiar faces as he was taken to the Benalla lock-up.[8]

The township of Benalla was quite close to McBean's Kilfera run, around ten miles further west. Nicolson and Hare decided to take advantage of this development. They visited young Kelly in the Benalla lock-up to see if *he* would give up Power, but he wouldn't. Hare dismissed him as a 'flash, ill-looking young blackguard'. They returned to Melbourne, to wait for details about the next meeting with their fiz-gig, Jack Lloyd.[9]

Ned Kelly stood trial in Benalla on 12 May for two separate charges of robbery.

The first charge was for assisting Power in the McBean robbery. Robert McBean appeared as a witness, but said that he could not identify Kelly as Power's assistant because 'the lad had his back to me the whole time'. That case was dismissed.

The second charge was for robbing a wool sorter named Joseph Bolwoski, bailed up at gunpoint as he walked home after work near Seymour. Kelly had allegedly aimed a double-barrelled shotgun at Bolwoski while Power searched him, robbing Bolwoski of £5, a pistol, some powder, bullets, caps, and various other small items.[10]

The prosecutor admitted he had no witnesses. The police had made extensive inquiries, but Joseph Bolwoski had vanished. Since the victim, who was the only witness to the crime, could not be found, that case was also dismissed. Kelly was then transported to Kyneton, further south, to face a third charge of armed robbery.[11]

It was alleged that he and Power had bailed up two herdsmen named Murray and O'Leary, keeping them hostage until after dark. It has sometimes been said that Kelly was a kind of Robin Hood, but he and Power were not above robbing poor rural working men or struggling shopkeepers. However, like Joseph Bolwoski, the Kyneton witnesses could not be found.[12]

Nicolson lived in Kyneton, as he was the head of Kyneton police district. When Kelly was transferred to the lock-up there, Nicolson visited him a second time, to try to get him to turn on Power. Kelly provided some useful snippets. He warned Nicolson to be careful when approaching Power's encampment, because there was a hollow tree that could be used as a guard house, with holes in the trunk for shooting at intruders. Nicolson called it 'Power's watchbox'. In the process of gaining information from Kelly, Nicolson must have revealed that Power's capture was imminent; because he engineered the court proceedings to retain Kelly for an extra week, due to the risk that Kelly would return to warn Power.[13]

In Melbourne, Frank Hare added two personnel to the team: his clerk, Sergeant Montfort; and a blacktracker named Donald.[14] He sent them to Benalla in advance, where they slept at the police barracks while awaiting instructions. The local police remained in the dark.

Jack Lloyd was ready to meet. Hare sent an enciphered telegram instructing Montfort and Donald to go to Kilfera Station on Sunday 29 May. Hare and Nicolson arrived at the farmhouse the night before. Montfort and Donald arrived on the Sunday. A nervous Jack Lloyd was there as well.[15]

4

It takes a thief to catch a thief

On Thursday 2 June, the search party of five men left Kilfera Station: Hare, Nicolson, Montfort, Donald, and Jack Lloyd as their guide. Before they left, McBean provided £15 for Lloyd to pay Power in exchange for the gold watch. To avoid attention, they took a circuitous route through hills and forests, avoiding roads and farms.

On Friday, they came to the boundary fence of the Glenmore Run. The large station on the upper reaches of the King River was the property of the Quinn family.

With the death of James Quinn senior from dysentery a year earlier, the Glenmore Run was now held in his wife's name, but effectively under the control of his many children, Ned Kelly's aunts and uncles.

James Quinn senior had not only worked hard, he had saved and made astute investments. But his children had not continued in the same way. The Glenmore Run remained forested and uncleared, the buildings and fences run-down. Its potential remained untapped.

The police search party made camp in a secluded spot several miles from the farmhouse.

With McBean's £15 in his pocket, Jack Lloyd left them and went to the Quinn farmhouse. The three police and the blacktracker waited for his return, dining on cold provisions.

Jack Lloyd returned on Saturday evening, and reported success. He pulled out a small object wrapped in a handkerchief from his pocket. He opened it and showed them: it was the gold watch that Power had relinquished for the £15. Lloyd had been escorted to Harry Power's hideout to do the exchange, and could now lead them there. It was up in the ranges behind the Glenmore Run, and it could only be accessed, as far as he knew, by the gully where the Quinn farmhouse was situated. He said that on the approach to Power's hut was a hollow tree with a bed in it—although it was unoccupied.

But they could not get past the farmhouse undetected because the Quinns kept dogs that would bark at intruders, sounding the alarm. There was also a large peacock that roosted on the roof which would make a shrill cry if it saw them.

Hare dismissed those concerns. As he saw it, having come so far, they had no alternative but to try.

Jack Lloyd was terrified. If the Quinns saw him with the police, he would be in deep trouble. He wanted to leave, but Hare made him stay. He ran off. With Donald's help they tracked him down. Hare threatened to shoot Lloyd if he tried to escape again. They went through the pass into the valley of the Glenmore run, and from there travelled through an endless succession of creeks and ferns; the ride to the farmhouse seemed to take forever. Lloyd was leading them astray: they were lost.

Hare asked Donald if he could take them back to where they had started.

Donald said simply, 'Yes, you've been going around in circles all night.'

He led them to the spot where they had camped, and from there to the Quinn farmhouse. As they were making plans to sneak past and into the ranges, there was a huge downpour.

It was a stroke of luck: they slipped past the Quinns' farmhouse unnoticed.

If they wanted to catch Harry Power, they knew they needed to find him before sunrise. But in the dark, wet forest, again Lloyd could not find his way. He broke down and cried.

Hare asked Donald if he could locate the tracks that Jack Lloyd and the Quinn brothers had made the previous day. Donald set out, returning a while later to report success. He then led the way, while Lloyd hung back, miserable and waiting for another chance to escape.

It was daybreak when they found the hollow tree with the bed inside it.

They scanned the cloudy sky for signs of smoke, in case Power had lit a fire, and Donald said he could tell there was a fire up along the mountain.

They left Lloyd at the hollow tree while Donald led them higher up the ridge, where they discovered a gunyah. They could see the feet of a man lying on a bed inside.

The three officers rushed the gunyah, grabbed Power by the ankles, and dragged him outside. He had been fast asleep, and howled in surprise when they grabbed him. They arrested him and slapped on some handcuffs.

Power asked who they were, and how they got up there.

'We're from Melbourne, and came past the Quinns' house,' Hare told him.

Power replied, 'No fear. You couldn't have passed without the dogs and peacock giving the alarm.'

'We did pass them.'

They searched Power's gunyah, where they found his double-barrelled shotgun slung from a pole and pointing down the hill. If he had been awake, he could easily have shot them.

They were all hungry and asked him for some food. Power said, 'If you go to that tree, you'll find some fine corned beef.'

And so they did. They also found tea, sugar, and bread in the tent.

Donald said with delight, 'Oh golly, what a feed we shall have!'

They had a hearty breakfast before taking Power back down the mountain. When they returned to the hollow tree, Jack Lloyd was gone.

In the valley below, as they reached the Quinn farmhouse, the dogs barked and the peacock shrieked. The Quinns sullenly watched the procession of police ride by with Harry Power in handcuffs.

Power was very talkative, relating bushranging stories as they rode to Wangaratta. The stories made his escapades sound like good, harmless fun.

It was late Sunday morning, and the Wangaratta church services were all finishing. Word spread quickly and the townsfolk hurried from church to see the famous bushranger brought into town.

Power called out to bystanders, 'They have got poor Power at last! But they caught him asleep.'[1]

When the time came for Power's trial at Beechworth Courthouse, the three police transported him to Beechworth in Frank Hare's horse and buggy, with Power again regaling Hare with tales of his exploits.

As they neared Beechworth, Power thanked Hare for treating him so well. As a gift of gratitude, he offered Hare his magnificent black mare, describing where the horse could be found in the Warby Ranges. Hare asked him where he had acquired her.

Power answered, 'You mustn't ask me that question.'

'Did you get her on the square?' Hare persisted.

'No.'

'Then I can have nothing to do with her.'[2]

They arrived in Beechworth with Nicolson at the reins of the buggy and Power beside him. Montfort and Hare followed on horseback. (This arrangement was probably at the insistence of Nicolson, who liked to remind the others that he was the most senior of the three.)

A crowd had gathered near the courthouse to watch Power's arrival. He doffed his hat and bade them 'Good morning!'.

Harry Power was tried for robbery under arms, specifically for bailing up the Buckland coach and its passengers. He pleaded guilty and was sentenced to fifteen years imprisonment. He did not face trial for any of the hundreds of other robberies and assaults he had committed. It may be that the police considered that, given his age (he was about 50) and the long sentence, there was no point in further prosecutions.[3]

He was transported to Melbourne by coach and regaled Frank Hare, who accompanied him on the journey, with yet more stories of the bushranging life. Hare later published much that Power had told him in his book, *The Last of the Bushrangers*.

Harry Power was ultimately deposited back in Pentridge Prison, from where he had originally escaped. Reporters remarked on his cheerfulness, politeness and courtesy towards his captors.[4]

Two days before Power's capture, Ned Kelly had been released from Kyneton lock-up. Journalists drew the obvious conclusion that the old bushranger had been betrayed by his protégé, and Harry Power came to the same conclusion. He publicly badmouthed Ned Kelly for years. There was some truth in that: Kelly had revealed some information to Nicolson (although exactly how much is unclear) and was paid £3.[5]

Soon after returning home, Kelly wrote to Sergeant Babington in Kyneton:

> I would like to know what you and Mister Nickelson would do for me I have done all circumstances would alow me which you now try what you can do answer this leter as soon as posabel direct your letter Daniel Kelly Gretta post office that is my name no more at present
>
> Every one looks on me like a black snake send me an answer as soon as posable[6]

Jack Lloyd was a lucky man. Ned Kelly was the suspected fiz-gig, and Lloyd was in the clear. The reward money was placed in the care of a trusted person, who doled it out to him in small amounts when required.

Four years later, Jack Lloyd hacked his neighbour's horse to death, and was sentenced to three years in prison. After his conviction, Beechworth's *Advertiser* exposed him as the fiz-gig who betrayed Power:

> **We have heard a great deal of Superintendent Nicolson's magnanimity in refusing the £500 reward for Power's arrest, when, in point of fact, the £500 was guaranteed in writing—there is no harm in saying it now, as the informer is secure in Pentridge—to the notorious Jack Lloyd, on condition of his putting Inspector Nicolson's hand upon the bushranger's shoulder.[7]**

Three years later, having served his time, Lloyd was released. Within weeks, his dead body was found on the road between Greta and Winton. The story was that he fell off his horse, drunk. There were rumours that he was pushed out of the saddle by a man riding beside him, but no concrete evidence ever surfaced.[8]

Stock Thieves

5

Constable Ward

Michael Edward Ward was born in Roscommon, Ireland, on 5 December 1845, the year that the potato blight came. The blight's arrival from North America coincided with unusually cool, wet weather that facilitated its spread. Ireland's rural poor, who subsisted on potato, watched their crops rot in the fields year after year. More than a million people starved to death. Many others emigrated to America, Australia and elsewhere.

Michael's family survived. They had a larger-than-average farm of about 30 acres, and his father supplemented their income at a local quarry. But life was tough for them.[1]

At the age of twenty, Ward left Ireland for Tasmania. His fare on the *Marco Polo* was paid by a local woman named Anne Shanny, of Moore. His travel documents listed his occupation as 'shepherd'. After a short stay in Tasmania, he went to New Zealand for two years, then arrived in Melbourne, where he found work as a storeman. In October 1869 he enlisted as a mounted constable and was sent to Beechworth.

Michael Ward is often described in history books as having a manicured, waxed moustache. This is due to a photograph taken when he was much older, decades after the events described here, when he wore spectacles and sported a well-groomed, curly moustache. Nobody actually knows what he looked like when he was young, whether he had a moustache all his life, or whether he cultivated it in later life. All that is known for certain is that he was handsome and well-groomed.

He arrived in the district when Harry Power was at large with the young Ned Kelly, and was quickly assigned to a search party led by Sergeant Bowes Wilson. With that patrol, he camped for 'days and weeks' in the wilderness of a strange, unfamiliar country.[2]

Where Ireland had lush, undulating plains, northern Victoria had dry, rocky hills. Instead of green fields cut with ash tree hedgerows, here the landscape was littered with straggly eucalypts and powdery wattles.

The search party never came close to finding Harry Power, who had the advantage of local knowledge and a network of allies. Wilson's patrol was ultimately sidelined by Standish's secret operation, run by Hare and Nicolson, to catch the bushranger.[3]

Ward was enlisted in another patrol three years later. Three men robbed a bakery, stole a gun, then shot and killed a publican with it because he refused to serve them. They fled into the bush. Under the command of Superintendent Brown, Ward and several other constables chased the murderers through the Pilot Ranges, north of Beechworth, catching them near a place called Watchbox Swamp.[4]

The scrubby mountain ranges were damp and cold in winter, but summers were blistering. During a December heatwave, while escorting a prisoner to the lock-up, Ward collapsed from sunstroke. The local newspaper noted with concern, 'Constable Ward is a useful officer, and the force could ill afford to lose him.'[5]

Like all unmarried policemen, Ward lived in the police barracks in Beechworth, subject to police rules and regulations every hour of every day. Beds were inspected, curfews were enforced, uniforms were expected to be in good shape. He worked eight hours a day, seven days a week. Policemen did not even get time off to attend church. He was retained in the Ovens district, rotating through the various towns and villages: Wangaratta, Eldorado and Greta.

Most of Ward's police colleagues were Irish too, with a smattering of Scots and a few others. Australian-born men simply did not sign up.

They shunned police work as a low-paid job for foreigners, and Irishmen in particular.

This curious phenomenon was not unique to Victoria. The police forces of New York and Boston were, at later times, famously dominated by Irish immigrants, as were forces in Canada, Scotland and elsewhere. The lure of police work for Irish expatriates worldwide has never been fully explained, but in the case of Victoria, it was partly because the conditions—meagre and harsh as they were—were superior to those for police in Ireland.[6]

Life in the Victorian police was regimented along military lines. There was an ongoing political struggle over the identity and role of the force. The previous commissioner, McMahon, preferred a quasi-military role, like the Irish constabulary; the current commissioner, Captain Standish, and others favoured a more community-based policing style, modelled on the London metropolitan police—the 'bobbies'. The result was a mixture. McMahon had left the force but he was now a parliamentarian and continued to impose his vision.

As was typical for constables, Ward was periodically reprimanded for the usual petty infractions. Being absent without leave from the barracks; not reporting when returning to the barracks; being twenty minutes late for morning stables; using 'insolent language' to the officer-in-charge when an application for leave was refused.[7]

His job entailed hard work across the full range of rural Victorian life, from neighbourhood disputes to serious crime. He arrested murderers, horse thieves, burglars and child molesters. He intervened in a dispute over the ownership of hens; caught a backyard clothesline thief; and when someone was hit by a train, he collected the strewn body parts and took them to the morgue.[8]

When a maid was charged with the theft of two pillows from a wealthy landowner, Ward appeared as a witness for the defence, testifying the maid had told him, 'she was sorry she had two pillows in her box . . .' When it emerged that the maid had not been paid by her employers, the case was dismissed.[9]

The job involved not just dealing with crime. He received a tip-off about an abandoned child in a bush hut near Beechworth. He and another constable broke down the door to discover an emaciated three-year-old girl. They carefully wrapped her up and took her to Beechworth hospital.[10]

When a little boy became lost in the bush, Ward was energetic in the search, earning praise in the news for having done 'yeoman's duty'. The little boy was located, having fallen down a deep hole. Three weeks later, he transported another boy, who had been injured in a horse-riding accident, to Beechworth hospital.[11]

On another occasion, he and another constable were assigned to catch 'the Wild Man of the Woods', after numerous sightings of an almost-naked man brandishing a butcher's knife. They found the Wild Man living in a remote bush hut. He put up a fight but they wrestled him down and took him to the Beechworth lock-up, where he became quite talkative. His name was John Leahy, from the south of Ireland, and after coming to Victoria had fallen on hard times.[12]

During torrential floods on the Ovens River, word came through that some Chinese men were trapped. Ward travelled down the river with two local men in a boat and rescued the men from the roof of their house, delivered them to Wangaratta, then went out again to rescue five more people from the roof of a tobacco-shed. He received a commendation for 'gallant conduct displayed in the rescue of several persons whose lives were imperilled by the floods'.[13]

One day in Beechworth, a horse broke free of a buggy and galloped 'at a furious pace' down the street. Michael Ward, who happened to be nearby as it charged past a bank, grabbed the reins and brought the feisty animal under control.[14]

Ward was to play a central role in the hunt for Ned Kelly and his gang, but those calamitous events were still a few years away.

In the meantime, Ned's criminal career progressed, and his network of thieves and smugglers expanded, and other police suffered the brunt of his violence.

Michael Ward was held in such esteem that when a senior bureaucrat lodged a complaint against him for accidentally kicking his suitcase at the station, the newspapers rallied to his cause, one stating, 'Constable Ward has gained great goodwill in the discharge of duties, not always of an easy and pleasant nature, and we have no doubt that the department will consent to his receiving from his friends in Beechworth and the neighbourhood some testimony of their appreciation of him.' Even *Melbourne Punch* took the side of the accused constable. The Police department dismissed the complaint.[15]

Ward became well acquainted with Ned Kelly, Ned's brother Dan, their relatives the Quinns, and their other relatives and friends, who were all familiar faces in the district courtrooms. He let Ned off with a warning on one occasion rather than arresting him for causing a public disturbance. In his early years as a constable, he did not arrest either of the Kelly brothers. That task fell to others, who were sometimes subjected to the Kellys' wrath in response.[16]

One Sunday in Wangaratta, Ned Kelly caused a disturbance outside a church, riding a feisty, unbroken horse. Rather than arrest him, Ward gave him a warning, and told him 'he had better find another place for showing off his horsemanship'. Kelly took the invitation literally, kicking his spurs into the animal to gallop away, but the animal bucked. Some locals believed that the embarrassing moment caused Kelly to bear a grudge against Ward from then onwards.[17]

6

Kelly and the cops

Even before he and Harry Power bailed up Robert McBean in March 1870, Ned Kelly had had run-ins with the law. His parents were not exemplary role models in that respect.

Ned's father, John 'Red' Kelly, had been transported to Van Diemen's Land (renamed Tasmania in 1856) for stealing two pigs. His seven-year sentence, of which he served four, was probably lightened by his decision to inform on a fellow thief named Patrick Regan, who was shot by police.[1] Given his ticket of leave in 1845, Red moved to Victoria, where he married Ellen Quinn, and took up farming and drinking. They lived in Beveridge, then Avenel, where Red was sentenced to six months' imprisonment for stealing a heifer. He died of alcohol-related illness in 1866.

Ellen Kelly had a violent temper. In 1866, soon after Red's death, she was found guilty of verbally abusing another Avenel resident, and fined £2. In early 1867 she and Red's sister Ann Ryan got into a physical fight; both of them were charged, convicted of assault and fined. Three months later, Ellen assaulted her landlord and wilfully damaged the rental property she was living in, and was fined again.[2]

After Ned was accused of stealing a horse, Ellen and her children left Avenel, possibly to avoid charges being laid. They relocated northeast to Greta, the vicinity of Ellen's dysfunctional criminal family, the Quinns. They moved in with Ellen's sisters and their children, who were renting a large old former hotel.

One day, Red's brother James, recently released from gaol for cattle-stealing, visited the old hotel and made a pass at Ellen. She whacked him with a gin bottle, then chased him down the street with a stick. He returned and burned down the hotel.

James was charged with attempted murder and sentenced to death. Redmond Barry, the judge who sentenced him, was well known for acquitting the men charged with treason after the 1854 Eureka Rebellion, and for representing Aboriginal people *pro bono*. He was not feeling lenient this time; however, in his summation he made it clear it was intended as a commuted sentence, to send a message, and not an actual execution. James Kelly was never released and died in a Melbourne lunatic asylum in 1903.

Ellen purchased a nearby selection of land on Eleven Mile Creek Road. Instead of farming, she made money by running a sly grog shanty and roadside inn.[3]

The Kelly shanty was a one-room hut. The 'rooms' inside were merely partitions separated by hessian. But despite its rudimentary accommodation, it did a roaring trade with passing traffic between Melbourne and the Beechworth goldfields. Her shanty became a hangout for criminals. It was described as 'a groggery and gambling hell'. There were multiple stories of travellers being fleeced of their cash or having their horses stolen, and of violent brawls.[4]

In 1869, when Harry Power was on the loose, and being harboured by Ellen's brothers, a Chinese man named Ah Fook arrived at the Benalla police station with a note that simply said, 'Kelly, 11 Mile Creek, robbed me'. The note was written for him by a local who'd taken pity on Ah Fook.[5]

With the help of an interpreter, Ah Fook explained what had happened to him. He had been walking along Eleven Mile Creek

Road when Ned Kelly sprang out from behind a bush, calling, 'I'm a bushranger. Give me your money or I'll beat you to death!'

Ah Fook handed over ten shillings, but Kelly beat him up anyway. Ah Fook had the bruises to prove it. Sergeant Whelan of Benalla went to the Kelly property accompanied by another constable, Ah Fook and an interpreter. As they approached, Ned Kelly burst out the door, sprinting away towards the back fence and the forest beyond. As Whelan galloped in pursuit, someone at the house released dogs that ran up and harassed him, slowing him down.

Despite the dogs, Whelan caught Kelly, whose only remark on being arrested was that if the fence was a little nearer, he would have got away.[6] When, back at the Kelly hut, the sergeant read out the warrant, Kelly said, 'That bloody Chinaman who passed yesterday did this!' He said that Ah Fook had insulted a woman at the hut and 'I took a stick to him, but I never hit him.'[7]

At the trial, despite the corroborating evidence of the bruises and the note, it was Ah Fook's word against Ned Kelly's. Or rather, it was Ah Fook's word against Ned Kelly, Ned's sister Annie and two of Ned's mates, who all insisted that Ah Fook was the aggressor. They said he turned up out of the blue, demanded a glass of water, then punched Ned Kelly, who ran away and hid. After telling everyone nearby he would return to burn down the house, Ah Fook then stormed off, they claimed.

Nobody believed it. Even the magistrate, A.C. Wills, indicated he didn't believe it, but he found Ned Kelly not guilty anyway. Perhaps Wills had no choice but to acquit, but he had a long record of dismissing cases where guilt was obvious, and of relying on questionable witnesses to do so.[8]

Six months after Power's capture, Ned's first serious charge was laid against him.

Jeremiah and Catherine McCormick were two ex-convicts who made a living as hawkers and had camped at Greta. It had been raining hard and the ground was boggy. One of their horses went missing, and they learned that Ned Kelly and his mate Ben Gould had taken it to free a bogged wagon. They retrieved the horse, but it was missing its cloth cover. When Kelly rode past, Jeremiah accused him of stealing the horse and cover, and keeping the cover. Kelly said that his uncle Jack Lloyd was responsible.

On Sunday evening, the McCormicks were packing up their cart in Greta, covering it as protection against the rain, when they met Jack Lloyd. McCormick asked him about the horsecloth, but Lloyd said he didn't have it.

Then Ned Kelly rode past again. Lloyd stopped him and demanded to know why he was telling lies. They argued. In anger and frustration, Catherine McCormick hurled a stick in Kelly's direction. Kelly wheeled his horse around and rode towards the McCormicks.[9]

Kelly shouted, 'I'll ride my horse over you and kill the bloody lot of you, you bloody wretches!' Then he charged his horse at Jeremiah McCormick and knocked him over.

Kelly rode about ten yards off, then turned again and shouted, 'Come on, you old bugger and fight me! I've got your cover. Do your bloody best about it! You want doing over.'

Later Ned reappeared across the street. He gave something to his cousin Tom Lloyd and pointed at Catherine. Tom crossed the street and gave her a small parcel, containing two bullock's testicles, and an obscene note saying, 'Your husband can tie them to his cock so he can shag you better next time.'

Kelly departed, but the McCormicks were terrified that he would return. Jeremiah sat by his wagon with a loaded revolver late into the night, until he eventually decided to seek protection from the police.

Edward Hall was a burly, overweight but tough constable from Ireland who had been assigned to the Greta station in August. Within weeks of Hall's arrival, Pat Quinn, one of Ned's uncles, had beaten him unconscious with a stirrup iron in the Greta police yard.

McCormick showed Constable Hall the note Kelly had given his wife.

He said he was afraid to press charges against Kelly, but Hall persuaded the McCormicks to accompany him to Wangaratta Courthouse the next day, where Jeremiah made a sworn statement that he was in fear of his life. On the basis of that statement, Hall charged Kelly with assault and using obscene language.

At the Wangaratta police court, Kelly was sentenced to six months' hard labour: three for the assault, and three for the obscene note. For the successful arrest and conviction of Ned Kelly, Hall was commended, and was given a £5 bonus.[10]

In his report on the matter, Hall revealed that he had learned that Ned Kelly had been trying to obtain firearms and was planning to 'take to the bush' with a man named Billy Cooke (previously known as Allen Lowry, he had changed his name after his recent release from Pentridge prison), who would soon arrive in the district. Hall concluded, therefore, that putting Kelly behind bars 'will save the police a good deal of trouble over the summer months'.[11]

Ned Kelly served four months of his six-month sentence. Soon after his release, Constable Hall learned from an informer, a horse thief named James Murdock, that Kelly had been boasting that the horse he was riding was stolen.

A few days earlier, a horse breaker from Mansfield named Isaiah Wright (known to all as 'Wild' Wright) had lodged at the Kelly shanty. Wright was a tall, strapping horse thief from Mansfield, about 40 miles south of Greta. Overnight, his chestnut mare wandered away because he had not bothered to tether it. He borrowed another horse from Kelly to return home on and told Kelly that if he found the chestnut mare he could keep her. Ned's brother-in-law Alex Gunn and a family friend named William 'Brickey' Williamson found the mare, so Kelly kept it.[12]

Several times, Constable Hall saw Kelly riding the chestnut mare around Greta. The mare matched the description of a horse recently stolen in Mansfield, whose theft had not yet been reported in the police gazette.[13]

He tried to entice Kelly off the horse by asking to talk, but Kelly rode away each time.[14] On 20 April, Hall tried a different tactic. He stopped Kelly on the bridge, said there were some parole papers that he needed to sign, and told him to come with him to the police station. He walked alongside, believing that Kelly was complying.

When they neared the station, Kelly said, 'Bring them out.'[15]

Hall replied, 'No, you can't write here. Come inside.'

Kelly said, 'No, I won't.'

Hall gave up on the deception, and told Kelly he was under arrest for riding a stolen horse.[16]

Kelly said, 'I'll see you damned!' He turned the horse around to ride away. Hall rushed forward, grabbed his clothing, and pulled him from the horse. Kelly shed his clothes and bolted. Hall drew his revolver, pointed it, and called to Kelly three times to stop running or he would have to shoot.[17]

Kelly stopped, turned around and stood facing Hall. He dared Hall, 'Shoot and be damned!'

Hall fired.

Hall fired at Kelly a second time, and then a third, but Kelly was miraculously unharmed.

The 'miracle' might be explained by the wording of Kelly's later description of the event: 'Hall got up and snapped three or four caps at me and would have shot me but the Colts patent refused.' A misfire, perhaps, except that Kelly then admitted: 'When I heard the caps snapping, I stood until Hall came close.'[18]

The term 'snapping caps' was sometimes used to refer to the firing of blanks or empty cartridges. The police kept stores of blanks and used them to train their horses not to panic at the sound of gunfire. Furthermore, ammunition was expensive, and constables had to account for it all, and sometimes pay for it themselves. It is possible that Hall and Kelly both knew the gun was harmless. It would certainly explain why Kelly dared Hall to shoot, and why he simply stood there while Hall fired three times at close range.

Kelly rushed forward, punched Hall in the face, then lunged for the gun.[19]

They wrestled. Hall was heavier, but Kelly was stronger. Hall hit Kelly on the head with the revolver five times. He said later, 'It seemed to have very little effect on him.'

They crashed into a fence. Kelly bit Hall. Hall screamed and called out for help. Kelly threw Hall to the ground, straddled him, wrenched the revolver from Hall's hand, turned it on him, and said, 'Now I'll let you have it!'

Several men came running to assist Hall and pulled Kelly off the constable. They dragged him to the Greta lock-up, while he struggled and kicked all the way.

Hall needed reinforcements, because several of Kelly's acquaintances were outside, riding around the police station 'like wild savages' and calling out that they were going to come in and rescue Kelly from the lock-up. He telegraphed Sub-Inspector Montfort at Wangaratta:

> I have arrested young Kelly after a desperate row with him for horse stealing. I struck him on the head with the revolver in self defence while arresting him, he is now in the lock up, please send a doctor and two constables. I cannot open the lock up until the latter come you will oblige me if you telegraph the occurrence to Superintendent Barclay.
>
> E Hall 569 S.C.
>
> Let the doctor come at once. E.H.[20]

Constable Arthur was despatched from Wangaratta, accompanied by Dr Hester, while Constable Thom was despatched from Benalla. The next morning, Kelly was taken to Wangaratta in a cart with a mounted escort.

Hall rode with Kelly in the cart to the Wangaratta lock-up. Kelly told him he didn't steal the mare, but would take the fall for it rather than 'split' on another thief.[21]

He said, 'I can do as bloody a lagging as any man in the country, and I'd do it before I'd put anybody else into it.'[22]

In reporting on the events, the Beechworth-based *Advertiser* described Kelly as 'a candidate for the gallows'.[23]

The Mansfield larrikin who had given Kelly the horse, Wild Wright, was Hall's next target. Two weeks after arresting Kelly, Hall saw Wild Wright riding along the main street of Greta and followed him on foot to the local blacksmith. Wright saw him and rode away, so Hall ran back to the police yard and called for Constable McInerney to hurry out. They rode off in pursuit and caught up with Wright, but he galloped ahead. Hall and McInerney fired their revolvers at him, but missed. They chased him for miles through the bush, but eventually lost him and returned to the station.

Hall suspected that Wright was probably lodging at the Kelly shanty, so he and McInerney visited there at one o clock in the morning. They found Wright in the bedroom of Ned Kelly's sister Annie. When the police entered the house, he hid behind the bed, but was easily seen. Hall arrested him.[24]

As they led him away, Wright said, 'If I had a weapon to defend myself, I would have dropped one or two of you.'

Hall took him to Wangaratta lock-up. Through the barred windows, Hall pointed to the chestnut cob outside, and asked Wright if he recognised it. Wright said he had never seen that horse before in his life.[25]

Hall next arrested Annie's husband, Alex Gunn, who had assisted Wild Wright in another recent horse theft near Mansfield.

At the trials in August, there was a public falling out among thieves. James Murdock testified against Ned Kelly. Brickey Williamson, who had assisted Kelly in catching the stolen horse, testified against Wild Wright, who in turn testified against Gunn.

Gunn was sentenced to eighteen months for horse stealing. Wild Wright was given eighteen months for illegally using a horse and Ned Kelly was given three years for feloniously receiving a stolen horse. It appears unfair to modern eyes that Ned received a longer sentence for what sounds like a lesser crime. However, receiving a stolen horse was considered to be the more serious offence. Horses were often 'borrowed' without the owner's consent, to be returned later, and this was what Wild Wright had done. On the other hand, the black market in stolen horses was a nefarious, organised criminal enterprise.

Within days of the sentences being handed down, Constable Hall was transferred out of the district, never to return. He had crossed powerful men and his position was no longer tenable. In January 1871, he had found a stolen horse on the property of a wealthy farmer named William Prentice. He removed the horse, and charged Prentice with illegally using a horse. After beating the charge, Prentice complained to the district police chief, Superintendent Barclay, who launched an internal investigation into Hall's conduct. Then, after arresting Ned Kelly, Hall became concerned for his safety, particularly given the savage assault he had previously suffered from Ned's uncle, Pat Quinn. Hall requested, and was granted, a transfer to Geelong. On his departure, local selectors banded together to present him with a monetary gift for his services to the community.[26]

7

Constable Flood

Constable Hall was replaced by another Irishman, Ernest Flood.

Flood had been born in Kilkenny on 6 June 1843, the sixth child of William, a doctor, and Mary. At the age of eighteen, he departed Ireland for Australia, hoping to make his fortune in the Victorian goldfields. He found mostly mud, not riches, so moved to Melbourne in search of work. Flood lived in St Kilda for a few years, then in 1867, needing a regular income, joined the police.[1]

Trim and good looking, Flood had black hair, hazel eyes and olive skin. He dressed smartly and was a groomsman by trade. He loved athletics and was a respected long-distance runner. He had been married for just over a year, and his wife, Mary, had given birth to their first child, Ernest junior, in July. Mary and Ernest junior remained in Yackandandah, awaiting accommodation arrangements in Greta.[2]

Before long, Greta was reclassified as a two-constable station, and Flood was joined by Constable Mullane, also born in Ireland.

It wasn't long before Flood encountered the Kelly family. In September a hawker named Max Krafft complained that two of his horses had been stolen by the younger Kelly boys, Dan (aged ten) and Jim (aged twelve). When Flood located Dan and Jim, they were riding Krafft's horses and galloped away when he approached, but Jim's horse refused to jump a fence and Flood caught them.

When the case was heard at Wangaratta police court, Ellen Kelly eyeballed the hawker and asked if he *really* thought the boys intended

40

to steal those horses. Krafft folded. No, he said, he didn't think that at all. The case was dismissed.[3]

Ellen was in court again a month later, this time in Benalla, suing a butcher named Bill Frost for paternity payments for her youngest child, Ellen junior. She claimed that Frost had slept with her on numerous occasions, had promised to marry her, had got her pregnant, and had even bought baby clothes. Frost claimed that Ellen was sleeping with several men, not just him. He had issued a subpoena for a witness named Wirey Hogan who would back that claim, but Wirey failed to appear.

The magistrate found in Ellen's favour.[4] Ellen and her supporters celebrated the decision by stampeding on horseback through the streets of Benalla, terrorising the town for three days. Sergeant Whelan of Benalla charged all of them with furious riding in a public place. The charges were heard a week later before Walter Butler, the same magistrate who had heard Ellen's paternity case.

Ellen's lawyer asked Sergeant Whelan if Benalla was actually a township, and therefore a 'public place'. When Whelan said that yes, Benalla was a township, Ellen's lawyer asked him to produce the official documents of gazettal. The perplexed sergeant could not.

Walter Butler banged his gavel. Case dismissed.

It was reported in the news that 'the offenders left rejoicing'. The *Advertiser* commented sarcastically that anyone previously fined for that offence should now get a refund.[5]

The demand for an obscure government document proving the designation of the township was ludicrous, and Butler's outrageous ruling on it makes no sense unless corruption or coercion was involved.

Sadly, Ellen's victory was short-lived. Baby Ellen died of diarrhoea less than three months later, in January 1872.[6] In the 1870s, a staggering 12 per cent of babies born in Victoria died before their first birthday. The menace of infant mortality struck all classes and races, and the biggest killer of babies was the scourge of diarrhoea.[7]

It was around this time that Ernest Flood met Annie Gunn. They were both married with spouses far away. Annie's husband, Alex Gunn, was serving time with her brother, Ned Kelly. Flood's wife would not relocate to Greta until later in the year.

Allegations of an affair between Ernest and Annie emerged in January 1872. Annie attended Benalla court in a case in which she was the victim. Flood offered to accompany her home.

Mr and Mrs Short, tailors in Benalla, filed a report with the district police headquarters of an affair between the two. They produced a note that Flood had given them:

> *Mrs Short*
> *Please give the bearer any dress that she requires and charge the same*
> *to me.*
> *Ernest Flood.*[8]

There was an internal inquiry. But the Shorts were found to have been attempting to blackmail Flood, and had made their accusation only after he had refused to yield. They had lied in their statements, and contradicted themselves repeatedly, and were drunk when making the complaint. Flood claimed that Annie Gunn had been acting as an informer for him, and that the dress was payment for information.

Flood was cleared. The district police chief Superintendent Barclay lamented that 'Though active enough I am afraid he is greatly wanting in discretion and stability.' Captain Standish agreed he had acted with indiscretion and that the case had damaged Flood's reputation in the Greta community, but suggested giving him another chance there. Flood remained in Greta. His wife relocated there, and they had another baby boy in March 1873.[9]

Several weeks after the inquiry, Annie Gunn fell pregnant. Maybe it was to Flood; maybe it was to someone else. She gave birth to Annie junior on 9 November 1872, with her husband Alex Gunn, still serving time, as the registered father. Two days later Annie died from postnatal complications. The baby was taken into the care of Ellen Kelly, but died a year later from diphtheria.

The day after Annie Gunn's death, Flood received a report that Ellen Kelly and her friend Jane Graham, a 21-year-old prostitute who resided at the Kelly shanty, were in possession of a stolen saddle. He went to Eleven Mile Creek, searched the property, found the saddle, then charged both women with possession.[10]

They appeared in Benalla police court before Walter Butler, the same magistrate who had dismissed the furious riding case against Ellen and her supporters a year earlier. He dismissed these charges against them too. His reasoning was that, although the saddle was definitely stolen, the women assured him they didn't *know* it was stolen.[11]

From his prison cell, Ned Kelly nurtured a hatred of Flood, and later threatened to roast the constable over a fire if he ever caught him. He never said why. Maybe he didn't like Flood's black hair and dark skin. Or maybe he resented Flood enticing Annie to testify against thieves.

Ned's anger is widely believed, for want of a better theory, to have stemmed from Flood's rumoured affair with Annie. If so, it apparently didn't occur to Ned that his sister was a grown woman who might find a handsome young policeman attractive while her dirty, rough, horse-stealing husband languished in prison.

In November 1873 Flood was transferred to Oxley, near Wangaratta, and replaced at Greta Station by Constable Michael Ward. Flood was later removed from the district entirely after coming into conflict with a powerful and unpleasant squatter named Brown, who was friendly with Superintendent Hugh Barclay. The details of the dispute are unavailable, but the gist seems to be that Flood tried to retrieve a stolen or stray horse that was found in one of Brown's paddocks.[12]

The local magistrates, impressed by Flood's work, sent a petition to Captain Standish to attempt to prevent his removal, as did the residents of Oxley district, but the Chief of Police, acting on the advice of his officer, did not relent. At the 1881 Police Royal Commission into the Victorian police, arising from the Kelly outbreak, a magistrate declared that removing Flood was one of the critical errors that led to the fatal chain of events to come, because those who replaced him allowed stock theft to run rampant.[13]

The following year the Quinn family sold the Glenmore Run and scattered across the Ovens district. With their departure, the lazy, inept inspectors Barclay and Brooke-Smith recommended to Standish that Glenmore Police Station be closed and relocated to nearby Hedi. Its closure in 1875 was later identified as another key error that allowed crime to flourish, leading to the Kelly outbreak.[14]

8

A tale of two Irishmen

In 1835, John Batman had sailed into Port Phillip Bay, built a house in scrubland, and founded the city of Melbourne. More settlers followed, and there was soon a rush to establish farms on fertile land. First in, best dressed. Before long, vast swathes of land were in the hands of a small number of farmers, known as squatters. The rights and wishes of the original Indigenous owners were not taken into consideration.

The chaotic land grab wasn't sanctioned, hence the term *'squatters'*: they didn't ask anyone's permission to do what they were doing. An enterprising man (they were all men) would cross over a range, find a valley, and simply declare it to be his. When the explorer Major Thomas Mitchell reached the south-western coastline of Victoria in 1836, he found a thriving community at Portland that nobody had known existed, established by the Henty family.

Fleet-footed men carved up the colonies while the colonial administrators dozed and only woke up to the problem far too late. Too much land was held by too few.

The early squatters aspired to be a colonial aristocracy, but their grass kingdoms were soon under siege. By the time Victoria was separated from New South Wales in 1850, there were already calls to 'Unlock the land!' The squatters played it well, at first. While colonial governors dithered about how to deal with the problem that had snuck up on them, the squatters sent lobbyists to London, where the laws were still being made. An 1846 statute allowed them to keep their squatting runs, but they all had to go onto fourteen-year leases.

The land was still officially Crown land, and the government could sell it off, or do anything else with it, as deemed necessary.

The gold rush of the 1850s brought an influx of people, and the gold bust turned those newcomers into malcontents. Crown land was unlocked and sold in small selections in auctions or ballots to help the working class get a start as landholders. Anyone who already owned land—whether squatter or selector—was specifically excluded from this selection process. Squatters fought back, finding loopholes in the laws. They employed 'dummies' to bid on land on their behalf, then bought the land off the dummies. Mostly, this was done on a small scale: a squatter's son, or daughter, or mate's mate, could be used to protect a valuable piece of the run.

Land boards resolved these disputes. Sometimes both parties accused each other of dummying. Selectors used dummies, too, to acquire additional selections. Another source of discontent was 'peacocking'. That was when a choice piece of land, such as a river frontage, became available. Without it, nearby land would be worthless. Those selections would command a premium, with fierce competition from both squatters and selectors, and all sorts of dirty tricks would come into play.

Robert McBean's Kilfera Run, being near towns and major roads, had portions sliced off and sold to selectors. The soil on Kilfera was not very fertile, thus the selectors struggled.

The most successful squatter in all of Victoria, for a while at least, was Irishman Hugh Glass. He had arrived in Melbourne with nothing. He became a successful merchant, then began brokering land deals, then speculating on land, then purchasing squatting runs from squatters going out of business or wanting to cash out. Hugh Glass conducted dummying on an industrial scale, sometimes flooding a selection with as many as 50 paid dummies.

He became the richest man in Victoria. His spectacular Melbourne mansion, Flemington House, had a Corinthian colonnaded portico, a ballroom, an artificial lake and a landscaped garden sloping down to Moonee Ponds Creek. Needless to say, he joined the Melbourne Club.

To the public, Hugh Glass had become the epitome of the greedy, rich squatter, even though he had never squatted as such.

Then, scandal erupted. It came to light that certain politicians were in the pay of Hugh Glass. A parliamentary inquiry found him guilty of corruption and had him imprisoned. He was freed after the Supreme Court intervened, and the Chief Justice ruled that parliament had violated the separation of powers. Judges send people to prison, not politicians.

Even before the scandal, the edifice was toppling. Like Icarus, Glass had flown too close to the sun. He was over-leveraged, and had overpaid for substandard properties. His dummying practices, the bête noir of political debate, were a drain on his cash flow. In 1869 his estate was liquidated by trustees. That same year, his infant daughter died, and he developed cancer of the liver. He died in 1871 from an accidental overdose of a painkiller.[1]

Hugh Glass's bribes were a doomed attempt to thwart progress. The tide was flowing out for the old squatter model, washing their monopolistic structures away like driftwood. There were heated parliamentary debates, petitions and activist groups on both sides. Flaws in earlier bills were addressed in later ones. Each new bill chipped more off the big old blocks.

To ensure selections went to genuine applicants and to stymie aspiring land moguls, selectors were required to reside on their selection. This had unintended harmful consequences because many selectors travelled to earn money as shearers and labourers during the off-seasons. For this reason, land boards looked the other way, and the provision was eventually abolished in 1878.[2]

Hugh Glass had purchased a squatting run near Greta called the Myrrhee Run. In the wake of his bankruptcy, the Myrrhee Run was transferred to the Union Bank, and sat idle. Unfenced and neglected by the bankers, it became an unofficial commons—a place where anyone could graze their animals for free. It was also an excellent place to put stolen cattle or horses temporarily, before moving them on. Ned Kelly, and his uncles, brothers, cousins and friends put those free pastures to good use in their criminal activities.

It is sometimes said that Ned Kelly was a sort of Robin Hood who championed the selector cause. He was not. The political struggle between squatters and selectors was titanic, but by the time Ned was wearing long trousers, it was already over, and the selectors had won.

The image of the oppressed selector shaking his fist at the wealthy squatter is powerful but misguided. Few selectors went bankrupt (fewer than one in five was late on even a single rent payment), and most purchased their selections outright at the end of their lease periods. Their biggest problem was not rich neighbours but stock theft. Ned Kelly didn't target squatters in some grand class war. Selectors were just as likely as squatters to have their horses and cattle stolen by the likes of Kelly and his mates.[3]

Respectable selectors were hard-working and honest. They traded at the stock auctions. At agricultural shows, they exhibited livestock, competed in egg-and-spoon races and bought toffee apples for their children. The Kellys were the sort of people that respectable families gossiped about over scones and tea after church. But Ned Kelly enjoyed the support of an expanding larrikin criminal underclass, known as the Greta Mob.[4]

The same year that Hugh Glass came to Victoria, another young Irishman like him came with similar aspirations, but without his ruthlessness.

When James Whitty stepped off the *Coromandel* on 10 June 1840, he had no money, and was illiterate. His brothers Patrick, John and Mark soon followed him from Ireland.[5]

Over the next two decades, they accumulated land around Whittlesea, near Melbourne. Patrick built a bluestone hotel that he named the Sir Henry Barkly Hotel after the then Victorian governor. James purchased an abandoned selection at Moyhu—near Greta— and relocated there with his wife and several children. His brothers followed suit.

James Whitty was a successful farmer. On his 352-acre block, he built a six-room brick house with a detached kitchen, a well and splendid gardens. True, it wasn't as spectacular as Flemington House, where Hugh Glass resided in Melbourne. But it was a mark of success.

The Whitty family befriended two other large Irish families in the north-eastern district, who, like them, were acquiring selections, working hard, making smart business decisions and generally doing well. They were the Byrne family and the Farrell family (not to be confused with the squatter Dominic Farrell of Whitfield).[6]

The Whitty, Byrne and Farrell families were regular attendees at Catholic mass. Their children regularly attended school. They were involved in community organisations. They acquired selections near each other or adjacent to each other, engaging in cluster farming, an emulation of sorts of the Irish clan structure.

All three families prospered.

Ned Kelly hated them.[7]

It must have been so confusing and enraging. His parents had come from Ireland with nothing too. His mother had a selection, and his grandfather owned a squatting run. Why, then, were things so different? Why were the Whittys, Farrells and Byrnes so prosperous, so happy, when his life was nothing but misery and hardship?

He hated those families, and most of all, he hated their elderly patriarch, James Whitty.

9

Michael Ward joins the detective force

On a chilly autumn evening in 1876, Constable Michael Ward was on desk duty at Beechworth police station when a miner named Sandy Doig reported a crime. He said he'd been walking home from work when he heard a cow making noises of distress ahead. As he neared, he saw two men in the gloom, carving up a cow's carcass. When he approached, he recognised them as two local youths, Aaron Sherritt and Joe Byrne (unrelated to the extended Byrne family near Greta). Both Sherritt and Byrne would become associates of Ned Kelly.

When Sherritt saw Doig coming near, he cut the brand out of the cow's hide and hid it. Doig said sarcastically, 'You call yourself a butcher?' Byrne and Sherritt ignored him and resumed carving.[1]

Ward did not find the culprits or the carcass that night: Byrne and Sherritt were long gone. The next morning, he and another constable visited Joe Byrne's mother's selection, where after a search, they found a cow's forequarter and hindquarter. They also found, hidden in a zinc bucket in the outhouse, a cow's head and horns. Ward kept searching, wandering through the grass. Some distance away from the house, he found a fresh piece of cowhide on the ground. He claimed it as evidence.

Ward asked Joe Byrne's mother, Margaret, how she came by so much cow's meat. She admitted Joe and Aaron had brought it last night, but said it wasn't stolen. It was one of Aaron's cows that the boys had slaughtered.

'Where are the boys now?' Ward asked. Maggie Byrne said she had no idea, adding that Joe didn't live there.

Ward persisted: 'Where does Joe live?' Again, Maggie Byrne claimed she didn't know.

Ward's next call was to the Sherritt household. The Sherritts also had a large quantity of meat that they could not account for. Ward found a piece of cowhide on the grass, and another that had been used to patch a hole in the wall. He took them both. They spoke to a neighbour of the Sherritts', Jane Batchelor, who told them she had lent the boys butchers' knives.[2]

Back at the station, Ward put the cowhide pieces together like a jigsaw, recreating the entire skin of the animal. In doing so, he clearly saw that one section was missing: the part where the brand would have been. He had confirmed Doig's statement with physical evidence.

He located Byrne and Sherritt and arrested them both for possessing stolen meat. They faced court a week later.[3]

Ward's systematic investigation, including his cowhide jigsaw puzzle, was the foundation of a compelling prosecution case. Byrne and Sherritt were both sentenced to six months' hard labour in Beechworth Gaol.

While in Beechworth Gaol, Joe Byrne and Aaron Sherritt became friends with Jim Kelly, one of Ned Kelly's younger brothers. It was only much later that Michael Ward realised that the criminal organisation that would eventually morph into the Kelly Gang had its genesis at this time in this gaol.[4]

Within weeks of their release, Byrne and Sherritt were in trouble again. A constable saw Sherritt in Beechworth with two horses and a dray, and noticed that one of the horses appeared to be lame. The constable stopped Sherritt, inspected the animal, and discovered it had an appalling injury: the skin on its right shoulder was stripped bare where Sherritt had cut away the brand, presumably because the horse was stolen. When Sherritt subsequently appeared in court charged with animal cruelty, the magistrate gave him a stern lecture and fined him £5.[5]

Two weeks later, Sherritt and Byrne appeared in court before Judge Hackett charged with maliciously wounding a Chinese man named Ah On. It was alleged that they taunted Ah On at a swimming hole near the Chinese camp next door to the Byrne selection, and threw rocks at him. A rock thrown by Sherritt hit Ah On in the head, causing serious injury, and he fell to the ground. Dr Fox of Wangaratta, a witness for the prosecution, testified that he had examined Ah On's injuries and found that his cheekbone was broken in five places; he was permanently disfigured. Dr Fox further stated that Ah On now had trouble chewing and might never completely recover. Several residents of the Chinese Camp testified that the violent attack was unprovoked.

But Byrne and Sherritt produced some counter-witnesses. Byrne's mother testified that she saw the whole thing, and that Ah On had started it by chasing Sherritt with a bamboo stick. She also said that Sherritt had merely thrown a stick in return, not a rock. Aaron Sherritt's mother testified that Aaron wasn't even there; he was at home with her the entire time. Aaron's brother William, and Joe's sister Mary, both testified that they saw what happened and that Aaron did nothing wrong. The jury, perhaps directed by Judge Hackett, claimed to be persuaded by these lies, and found Byrne and Sherritt not guilty.[6]

Dan Kelly also had some luck before Judge Hackett at the Beechworth general sessions. He stood accused of stealing a saddle from a hotel in Benalla the previous May. The victim was no wealthy squatter; the owner of the saddle was a struggling itinerant wool sorter named Sidney Smith. During his stay at the Liverpool Arms Hotel, he had left his saddle in the kitchen for safekeeping, but it was gone in the morning. Months later, on New Year's Eve, a constable in Benalla noticed Dan Kelly riding a horse fitted with the stolen saddle.

Dan's lawyer produced a string of shady defence witnesses, including Jack Lloyd, Bill Skillion (Dan's brother-in-law) and Ned Kelly. Their version was that Dan had bought the saddle innocently, from a traveller named Roberts who lodged at the Kelly shanty. He had no first name. Just 'Roberts'. Ned Kelly testified that he had searched high and low for Roberts, so as to clear his brother's name, but sadly Roberts could not be found. If only someone could find the mysterious Roberts this whole thing could be sorted out.

After Ned's testimony, Judge Hackett addressed the jury, instructing them to find Dan Kelly 'not guilty'. He said, 'I don't see why he is here at all. He has given a perfectly fair account of how he came into possession of the saddle, and the whole of the evidence corroborated that account.'[7]

The jury did as instructed, returning a verdict of not guilty.

Michael Ward was twice recommended for transfer into the detective force. On the second occasion, he was accepted, but changed his mind at the last minute, deciding that he would rather stay in Beechworth as a humble constable. In 1877 there was a major expansion of the detective force, and because he had previously been recommended, was transferred whether he liked it or not. He therefore had to relocate to Melbourne.[8]

The Hibernian Society, a prominent Irish club, held a St Patrick's Day ball in Beechworth each year. In 1877, for reasons lost to history, the St Patrick's Day ball was delayed until June, but was a success.

During an intermission in the dancing, Mr Hiram Horrocks, postmaster at Eldorado and president of the Beechworth shire, asked for everyone's attention. He announced that, as everyone knew, the much-loved Constable Michael Ward had been promoted to the detective force (*applause*). Therefore, Horrocks continued, Beechworth would sadly be deprived of the constable's services. (In fact, Ward had already transferred to Melbourne earlier in the year, and had returned to Beechworth for this event.)

An *Advertiser* journalist at the ball later wrote: 'Mr Horrocks . . . in a few well-chosen words, spoke of Mr Ward's zeal and efficiency when in the police force, and of his sterling worth as a man.'[9]

Horrocks presented Ward with a purse of sovereigns, collected by citizens of Beechworth as a parting gift. In his acceptance, Ward said that the happiest days of his life had been spent in Beechworth, where he had had plenty of work (*laughter*), and had made plenty of friends (*applause*).

Ward thanked everyone in the room for the gift: 'Not just for its intrinsic value, but also for the kind feeling which prompted its being given.'

In reporting the event, the *Advertiser* gushed its own endorsement of Michael Ward:

We may add our tribute of esteem to Mr Ward, who lately was fittingly transferred to the detective department after a period of faithful service as a mounted constable, and it is no exaggeration to say that a better never served in this district.[10]

He then departed Beechworth for a new life in Melbourne, not knowing that events were already in motion that would bring him right back.[11]

10

The Whitty raid

In 1877, Victoria's crime rate was at an all-time low. Among the factors to explain this were: the decline of the gold rush; the exodus of young men as the goldfields were mined bare; police reforms over the past three decades, and the force's old, corrupt guard being slowly replaced by young immigrants who took their job seriously. Newcomers like Constable Flood and Detective Ward. The force also now had a core of competent officers and potential future leaders, including the Power-catching trio of Nicolson, Hare and Montfort.[1]

From his headquarters in the Melbourne Club, Captain Standish enjoyed popular support for the improved state of things. Crime was down, and the force was far less embarrassing than it had been.

Standish was slowing down. His eyes, which once sparkled with intelligence, were now clouded over, dulled by hard living, hard drinking and years of burning the candle at both ends. He was complacent. Had he stepped down—or been removed—he could have retired with a legacy of modest reform and decades of stable leadership. But he enjoyed the salary, the status and the lifestyle. And besides, was he not very good at the job? Didn't everyone think so? Everyone, of course, other than a handful of stern-faced wowsers like the politician Francis Longmore.

But although *most* crime was down in *most* parts of the colony, there were signs of trouble. Horse stealing was on the rise: in the first half of 1877, the *Victorian Police Gazette* reported more than 300 horse thefts across the colony. Tellingly, almost a third of those thefts occurred within 60 miles of Greta. Likewise, cattle theft in north-east Victoria in 1876 and 1877 had jumped by a third compared to previous years.[2]

A sophisticated criminal network was operating on both sides of the border. Victorian police in the north-east began working with their New South Wales counterparts across the river. Investigations were hampered by the reluctance of witnesses to testify, but the shape of the network came into view.[3]

Horses stolen in Victoria were being moved into New South Wales. Brands were altered, documents forged and the horses resold. Often they were sold back into Victoria as different animals, with a fake historical chain of ownership. Behind it all, there was talk of a mastermind, a man known only as 'Thompson'.

The thieves stole from the rich, and they stole from the poor. A farmer would wake to find that a prized mare had vanished; a merchant would lose a flea-bitten workhorse; a labourer's scrawny nag would disappear. The thieves raided the large, wealthy squatting runs too, netting several high-value horses in a single night.

In March 1877, five horses with a combined value of £60 were stolen from a Wangaratta station. Later that month, two horses with a combined value of £50 were stolen from nearby Chiltern. The value of the horses taken in those two raids alone was more money than a miner, then earning about £2 a week, would see in a year.[4]

One night in August, the thieves raided the nearby Myrrhee Run, taking eleven horses with a total combined value of £200. Six of the horses belonged to James Whitty, who currently had possession of the run.[5]

The Myrrhee Run, after the collapse of Hugh Glass's property empire, had become a kind of commons, used by local farmers as free grazing land and by stock thieves as a holding place for stolen stock. Six months earlier, James Whitty and Andrew Byrne had taken a five-year lease on it. (Andrew Byrne was one of the prosperous extended

Byrne family around Moyhu, unrelated to the criminal Joe Byrne of the Beechworth district.)

With rent payments to make, the new owners couldn't allow the free-for-all practice on the run to continue. They placed a newspaper advertisement in February to inform the farming community of the changed conditions. Specifically, they threatened to impound any stock they found grazing on the run; the owners would then have to pay a fee to the local poundkeeper in order to retrieve their stock.

At the same time, they were willing to sublease pastures to other farmers. For this reason, some of the stolen horses belonged to neither James Whitty nor Andrew Byrne, but to selectors who were paying for use of the run.

In his role as inspector of police stations, Superintendent Nicolson visited the Greta police station in April, and was appalled. The station was dirty, the police were dishevelled, and there was no evidence of any actual police work being done. Senior-Constable Thom had a crushed hat, a soiled uniform and was sporting a wild, untrimmed bushman's beard. His subordinate, Constable Hayes, was similarly unkempt. If these two buffoons were the best the police could offer in response to professional horse thieves, then the battle against crime was surely lost.[6]

On his return to Benalla, Nicolson decided to go via Eleven Mile Creek Road, and visit that notorious hotbed of crime, Ellen Kelly's shanty. Constable Hayes accompanied him there, then afterwards returned to Greta. Nicolson wrote a report to Standish about the visit:

> She lived on a piece of cleared and partly cultivated land on the road-side, in an old wooden hut, with a large bark roof. The dwelling was divided into five apartments by partitions of blanketing, rags, etc. There were no men in the house, only children

and two girls of about fourteen years of age, said to be her daughters. They all appeared to be existing in poverty and squalor.

She said her sons were out at work, but did not indicate where, and that their relatives seldom came near them. However, their communications with each other are known to the police. Until the gang referred to is rooted out of this neighbourhood one of the most experienced and successful mounted-constables in the district will be required in charge at Greta. I do not think that the present arrangements are sufficient.[7]

Before parting ways, Nicolson told Hayes, 'Never go near that house alone, and tell other police that come to Greta never to go near that house alone. Always have a second constable with you.'[8]

He had previously given the same advice to Thom, and instructed him to spread the word around. There is no indication that either Hayes or Thom ever passed the word to anyone. Neither constable had any intention to visit the Kelly shanty under any circumstances, for any reason, alone or otherwise.

The reason for Nicolson's advice was that a constable without backup was vulnerable both to aggression and to the levelling of spurious accusations. In the near future, a young constable named Fitzpatrick would prove both of those concerns about the Kelly shanty to be well-founded.

Nicolson had Senior-Constable Thom removed from Greta, to be replaced by Constable Strahan. He gave young Constable Hayes a second chance, believing that he had been led astray by Thom and might turn into a capable policeman under the right supervisor.

In his report on the situation to Standish, Nicolson noted that the ineptitude of the Greta police was partly counterbalanced by Sergeant Steele in Wangaratta, a competent and hard-working officer who monitored the Greta crime hotspot to the best of his ability, despite being in a different jurisdiction.

Nicolson's advice to the officer in charge of the district, Inspector Brooke-Smith, was essentially a zero-tolerance policy. He suggested that all crimes committed by the Kellys and their associates should be prosecuted, including minor crimes. His reasoning was that they obtained social status—or as he called it, 'flashness'—by visibly flouting the law. The lack of effective policing, and the reluctance to press charges, was enhancing their power and prestige. However, he stressed that any crackdown should be strictly by the book: it had to be done 'without oppressing the people, or worrying them in any way'.[9]

Inspector Brooke-Smith was of a similar mind to constables Thom and Hayes. As far as he was concerned, the best way to deal with the Kellys was to ignore them.

In November there was a breakthrough in the attempt to curb the theft of horses, thanks to the diligent work of a policeman across the border. It was in part due to liaison between the Victorian police in Wodonga and Superintendent Singleton in Albury, who realised that horses were being moved across the border when the river was low.[10]

In the river town of Howlong, on the New South Wales bank of the Murray, Sergeant Larkin was inspecting the paperwork for a local horse sale when his suspicions were aroused. He was on the alert because the river had dropped after an extended dry spell.

The description of one of the horses for sale matched one of those stolen from the Myrrhee Run. The seller was listed as James Kennedy, so Sergeant Larkin decided to pay Mr Kennedy a friendly visit.

When he was asked about the horse sale, Kennedy said he was selling it to a man named Howard, but the sale had not yet been finalised. In that case, Sergeant Larkin said, the horse should still be here. Could he please see the animal in question?

It was a simple enough request (if the sale was legitimate), but Kennedy lost his cool. He told the sergeant that he had no right to demand to see the horse.

Larkin defused the situation: no need to see the animal. Could he merely have a look at the receipt of sale? Kennedy found the paperwork and handed it over. Larkin immediately confiscated it, and said that if he wanted it back, he'd better bring that horse to the police station tomorrow morning.

As soon as he returned to the station, Larkin sent a telegram to the Victorian police, asking the owner, James Whitty, to get to Howlong as fast as he could, to identify a potentially stolen horse.

The next day, Kennedy brought in the mare, hoping to get his papers back, but Larkin impounded the animal, then brought James Whitty to the police yard to inspect it. Whitty recognised it as his horse, but the brand, KY, was different. They took a close look at the brand, and saw that it had been cleverly altered from the original W.

Larkin arrested Kennedy, then went looking for more of his horses. He found three other horses owned by Kennedy with altered brands: one branded AW; another branded FK; and a third branded WB. Under interrogation, Kennedy said that he bought all the horses fair and square. He had obtained the horse branded WB from a man named Studders.

Larkin tracked down Studders and arrested him. Two thieves down.

When questioned, Studders said he bought the WB horse on the Victorian side of the border from a German farmer named William Baumgarten. Larkin conveyed everything he had learned to the police in Wodonga. From here, he could progress the investigation no further, as it was a Victorian matter. The Victorian police had been slack or incompetent, or both, in stopping horse theft, but now it was time for a couple of them to shine.[11]

William Baumgarten's selection was in a quiet valley by the river, several miles downstream from Albury and Wodonga.

Constable William Bell of Wodonga police visited the selection, dressed in plain-clothes, posing as a potential customer. He asked Baumgarten if he had any horses for sale. Baumgarten said no. Bell said he was surprised by that, because his good mate Studders had sent him here.

Baumgarten fell for it. They went to a secluded paddock with a black mare and a filly in it. Bell checked the animals over carefully, as if considering whether to buy them. A black mare branded WB on the shoulder, and a filly branded AN near the neck. As casually as he could, he asked Baumgarten where he got them.[12]

Baumgarten replied, 'From a man named Thompson.' He produced the receipt of sale. which showed the previous owner's name to be Thompson.

Bell said he was interested, and would return to buy both horses. He left at a leisurely pace, then as soon as he was out of sight, hurried to Wodonga as fast as he could. Then he and Constable Stowe (also in plain-clothes) returned to Baumgarten's property and arrested him.

Three down.

They searched the property, looking primarily for branding irons, since the brands were clearly being altered somehow, but they found none. They searched Baumgarten's father's property too. He had branding irons but they were legitimate and did not match any brands on the stolen horses.

The horse branded WB was a Whitty horse; the B had been appended to the original brand that had simply been a W.

Stowe interrogated Baumgarten in the Wodonga lock-up. He asked about the receipt of sale: where and how did the sale take place? Baumgarten told him that Thompson was passing through the area with a lot of very nice horses. He had stopped to chat, and had asked Baumgarten if he'd like to buy any horses. They were beautiful animals, so naturally Baumgarten said yes. A few days later he noticed the brands were wrong, but even then, it didn't cross his mind that they were stolen.

Stowe didn't buy a word of this. Baumgarten's selection was a backblock, not on the way to anywhere. He said sarcastically, 'It's a curious place to sell horses.'[13]

Stowe wanted to know more about Thompson, but Baumgarten had nothing more to say. He was then transferred to Wangaratta lock-up for his case to be heard in the jurisdiction where the horses had been stolen. There, he was again interrogated, this time by Sergeant Arthur Steele.

II

Sergeant Steele

Arthur Maude Loftus Steele had been born in Ireland in 1836.[1] He came from a large family of career soldiers. His father had risen to officer rank in the British army, and his brothers had all enlisted too. One brother died in the Crimean War.

He was an excellent policeman: everyone agreed on that. The mystery was only why he had never been promoted beyond sergeant. Perhaps it was because he wasn't a member of the Melbourne Club or other exclusive circles. He didn't have the ear of politicians or Supreme Court judges, and would never be invited to a card game with Captain Standish. He had been a constable in Wangaratta for nineteen years before finally being promoted to sergeant the previous year, in 1876 at the age of 40. He could at least be glad that he had not been transferred back and forth across the colony, but instead had been allowed to settle and put down roots.[2]

Steele's focus was on the receipt of sale. He showed it to Baumgarten and asked him: did Thompson sign this receipt?

Baumgarten said he did. The signature on the form was Thompson's.

When Steele asked him to describe Thompson, Baumgarten said he was a tall man with a fair complexion.[3]

Steele then asked Baumgarten how he paid for the horses. Baumgarten said he paid Thompson £42: a cheque for £18 and the rest in cash. Baumgarten also let slip that his brother Gustav had also acquired some of Thompson's horses.

Sergeant Steele visited Gustav's property where he found more stolen horses from the Whitty raid, and also discovered a man there named Joseph Brown, who matched the description provided by Studders of another suspect involved in the thefts. Steele arrested both Gustav Baumgarten and Joseph Brown.

Four, five.

Yet they were still no closer to finding Thompson.

Perhaps Baumgarten's cheque was the key. Thompson would have to cash it sometime. After further inquiries Steele learned that the cheque had already been cashed, and not at a bank, but at a hotel in Benalla owned by William Cain. He spoke to Cain, who seemed to be unaware that by cashing the cheque he had facilitated money laundering. A customer named Thompson had requested to cash it, and Cain had done so, depositing it with the bank sometime afterwards. It all seemed aboveboard, because Baumgarten had gone to the hotel with him, and witnessed Thompson's signature on the back.

Did William Baumgarten really help the mysterious Thompson cash his cheque? No, because Baumgarten was in custody at the time. Someone had accompanied Thompson pretending to be William Baumgarten.

A Melbourne detective named Joseph Brown, ironically with the same name as the man arrested by Steele, had been despatched to the district to investigate organised horse thieving.[4]

Detective Brown started by investigating all the horses that Sergeant Larkin had seized from Kennedy. There was a mix of brands, and not all had come from Baumgarten. Instead, Kennedy seemed to Brown to be a fence with access to multiple channels for stolen stock.

He followed the trail leading from another of the horses that Larkin had seized from Kennedy. This animal had been stolen from Bill Frost, the man whom Ellen Kelly had taken to court for paternity payments, and who had earned the eternal enmity of the Kelly family. Since his breakup with Ellen, Frost had been a frequent victim of crime. He had been shot in the face (he said the shooter was a station cook who had recently left town and who was never located), and he'd had multiple horses stolen.

Brown studied the receipt of sale of Frost's horse, which stated that Kennedy bought it from a man named 'Ryan'. The purchase had taken place at Sheek's farmhouse near Benalla, although Sheek himself wasn't home at the time.

Brown quickly learned that 'Ryan' another alibi of Billy Cooke (once known as Allen Lowry), a hardened criminal and long-term friend of Ned Kelly. He heard that Cooke was in Barnawartha, close by the Baumgarten properties. Brown hurried there, found Cooke and arrested him.

That brought the tally to six.

Cooke said, 'I knew you were going to arrest me. I knew I was wanted, and I came to give myself up to Constable Robinson or Constable Larkin at Howlong.' If true, he was too slow: Brown didn't give him a chance to turn himself in.

Brown found another witness against Cooke. A farmer named Peterson had seen Cooke and several other men with eleven horses. They had asked Peterson if they could keep their horses in his paddock for a few days, and he had let them. The descriptions of two of Cooke's accomplices sounded like Dan Kelly and one of the Lloyd brothers.[5]

Each arrest led the police deeper into the network, and uncovered more participants. Michael Miller (alias Woodyard), David Morgan and John Collinson Gibbs were all arrested. That brought the number of arrests to nine.

As the investigation progressed, someone started tying up loose ends. Two decapitated horses were found in a lagoon on the Murray River, the brands cut from the carcasses. A few days later, the mutilated body of a stolen horse was discovered in the Murray River near Howlong. Another dead horse was discovered in a river bend near Barnawartha, close to the Baumgarten properties. The burned and charred corpses of four more horses were found near Barnawartha in January 1878.[6]

The thieves were dumping their inventory.

Dan Kelly and his cousin Jack Lloyd junior were identified as suspects in the Whitty raid and warrants were issued for their arrest. The police had not yet established the identity of the ringleaders, although Sergeant Steele suspected Ned Kelly's involvement. Indeed, Thompson was later proved to be Ned Kelly, and the man with him when he cashed the cheque was Joe Byrne.

The Fitzpatrick Incident and Its Aftermath

12

Constable Fitzpatrick

Constable Alexander Fitzpatrick was a rarity: a Victorian policeman born in Victoria. At the time he joined, there were only 30 other Victorian-born men in the entire force of over a thousand.[1]

Fitzpatrick was born on 18 February 1856 in the mining village of Mount Egerton near Ballarat to English parents Charles and Jane. Charles was a carpenter. Young Fitzpatrick was an expert horseman who, in his own words, could 'ride like a centaur'. He worked as a boundary rider for a time, and through that came to the notice of prosecutor Charles A. Smythe, probably as an employee. Smythe was so impressed that he personally recommended Fitzpatrick to Captain Standish for recruitment. *This* was the sort of young man they needed more of in the force.

Upon enlistment in 1876 he spent three months at the Richmond barracks and was then transferred to Benalla, under the supervision of Sergeant Whelan. His fiancée, Anna, stayed behind in Frankston, south of Melbourne. Fitzpatrick already had a child from a failed relationship with a woman from a village near his home town, for whom he paid child maintenance out of every pay cheque.[2]

Ned Kelly was blind drunk when Fitzpatrick first met him in September 1877. Fitzpatrick arrested him for public drunkenness, escorted him to the lock-up and, as he described it later, 'looked after him and treated him kindly'. He declined to press charges, and he believed Kelly was grateful for his leniency. He felt he had formed a rapport with Kelly.[3]

Ned Kelly enjoyed relating a story about how, the morning after one occasion of being arrested for drunkenness (perhaps a different occasion), as he was being escorted to the courthouse, he made a dash for freedom and ran into a bootmaker's shop. He claimed it took four police plus the bootmaker to subdue him, and that he kicked Fitzpatrick into a wall. He also claimed that (either in that brawl or another) Constable Lonigan subdued him with a 'dirty grip' on his genitals.[4]

Two weeks later, a warrant was issued for Ned's younger brother Dan and their cousins Tom and Jack Lloyd (junior) for assault, robbery and malicious damage. It transpired that Dan Kelly was employed or contracted to deliver meat to the Goodmans' store in Winton, a small village outside Benalla on the way to Glenrowan. Dan had arrived drunk, with his cousins in tow. Amelia Goodman became frightened of them, so she bolted the door, but they broke through it. They subsequently did significant damage to the store and the contents.[5]

Amelia's husband, Davis, was out. Her eleven-year-old son was there, and a young hawker named Moris Solomon, who tried to stand up to the intruders.

Dan asked Moris, 'Who are you?'

He answered, 'I'm only a stranger, but I don't see why you should annoy a married woman like that.'

Dan told Moris to get out of there. He said he needed some potatoes, and told Moris to go and fetch some potatoes for him from the store, which adjoined the room they were in. Not wanting to be left alone, Amelia said she would get the potatoes.

As soon as Amelia had left the room, the youths allegedly bashed Moris, causing his head to bleed.

Amelia's baby started crying, so she went into the bedroom to breastfeed. While she was in there, the boys carried on outside the door, making lewd comments. The other two pushed Tom into the bedroom towards her, allegedly with his penis out.

Her eleven-year-old son ran to get help. The schoolmaster soon came, but the three chased him away. She shut the door again but they smashed it open again, this time tearing it completely off its hinges. She escaped through the back door and ran to a neighbour for help. When she returned with the neighbour, the three youths had fled.

Warrants were issued for Dan Kelly, Tom Lloyd and Jack Lloyd. The police went to their homes, but the boys were not there. Searches were conducted across the district, but the boys could not be located. Two weeks later, while travelling into Benalla, Fitzpatrick met Ned Kelly, and spoke to him about the case. Kelly said that the district superintendent had asked him to 'give up' Dan, Tom and Jack to the police.

Blatantly flattering the young constable, Kelly said, 'If I gave them up to anybody, I'd give them up to you,' but then added, 'I'll keep them out of the road for twelve months, in defiance of all the police.'

Fitzpatrick told Kelly he should give the boys up, reassuring him, 'I don't think there's anything serious against them.' That was not true.[6]

The next day, Ned Kelly returned to Benalla accompanied by Dan and the Lloyds, who surrendered themselves at the police station.

Fitzpatrick believed that he was responsible for the young men coming in to face justice; he believed his kindness in not pressing drunkenness charges, and his persuasive powers in his conversation on the road to Benalla had achieved what the entire district police force had failed to do. He believed that he had proven that charm, friendship and a lenient attitude could achieve more than a gung-ho attitude.

Fitzpatrick was naive and gullible to believe that he had persuaded Ned to bring the boys in. A more likely factor was the weakening of the case against them: during the two weeks they were in hiding, the prosecution witness Moris Solomon had disappeared. The only remaining witnesses were Amelia and her eleven-year-old son.[7]

At their court appearance on 19 October 1877, they were found not guilty of unlawful entering, but were found guilty of wilfully damaging property, and sentenced to three months' imprisonment in Beechworth Gaol, plus a fine of £2 2s each, in default of which they would have to serve a further three months.

Tom Lloyd's trial for assault and attempted rape was held on 28 February.[8]

Amelia Goodman testified against him. Her eleven-year-old son bravely took the stand and testified too.

The witnesses for the defence were the accused, Tom Lloyd, and his brother Jack. Their version of events was that everyone sat around drinking gin, then all shook hands before departing. The magistrate, Justice Bindon, told the jury he did not believe that there was a case against the young man. He added that if there *was* any case to be heard, 'there was at most but evidence of a common assault'.

The jury found him guilty of assault, but not of attempted rape. Bindon gave him a four-month sentence in Beechworth Gaol.

Moris Solomon was never seen again.

In Wangaratta, while Sergeant Steele hunted for the mysterious Thompson, the first cases involving the Baumgarten ring were heard in court in November. Whereas the investigations had been exemplary, the prosecution was a shambles.

The eyes of magistrates, jurors and court reporters glazed over as the trials bogged down in a disorienting swamp of details. Altered brands; forged receipts; fake names; fake identities; river crossings; and with the ever-mysterious Thompson shimmering in the background.

Adding to the prosecutors' headaches, the Benalla poundkeeper, Alexander Whitla (nicknamed 'Whitlow'), had vanished. A key witness for the prosecution, he could potentially identify individuals who had delivered and collected stolen animals from the pound, but he could not be found anywhere.[9]

When the Baumgarten brothers were tried in February 1878, the jury failed to reach a verdict; the brothers were discharged but committed for retrial.

An eyewitness confirmed that Thompson was Ned Kelly, and on 15 March, a warrant was issued in Chiltern for Kelly's arrest. A witness recalled that two of the men transporting the Whitty horses to the Baumgartens' properties bore a strong resemblance to Dan Kelly and Jack Lloyd. Warrants were therefore issued on 5 April 1878 in Chiltern for the arrest of Dan Kelly and Jack Lloyd.

In his first twelve months of service, Fitzpatrick had impressed his colleagues and superiors. His evaluation in March described him as 'a young constable and likely to prove a useful one'. Constable McIntyre described him as a 'decent young fellow' and later testified that he 'never saw anything wrong with Fitzpatrick'.[10]

In early April he was assigned duty at a horseracing event in Cashel. Meanwhile at the Greta police station, Senior-Constable Strahan became ill and was granted sick leave. Sergeant Whelan received a telegram from the district chief that Fitzpatrick was being temporarily transferred to Greta to fill in during Strahan's absence.

Whelan did not anticipate Fitzpatrick's return until Sunday at the earliest, so he despatched Constable Healy to Greta in the meantime, instructing him to return on Monday, when Fitzpatrick would be back. The Cashel races finished on Saturday afternoon, so Fitzpatrick slept at the Cashel police barracks on Saturday night, then returned to Benalla the next day, arriving on Sunday afternoon.

Healy's presence in Greta meant that Fitzpatrick was not required there until Monday. He arranged with Whelan that he would stay Sunday night at Benalla barracks and ride to Greta on Monday.

As he perused the latest *Police Gazette*, he noticed the warrant for Dan Kelly's arrest.

Coincidentally, while at Cashel he had seen Dan Kelly, who was attending the race event, and had seen him again when returning to Benalla. Dan was riding a bay mare on both occasions. Fitzpatrick told Sergeant Whelan that on his way to Greta he planned to stop in at the Kelly shanty and arrest Dan Kelly. Whelan had misgivings, because he considered the Kellys to be dangerous.[11]

He endorsed the plan, but warned Fitzpatrick to be careful. He knew that Fitzpatrick had no choice but to attempt the arrest. The police regulations were crystal clear: they were required to arrest a wanted offender when the opportunity arose, with or without a physical copy of the warrant in their hand.[12]

Fitzpatrick set out on Monday morning, no doubt excited by his responsibility as officer-in-charge, and of the opportunity to bring in Dan Kelly a second time.

13

The Fitzpatrick incident

Constable Fitzpatrick left the Benalla police yard on horseback at 2 p.m. on 15 April 1878. He rode north-east along the main road, then stopped a short way out of town at David Lindsay's Hotel in Winton, where he had a brandy and lemonade, and sought information on the Kelly brothers. After finishing his drink, he rode east along Eleven Mile Creek Road in the direction of Greta. He reached the Kelly shanty between 4 and 5 p.m.

Fitzpatrick was later accused by the Kellys of arriving drunk, his visit to Lindsay's Hotel seemingly corroborating their accusation. However, if that was true, he would not have arrived when he did. Police were required to always ride their horses at walking pace, 'except upon an emergency'. At walking pace, a rider with a heavy pack would take about two hours to ride the eleven miles from Benalla to Eleven Mile Creek, so Fitzpatrick can only have spent a short time in Winton.[1]

Fitzpatrick dismounted and went to the door, hoping to find Dan Kelly, but the only people home were Ellen Kelly and three children, including fourteen-year-old Kate. He chatted to Ellen for about an hour, stalling for time, hoping that Dan would arrive while he was there. Then he heard the sound of woodchopping from up the hill, so he investigated, in case it was Dan chopping. It was the Kellys' family friend, Brickey Williamson.

As an excuse to talk, Fitzpatrick approached and asked if Brickey had a splitter's licence. Brickey said he didn't need one, because this property was a selection, where a licence was not required. They talked for about ten minutes. It was now dusk. Fitzpatrick gave up on arresting Dan Kelly, mounted his horse, and set forth towards Greta once more.

As he rode away, Fitzpatrick saw, through the gloom, two horsemen riding towards the Kelly shanty. The riders entered the slip panels into the Kellys' yard. Fitzpatrick wheeled around, and followed them. By the time he reached the yard, only one man was there. It was Bill Skillion, the Kelly boys' brother-in-law, leading two horses. There was a third horse nearby that appeared to have been ridden recently, so he asked Skillion who had been riding it.

Skillion said he didn't know.

Fitzpatrick looked closer at the third horse and recognised it as the bay mare that he had seen Dan Kelly riding a few days earlier. He said, 'That's Dan's horse. Where is he?'

Skillion said, 'Up at the house, I suppose.'

Fitzpatrick returned to the Kelly shanty. He stood out the front, and called out, 'Dan!'

Dan Kelly emerged, his hat and coat off, holding a knife and fork.

Fitzpatrick said, 'I'm going to arrest you on a charge of horse stealing, Dan.'

Dan said, 'Very well. You'll let me have something to eat before you take me?'[2]

Fitzpatrick said, 'All right.'

As they went inside, Dan said, 'I've been out riding all day.'

His mother Ellen was still inside, as were Kate and the two younger girls. Ellen whispered something to the girls, who ran out of the house to the back. Dan sat down to finish his dinner.

Ellen was furious that Fitzpatrick's earlier friendliness had merely been a ruse in order to arrest Dan. She shouted abuse at Fitzpatrick: 'You're a deceitful little bugger! I always thought you were!' Then she said, 'You *will not* take him out of this tonight.'

Dan said, 'Shut up, mother! That's all right.'

Behind Ellen, the fireplace flickered.

Fitzpatrick was momentarily distracted by Bill Skillion walking past the house, leading a horse.[3]

Ellen raged at Fitzpatrick. Picking up the fire shovel, she raised it at him menacingly, moving towards him, to drive him out the door.

Ned later accused him of drawing his revolver and shouting, 'I'll blow your brains out!' Maybe he did, with the situation heating up, and with his pulse pounding like a marching drum.

Fitzpatrick was unsuccessfully trying to assert his authority, to rein in an out-of-control situation. He was about to learn the same hard lesson that Constable Hall had learned seven years earlier: the Kellys never backed down.

Ned Kelly appeared in the rear doorway with a pistol, and fired. It seemed to be a warning shot, as the bullet zipped past him into the far wall.

Surprised and shocked, Fitzpatrick spun around to face Ned.

Ellen smashed the fire shovel against his head, knocking his helmet down over his eyes.

Temporarily blinded by his helmet, Fitzpatrick raised his arm in Ellen's direction to fend off a second blow from the shovel. Ned fired again, hitting Fitzpatrick in the wrist.

He was firing wide again to scare Fitzpatrick, but the policeman's arm flailed wildly in the air to defend against the shovel, intercepting the bullet.[4]

Fitzpatrick pushed his helmet off his eyes and reached for his gun, but it was not in the holster. Dan was on his feet nearby, holding it.

Ned approached, pistol still raised.

Fitzpatrick grabbed the muzzle and pushed it away, exclaiming, 'You cowardly wretch! Do you want to murder me?'[5]

Ned tried to wrest the pistol out of Fitzpatrick's grip. As they tussled for it, Ned's gun discharged a third time, hitting a wall.

Brickey and Skillion had entered the room. There were now four men aiming guns at Fitzpatrick, including Dan who was brandishing Fitzpatrick's police-issued Webley.

Ned Kelly said, 'That'll do, boys.' He turned to Skillion and said, 'You bugger, why didn't you tell me who was here? If I'd known it was Fitzpatrick I wouldn't have fired. If it had been any of the other buggers, they wouldn't leave here alive.'[6]

Ned's insincere flattery of Fitzpatrick rang hollow in the aftermath of the fight. Ned was already moving to smooth it all over with the young policeman. There was some truth in what he said, because he had been led to believe a different policeman was in the house.[7]

Kate Kelly, who had been there the whole time, sat down and cried.[8]

Fitzpatrick's wrist was still bleeding. He felt dizzy. He fainted.

When he regained consciousness, he was on the floor. He did not know how long he had been out. He could hear people talking near the fireplace.

He heard Kelly say, 'Bill would have given that bugger who went by a pill the other day.' ('*Pill*' meant bullet. Joe Byrne's alias was Billy King, or Bill.)[9]

Skillion said, 'What, the Benalla cove?' (Sergeant Whelan.)

Kelly said, 'No, Sergeant Steele. And I've got a pill for him yet.'

Skillion and Brickey left.

Fitzpatrick got up. The only other people in the room were Ned and Ellen.

Ned said to him, 'I'm sorry this happened. It will get me into trouble. I'll get it pretty heavy.'[10]

Fitzpatrick saw a bullet hole in the bark in the wall, near where he had been attacked.[11] Seeing his disassembled revolver on the table with the bullets removed, he put it together again. Ned came over and took it out of his hand. He asked Fitzpatrick if he had any bullets other than the ones in the revolver. Fitzpatrick said he didn't.

Ned examined Fitzpatrick's wrist. There was a bullet lodged in it. He said, 'Here's the bullet, we must have it out.'

Fitzpatrick said it was fine, and he would take it to a doctor.

Ned said that wasn't possible. 'You can't go away with that in your hand.'

Ned produced a rusty razor to cut it out, but Fitzpatrick offered his penknife, which Ned used instead. He cut the bullet out of the wound. It was a small, pointed ball. Ellen Kelly then bandaged Fitzpatrick's wrist.[12]

Ned complimented him: 'You're very plucky to suffer the pain.'[13]

These seeming acts of kindness were designed to remove the evidence, ameliorate the injury and make the incident go away.

Fitzpatrick went outside and sat on a log. It was a cold, starry night with an almost full moon. The ground was soggy from recent rain.[14]

Ned followed him, and said, 'Now, I spared you; now you spare me. How will we manage to say you were shot?'[15]

Fitzpatrick said he wouldn't mention who shot him.

Ned said, 'You'd better say you went up to arrest Dan, and he was with Williamson, and you were putting the handcuffs on, and you had your revolver out, and it went off and shot you. And Dan took your ammunition from you.'

But then Ned had a better idea. He asked Fitzpatrick if he knew Whitlow. That was a reference to the Benalla poundkeeper, Alexander Whitla, a prosecution witness in the horse-theft trial who had been missing for six months. Fitzpatrick had never met him because Whitla had disappeared soon after his arrival in Benalla.

Ned persevered anyway. 'Say this. Two men rushed from behind a tree as you were arresting Dan. Describe them as two big men, one of them like me, so they'll think it's my brother Jim, and the other Whitlow. And then say, 'I heard one of them sing out, "*Oh! Whitlow! You've shot him!*"'.'

Kelly explained that the reason for using Whitlow and Jim Kelly was that both of them were 'miles away'. Ned knew something that the authorities didn't, namely that his brother Jim was locked away in a New South Wales prison under a false name. He knew that it was safe to finger Jim as a suspect, because Jim would not be found. Clearly, Ned knew that Whitlow was similarly unobtainable.

Ned enthusiastically encouraged Fitzpatrick to report that Jim Kelly and Whitlow were responsible because nobody could prove the story true or false. He instructed Fitzpatrick to get out his notebook and write all this down. Fitzpatrick played along.

Ned was on a roll. As he enacted his moonlit drama, he had Whitlow confess to stealing various horses in the district. Whitlow even confessed to stealing horses from Bill Frost, Ellen's poor ex-lover, whom the family continued to persecute. Ned made Fitzpatrick write that down too.

Fitzpatrick wanted to leave. He asked for his revolver back. Not yet, Ned told him. He said the others were bringing his horse around, as they had hidden it in a rear paddock while Fitzpatrick was laid out on the floor.

Ned said, 'If you do say I shot you, you'll get no credit for it. The government won't reward you. But I'll make it worth your while. I'll give you a few hundred, which I'll have after the Baumgarten case is over. They only want me to keep out of the way until the case is over.'[16]

Ellen had come out. She interjected, saying to Ned, 'You'd better tell him that if he does mention it, his life will be no good to him. We have plenty of friends to do for him.'

Dan Kelly and Bill Skillion arrived with Fitzpatrick's horse. Dan returned his handcuffs, and Ned returned the revolver. Fitzpatrick mounted his horse, and rode down to the road. Then, instead of proceeding to Greta, he turned west, back towards Benalla.

About two and a half miles along the road, he turned and saw two riders following him. He believed they were Bill Skillion and

Brickey Williamson, tracking him down after a change of heart about letting him go.

He spurred on, and rode hard until he arrived once more at David Lindsay's pub at Winton. To calm his nerves, they offered him a glass of brandy, which he gratefully accepted. The publican later testified:

> I saw Fitzpatrick at my house between 10 and 11 at night. He came on horseback. He appeared faint and weak. He sat down beside the house. He had his hand bandaged up. I undid it and wet the cloth and bandaged it up. He told me how it occurred. It was bleeding there. Gave him some drink. He could not take it at first. He was quite sober.[17]

David Lindsay accompanied Fitzpatrick to Benalla. They rapped on Sergeant Whelan's door at about 2 a.m. Whelan examined his arm, and 'saw a mark like a bullet wound'. He sent for Dr Nicholson, and took Fitzpatrick's statement.[18]

As Nicholson treated Fitzpatrick, he smelt the whisky that he had consumed at Lindsay's Hotel, although Fitzpatrick did not appear drunk and there was no indication that he had been drinking heavily.

The next morning, Sergeant Whelan fired off a telegram announcing the attack on Fitzpatrick by Ned Kelly and Ellen Kelly. He and Fitzpatrick went to the Benalla courthouse, where Whelan issued a warrant against Ned Kelly for attempted murder, and warrants against Ellen Kelly, Dan Kelly, Bill Skillion and Brickey Williamson for aiding and abetting.[19]

14

The arrest of Ellen Kelly

Sergeant Steele was on duty at the Wangaratta police station on Tuesday morning, 16 April 1878. Inspector Nicolson was in town, and only moments earlier, Steele and Nicolson had been talking about Ned Kelly, who was wanted for charges of horse stealing. Steele had told Nicolson that he believed Kelly would 'take to the bush'.[1] In other words, he would hide in the wilderness, emerging to engage in acts of bushranging.

Nicolson had briefly stepped out of the office when a telegram arrived from Benalla:

> Constable Fitzpatrick attempted to arrest Daniel Kelly at his mother's near Greta at 6 o clock yesterday evening. Ned Kelly fired two shots from a revolver at him, the second ball lodged in his left wrist. William Skillion and Williamson alias Brickey were there armed with revolvers and presented them at him. Mrs Kelly struck the constable with a shovel on the head. In throwing up his arms he received the ball. Description: Skillion, Irish, 26 years, stout build, round shouldered, fair complexion, wears all his beard cut very short, all identifiable. Both dressed in bush dress. Mrs Kelly is well known to district police. Offenders will most likely make for New South Wales. Warrants will issue at once. Constable here not in danger.[2]

When Nicolson returned, Steele showed the telegram to him. To Steele's surprise, it didn't alter Nicolson's travel plans. Nicolson's attitude was that it was not his district and therefore not his problem. As the inspector of stations, he had planned to visit the Bright station that day, and was not going to be sidetracked. He bade Steele good day, and then departed for the railway station to catch the late morning train up the mountain to Beechworth. From there he rode to Bright.[3]

It was curious that Nicolson would tour the smaller stations, acting like a martinet by terrorising the hapless constables for minor infractions, but he seemed to have no problem with the rampant laxity and incompetence of senior officers, such as Inspector Brooke-Smith in Wangaratta.

Steele stayed beside the telegraph machine, awaiting further instructions. None came.

He found Detective Brown and showed him the telegram. They left immediately for Greta Police Station.[4] Senior-Constable Strahan was there, having returned from leave early, presumably having been instructed to do so. He joined them as they rode to Eleven Mile Creek.

Steele knew that warrants were issued—Whelan's telegram said they were being issued—so they could, in theory, barge right in and arrest everyone. But they wanted to catch the Kelly brothers, and in particular Ned, so they stopped on a nearby hill and sat and watched the Kelly shanty. The suspects didn't seem to be home, and there was no sign of them for the rest of the day.

At nine in the evening, they rode down to the shanty.

Ellen and Kate were home.

Steele asked Ellen if she had been present when her son Ned shot Fitzpatrick.

She replied, 'It would be hard for me to see him, when he wasn't at my place.'

Strahan asked with surprise, 'Do you mean to tell me that Constable Fitzpatrick wasn't at your place?'

Ellen replied to Strahan, 'I haven't seen Constable Fitzpatrick since you and him was at my place, and that's over a month. And as for seeing my son Ned, I haven't seen him for the past four months.'[5]

Kate endorsed her mother's statements.

They arrested Brickey Williamson at his selection next door.

They also went to the adjacent Skillion property on the other side and arrested Bill Skillion, who told them he had nothing to do with it and wasn't there. He said he saw Fitzpatrick riding past his house at about five in the evening towards the Kellys' place.

The two constables returned to the Kelly house; but there was no sign of Ned and Dan, so they took Brickey and Skillion to the Benalla lock-up.

On the way, Brickey said that he had a conversation with Fitzpatrick about a splitter's licence, but that was the extent of his interaction. The last time he saw Fitzpatrick, the constable was crossing a paddock after Dan Kelly. He didn't hear any gunfire.[6]

Steele, Brown and Strahan returned to the Kellys' place at one in the morning. Ellen was still awake. Steele told her that he was arresting her for her part in the assault on Fitzpatrick.

Ellen asked what Fitzpatrick claimed she did.

He told her, 'He accuses you of striking him on the head with a shovel.'[7]

She admitted doing it. She explained, 'I know I've a damn bad temper. You wouldn't like to see a son of your own taken away. If they once got him into gaol, there's no telling what those bloody wretches would swear against him if they got him in. He got into it innocently.'[8]

Kate was awake, despite the late hour, and distraught. Steele talked to her privately. She confided that the only reason they didn't kill Fitzpatrick was because of her: she had cried and begged them not to.[9]

Steele took Ellen Kelly to the Greta lock-up.

The three prisoners were moved to Benalla on Wednesday afternoon, to appear at the Benalla police court on Thursday. At the preliminary hearing, Magistrate F. McDonnell ordered them to be remanded in Beechworth Gaol awaiting a full hearing.[10]

A fortnight after the incident, the Victorian government issued a notice of reward of £100 for anyone providing information that led to Ned Kelly's arrest.[11]

15

Ward undercover

Detective Michael Ward and Constable Ernest Flood were redeployed to Benalla to work on the Kelly case. Both had previously served in the Ovens district; both knew the Kellys; and both were young, energetic and smart. They reported to the very top, directly and secretly. Flood reported to Standish; Ward to the chief of detectives, Inspector Secretan.

Ward arrived at Benalla Railway Station on Thursday, three days after Fitzpatrick was shot. It was the day of the preliminary hearings and the Kelly sisters, Kate Kelly and Maggie Skillion, were in court. Ward believed—or hoped—that Ned and Dan might sneak home for a visit that evening for an update. He watched the Kelly sisters ride out of town in their horse and dray, waited a little while longer, then left in the same direction—towards Eleven Mile Creek. He was accompanied by Senior-Constable Strahan and two others.

The light was fading, and bad weather was coming in. By the time they turned onto the Greta Road at Winton it was raining hard. Two miles out of Winton, they came across a dray with no horse attached, but with two bags of flour and other personal items on it. They searched nearby and found Kate and Maggie sitting on a log, drenched. They had crashed their horse and dray in the dark, and their horse had galloped off. In the dark night storm, they were lost and could not find their way home.[1]

They recognised Ward and Strahan. Ward offered Kate some whisky from a bottle to warm her up, which she accepted.[2]

Ward assigned the two other constables to escort the women home, while he and Strahan parted company with them, pretending to go elsewhere. Instead, Ward and Strahan went to a hill near Eleven Mile Creek where they could watch the Kelly house. They stayed there and watched all night, but there was no sign of Ned or Dan.[3]

In the weeks that followed, Ward rode around the district making inquiries. He soon learned that the Kelly brothers might be hiding near Ryans Creek, or its tributary Bullock Creek, down south in the Wombat Ranges between Greta and Mansfield.

Power had once hidden in the sparsely populated hills and valleys of the Wombat Ranges, protected by the Quinn family, who then lived at the edge of the ranges. The Quinns had long since sold the Glenmore Run, and Power was in prison, but the forested valleys of the ranges offered myriad hideaways.

He searched Bullocky Gully with no luck, then organised a search party in early June that went south from Greta into the Wombat Ranges. He was accompanied by Strahan as well as constables Twomey, Hayes and Whitty. They camped at Ryans Creek for three days, conducting searches of the surrounding creeks and valleys.[4]

They were not in uniform: it was against policy to wear uniform on multi-day search patrols like this. Police had to purchase their own uniforms, and they weren't a cheap purchase on a meagre constable's wage. Further, uniforms worn on camping trips would come back soiled and damaged, reflecting poorly on the constables wearing them, and also on the public perception of the force.

They did not find the Kelly brothers.

While Ellen, Brickey and Skillion awaited trial, Constable Flood visited the Kelly shanty on 13 May, accompanied by Constable

Fitzpatrick and Sergeant Steele. They conducted a search. They found no firearms, but Flood found a bullet mould. Fitzpatrick reconstructed the events of a month earlier. They inspected the walls where the two bullets that didn't hit him would have gone. They found no bullet holes. However, two sections of the bark wall had been replaced with new strips of bark.[5]

Back at the Benalla station, Flood used the mould to make two lead bullets and examined them. They were small, pointed balls that matched Fitzpatrick's wound. There was subsequently much speculation that perhaps the wound was caused by Fitzpatrick's own weapon, but that was not credible. A discharge from a Webley into his wrist at point blank range would have ripped a substantial—potentially lethal—hole in his arm, whereas Kelly's small-bore, low-powered pistol could have inflicted a non-fatal wound.[6]

Ward established a network of agents and informers across the district, but one of his agents was quickly exposed.

A painter named Charles Askew arrived from Melbourne in early May, gaining employment in Winton, all expenses being covered by Ward. Somehow, the criminals found out. Maybe Askew blabbed.

Jimmy Quinn was the Kellys' standover man. If someone was making trouble, he would take care of it. If someone was suspected of being a police informer, Jimmy would see to it that they didn't inform anymore.

Askew was on the main street of Winton when Jimmy Quinn rode up and offered to fight him for £1. Askew declined. Jimmy jumped off his horse and came at Askew, landing solid punches. Askew fell; then, as he tried to get up, Jimmy kicked him, and he fell again. Askew got to his feet and ran to a nearby house. The woman refused to help. Jimmy caught up with him and beat him senseless.

Jimmy then went into hiding in a remote place along Black Range Creek. Ward and Flood found him there and arrested him. When Ward told him what he was being arrested for, Jimmy said he didn't know anything about it.

Jimmy appeared at the Benalla police court before magistrates Wyatt and McKellar. They set bail at £100, awaiting trial. Three months later, a jury found Jimmy not guilty. That's how things went in the Ovens district.

Ward returned to Melbourne and waited for news. One of his agents, a blacksmith near Beechworth, contacted him in late August. He said he had seen Ned Kelly passing by The Woolshed district's commons with a gun under his arm and a revolver strapped to his saddle, riding in the direction of Joe Byrne's mother's house.[7]

Ward notified Inspector Secretan, who instructed him to return north to follow up on the lead. He didn't leave immediately, however, but remained in Melbourne for two more weeks, growing his hair and beard out, and making preparations. This time he went incognito, disguised as an itinerant worker: a butcher, a splitter or simply a swagman. When he returned to the district on 9 September, he was unrecognisable.[8]

Secretan gave Ward total latitude in his actions. Two blacktrackers were posted to the district, for him to call on if needed. His local contact was Constable Flood.[9]

The trail was already cold. He learned that, although the Kellys had been in the vicinity of Beechworth, they were now in New South Wales. When they returned, he would make a move. In the meantime, he travelled through the district in disguise, looking for other clues. He even encountered Kate Kelly on one occasion, but she didn't notice or recognise him.

Undercover life would have been rough for Michael Ward. Swagmen were an ever-present feature of the colonial landscape, travelling as they did from town to town with their bed-rolls—their 'swags'—on their backs, a billy can dangling. They were former gold-miners, broke after the gold bust, or immigrants in search of seasonal work, or roaming criminals. Many were destitute, while others carried large hidden stashes of cash.[10] The valleys and mountains around the Ovens and King rivers were cold in winter, dangerous for camping out with only a swag; many swagmen stayed in workers' huts on squatting runs and large selections. Sparse and rudimentary, they at least offered protection from rain and frost. Those who slept rough in the ranges sometimes died of exposure.

The risk of his cover being blown was greater near the towns of Beechworth and Wangaratta, where he had served for years as a constable. The highland settlements of the Upper King Valley and the scattered villages in the lower reaches of the Snowy Mountains were safer bets.[11]

As a splitter he was cutting logs, which was backbreaking work available year-round. It is likely that, with the arrival of the shearing season in spring, Ward joined the influx of swagmen to the crowded workers' huts on the sheep stations. Shearing was hard work, but not as hard as splitting, and with an Irish accent like Ward's it would have been easy to blend in with travelling workers from across the colonies.

In the interim, the Ovens district chief inspector, Chomley, was replaced by John Sadleir, who had been the officer in charge at Mansfield.[12]

Like almost everyone else in the force, John Sadleir was born in Ireland, but unlike most of them, his Tipperary relatives were well-to-do. He joined the Victorian police in 1852, only a month after arriving in the colony, as part of the drive to recruit 'gentlemen' to counteract the predominance of violent, indolent ex-convicts, ex-convict guards and drunks.

He was immediately promoted to sergeant, soon followed by further rapid promotions to sub-inspector, inspector and superintendent. He had never been a constable; had never done late-night foot patrols of Melbourne hotels; had never whiled away time as the sole cop in a mountain village; never served as a stagecoach guard.

Even Standish, with his posh family background, had spent a few years as a starving miner in Ballarat and a goldfield merchant in Beechworth, but those experiences were also beyond Sadleir's realm. For him, life was meant to be easy.

He was favoured by the establishment because of his class background, but also because he was earnest and dependable, and because he was trained in community-focused 'bobby'-style police methods. He was a nice, well-meaning man, who attended church, didn't drink, didn't brawl and didn't shirk duty when it was required of him. He was neither lazy nor corrupt. All these things put him above the competition for promotion. The only downside, and it was a trifling matter compared to his many strengths, was that he wasn't particularly bright.[13]

Secretan briefed him about Ward's arrival in the district, instructing him to keep the information to himself. He was never informed of Flood's role as Ward's point man. Sadleir asked Secretan if he could at least tell one or two highly trusted officers about it: he didn't want to keep it a *complete* secret. Secretan reiterated that, no, he could not tell anyone.[14]

The operation was Standish's idea, and Secretan confided that he doubted it would come to anything. He told Sadleir, 'I hope the move will be successful, for it begins to look rather doubtful. Still, must hope for the best.'[15]

Sadleir was excited to hear Ward's theories about Kelly's possible haunts. He was familiar with the Wombat Ranges from his years living in Mansfield, knew that criminals rode the forest trails there, and knew there were many places to hide.

Sadleir made contact with his former colleague in Mansfield, Sergeant Michael Kennedy. He told Kennedy that a patrol 'has been proposed' (without saying by whom), and he sought Kennedy's opinion on it. In fact, Ward had *already* organised and led such a patrol.[16]

Kennedy agreed with Sadleir's theory that the Kellys were in the Wombat Ranges. He suggested that they might establish a base camp at a place called Stringybark Creek:

> The distance from Mansfield to the King River is so great, and the country impenetrable, that a party of men from here would, in my opinion, require to establish a kind of depot at some distance beyond the Wombat—say Stringybark Creek, seven miles beyond Monk's. By forming a camp there, it would enable the party to keep up a continuous search between there and the flat country towards the King River, Fifteen-mile Creek, Hollands Creek.[17]

Kennedy added: 'I feel sure, by efficiently carrying out this plan, Kelly would soon be disturbed, if not captured.'

Under Sadleir's direction, Kennedy led multiple patrols through the Wombat Ranges over the next few months, although Ward had learned that the Kellys had crossed the border north. These patrols had the potential to ruin Ward's plans because if the Kellys learned that the police were monitoring the ranges, they might not return.[18]

Sergeant Kennedy, who knew nothing of Ward and received only cryptic advice from Sadleir, went out with constables McIntyre and Johnston, riding through the wooded winter valleys of the upper King River. But he found no sign of the Kelly brothers.[19]

16

The trial of Ellen Kelly

The hearings for Ellen Kelly, Brickey Williamson and Bill Skillion took place in the Benalla police court on 16 May 1878. The presiding magistrates were McBean, O'Donnell and Roe.[1]

The lawyer for the accused, Zinke, reserved his defence. These hearings were to decide whether the cases would go to trial, which they almost certainly would. There was no need to play all his cards quite yet.

Zinke and his clients patiently listened while the prosecution outlined the case in detail. Zinke noted details that could be exploited at trial.

He noted that Constable Fitzpatrick had stopped at Lindsay's Hotel on the way to Eleven Mile Creek, and again on the return to Benalla, consuming alcohol on both occasions.

He noted that Skillion was alleged to have been in the house brandishing a firearm when the shooting occurred.

When Dr Nicholson testified about treating Fitzpatrick's wound. He said,

> There appeared to be a bullet wound. The bullet had apparently entered at the outside of the wrist at the end of the bone, then moved upwards in a slanting direction across the wrist and lodged in the back of the wrist under the skin. The entrance wound was slightly elongated in the course of the bullet. At the exit end, there was a clean incision, a little more than half an inch in length. The incision was not in a straight line, but slightly curved to the left.[2]

Zinke cross-examined him: 'Would you *swear* it was a bullet wound?'

As a man of science, and with all the circumspection he believed was due in a courtroom, Dr Nicholson replied, 'I could not swear it was a bullet wound, but it had all the appearance of one.'[3]

Zinke made note of that. Clearly, Dr Nicholson believed Fitzpatrick's account, but the fact that he would not *swear* it was a bullet wound . . . that could be useful.

Brickey and Skillion were remanded in custody to await trial at the Beechworth Assizes in October. The Assizes, also known as the General Sessions, were presided over by a Supreme Court judge and were reserved for major cases. Ellen was granted bail while awaiting trial, set at £100. She made bail in June after it was reduced to £50, thanks to the generosity of a local squatter. In reporting her release, the *Advertiser* mentioned that she had a baby with her:

> It was an act of charity, as the poor woman, though not the most reputable of characters, had a babe in her arms, and in the cold gaol without a fire, it is a wonder the poor little child lived so long during this bitter wintry weather.[4]

None of the police reported seeing a baby at the house at the time of the incident or the arrest, and no baby was taken with Ellen to the lock-up, but Beechworth Gaol records show that she had an infant with her. It is possible that it was Kate's baby, whom Ellen was wet-nursing.[5]

The Beechworth Assizes were held over two days in October, before Justice Redmond Barry. A jury was empanelled and the three cases were tried together.[6]

After Fitzpatrick had testified, Ellen's defence barrister, John Bowman, went hard.[7]

Had he been instructed to go to the Kellys? No, Fitzpatrick replied, he hadn't.

Did he have a copy of the arrest warrant? No.

Did he, perhaps, have a brandy or two during his visit to the Kellys? No.

Did he concoct the entries in his logbook? No.

Did he actually expect people to believe his story? Yes, Fitzpatrick replied, he did.

Bowman accused Fitzpatrick of being so drunk at the time he didn't know what was going on. He told the jury that Fitzpatrick had no business being there, because he didn't have a physical copy of the warrant.

In fact, he didn't need a copy of the warrant. Arrest warrants don't work like search warrants, and the same applies today. Knowledge that the warrant exists is sufficient cause to arrest.

Lindsay testified that Fitzpatrick wasn't drunk, even though he had a brandy at the hotel to calm his nerves. Dr Nicholson also testified that he wasn't drunk, but Bowman got him to admit that he could smell brandy while treating him.

Bowman followed up on the weak point identified by Zinke, questioning the doctor if he would swear that the wound was caused by a bullet. The doctor answered as he had in the May hearing. The jury, who heard his reply firsthand, must have realised that this line of questioning was a dead end. It didn't impact the result of the trial, but landed a rhetorical blow when it was reported in the press.

The journalist for the *Advertiser* in court that day jotted a summary of Nicholson's final word on Fitzpatrick's wounds: 'They might have been produced by a bullet'.

It sounded more dubious than the doctor's earlier, verbatim testimonial record—'I could not swear it was a bullet wound, but it had all the appearance of one'—and hence failed to capture his opinion, which, given his previous testimony, was that Fitzpatrick was shot. That journalistic scrawl is often interpreted as suggesting the doctor was hedging, when he was simply being misrepresented.

Bowman pressed the doctor about the seriousness of the injury, inducing him in an unguarded moment to describe it as a 'skin wound'. He asked the doctor if Fitzpatrick had lost much blood. Nicholson answered that he hadn't.

Then there was the question of the shooting itself. Bowman alleged that Ned Kelly had not intended to shoot Fitzpatrick (which may have been true: Ned may have intended it to be a warning shot). How, then, could these accused people be complicit in an unintentional act?

Bowman's final line of defence was that Skillion was not even present. He declared that if he could prove Skillion wasn't there, then the entire case was discredited. He called two witnesses, Joseph Ryan and Frank Hearty, who testified that Skillion was with them all day. They admitted that they all eventually visited the Kellys that evening, but by then 'the row was all over'.

And that's where Bowman's case fizzled. Ryan and Hearty both admitted to buying a horse from Ned Kelly that day. It wasn't a crime to buy a horse, even from Ned Kelly, but it certainly undermined their credibility. Then, under cross-examination, Joseph Ryan admitted that he was Ned Kelly's cousin.

The jury retired for two hours, then returned a verdict of guilty for all three.

Bowman's accusation that Fitzpatrick was a drunkard did not sway the trial, but the mud stuck: it is commonly, but wrongly, believed that Fitzpatrick ultimately died of cirrhosis of the liver.[8]

Justice Barry sentenced Brickey and Skillion to six years in Pentridge, and sentenced Ellen to three years.[9]

Standish wrote, much later, that he believed that an injustice had been done to Brickey Williamson, who should not even have been charged. He explained:

> Though I entertained that opinion at the time, I did not of course think it proper, as head of the Police Department, to offer my remarks on the verdict of the jury or the sentence passed by a Judge of the Supreme Court.

He also pushed for a remission of sentence for Brickey, commenting, 'It strikes me as astonishing that he was convicted of the offence at all'.[10]

Afterwards, in the Beechworth gaol yard, Ellen Kelly spoke to Brickey through the bars of Brickey's cell, telling him, 'They will play up. There will be murder now.'[11]

Seeking the Kelly Brothers

17

Border crossings

A tip-off came Michael Ward's way in October. The Kellys had returned from across the New South Wales border and were back in the Wombat Ranges. Ward notified Secretan, who contacted Superintendent Sadleir. Apparently, Sadleir was hoping to catch the Kellys in Beechworth at their mother's trial.

Secretan wrote to him:

> I have reliable information that the Kellys have not been in Victoria for a considerable time, but are expected immediately. I believe if they do come that Detective Ward will be in a position to effect their arrest. I think your men are merely guessing that, as the trial of their mother is coming on now, they are likely to be about. I should have written you before, but really had nothing positive until yesterday. Faithfully yours, FREDK.[1]

Ward went south, along the valley of the King River, to the ranges. He set up camp at Power's old hiding place, now known as Powers Lookout, and explored. He learned that the Kellys were around, somewhere nearby. He wasn't sure where, but believed they were camped near the King River.

He was correct that they were close by, but not about them camping by the river. They were hiding in a log hut a few miles west of the King on Ryans Creek, where Ward had searched for them six months earlier.

Ward broke camp and returned down the valley to Moyhu, where he gave a message to his contact (Constable Flood), who relayed it to Secretan on 15 October. Ward suggested enacting the plan they had considered in winter, with two separate patrols going into the ranges in a pincer movement. One group would leave from Greta on the north side of the ranges, the other from Mansfield on the south.[2]

The next day, Secretan instructed Sadleir to send patrols into the ranges:

> [send patrols from] Greta, Fifteen-mile Creek, and thence to Mansfield, as it is now (on the 17th October), alleged that one or both of the Kellys are about there, and, if not, this move will cause commotion in their camp.[3]

He forbade Sadleir to tell anyone about Ward's presence in the district.[4]

Through Flood, Ward was notified of the plan. The message included a suggestion from Secretan that he accompany one of the patrols.

Ward didn't do that. Instead, he returned to Powers Lookout and on Saturday 26 October set up camp there again. He reasoned that if the Kellys were discovered and chased out of the ranges, there was a good chance they might come there. If they did, Ward would be there, waiting to arrest them. If not, he would simply join up with the Mansfield patrol, led by Sergeant Kennedy, as it came down out of the ranges.[5]

He inscribed his name and date into the rock face.[6]

Then he sat on the lookout, the King Valley spread before him, the river twisting out of sight towards the Ovens River. He dared not light a fire for fear that the smoke would betray his presence. He snacked on cold food from his pack, with a flask of water and a flask of brandy beside him, listened to the birdsong, and waited.[7]

18

Into the Ranges

Mansfield was a sleepy little country town surrounded by rolling, fertile fields and ringed by forested mountains. To the east stood Mount Buller, snow-capped each winter.

Crime was relatively low. The locals attributed this, in part, to an association of Mansfield graziers and business folk called the Stock Protection Society. They had established a fund to reward police (or anyone willing) for catching stock thieves and for returning stolen horses and cattle. A policeman's pay was paltry, especially when compared to the profits of the wealthiest landowners. The occasional £5 bonus was motivating for the police, yet was a mere line entry in the accounts of the Stock Protection Society. It was, for the land-owners, money well spent. Sergeant Michael Kennedy had been the recipient of several such bonuses.[1]

John Sadleir had been the officer in charge at the Mansfield station until a few months earlier. Now the district chief in Benalla, he had been replaced by Inspector Pewtress.

On 21 October, Sergeant Kennedy received a telegram from Sadleir outlining the final arrangements for the planned patrols into the Wombat Ranges. Kennedy had been chosen to lead the Mansfield patrol. The other three members of his patrol would be constables McIntyre, Michael Scanlan and Thomas Lonigan.

McIntyre was a constable in Mansfield. Scanlan and Lonigan, chosen because they could recognise Ned Kelly, arrived for the patrol from Mooroopna and Violet Town respectively.

Lonigan was fearful that he might not return. As he departed from Violet Town, he returned three times to say goodbye to his wife. And Scanlan, before leaving Mooroopna, asked a mate to look after his dog if he didn't come home.[2]

Sergeant Kennedy was troubled too. Gesturing at the WANTED poster of Ned Kelly on the wall, he muttered, 'I don't like the look of that man.'[3]

Only McIntyre was unconcerned. The way he reasoned it, Ned Kelly had spared Fitzpatrick's life. He had even removed the bullet from Fitzpatrick's hand. McIntyre thought that surely these things proved that Ned Kelly was not a man of violence.[4]

McIntyre had never met the Kellys, but he did know their associate Wild Wright, who lived locally. After the Fitzpatrick shooting, he had made inquiries at the Wrights' house about the Kellys' whereabouts.

Wild Wright had said he knew where they were, but would not betray Ned Kelly 'for all the money in Australia'. Then he said, 'Ned Kelly is mad, and you'll see it one of these days. I tell you, McIntyre, he's mad.'[5]

Despite that earlier warning, McIntyre persuaded himself that everyone was far too worked up about the supposed risk that Ned Kelly posed.

A gold escort came through town, escorted by Senior-Constable Kelly (no relation) armed with a Spencer rifle. Kennedy asked to borrow the Spencer. Senior-Constable Kelly handed it over reluctantly, because now *he* was lightly armed, and if bailed up on the journey to Melbourne, would be in deep trouble.[6]

The standard-issue Webleys were powerful, high-quality handguns, but revolvers are best at close range. In the wild hills of the Wombat Ranges they would be ineffective. With this in mind, Kennedy also borrowed a shotgun from the vicar, Reverend Sandiford. To McIntyre's eyes, bringing the Spencer *and* the shotgun along with them was an overreaction. As far as he knew, the Kellys were merely horse thieves, not murderers.[7]

McIntyre said later:

Our party did not know what was going to occur. We went to search for and if we found them, which was doubtful, arrest two men, one of which was armed with a revolver and was likely to resist arrest with that weapon, the other was an individual who was not looked upon as being dangerous. It was never for a moment suspected by us that these two men had any associates, and I believe there was not a man in our party who intended to shoot Ned Kelly unless in defence of his own life, or as a last resource in effecting his capture.[8]

They trained their horses for two days in preparation.

The day before they departed, McIntyre encountered Wild Wright's mute brother, Dummy Wright, on a Mansfield street. Dummy gestured at him, making a gun shape with his hand and clicking sounds with his mouth. Was it a threat or a warning? McIntyre recalled that Dummy 'seemed quite distressed'.[9]

At dawn on Friday 25 October, the four men saddled up and rode out of town, heading north. A stranger watched them leave.[10]

It was wild, uninhabited country, the hills carpeted with thick forest and an undergrowth of scrub and ferns. An early frost and chilly morning air gave way to bright sun and a warm afternoon breeze that smelt of spring pollen.[11]

They travelled on the Benalla Road, then turned onto Wombat Road, and then onto Mount Battery Run. The only house they passed was the home of Mr Martin, near Bridges Creek, where they left the road and travelled along the creek for a while, then followed a blazed line of trees to the abandoned gold-diggings on Stringybark Creek, which they reached at about 2 p.m. There they found a campsite at a place called Burnt Hut, used by prospectors back when there was still gold to be found.[12]

Sergeant Kennedy's plan was to use the camp as a base for patrolling for a few days before moving deeper into the mountains to the east and north, where the Kelly brothers were more likely to be found. They had no idea that the campsite they had chosen was only one mile away from a hut where the Kelly brothers were staying.

Kennedy took the rifle and went out alone for a couple of hours. On his return, Kennedy told McIntyre he had seen several kangaroos down at the creek and handed the rifle to him, telling him to go and see if he could shoot one. McIntyre went down to the creek, but could not see any kangaroos, so he returned without firing the rifle.[13]

This was the only opportunity that McIntyre ever had to fire a Spencer rifle and he did not take it. The Spencer took a cartridge with seven bullets. A lever fed a bullet from the cartridge into the breech. In the hands of a trained expert, it was a formidable weapon, but few police were familiar with it. None of the four had ever fired a Spencer rifle and, as it happened, none of them ever would.[14]

The campsite was known as Burnt Hut because of the charred remains of a building nearby. They pitched a tent in the north-west corner of the clearing, with the creek about 70 yards away to the east. Down the other end of the clearing, to the south, the ground dropped to a shallow bog covered with tall reeds.

Standing in front of the tent and looking across the clearing in the direction of the creek, to their left was a huge old log that ran along the campsite's northern edge. Another log lay across it at right angles, creating a nice wind shelter for cooking. They started a campfire in the nook where the two logs met.

They slept on oilcloths in their tents. Nobody kept guard during the night.[15]

At first light McIntyre was awake, and went down to the creek, taking the shotgun with him as a precaution. On his return up the hill, he heard Kennedy calling for him. His mare had broken its hobbles and all the horses were in disarray.

Kennedy announced that he and Scanlan would go out on patrol, leaving Lonigan and McIntyre at the campsite. He instructed Lonigan to look after the horses and McIntyre to make the tent more comfortable with grass and ferns, and also to cook some bread.[16]

Kennedy said to McIntyre, 'Mac, don't be uneasy if we're not home tonight.' Then he and Scanlan departed north on patrol.[17]

McIntyre stoked the fire and began baking bread.

Lonigan sat and read *The Vagabond Papers,* a series of interviews of Pentridge inmates by an anonymous Melbourne journalist known only as the Vagabond. The interviews had been published as a serial in *The Argus* the previous year, and were now available in book form.

The interview with Harry Power was most interesting. The old crook had confessed to the Vagabond, 'I've led a very wicked life, Sir.' But in the tales he told of his bushranging days, he was a gentleman who abhorred violence and who said, 'Good morning, ma'am!' when entering a woman's home with a gun.

Enraptured by his self-serving lies, Vagabond said of Power:

Courage, when unaccompanied by brutality, commands my respect, and Power boasts that he never shed blood, except in self-defence, never killed a man, and never insulted a woman. 'I was never a brute,' said he, and enquiries among the warders satisfied me that he spoke truthfully.[18]

Indeed, in the rosy view of the Vagabond, the old-fashioned bushranger was a cut above the modern criminals:

His courageous crimes stand out in such contrast to the mean forgeries and breaches of trust now of daily occurrence, that Power is the hero of Pentridge.[19]

Thus began the myth of Harry Power, forever after described as a gentleman bushranger, rather than the desperate, violent misogynist that he was.

Ned Kelly was mentioned. Power apparently told the Vagabond, '. . . he was no good, and he helped sell me out at last. They say that he or one of the Quinns was dressed up as a blacktracker to deceive me. God will judge them for taking blood money.'

Surely Power knew that the true fiz-gig had been exposed as Jack Lloyd, a man who met a sudden and mysterious death only weeks after being released from Pentridge. Yet there was no mention of Lloyd in *The Vagabond Papers*, only accusations of betrayal from Power against Ned Kelly. Perhaps, as Lonigan shared bits and pieces with his colleague while the bread baked, McIntyre found even more reason to be reassured about Ned's character.

Lonigan was startled by a sound from the creek. McIntyre told him it was nothing, just wildlife, probably a kangaroo or wombat crashing through some undergrowth. To show Lonigan there was no reason to be afraid, he picked up the shotgun and wandered down to the creek to investigate. And just as he expected, he found nothing.

Nothing, except for a flock of lorikeets. Remembering Kennedy's earlier invitation to shoot a kangaroo, he took aim at the parrots and fired, killing two, which he collected and returned to the campsite to cook for dinner.[20]

Lonigan remained on edge. He pulled his revolver out of his pack and strapped it to his side. McIntyre placed the shotgun inside the tent and returned to baking bread. His revolver remained in the tent, in his pack. Unlike Lonigan, he was unarmed.

19

Stringybark Creek

It was late afternoon at the campsite by Stringybark Creek. Kennedy and Scanlan hadn't returned yet. McIntyre suggested they stoke the fire to guide the others. He and Lonigan soon had it roaring away.

McIntyre filled up a billy and put it on the fire to make tea. In doing so, he was facing north, his back to the clearing. Lonigan was on the other side of the fire, facing the clearing, but like McIntyre, was transfixed by the flames and busy cooking.[1]

McIntyre heard someone behind him shout, 'Bail up! Throw up your arms!'[2]

His first impression was that it must be Kennedy and Scanlan, playing a joke.[3]

McIntyre turned. Four men, two with rifles and two with shotguns, were approaching through the spear grass at the other end of the clearing. One of them—Ned Kelly—had a rifle pressed against his shoulder. McIntyre thrust his arms out horizontally. As soon as he did, Kelly's aim swung to the right, to Lonigan.[4]

McIntyre turned his head. Lonigan was running away, fumbling with the buttons on his revolver case, trying to get out his weapon. He had only taken a few steps when Kelly fired. McIntyre turned and saw Lonigan fall.[5]

Lonigan cried out, 'Oh Christ! I'm shot!' As he lay on the ground, he made some loud, laboured gasps, then was silent.

106

McIntyre started to lower his arms. The four men rushed towards him and surrounded him, shouting, 'Keep up your hands! Keep up your hands!'[6]

Ned Kelly, with a rifle in one hand and a revolver in the other, asked if he was armed. He said no.[7]

Kelly asked where his revolver was. He replied, 'At the tent.'[8]

On hearing that, Dan Kelly rushed over to the tent, aiming his rifle at it, and shouted into the tent, 'Come out here, you bloody bastards!'

McIntyre told them there was nobody inside.

Ned Kelly asked, 'Where are the others?'

McIntyre replied, 'They're out.'

Ned ordered McIntyre to raise his hands high up above his head. Then he searched him thoroughly around the body, down the legs, and even in his boots. No weapons.

Kelly leant his rifle against the log and leapt over it to inspect the body of Lonigan. McIntyre noticed that the weapon was within his reach. Someone else noticed, too. Behind him, from the tent, one of the others called out, 'Ned! Look out! Or that bastard will be on top of you!'[9]

Kelly rushed back, picked up his rifle, and said, 'You'd better not, or you'll soon find your match, for you know I'm a match for any three men in the police force.'

Then he went back to inspect Lonigan.

Lonigan was dead. Kelly took his revolver.

Looking down at the body, Kelly said regretfully, 'Dear, dear. What a pity that man tried to get away. What made that bugger run?'[10]

As he returned, Kelly had a strange expression on his face. McIntyre believed, or assumed, that it was a look of remorse. Maybe he hadn't planned to kill Lonigan, McIntyre thought. Maybe the plan was merely to take them all as prisoners but spare their lives.[11]

Kelly was calm and held his weapon steadily. The two other men, whom McIntyre did not recognise, were equally cool. But Dan Kelly was excited and making short, almost hysterical laughs.[12]

Dan Kelly said, 'Did you see how he caught at his revolver?' He re-enacted Lonigan's last moments, moving his hand to his hip the way Lonigan had when fumbling for his revolver, and exclaimed, 'Like that!'[13]

Ned Kelly entered the police tent, emerging a short time later with McIntyre's revolver and the shotgun.[14]

Ned told McIntyre to put his hands down and sit on the log.

Dan Kelly came from the tent with some handcuffs he had found there, saying 'Here, we'll put these on the bugger.'

McIntyre refused to hold out his hands. He appealed to Ned: 'What's the use of putting these things on me? How can I get away and you all armed as you are?'[15]

Ned said, 'All right, don't put them on him.' He tapped his rifle. 'This is better than handcuffs.' Then, addressing McIntyre, he said, 'But don't you try to get away. If you do, I'll track you to Mansfield and shoot you at the police station.'[16]

They found the tea, and helped themselves, but before Ned partook, he gave some to McIntyre and told him to drink. It seemed like an act of generosity until Ned revealed that he was worried about poison. Ned asked him if there was any poison in the camp. McIntyre told him there wasn't. They also feasted on the fresh bread that McIntyre had cooked.[17]

Having discovered the shotgun, Ned Kelly opened it, tipped out the shot, and replaced it with cartridges of his own. Then he handed it to one of the others.[18]

Ned proudly showed McIntyre his rifle, commenting, 'That's a curious old gun for a man to carry about the country with him.' The stock was fractured, repaired with a coil of wire. The stock and barrel were also bound together with wire.

McIntyre said, 'Yes, perhaps it's better than it looks.'

Kelly boasted, 'I'll back it against any rifle in the country. I can shoot a kangaroo at a hundred yards with every shot with it.'

Kelly and his men had, by McIntyre's estimation, five rifles (Kelly had two while the others had one each), three revolvers and a double-barrelled shotgun. McIntyre calculated therefore that the gang could fire a total of 25 rounds, and maybe 37 rounds, without having to reload.[19]

Kelly pointed towards the log. 'Who is that over there?'

McIntyre said, 'Lonigan.'

Kelly shook his head. 'It's not Lonigan. I know Lonigan well. And I'll put a hole in you if you don't tell me the truth.'

When McIntyre repeated his answer, Kelly said, 'I'm glad of that, for the bugger once gave me a hiding in Benalla.'

Dan commented wryly that Lonigan wouldn't be locking up any other poor fellows again.[20]

Much later, Kelly elaborated on the hiding he had received from Lonigan in Benalla. As he told it, he had been arrested one night for being drunk, and as he was escorted to the courthouse the next morning, he made a run for freedom. It took four constables to bring him under control (so he said), and even then it was only because Lonigan played dirty by grabbing him by the balls.

Kelly later claimed he had suffered pain in that private area after the incident, but the day he shot Lonigan, the pain lifted and he never suffered from it again. Superstitious nonsense, but no less insane than suspecting McIntyre had poisoned the tea.[21]

Kelly informed McIntyre that he would now execute him. He stood up and aimed his rifle at McIntyre, but then lowered it without firing. He made the same threat and prepared to kill him several more times.[22]

The gang enjoyed the meal and complimented McIntyre on his cooking. McIntyre took the compliments with grace. The shock of Lonigan's death had somehow thrown him into an altered mental state. A calm state. He said later, 'I felt abnormally cool and observant. I did not address a single word to these men unless in reply to their questions, except my remonstrance against being handcuffed.'[23]

One of the men, whom McIntyre later learned was Joe Byrne, asked him for some tobacco. He gave Byrne some tobacco, then they shared a smoke from McIntyre's pipe.

While the others raided the tent supplies and scouted through the nearby scrub, Ned Kelly interrogated McIntyre. Ned knew all about the patrol. He knew there were four of them; that they had come from Mansfield; what their horses looked like; and that they had brought a rifle with them.[24]

However, he did not know their identities. When McIntyre told him the names of the other two, Kelly said had never heard of Sergeant Kennedy, but commented that Scanlan was a 'flash bugger'.

'Who has the rifle?'

'Kennedy.'

McIntyre said he hoped they wouldn't shoot Scanlan and Kennedy in cold blood.[25]

Kelly said, 'I'm no coward. I won't shoot any man who holds up his hands to me.'

'Do you intend to shoot me?'

'What should I want to shoot you for? I could have shot you half an hour ago if I liked.'

Kelly said that, at first, he thought McIntyre was Constable Flood. 'If you had been, I would have roasted you at the fire.'[26]

McIntyre became certain that Kelly and his men had been spying on them ever since their arrival at Stringybark Creek.

Kelly warned him, 'There's a good man down the creek, and if your mates come across him, you'll never see them again.' McIntyre never saw anyone else there, and never learned who that 'good man' was, or even if he existed.[27]

Kelly said, 'That bloody Fitzpatrick has been the cause of all this.'

Referring to Brickey Williamson and Bill Skillion being found guilty of assaulting Fitzpatrick, he said, 'Those people that were lagged at Beechworth were lagged innocently. They had no more revolvers in their hands that night than you have, and that's the cause of me and my two brothers turning out.'

He asked McIntyre, 'What became of the Sydney man?' This was a reference to George Gibson, who had shot and killed a policeman in New South Wales two months earlier.[28]

Sergeant Wallings and two constables had gone to a hotel near Dubbo to investigate a sighting of a well-known horse thief in those parts. Gibson was not the man they were looking for, but he fled the hotel when the police arrived and when pursued, turned and shot Sergeant Wallings in the chest with a rifle.[29]

When two police located him in October, he again tried to run, and had again turned and opened fire, but on the second occasion was killed in a shootout with police after he had commenced firing at them.[30]

McIntyre said, 'He was shot by the police.'

Kelly said, 'If they shot him, they shot the wrong man.' [31]

He then said, 'I suppose you buggers came out here to shoot me.'

McIntyre said, 'No. we came out to apprehend you.'

He said, 'What brings you out here at all? Isn't it a shame to see such fine strapping big fellows like you, in a lazy loafing billet like the police force?'

McIntyre said, 'We were ordered to come out.'

Kelly said, 'Well, if I let you go, you'll have to leave the police.'

McIntyre said that he would.

Kelly told him, 'The best thing would be for you to get them to surrender. If they escape, I'll shoot you. If you let them know in any way that we are here, you will be shot at once. If you get them to surrender, I will allow you to go in the morning. But you'll have to go on foot as we want your horses. We'll handcuff you up all night as we are going to sleep here ourselves.'[32]

McIntyre no longer believed these promises of letting him live. It was now abundantly clear to him that they intended to leave no survivors.[33]

He promised he would try to persuade the other two to surrender, but only if Kelly was telling the truth about letting them live. McIntyre said, 'I'd rather be shot a thousand times than sell my mates, one of whom is the father of a large family.'[34]

Kelly said he would not shoot them. McIntyre then asked, 'You won't allow any of the other young men to shoot us?'[35]

Kelly said with a shrug of indifference, 'They can please themselves.'[36]

Pointing to the horses, Kelly asked, 'Who owns that brown mare over there?'[37]

McIntyre said, 'She's mine.'

Kelly replied, 'She's mine now. That's the one I'm going to take. Is she any good?'

The mare was an old, slow stumbler, but McIntyre replied, 'Pretty fair.' Kelly could find out for himself.

While Ned Kelly sat nearby, and the others rifled through the tent, McIntyre's gaze was drawn to the body. Lonigan's face was now white with the pallor of death.[38]

McIntyre silently prayed. He was not a religious man. He had been raised in the Church of England but in adulthood had rejected the church's teachings in favour of a worldview based on reason. But at that moment, looking at the body at the edge of the clearing, under the darkening sky, he searched for a connection between 'the immensity of a Creator and the frailty of mankind'.[39]

He did not know what to do.

If he warned Kennedy and Scanlan of the danger, he would be murdered. Kelly had bluntly told him so. But if he did warn them, even if it cost him his life, would he be able to save them? Probably not. Neither Kennedy nor Scanlan had any expertise with firearms. In the sixteen months since McIntyre had been at the Mansfield police station, he had never once known Kennedy to fire a single shot. And then there was the incident yesterday with the shotgun and the kangaroos. Kennedy had passed the shotgun to McIntyre, revealing his unwillingness to use it himself.[40]

The best thing was for them to surrender, and at least survive the initial encounter. Then play for time, maybe.

Horses were approaching.

Kelly said, 'Here are the others coming, lads. Take your places.'

He told McIntyre, 'You sit down on that log, or I'll put a hole through you.[41]

The four concealed themselves around the clearing. Kelly hid behind near McIntyre, who sat glumly waiting for the horsemen to arrive.

McIntyre heard Kelly hiss at him from behind the log, 'I've got a rifle here for you if you give them any warning.'

He pleaded, 'Don't shoot the men! I'll get them to surrender.'

Kennedy appeared first, then Scanlan, about two horse-lengths behind him.

As he had been instructed, McIntyre got to his feet and walked towards them, ready to explain the situation, and to tell them they must surrender. He neared Kennedy, but before he opened his mouth, Ned Kelly stood up from behind the far log and shouted, 'Bail up! Hold up your hands!'[42]

Momentarily, Kennedy thought it was a prank, just as McIntyre had. He grinned and playfully reached for his holster, believing it was Lonigan calling out to him.

Kelly fired.

McIntyre said to Kennedy, 'I think you had better dismount and surrender, as you're surrounded.'[43]

McIntyre looked over his shoulder and saw Kelly changing rifles. The other gang members had broken cover and were advancing.

Kennedy hugged the neck of his horse, then rolled from the horse on the off side, away from Kelly but towards the other three.

As he got to the ground, he surrendered, shouting, 'It's all right boys! Stop it! Stop it!'[44]

The gang opened fire.

Scanlan had pulled up and was dismounting. He had one foot still in its stirrup, and was swinging to the ground, when the four armed men opened fire. He got flustered, let go of his horse before he had completely dismounted, and stumbled. He fell over. He got up quickly and ran towards the cover of some nearby trees. But as he ran, he tried awkwardly to disentangle himself from the Spencer rifle. He tripped and fell over again.[45]

Scanlan was on his hands and knees when Kelly took aim and shot him, hitting him in the side of his chest. A large spot of blood appeared on his grey coat.

He slumped to the ground and died.[46]

Kennedy's horse took fright and galloped towards McIntyre.

McIntyre grabbed the reins, jumped onto the horse, and rode it out of the clearing. It was a split-second decision.

Behind him, he heard Dan Kelly shout, 'Shoot the bugger! Shoot the bugger!'

The horse plunged forward, causing McIntyre to lose a stirrup. He leant forward to get it back over his foot. Believing that McIntyre had slumped from a bullet wound, Dan Kelly cried out in excited joy.

There was a storm of gunshots, but he did not know if they were meant for him.[47]

Sometimes history can turn on the smallest details. A horse that takes fright; an opportunity seized; a bullet that misses its mark. Had McIntyre not escaped, nobody would have ever known what became of those four troopers who rode into the ranges from Mansfield in 1878. They would have simply vanished.

Like Moris Solomon, perhaps. Or Whitlow.

20

McIntyre's flight

McIntyre rode north along the creek for about half a mile, then turned west into the setting sun, hoping to reach the Benalla Road, which he estimated was about ten miles away. He dared not slow down. The killers had Scanlan's horse at their disposal, saddled and ready to ride, and they were expert bushmen.[1]

The forest was too thick for him to guide the horse, so he 'gave him his head.' He made good ground for a while, but they were soon in dense undergrowth. The horse jumped over logs and wove through thickets. McIntyre leant to the left, then to the right, dodging branches. He dismounted and led the horse on foot for a while, then remounted.[2]

As he burst through some scrubby undergrowth, he saw a tree in front of him with wide, low, splayed branches. He didn't stop the horse in time. A branch hit him in the chest, or rather he hit the branch, and he fell backwards off his saddle. His head hit the ground.

He lay on the ground for a while, in a state of dazed confusion, and had the illusion he was swimming in a sea of blood. When he came to his senses, his eyes were welled with blood, and his mouth tasted of blood.

He found the horse a short distance away and mounted it. The horse refused to budge. He coaxed it into a walking pace. Maybe it was injured from a bullet wound, or from the ride. McIntyre, dismounted, removed the saddle and bridle, and tossed them into some thick ferns where they wouldn't be found, then sent the horse away.

After resting in a hollow tree, he walked towards the setting sun, and found a wombat hole. He crawled in, took out his memo book, and wrote an entry:

Ned Kelly, Dan, and two others stuck us up today when we were disarmed. Lonigan and Scanlan are shot. I am hiding in a wombat hole until dark. The Lord have mercy on me. Lanigan tried to get his gun out.[3]

Then he concealed the memo book in his clothes near his chest so that if he was killed, there was a chance his killers wouldn't discover it.

He heard the sounds of men and horses nearby. At least, that's what he thought he could hear, but he wasn't certain. Whoever or whatever they were, they went away. When night fell, he crawled out of the wombat hole and set out for Mansfield. His plan was to head west until he found the Mansfield–Benalla road, then follow that home.

Before the light had completely faded, he had picked out a star in the west as his guide, which he now headed towards, making sure he kept it in view. As it sank below the horizon, he picked another star above it to guide him. He stumbled among some logs and ferns, and when he looked up again, he could not find his guiding star. He got a compass and three matches out of his pocket. The first match failed to light, but the second allowed him to read the compass and get his bearings again.[4]

He waded through streams. His wet boots chafed, so he took them off and walked barefoot. He crossed gullies, clambered over logs and climbed hills. In the pre-dawn light, he heard rustling and saw several figures nearby. He thought they were men, but as he crept forward cautiously, he saw that they were kangaroos.[5]

Dawn broke. Before him, open country sloped down to the south-west towards Dueran, a station about five miles north of Mansfield. He thought he had been going west, but he had been going south. He fixed his eyes on the Dueran homestead and trudged towards it.[6]

Around mid-morning he lay down by a creek feeling hot, tired, and doubtful that he would make it back to Mansfield alive, so he wrote another entry in his book:

I have been travelling all night, and am very weary.

Nine a.m., Sunday: I am now lying on the edge of the creek named Bridge's.[7]

A rest and a drink from the creek perked him up enough to continue.

Around 10 a.m. he saw a hut with smoke coming out of the chimney, and a woman and child standing in the doorway. Above all, he was looking forward to a nice cup of hot tea. But as he got closer, the woman and child disappeared—as if they had never existed. He wondered if his mind was playing tricks, although he could still see smoke clearly rising from the chimney.

When he reached the house, he discovered that it was abandoned. There was no smoke, no fire, no woman, no child. The place was empty.

At around noon, McIntyre stumbled into the proximity of Dueran Station. Two of the horses in the yard looked remarkably like the police horses they had taken to Stringybark Creek. They weren't, but that's what the foggy, concussed, sleep-deprived McIntyre thought he saw.

He circled wide around the station, taking care not to be seen, then shuffled down the road towards Mansfield.

He arrived at McCall's farmhouse about a mile and a half outside of Mansfield at about 3 p.m. Mr McCall was hosting a Sunday afternoon party, with several ladies sitting outside at the front of the house.

As McIntyre stumbled towards them, they stood and stared with astonishment. They did not seem to recognise McIntyre, who could barely walk, and who was muddy, ragged, barefoot and covered in blood.

When McColl came forward to meet the unwanted arrival on his lawn, McIntyre said to him, 'Have you got any firearms?'

Everyone was alarmed.

Glancing nervously at his guests, McCall replied, 'No.'

McIntyre said, 'I belong to the police. And surely you have got a gun.'

Recognising McIntyre, McCall said, 'I know you're a trooper, but we have no gun.'

McIntyre told them what had happened.

He sat down. They brought him tea and refreshments. A neighbouring farmer named Byrne (no relation to Joe) arrived and took McIntyre into town with his horse and buggy.

At the barracks, McIntyre searched for Inspector Pewtress. Only Constable Meehan was there.

The inspector was at home, in bed with a cold. Sadleir hadn't informed Pewtress about, nor asked for his approval for, the Stringybark Creek patrol. Pewtress had been in Melbourne on unrelated duty the previous week, and had only learned of the patrol when he arrived in town on Saturday, finding no sergeant and just two constables at his station.

Pewtress opened the door, took one look at the tattered, bloodstreaked man before him, and exclaimed, 'Good God, McIntyre! What's happened?'

McIntyre said, 'They are all killed, Sir. Everyone shot by the Kellys but me.'

After McIntyre had given a verbal and written report, Pewtress hurried to the telegraph office. There, he composed telegrams to Sadleir in Benalla, and the chief commissioner in Melbourne.

To his credit, Pewtress recognised his limitations. He had arrived from England in 1852, one of the 'London Fifty', the imported, high-quality London bobbies who, it was hoped, would lift the standard of the Victorian force and bring a focus on community policing rather than militarism. Unfortunately for him, the requirements of the job had suddenly swung in the other direction. He had been in

Mansfield less than six months. He needed expert support, ideally from Superintendent Sadleir himself, who had lived in Mansfield for years.

His message to Sadleir said, in part:

> I think it is near useless to send a handful of constables after four well-armed bushrangers and without ample provision. I know nothing of bush life and am therefore unable to guide men to the course they should pursue and might through ignorance lead them into danger and perhaps death.[8]

The message to Melbourne went through, but not the one for Sadleir in Benalla. The operator explained that, as it was Sunday, there was nobody in the Benalla telegraph office. Pewtress rewrote the note to Sadleir, handed it to Constable Meehan and instructed him to deliver it to Benalla on horseback. Meehan rode off, unarmed.

That left three police remaining in Mansfield: Inspector Pewtress, Foot Constable Allwood and Mounted Constable McIntyre.[9]

Pewtress also sent an urgent message to the chief commissioner, Captain Standish.

There was a reason Constable Meehan had not been assigned to the Stringybark Creek patrol. He was a layabout and a drunk who was known to visit a local hotel for brandies before lunchtime. In briefings, superiors could smell alcohol on his breath. He was on familiar terms with the Quinns and other miscreants, but not enough to feel safe from them. He was a loafer, not a crook, and as such, had the respect of neither police nor criminals.

Heading out, two associates of Ned Kelly passed Meehan; they were heading in the opposite direction and eyeballed him suspiciously. Further along, he believed he was being followed by two riders. He stopped at the house of someone he knew to get a weapon, but they weren't home, so he doubled back to another friend's house. They weren't home either. It was dark now. There were two riders loitering on the road nearby, but he couldn't tell if they were the same as before.

Perhaps inspired by McIntyre's actions in the ranges, he set his horse free and continued to Benalla on foot. On the way, he got lost in the bush.

Fears were held for his safety, but after he appeared safely in Benalla, and his horse was eventually retrieved, he was the subject of derision. There were reports that the two men following him were merely local farmers.

When interviewing him some days later, after his escapade had become public knowledge, Sadleir asked him pointedly, 'Meehan, wouldn't it be better for you then, that you were shot, than to be out all night in the bush?'

Meehan did not concur. Embarrassment was better than death.

Waiting near Powers Lookout, Michael Ward expected the Kennedy patrol, but they did not come. A group of riders appeared, but they were the squatter Harry Connolly and his workers.[10]

On Tuesday 29 October, after waiting for three days, he started north for Moyhu. On the way he met the Greta patrol, led by Shoebridge. After he revealed his identity to them, he asked if they had found Kennedy's patrol, but they had not, and were equally confused.

He stopped at the Chinese Camp, where a woman on horseback found him and handed him a letter from the Greta patrol, informing him of the murders at Stringybark Creek. He immediately set out for the Wangaratta police station to report for duty.[11]

21

Three inquests

The search party to find Kennedy was led by Inspector Pewtress, and also comprised Constable Allwood and several volunteers. The local doctor, Samuel Reynolds, advised that Constable McIntyre was unfit for duty, but McIntyre ignored his advice and insisted on going too. Dr Reynolds also joined them, not for McIntyre's sake, but in case Kennedy needed treatment.[1]

All the Mansfield police weapons had been taken on the Kennedy patrol. Consequently, the search party was completely unarmed. Furthermore, in their absence, Mansfield was left without any police.[2]

They departed Mansfield in the late Monday afternoon, two days after the shootings, reaching Monk's sawmill at sunset. Monk happened to know Ned Kelly personally and was shocked when Pewtress told him what had happened. Monk offered to guide them to Stringybark Creek. Two employees at the mill named Lopdell and Duncan came too.

A light, drizzling rain fell. There was no moonlight to aid them. Pewtress periodically checked on them, calling 'Where is Mac?' and 'Where is Allwood?'

A mile from the Burnt Hut campsite, they dismounted and walked. Horses might give away their approach.

At last Monk announced they'd reached the Burnt Hut campsite on Stringybark Creek. Visibility was so poor that they had to take his word for it. The drizzle had become a steady rain.

McIntyre wandered about, looking for things he remembered: the tent, the crossed logs, the fireplace and the bodies. Pewtress became impatient and sceptical.

Monk found a pile of ashes. He called out, 'Here is where you had your fire.'

McIntyre hurried over, but it was wrong. There were no logs here. He was certain that his fire had been next to the logs. He said, 'We had no fire in the open.'

Monk inspected the ashes, and realised it was no fireplace. 'This must be the remains of your tent.' It was. There were remnants of the tent as well as some papers, but the rest had been reduced to soggy ash. They later found Kennedy's notebook nearby in the mud, with some pages torn out.

From the remains of the tent, McIntyre got his bearings. He soon found Lonigan's body, then Scanlan's body. Scanlan lay where he had fallen, but Lonigan's body had been dragged several feet. The pockets of both dead men had been turned inside out and the contents taken. Their firearms were gone. Lonigan's wedding ring had been removed.[3]

It was dark so they waited until daylight, sitting on a log, huddled against the rain. When morning came, they searched for Sergeant Kennedy up and down the creek, calling out 'Cooee!' and hoping for a 'Cooee!' in return. None came.

Finally, they loaded the bodies of Lonigan and Scanlan onto Monk's packhorse and returned to the sawmill. Monk asked Pewtress not to publicise the assistance that he and his employees had given the police because he lived in a remote place and feared retribution.

Before the search party had set out from Mansfield, Pewtress had arranged for a man with dray and horses to meet them at the sawmill. They loaded the bodies onto the dray and transported them into Mansfield.

McIntyre was fading. He was too unwell to ride horseback, so Pewtress made him lie down in the dray, next to his dead companions.[4]

The bodies were delivered to the Mansfield morgue. McIntyre checked into the hospital, where he was examined by Dr Reynolds before returning to the barracks.

Pewtress arranged autopsies on the bodies of Scanlan and Lonigan. He transmitted an urgent broadcast to all nearby police stations, requesting backup. He also sent an updated report to Superintendent Sadleir in Benalla about the retrieval of the bodies, and stated the need to return to Stringybark Creek to search for Kennedy as soon as possible.

By Tuesday morning, six constables had arrived in Mansfield from nearby towns. Two priests, who were friends of Scanlan and Kennedy, also arrived. They were Father Scanlon and Father Kennedy; despite having almost the same names as the policemen, they were unrelated to them.

Pewtress was going around town recruiting volunteers to assist in the search for Michael Kennedy. His efforts were hampered by Wild Wright, who was also doing the rounds, warning people they would be shot if they assisted the police. Before setting out again with a search party, he instructed McIntyre to arrest Wild Wright.[5]

He was easy to find. Wild Wright was out on the main street, shouting and gesticulating at some newly arrived constables. Father Scanlon was nearby, watching.

McIntyre walked up to Wright and said, 'I've come to arrest you. I've seen my mates shot, and if you don't come quietly to the lock-up, I'll shoot you.'

Wild Wright held out his hands to be handcuffed.

As they crossed the road towards the lock-up, Wild Wright said, 'McIntyre, when I heard one of the police had escaped, I was glad it was you. I'm damned sorry for it now, but if you've escaped once, you won't next time.'

Wild's mute brother Dummy Wright was also arrested.

Father Scanlon later approached McIntyre and asked if his threat to shoot Wild Wright was genuine. McIntyre replied sarcastically, 'A little shooting would do him good, as he was talking so freely about shooting others.' The priest was unimpressed. McIntyre reassured him, 'I wouldn't have shot him, as I wouldn't have been justified.'[6]

Superintendent Sadleir arrived from Benalla later that day.

He discovered Wild Wright in the lock-up, and interviewed him. Wild told him that he didn't know where the Kellys were, but promised to find out in return for a payment of £30, if Sadleir released him.

Sadleir accepted the deal.

Wild Wright hurried away, mounted his horse, and sped north towards Greta.

McIntyre was heartened by Wild Wright's promise to assist, because to him it proved that virtue could be found in the darkest of hearts. He remarked philosophically, 'Few men, if any, are altogether bad.'[7]

No information was forthcoming from Wild Wright, but surely it was the thought that counted.

A magisterial inquiry into the deaths of Lonigan and Scanlan was held that afternoon. McIntyre's testimony was recorded by a clerk. His description of events was virtually identical to his earlier report to Pewtress.

Dr Reynolds, who had conducted the autopsies on both bodies, also testified. He stated that Lonigan's body had seven bullet wounds. Four in the left arm (at least two of which were caused by entry and exit of one bullet); one through the outside of the left thigh; one on the right temple; and one through the right eyeball. He concluded, 'Death must have been almost instantaneous from injury to the brain.'[8]

Reynolds found a bullet wound in the right side of Scanlan's chest, in keeping with McIntyre's account. The bullet had crushed through a rib, passed through the right lung taking pieces of bone with it, and lodged in the sternum. He stated that the resultant internal haemorrhaging would have caused rapid death.

However, Scanlan had three other bullet wounds: the right hip; the right shoulder, and the middle of the chest.

McIntyre was surprised by the number of bullet wounds. There had been plenty of shooting, but he had seen both Scanlan and Lonigan killed by a single shot from Kelly's rifle. Had there been a ritual shooting of the body, either to initiate one or more members of the gang, or to force their complicity in the murder? It certainly looked that way. However, Reynolds did not believe the injuries were inflicted after death. A likely explanation for Lonigan's multiple wounds is that Kelly shot Lonigan with a quartered bullet.[9]

Magistrate H.H. Kitchener found that Lonigan and Scanlan were murdered by Ned and Dan Kelly, 'and two other men, whose names are unknown'.[10]

McIntyre applied for, and was granted, warrants against Ned and Dan Kelly for murder.[11]

After the inquest, everyone walked across to the Catholic church for the double funeral of Michael Scanlan and Thomas Lonigan.

Lonigan's wife, Charlotte, arrived by coach from Violet Town just in time for the service, confused and distraught. She was heavily pregnant. She had left the other children at home.[12]

All business had been halted in Mansfield and it seemed as if the town's entire population was in attendance.

After the service there was a large procession to the graveyard. Michael Scanlan and Thomas Lonigan were buried at 2 p.m.

It was midnight when Tuesday's search party returned, having again failed to find Kennedy.

McIntyre's sleep was broken by their return, and also by the steady arrival of police from other localities, answering the call for assistance. Dr Reynolds came by, found him awake and exhausted, and sent him to the hospital.[13]

The Wednesday search party was the largest yet, with plenty of volunteers (now that Wild Wright had left town), and numerous newly arrived constables. They left at noon. The plan was for the entire party to camp at Monk's sawmill overnight, then recommence the search on Thursday morning.

Sadleir didn't go with them. He visited Sergeant Kennedy's wife to console her, then returned to Benalla that day. During his brief stay in Mansfield, Sadleir's only action was to release Wild Wright, a Kelly henchman who had threatened to murder several townsfolk.[14]

At noon on Thursday, search volunteer and shire president James Tomkin rode into town with news that Kennedy's body had been found. It had been discovered by another volunteer, Henry Sparrow, the overseer of a squatting run called Mount Battery Station, that morning.[15]

Tomkin had discovered the tracks left by Kennedy's horse as McIntyre escaped on it. As leader of one of the search teams, he decided to follow those tracks, on the theory that Kennedy had attempted to follow McIntyre. That was how the body was located by Tomkin's team.[16]

Kennedy was lying face-up in low ferns, in a clearing about a quarter of a mile north-west of the campsite, his head towards the campsite. There was a large hole in his chest. A police cloak had been draped over him. His face had decomposed so much that it was almost unrecognisable. One ear was missing.

Kennedy's pockets had been emptied. One item of particular value to him was a pocket watch, an heirloom that he carried everywhere with him. It was gone.

The body arrived in Mansfield late Thursday afternoon.

Michael Kennedy's daughter Mary was playing with a friend when the two girls saw the group of riders and a wagon approaching. She ran to tell her mother, Bridget. They hugged each other as the procession passed the house, the men's heads were bowed and their hats doffed. Seeing them ride along like that, Bridget Kennedy knew.[17]

Pewtress visited soon afterwards to deliver the terrible news.[18]

Given the state of decomposition, a post-mortem was conducted rather than a full autopsy. Bridget was not allowed to see the body of her husband: it was decided it would be too distressing for her to see him in such a gruesome state.

At the inquest on the morning of Friday 1 November, Reynolds testified that the cause of death was a gunshot blast to the chest, fired at very close range. He also stated: 'Deceased must have been facing the murderer as he was shot, as no wounds appear on the back, except the one carried by the charge passing through the body.'[19]

There were other wounds. Kennedy had a bullet wound in the right side of his chest, his face, and his temple. He also had a bullet wound in his armpit, suggesting that he had his hands up in surrender when shot.

Kennedy's missing ear was the object of sensational reports that suggested Ned Kelly had cut it off, but it may simply have been taken by a wild animal.

In his findings, magistrate Kitchener wrote, 'I find that Michael Kennedy was killed and murdered by some person or persons whose names are unknown, whilst the said Michael Kennedy was in execution of his duty as sergeant of police.'[20]

Kennedy's funeral was held after the inquest at the Anglican church. It was an ecumenical event, with clergy from the Presbyterian and Catholic churches in attendance, and even the Anglican Bishop of Melbourne, James Moorhouse, and his wife, Mary, who had come up specifically for the service. Father Scanlon conducted the service. Kennedy's wife, Bridget, tried to open the coffin to see Michael and had to be restrained.

Michael and Bridget's five children were dressed in their best. The babies, Jimmy and John, were too young to understand, but the three older children did. The oldest, Mary, was nine.

The crowd trudged through the rain from the church to the Anglican section of the graveyard. There they buried Michael Kennedy.

After Stringybark

22

Riders on the storm

On Wednesday 30 October—the day before Kennedy's body was found—a dark haired, scruffy bearded man had ridden into Wangaratta through sheets of driving rain. His horse was heavily laden, as if he had travelled a long way. He was drenched, yet looked as if he needed a wash and a change of clothes.

Severe weather had moved in across the region. The skies above Wangaratta and Beechworth had opened with wild storms the night before. Spectacular lightning flashed and streaked across the sky, including one that looked like a ball of fire. A strike shattered the verandah posts of one Beechworth house and set it alight. The deafening thunder had continued until dawn.[1]

The rider entered the Wangaratta police station, took off his cloak, and introduced himself as Detective Michael Ward. His undercover work was finished and he wished to report for duty.

It so happened that Superintendent Nicolson was there. He had been assigned control of the Kelly case by Captain Standish on Monday and as of today was based at Benalla headquarters.

Ward gave him the rundown. He believed that the gang would try to cross into New South Wales. Nicolson agreed. But with the weather so bad and the rivers rising, it might not be possible for them to cross the Murray.

Ward then rode east into the mountains to speak with a potential informer at Mount Blowhard, near Dinner Plain. He hoped to be back within a day or two, but widespread floods delayed his return until the following week.[2]

Under orders from Superintendent Nicolson, Senior-Constable Frank James led several mounted constables to Mansfield on Wednesday, in time to join the third search. They camped at Monk's sawmill, then Kennedy was found on Thursday. Pewtress and most of the others returned to Mansfield with the body, but Senior-Constable James and his men stayed and continued searching.

The few items that could be salvaged from the Burnt Hut campsite had already been taken. The charred remains of the tent had turned to mush. They explored further afield.

On a small plateau less than a mile away, where Ryans Creek cascaded down the mountain, they found the remains of another hut, which had been burned within the past few days.[3]

The plateau of about twenty acres had been cleared and fenced on three sides, the unfenced west side bounded instead by a steep mountain slope. There was evidence of goldmining in the creek. The sluicing was too extensive to have been conducted by four men in a period of a few months. This was an established, well-mined dig. Likewise, four men could not have done so much clearing and fencing in such a short time, particularly if they were also goldmining. Clearly the little mountain property predated the Kelly brothers' arrival.

On a tree beside the hut the name J. Martain was prominently carved. It was presumably the name of the person who had lovingly created this secret farm. But whoever he was and wherever he was, J. Martain no longer lived there.[4]

The hut was built with thick, round logs, each two feet in diameter. The door, made of thick slabs and plated with iron, had holes for firing a weapon. The hut was built, or had been recently modified, to withstand a siege.

The manner in which idle days in the mountains had been spent by the Kelly brothers in the six months they had been in hiding soon became clear. Trees in all directions had been used for target practice. Some trunks had targets marked on them with charcoal. There were cuts and holes where bullets had been dug out of trunks to be melted down and reused. There were thousands of bullet holes in trees.[5]

The search party rode north down the valley, stopping at the scattered farmhouses of the Upper King River, asking locals if they knew anything about the hut they had discovered, the farm, the gold-digging or the Kelly brothers.[6]

Nobody knew anything.

Ward's investigations resumed on Monday 4 November, a few days later than he had planned. Making inquiries in Oxley, he learned that four horsemen with two packhorses had passed through town on 27 October, the day after the murders. They were heading east.

The Ovens River was roiling from stormwater, and impassable in most places. If they were going east, they probably intended to cross the river at the Pioneer Bridge, and maybe head up into the mountains via Beechworth.

He visited the proprietor of the Pioneer Bridge Hotel, Mr Moon, who had seen them. One of them had come into the hotel and purchased a bottle of brandy while the other three waited outside in the rain with the horses. As Ward suspected, they had crossed the bridge. The next village on the road up to Beechworth was Everton.

There, he learned that the men had stocked up on sardines and horse feed, then ridden towards Sebastopol, the locality near Beechworth where Joe Byrne and Aaron Sherritt lived. Further inquiries convinced him that the fugitives had visited Sherritt's parents' house.[7]

He returned to Wangaratta to report these discoveries to Nicolson, but Nicolson had gone north, to Wodonga. There wasn't time to lose.

He caught the next train to Wodonga to brief Nicolson in person. There, on learning that Nicolson was over the border, he crossed the river to Albury, but Nicolson was on patrol and out of contact. The word in Albury was that Kelly and his men were on the Murray River, surrounded by police, and would soon be caught. Ward returned to Wodonga. He telegrammed instructions to Wangaratta and Beechworth police to guard their bridges overnight, then caught the train back to Wangaratta.

In Wangaratta, he made a startling discovery from the constables there. The four fugitives had been seen on the outskirts of town, on a track that went under the One Mile Bridge. They had apparently circled around the township, then ridden west towards the Warby Ranges.[8]

This changed everything. They *had* been up in Sebastopol, but weren't there now. And they weren't on the Murray, surrounded by police. They were in the Warby Ranges.[9]

Ward reported the information to Inspector Brooke-Smith, who apparently already knew all about it. Having briefed the town's most senior officer, Ward packed his horse and departed again, returning to the wilds of the upper King River and the foothills of the Wombat Ranges, where he hoped to interview a potential informant.

Sergeant Steele had heard from the Benalla railway master on Sunday evening that a young boy from the Delaney family was rumoured to have seen four riders on the track under the One Mile Bridge. Under instructions from Sadleir, Steele was now preparing a contingent of thirteen mounted constables for an expedition to Rats Castle, in the granite hills behind Beechworth, where the outlaws were reported to be hiding. Nicolson had received a report that someone had seen a horse branded with a bell near there, a brand that was thought to match one of the gang's horses. Sadleir had ordered a special train to transport Steele and his men up to Beechworth.[10]

The rumour about what the Delaney boy had seen came to Steele via Wangaratta's stationmaster, Henry Laing, who had telegraphed his counterpart in Benalla about it. Sadleir gave Steele permission to stop the train in Wangaratta for half an hour to learn more about this rumour, but Steele was instructed that, if there was anything to it, he was to inform Inspector Brooke-Smith and then continue to Beechworth.

When the special train ground to a halt at Wangaratta Station, Constable Twomey was on the platform, waiting to speak with Steele.[11] Twomey explained that Mrs Delaney, who lived near the One Mile Bridge, had heard horses approaching. She and her sons saw them pass under the bridge. There were four riders, plus a pack-horse, and four saddleless horses in front of them. The track under the bridge was treacherous, more so with the Ovens River so high and fast. They would have needed a local guide to show them the way, or they would have ended up in the river. Honest people did not use that little track under the bridge. Steele suspected that guide was probably Steve Hart.[12]

Nineteen-year-old Steve Hart was born near Beechworth to a large Irish immigrant family. He briefly worked as a butcher boy and occasionally competed as a jockey in Wangaratta races. In 1877, Sergeant Steele arrested him for multiple horse thefts. All charges were downgraded by the magistrate to 'illegally using a horse', and Hart was given a twelve-month sentence in Beechworth Gaol. After Hart's release, Sergeant Steele was pleased to learn that the young man was working with his father for an honest living. But one day he heard that Hart had quit. He had thrown down his axe, shouted, 'A short life and a merry one!' Then he left his parents' farm.[13] Steele asked Constable Twomey how many men were available in Wangaratta.

Twomey said, 'Six.'

Steele believed the riders were probably Kelly and his gang, and if so, they would make for the Warby Ranges. He instructed Twomey to deliver this information to Brooke-Smith immediately.[14]

Sadleir had been very specific in his orders to Steele: if the rumour needs further investigation, *inform Inspector Brooke-Smith, then proceed to Beechworth anyway.* It sure seemed like a hot lead. Steele wished he could follow it, but his hands were tied. If he made the wrong call—if he defied his explicit orders, stopped the train, and charged off to the Warby Ranges—and he was wrong, his reputation would be tarnished.[15]

Sergeant Steele signalled the engine driver to leave, then boarded the rear van.

As the train pulled away, Constable Twomey stood on the platform, boiling with impotent anger. He couldn't believe that Sergeant Steele hadn't changed his plans.[16]

Twomey knocked on Inspector Brooke-Smith's door at Kitt's Hotel at about 1 a.m. The bleary-eyed inspector told him to go back to the Delaneys to see if they knew anything else.

Twomey returned to Kitt's Hotel with his findings at daybreak. He had learned something new. One of the Delaney boys reported that the gang had crossed an old wooden bridge near their house in the direction of the Warby Ranges. Brooke-Smith muttered something about sending a telegram when the telegraph office opened in a couple of hours.

Later in the morning, Twomey received instructions via Constable Walsh that he was to visit the Delaneys again, to see if he could learn anything more. It was futile. The Delaneys had already told him everything.

By the time Steele had departed Beechworth for Rats Castle, the expedition was already hopeless. *The Argus* had gone to print in Melbourne that morning, stating, 'the party of ruffians causing so much excitement are lurking in the ranges known as Rats' Castle, near the Mares' Flats, Indigo Creek'. The tip-off came from Chiltern on Thursday, soon after Nicolson had learned it himself. Without a doubt, the leak had come from inside the police. Low-paid constables were susceptible to the charms of journalists offering cash.[17]

There was no trace of the outlaws around Rats Castle. They searched the Stanley Ranges further south-east, but found no trace there, either.

In Myrtleford, Steele received a telegram from Superintendent Sadleir that his patrol was required at Beechworth barracks immediately. Apparently, someone had received news of the outlaws.

On the evening of Wednesday 6 November, Standish arrived in Benalla from Melbourne to confer with Nicolson. As they chatted after supper at a Benalla hotel, they received an urgent despatch from Superintendent Sadleir. Sadleir's message stated that he had received information in Beechworth that the Kelly Gang had been seen at Sebastopol, and were there right now.

Standish and Nicolson hurried from the hotel. Standish ordered the stationmaster to urgently prepare a special police train for Beechworth. Nicolson readied all the available men at the barracks. A steam train could not depart at a moment's notice. It had to be fired up with a wood fire, then coal shovelled in, and its boiler brought to steam before it could move. They were soon on their way up the mountain rail track with nine mounted constables and a blacktracker, arriving at Beechworth at three o'clock in the morning.

At the arranged meeting place, Sadleir was there with more than 40 mounted police, including Sergeant Steele's patrol, which had been recalled from the mountains.

There were also two journalists, and a man whose face was covered in black boot polish, who appeared to be drunk. Sadleir told Standish and Nicolson confidentially that the man with the blackened face was his informer, who would take them to where the gang was hiding. Sadleir seemed to know where they were going, but didn't say.[18]

They departed at four o clock. Fifty mounted police rode through the bush with a noise like rolling thunder. They could be heard miles away. Sadleir stopped the great cavalcade on a rise overlooking a small hut.[19]

Sadleir announced, 'This is the house of the Sherritts.'[20]

At that point, Nicolson took charge. He sent several constables into the bush to search nearby; and others to the rear of the house, in case the outlaws tried to escape that way. He picked some to join him in the main approach, then led them in a charge at full gallop towards the hut. They jumped off their horses and ran to the door. Constable Bracken got there first. Nicolson pushed him out of the way. Bracken's gun went off. All the constables in the bush came at a gallop.

They searched the house, respectfully allowing Nicolson to go first. Nobody was home.

Regarding Bracken's gun discharging, Nicolson later (at a subsequent Royal Commission) explained why he had pushed the constable: 'It has been my custom—a well-known custom in the police force—that no one should go before me on any occasion of this kind.' As an adherent of the principle of 'leading from the front', he believed that he should put himself at risk before those under his command.

However, Nicolson's 'custom' wasn't so well known that Constable Bracken knew about it.

Someone suggested that the outlaws must have gone to the nearby Byrnes' property. That seemed plausible. Sadleir led the great cavalcade to the Byrne house, where he led a thorough search of the property. All they found there was a very cranky Mrs Byrne, who wanted to know on what authority they were searching her house.

The Great Sebastopol Raid was a public relations disaster for the police and an embarrassment to Captain Standish.

It was lunchtime, so Standish sent all the constables to a nearby pub for lunch. As he smoked his pipe outside, he noticed Sadleir talking to a man he didn't recognise. Nicolson informed him it was Aaron Sherritt, who they hoped to entice into undercover work. He urged Standish to talk to Sherritt himself, and to perhaps offer a share of the reward as an inducement.

Standish did so, asking Sherritt to help catch the gang in exchange for the reward money. Sherritt was noncommittal.[21]

Sergeant Steele was nearby. He could not hear what was said, but understood its purpose. Sherritt walked off with his axe slung casually over his shoulder, happening to pass Steele on his way. As Sherritt passed by, he pointed at the informer covered in boot polish, and told Steele menacingly, 'I know that dog.'[22]

23

The Warby Ranges

On the afternoon of Wednesday 6 November, Inspector Brooke-Smith finally organised a large patrol—of 22 mounted police—to follow up on the sighting under One Mile Bridge. More than two full days after the tip-off.

They rode north, the Warby Ranges on their left, to Peechelba. From there, they split into two groups. One group, under Detective Douglas Kennedy, crossed the ranges to Lake Rowan on the other side, while Brooke-Smith led the other group further north-west to the river town of Yarrawonga, then south to Lake Rowan the next day. They then proceeded back towards Wangaratta across a pass through the ranges.[1]

On the way out of Lake Rowan, they stopped at the property of a Kelly associate named Bryan. In the stockyard there, Constable Charles Johnston found evidence that the gang's horses had been there very recently, including hoof-marks and some horse-hair caught on a fence. He summoned Brooke-Smith by calling out 'Cooee!'.

The hoof-marks were very recent, 48-hours old at the most. Johnston and a man named Dixon followed the tracks for about two and a half miles, towards the Warby Ranges, returning to Brooke-Smith and the others by nightfall. They camped overnight, then Brooke-Smith announced that they should return to Wangaratta, stock up on supplies, and come back to follow the tracks with fresh provisions and blacktrackers.

Back in town, Brooke-Smith told Johnston to have the men ready at four in the morning, then he headed for Kitt's Hotel for the night. When Johnston roused him at the hotel at four o clock, he said to head on down, and he would be there immediately. He didn't come. Johnston roused him again at five, and again at seven. He instructed Johnston to take the men to Morgans Gap, and he would follow soon afterwards.

It wasn't until mid-afternoon when they saw Brooke-Smith ride leisurely up the hill towards them at Morgans Gap. They had spent the day restlessly waiting, but now, at least, they could start the chase. They rode to the nearby orange grove behind Bryan's place, and picked up the tracks, which took them to the summit of the Warby Ranges. There, they found a campsite, recently used. After inspecting the general state of the campsite, including patches of crushed grass and other telltale signs of usage—the blacktrackers declared that the outlaws had stayed there last night.

They were close. Perhaps they were *very* close.

They searched the surrounding forest and found a wandering horse. Its brand, B 87, identified it as Sergeant Kennedy's packhorse from Stringybark Creek. It was a tense moment. Despite losing an opportunity last night, they had the chance to redeem themselves. The gang were probably still in the ranges, and could be discovered if tracked immediately, but time was short.

The searchers triumphantly led the packhorse down to the foot of the ranges and showed it to Brooke-Smith.

He said, 'Who found it?'

Johnston said, 'The party was all together when we got the horse in the ranges.'

Brooke-Smith said, 'Right. Proceed to Wangaratta.'

They couldn't believe their ears, but back to Wangaratta they went.

Brooke-Smith was an officer once considered for the role of chief commissioner of police, which was ultimately given to Captain Standish. For all Standish's faults, and there were many, the colony had dodged a bullet.

Brooke-Smith slept in again the next morning until nine. Nicolson happened to be passing through Wangaratta, learned at least some of the situation, and had him kicked out of the hotel. Johnston and the rest of the patrol had already departed some time earlier as they wanted to, as Johnston put it, 'fight the bushrangers'.

Brooke-Smith had instructed them to return to Bryan's place and pick up the tracks from there. Johnston led a search into the ranges. Brooke-Smith, loitering behind, couldn't find them. To summon his men back, he fired his gun into the air. It worked. They came back fast.

Over the next four days they searched the Warby Ranges, picking up more tracks. They followed the outlaws to the outskirts of Glenrowan, then back into the ranges. It was thick scrub, but not too thick to search. The blacktrackers worked methodically. The ground was wet and soft from the storms. Deep hoof-marks were easy to find.

They found fresh orange peels. The gang had stocked up at Bryan's orchard, and had carelessly left a clue. They were still here, in the ranges. Despite all the screw-ups, there was still a chance that the police might catch them.

But they were thwarted by Brooke-Smith, who would direct them away from fresh tracks, make them go over old ground, or return to Wangaratta for the night.

Disgusted with Brooke-Smith's laziness and cowardice, Johnston soon applied for, and was granted, a transfer to Benalla.[2]

In the secluded upper King Valley, Michael Ward recruited a new informer: Pat Quinn.

Yes, *that* Pat Quinn, the man who, seven years earlier, had beaten Constable Hall with a stirrup iron in the streets of Greta. But that was then. In the meantime, Pat Quinn had been developing his selection and was beginning to prosper. He was applying to obtain freehold title on his property, which was granted early the following year. He had a wife and children to think about, and he had no interest in getting involved in Kelly's criminal projects.

Furthermore, Pat Quinn wasn't Ned Kelly's blood relation. He was from a different Quinn family, who had happened to marry a Glenmore run Quinn. He was willing to sell Ned Kelly.

Indeed, Quinn had already been informing on the thieves. A year earlier, he had ratted on Billy Cooke (formerly known as Allen Lowry, and sometimes as Ryan), which led to Cooke's arrest.[3]

Quinn told Detective Ward that he had met Ned Kelly on the road around the time of the Fitzpatrick shooting and conversed with him. He asked Kelly if he was involved in the horse thefts. Kelly denied it. Quinn said he didn't believe him, and advised him to hand himself in to the police.

Kelly said he wasn't going to do that. Then he told Quinn, 'If any man interferes with me, I'll shoot him.'

Quinn told him again the best thing to do was to give himself up, then he said, 'If anyone is advising you otherwise, it's for your bad and not for your good.'[4]

He had also heard that, despite Kelly's denials, Kelly had been at the house when Fitzpatrick was there, and had shot him, just as Fitzpatrick said.[5]

Ward told him that as soon as he had news of any importance to let him know. He assigned Quinn the codename '*Foote*'.[6]

Ward returned to Wangaratta, where he heard that the outlaws had been tracked through the Warby Ranges but had not been found. On 28 November, an informer of his named William Hopstead came into town, and told him that he had seen two horses in the ranges that might be the police horses from Stringybark Creek. With Hopstead and some mounted constables, Ward rode into the ranges and located the two horses. Hopstead was right. Both of them were police horses from the Stringybark Creek patrol.[7]

24

Uproar

From Collins Street bankers to Castlemaine blacksmiths, from Minimay mistresses to Mallacoota maids, the colony was in uproar about what the press called 'the Mansfield Murders'.

On Sunday 27 October, the day the news broke about the murders at Stringybark Creek, Victorian premier Graham Berry had met with Captain Standish, seeking Standish's opinion on two courses of action the premier had in mind. First, an increase in the reward from £200 to £500 per gang member. And second, an Outlawry Act styled on similar legislation in New South Wales brought into effect some years earlier, allowing anyone to shoot the four gang members on sight. Standish had liked both ideas.

In parliament, Berry had thundered:

> No effort will be omitted by the Government to stamp out these bushranging murderers or to ascertain the fate of Kennedy, whose disappearance is one of the most monstrous things that has happened in the colony.[1]

Berry was a progressive politician with an agenda of political reform: to lessen the power of wealthy landholders. Kelly mythology views Ned Kelly as a crusader for such causes, but the political champions of selectors and of land reform did not see him that way. Berry was no friend of Ned Kelly, whose actions disgusted and appalled him.

While not referring to the Kelly brothers by name, the *Felons Apprehension Act* created a legal mechanism to declare an individual an 'outlaw'. The criteria were that they had to be the subject of a warrant of arrest for a crime that attracted the death penalty, and that it was reasonably believed they would resist all attempts to be arrested. The attorney-general had to bring a claim to a Supreme Court judge, who could issue a summons. If the individual didn't appear, they would be outlawed, and anyone could legally shoot them on sight, if they were armed or reasonably thought to be armed, and could not be apprehended without risk to the apprehender.[2]

The bill had bipartisan support, although there were a few dissenting voices. One member questioned whether it changed anything in reality, because if someone actually succeeded in shooting Ned Kelly, there was zero chance they would be prosecuted. Another member worried about innocent people being shot by mistake; the attorney-general reassured him that the legislation had been copied word-for-word from the New South Wales version, where there had mercifully been no such tragic error.[3]

The act also made it illegal for anyone to 'voluntarily and knowingly harbour, conceal, or receive or give any aid, shelter, or sustenance' to outlaws, the punishment being up to fifteen years in prison.[4]

The *Felons Apprehension Act* (sometimes called the Outlawry Act) was passed by the Legislative Assembly on the Wednesday, and by the Legislative House the next night.[5]

The legal trigger was pulled the following Monday, when the Crown solicitor delivered an affidavit from Captain Standish to the chief justice of the Supreme Court. It declared that Ned Kelly, Dan Kelly 'and two men whose names are unknown' had murdered Michael Scanlan, Michael Kennedy, and Thomas Lonigan, and would resist all ordinary means to arrest them. The notice in the Government Gazette stated that the two unknown men were believed to be Billy King (between nineteen and twenty years of age) and Charles Brown (aged 21).

The police erroneously believed that Billy King was an alias of Wild Wright: it was an alias of Joe Byrne.[6]

The chief justice issued a summons for them to appear at Mansfield courthouse by 12 December or be deemed outlaws. Nobody expected them to show up, and they didn't, but the legal process had to be followed.[7]

There was saturation news coverage. Every newspaper in the colony carried daily updates, sometimes multiple daily articles, with correspondents reporting from Mansfield, Benalla, Wangaratta, Beechworth and elsewhere. There were feature articles about the history of the Kelly family and editorials denouncing their wickedness.

City journalists traipsed through the towns and villages around the Ovens district, talking to whoever would talk to them. They soon latched onto Michael Ward as a key figure. Every move he made was reported and syndicated across the colony. Not all of it was true.

'Strahan's party and Detective Ward returned to Wangaratta yesterday, after having been in the bush for sixteen days.'[8]

'Here we also met Detective Ward, as fine an officer as he is in the force. He had been out some seven weeks on important business, and was just making for Wangaratta.'[9]

'Detective Ward passed through Benalla last night.'[10]

'More troopers arrived by per train last night. Detective Ward went onwards; the troopers stayed in Benalla.'[11]

'Today Superintendent Nicolson left for Benalla, Superintendent Sadleir went to Beechworth and Inspector Brook-Smith [sic] to Yarrawonga, on the Murray; whilst Detective Ward went towards Glenmore.'[12]

'Detective Ward, who is an excellent bushman and knows the district well, and is also fully acquainted with the Kellys, continues to actively ferret out information.'[13]

The journalists wandered the district as if in a foreign country, never straying too far from the railway line, their connection to home. The district telegraph offices had never been so busy. The journalists were there every day, sending thousands of words daily to Melbourne, and receiving cranky demands from their editors, desperate for content. The public was hungry for news. It was common for feature articles in the city papers to start with a sentence along the lines of, 'There is no news to report on the Kellys today,' followed by a lengthy article of more than a thousand words.

The Melbourne *Herald* correspondent reprinted from a regional newspaper an interview with a Professor Nimshi 'of Wangaratta four years recent', who proffered commentary on Ned Kelly's skull:

> **The head of this man is non-intellectual. The base of the skull with the whole basilar section of the brain is a massive development of the lower animal proclivities, and which, being vastly in excess of the moral sectional measurement, inclines him to the perpetration of sensual animal vices; and which, with an adverse facial angle, prompts him to the commission of vicious brutal acts of outrage and aggressiveness. He has large organs of self-esteem and love of approbation, which gives self-conceit and vanity. If the one be wounded, or the other mortified, his animal nature would know no bounds. He would be likely under sudden surprise to commit the grossest outrages; and, being uncontrolled by any moral sentiment, stamps his character as wolfish and ravenous, his notions of moral right giving him a dangerous range of action.**[14]

Professor Nimshi was a self-proclaimed all-round scholar, being a phrenologist, a lecturer in astronomy and geology, and a 'curative mesmerist'. Such were the lengths that the Victorian journalists would go to for a story about Ned Kelly.

Local reporters knew the district and had been reporting on the Kellys and their associates for years. They took a dim view of these interlopers. The journalists at Beechworth's *Advertiser* analysed the locations visited by *The Age's* correspondent, gleefully announcing that he had claimed to have travelled an implausible, if not impossible, 288 miles in a single day. They proceeded to publish a parody of a city journalist:

> Secret information reached me at three o'clock in the morning that the Kellys were camped on the top of Mount Feathertop, where they were engaged in melting the snow, so as to swell the rivers and prevent the police from following them.
>
> I at once rose from my comfortable couch, and having primed myself with a raw beefsteak and a mixture of rum and gunpowder, placed a heavy brass cannon in my waistcoat pocket, and a few revolvers and rifles in my belt, and having mounted Pegasus, I strapped a torpedo in front of me, and a balloon in my rear.[15]

But mockery was no obstacle to the big business of Kelly reporting. The day after the Professor Nimshi expose went to print in Melbourne, *The Herald's* roaming correspondent found a sensational new angle on the Fitzpatrick shooting:

> Their story is, that so far as Fitzpatrick's wound is concerned, the fact was that he was behaving rather freely with one of Kelly's sisters, when his revolver went off accidentally, but that none of the family or their friends fired at him in any way.[16]

The article was about as fact-based as the interview with the esteemed professor. It was bogus in so many ways that it's hard to count. For starters, Ellen Kelly had already admitted that Fitzpatrick was there to arrest Dan, not to make out with her daughter. And Brickey, Ellen and even Ned himself all later admitted that Ned was present, and that he shot Fitzpatrick.

But some stories catch on. Some images stick in the mind's eye. A randy young cop making out with a farm-girl gets so excited that he accidentally discharges his gun. Wow! It had everything, right down to the bawdy metaphor of an exploding revolver in his pants. And best of all, it made sense. The cruelty and evil of Stringybark Creek were now comprehensible.

The article also took aim at Constable Flood:

> **It is alleged that the member of the force referred to has openly boasted that he seduced Kelly's sister; this in itself is enough to arouse to the fullest the passions of such men as the Kellys; and smarting under two such supposed grievances as the wrongful conviction of their mother and the openly boasted seduction of their sister, it can well be conceived that men whose training has been such as the Kellys' would, when opportunity offered, hesitate at no crime which would inflict punishment on the police force, members of which they blamed for their wrongs.**

It was sadly ironic that these malicious smears were directed against two good, hard-working cops instead of the many corrupt, lazy drunkards around them.

The following Wednesday, 13 November, *The Herald*'s allegations were raised in parliament by Donald Cameron MLA. He noted that 'statements had been made' that the behaviour of 'certain members of the police force' had led to the Mansfield murders. He demanded an inquiry to find out if there was any truth to the statements.[17]

Fitzpatrick's alleged molestation of Kate was at odds with the facts, and was contradicted by statements by Ellen, Brickey, Bill Skillion and even Ned. Yet the rumour took hold.[18]

Fitzpatrick's reputation never recovered.[19]

25

Agent McIntyre

On the day of Michael Kennedy's funeral, Constable McIntyre was instructed to check in to the police hospital at the Richmond Depot, Melbourne. McIntyre gave evidence at the inquest, but could not stay for the funeral. He departed by coach for Longwood escorted by two armed volunteers, Dr Reynolds and William Joseph Collopy, both of whom had assisted in the search. From Longwood Station he caught the afternoon train, arriving at the police hospital in the evening.[1]

Morning brought two unexpected visitors to his bedside: Chief Commissioner Captain Standish and Superintendent Frank Hare. Standish wanted to know all about the events at Stringybark Creek.

McIntyre blurted out, 'I could do nothing else, sir!'

Standish replied, 'It's all right, McIntyre, I'm satisfied with your conduct.'

They talked until lunchtime. When he told them about his injuries from the fall, Standish asked to see, so he lifted up his gown and showed them his back. The skin was completely black from bruises.[2]

Standish informed McIntyre that he had been formally transferred to the Melbourne precinct, and could not return to Mansfield. He explained that McIntyre was the only witness to the murders, and needed to be protected.

A reporter from *The Herald* visited him after lunch. He was still in bed. He reassured the reporter that he was in pretty good shape, and would be back on duty after a few days' recuperation.

The reporter wasn't so sure. The subsequent article said:

McIntyre has unquestionably sustained a severe shock to his nervous system, in addition to which the lower portions of his back and hips are perfectly black, caused by the fall he sustained from Sergeant Kennedy's horse after making his escape from the camp.[3]

McIntyre praised Sergeant Kennedy as 'a most brave and experienced officer, full of daring, yet possessing military caution in a high degree.'

In response, the reporter asked: if that was the case, why was no sentry placed at the campsite overnight?

McIntyre explained that they had no idea the Kellys were nearby. 'It was way out of their district where we camped.' He continued, 'The fact is, information had been received by us that the Kelly brothers were working by themselves near to Greta, and it had been arranged that a police party at Hedi should work the country towards Mansfield, and in the event of their not encountering the "boys", we should join forces and work back towards the head of the King River.'

The reporter also asked about him shooting the birds.

McIntyre replied, 'Yes, we fired at some birds on the morning of the murder, but I believe that it was the shots fired on the previous night which betrayed us.'

Other journalists came and interviewed him over the coming days. McIntyre enjoyed the attention, partly because his first job had been in a newspaper office in Ireland, and partly because some of his Irish relatives were in the news business.[4]

He gained favourable coverage for the most part, but the detail about hiding in a wombat hole continued to haunt him. He wrote later, 'I have often regretted that I mentioned this place of concealment, there was no necessity for it, I could very easily have said that I concealed myself without mentioning in what manner I had done so, it would have injured no person and saved me from many humiliating and vexatious remarks.'[5]

Two weeks later, mostly healed and quite bored, McIntyre applied for a transfer to Mansfield. Soon after he lodged the application, a hansom pulled up at the depot. (A hansom is a stylish, upmarket horse-drawn cab.) The driver entered with a note for McIntyre, which said:

> Will Constable McIntyre be good enough to come to the club in the hansom by which I send this note.[6]

McIntyre climbed in. After a short trip across the city, the driver delivered him to the front steps of the Melbourne Club. Captain Standish lived there now, having moved in permanently in 1873, and conducted most of his official business within its private rooms.

Standish first dispensed with question of McIntyre's transfer. It was rejected. On to more important matters.

McIntyre could help in other ways, not just charging around on horses in the bush. An associate of Ned Kelly, Billy Cooke was serving time in Pentridge for horse theft and might be willing to turn informer. McIntyre's job was to interview Cooke, then report back.

McIntyre visited Pentridge Prison on 25 November. Cooke was cooperative, and surprisingly well-informed about the Stringybark Creek murders. He told McIntyre that the two mystery gang members were probably Joe Byrne and Charles Harris. McIntyre asked what they looked like. Cooke's description of Byrne resonated, but his description of Harris didn't. Harris was aged about 30, but McIntyre remembered the fourth man being very young, perhaps twenty at most.

Even so, this was valuable information. McIntyre had learned the name of a third member of the gang.[7]

Cooke said that a year earlier, when the Baumgarten brothers were arrested, he visited Ned Kelly to inform him of the arrest. Ned scoffed that he didn't care if the Baumgartens were in the lock-up, because he was still free. He boasted that even if others went down, he would never be arrested for the Whitty horse thefts.[8]

Joe Byrne was at the Kelly house that day. Byrne told Cooke he was 'one of the principals' in the horse theft and smuggling scheme, and particularly the Whitty job, and told Cooke the names of several individuals involved on both sides of the border.[9]

The depth of Byrne's involvement was clear from an anecdote that Cooke related. Ned Kelly needed to cash a cheque he had acquired from the Baumgartens. He and Byrne went to a Benalla hotel, with Byrne pretending to be one of the Baumgarten brothers, in order to convince the hotelier to cash the cheque.

McIntyre asked whether Wild Wright was part of the Kelly's criminal circle. Cooke said that he wasn't trusted, because Kelly considered him a 'blathering fool'.[10]

Cooke told McIntyre of some locations they were likely to hide. He said they had planned to move into New South Wales, but were prevented by the floods.[11]

Constable McIntyre wasn't the only policeman working Pentridge, and Cooke wasn't the only informant. The day after the bodies of Lonigan and Scanlan were discovered, Detective Brown had the first of many private conversations with Brickey Williamson, also an inmate behind the bluestone walls. Captain Standish himself also met with Brickey on multiple occasions.

Brickey was a fount of knowledge. He provided descriptions of the gang's horses, including the brands. He gave the names of their associates, and who might be induced to betray them. He described the locations of hideouts.

He described how the Kellys' sister, Maggie Skillion, who lived on a nearby selection, had a white sheet permanently hung out on a line, so that when the police were about, she could bang on the sheet with a stick: a warning signal that could be seen from far away. Maggie was also providing them with provisions, which she would hide in a hollow log.

When he learned that Brickey was talking, Captain Standish visited Pentridge and met him. In mid-November, Brickey warned that Ned Kelly planned to rob a bank. Then, at the start of December, he provided more details. The gang was planning a bank robbery somewhere along the railway line between Melbourne and Benalla.

The likely targets were Seymour, Avenel, Euroa or Violet Town.[12]

Superintendent Frank Hare had recently been placed in charge of the Bourke district, which included Seymour and Avenel. The other two were in Sadleir's jurisdiction.

Hare recalled later that Standish instructed him to reinforce those towns against bank robbery in early December.

Seymour, the closest to Melbourne of the four, was the prime candidate. Of Seymour's three bank branches, the Colonial Bank was the most vulnerable to robbery. Brickey thought they'd probably hit Seymour, because Ned had been talking about robbing a bank there for ages. Usually there were only a foot constable and a sergeant in Seymour. Hare despatched three more constables there, including one in plain-clothes, with special instructions to monitor the Colonial Bank.[13]

Avenel had one bank branch and two constables. Hare sent a third constable with instructions that the three of them were to monitor the bank in plain-clothes around the clock. The bank managers in Seymour and Avenel were all notified of the risk.[14]

Beyond Avenel, Hare's jurisdiction ended. The next town up the line was Euroa, which was part of the north-eastern district. Euroa was also a prime contender for a robbery, because Ned Kelly had once worked in that vicinity as a labourer so he knew it well. But that was Sadleir's responsibility. Or perhaps, since Nicolson had charge of all things Kelly-related, it was Nicolson's responsibility.

Standish swore he sent the memo to Benalla. Nicolson swore he never received it.

But Nicolson was traversing the district, overseeing the entire police operation, and was rarely in Benalla. When he wasn't out with search parties, he was travelling from one place to another.[15] By contrast, Sadleir was in Benalla head office all day, every day. Having recently recovered from rheumatic fever, he was confined to desk duties. If Standish's message was overlooked, then it was Sadleir who overlooked it.[16]

The banks in Euroa and Violet Town were left unguarded, and the townships received no additional police protection. Meanwhile, the crowded barracks in Benalla, Wangaratta and Beechworth overflowed with newly arrived mounted constables, packed side by side on make-shift beds, impatient to chase bushrangers.

Euroa

26

Tip-off

A quiet offer was made to Senior-Constable Kelly at Hedi station by a local postmaster, to monitor the mail for anything suspicious. It was highly illegal, but the risk was on the postmaster. Naturally, the senior-constable was open to it.

The postmaster showed him an intercepted letter, supposedly from the editor of a border-town newspaper known to be sympathetic to the Kelly Gang, outlining plans to smuggle them across the Murray River. The author of the letter is not known, even today. The recipient (presumably a Kelly associate) was in the Greta district:

> Sir, I have been requested by E. and D. Kelly to do what I could to assist them in crossing here.
>
> I am to write to you to let you know the arrangements. They are to be at a time to be named at the junction of Indigo Creek and Murray, and there is to be a password, it is this—'Any work to be had?' 'Yes.' 'Where?'
>
> On the New-South Wales side one shall meet you. I will have a boat ready. There must not be any horses come to the river, if you should have horses they must be led by the bridge to a safe place already prepared for them. I will have four on each side of the river to watch upper and lower side. I have a place fixed where you will be safe. If you should want horses there will some be got for you. There are two says they will join you if requested. You must mind they will want money and I have got none. When you write, direct to Howlong for—(the signer)[1]

Senior-Constable Kelly forwarded a copy of the letter to Benalla police headquarters, and it arrived there on 8 December.

On reading the letter, Sadleir could hardly believe his eyes . . . or his luck. If true, this was the best chance yet to catch Ned Kelly and his gang, thanks to the carelessness of a newspaper editor. Sadleir must also have been thinking about the reward money, due to whoever was involved in catching or killing them. Technically, he was supposed to leave all things Kelly-related to Nicolson, but there, too, luck had gone his way, because Nicolson was out of town.

Sadleir made a note on 8 December, that:

> The envelope showed the Bungowannah and Albury postmarks of the 3rd instant.
>
> There is no fear of any action being taken by the writer or his confederates for some days, unless this a blind to cover movements already taken.[2]

That was a big 'unless', but he seems to have not considered the bigger 'unless': that the letter itself was a ruse. A local schoolmaster named James Wallace was a close friend of Joe Byrne. He and his wife ran a rural post office at Bobinawarrah, near Greta, as a side business. He was probably both the author of the letter and the person who showed it to Senior-Constable Kelly. By his own admission, Wallace created other letters with false signatures to assist the gang, and he was adept at forging the handwriting of others.

Sadleir made arrangements to catch the late train to Albury on Tuesday with Sergeant Harkin, with the intention of installing Harkin on special duty to watch out for this crossing. As he was making his last-minute preparations, Nicolson rode into the yard with a patrol of several mounted constables.[3]

Nicolson was exhausted. He had been working hard for the past month: patrolling, riding from town to town, organising search parties. The extensive riding about was taking a toll on his fragile health. This most recent excursion had been to the upper King River to meet Pat Quinn, whom Ward had recruited as an informant, but Quinn had not showed up. Nicolson felt ill and his eyes were inflamed.[4]

He needed nothing more than a good, long sleep in a comfortable bed; but, after listening to Sadleir's briefing and reading the mysterious letter, he knew he had to go north to Albury too. He packed a travel bag and accompanied Sadleir and Harkin to the railway station, to wait for the northbound train.[5]

It was eight o clock and quite dark when the train stopped at the platform. Among the disembarking passengers, they recognised a magistrate named Alfred Wyatt, carrying what looked to be a bouquet of flowers. Seeing them, Wyatt bustled up and asked to speak to Nicolson urgently and privately. The bouquet wasn't flowers, but a large knot of cable wire.[6]

Nicolson ushered him into a room in the stationmaster's building. Sadleir tried to follow, but Wyatt shut the door in his face.[7]

Once they were in private, Wyatt showed Nicolson the wire, and pointed out where they had been cut. These were telegraph wires from the line near Euroa, he told Nicolson. The telegraph had been cut, and he was sure that Ned Kelly and his gang had done it.

They re-emerged onto the platform, where Nicolson relayed Wyatt's concerns to Sadleir (who had in fact been standing right outside the door and was already completely up to speed). Nicolson instructed Sadleir to ask the guards and drivers whether they had noticed anything untoward at Euroa.

Wyatt was in a very agitated state, which predisposed Sadleir to discount everything he said. He would have been much more inclined to take the man seriously if he had been in a calm and sober state of mind.

Sadleir walked along the platform, speaking to some passengers, including some who had come from Melbourne, inquiring if anything was wrong along the railway line. They told him there were police at most stations, and there was 'no alarm whatever' along the line. He felt that he had learned enough.

He reported back to Nicolson, 'Everything was going on all right as usual at Euroa.'[8]

He and Nicolson boarded the train and took their seats. Wyatt watched them depart, holding his wire bouquet like a jilted lover.

Nicolson fell asleep almost immediately.

When the train stopped at Glenrowan Station about half an hour later, Sadleir noticed a man on the platform, lurking in the shadow of a recess in the building. He recognised the man: it was McDonnell, the owner of a hotel in Glenrowan, and a friend of Joe Byrne.

McDonnell was looking at him in a curious, suspicious manner. When Sadleir stared back at him, McDonnell retreated into the shadows, out of sight. The way he had looked at Sadleir, it was almost as if McDonnell was there to check that he was on the train.[9]

27

Wyatt's day trip

Earlier on that same Tuesday, 10 December 1879, Alfred Wyatt had caught the southbound train from Benalla to Euroa to preside over an afternoon session of licensing claims. This is how his afternoon and evening had unfolded.

Looking through the train's windows to the right, he could see the rolling plains of the Goulburn River basin stretched westward and northward. To the left were the forests of the Strathbogie Ranges, and beyond them, out of sight further east, were the Wombat Ranges and Stringybark Creek.

As the train started to slowly pull out of Violet Town, the station before Euroa, a man walked alongside the platform, trying to get his attention. The man called out, 'The lines are down!' He and another man then jumped onto the train and found Wyatt in his seat. As a well-known magistrate, Wyatt was a kind of authority figure, although he had no authority over the railways.

The man's name was Mr Watt and he was a telegraph repairer. He had tested the telegraph line at Violet Town and found there was no connection to Euroa. There were two telegraph systems: the government line ran down one side of the track, and the railway telegraph line down the other side. He asked Wyatt to keep an eye out on the right-hand side of the track, while he watched the other, looking for breaks.

About three miles before Euroa, the homestead of Faithfulls Creek Station slid into view on the right. It was an outstation of the sprawling Younghusband stock empire, one of Victoria's biggest

160

grazing conglomerates. In the open paddock near the homestead, six telegraph poles were down.

The driver slowed the train to a crawl. The passengers peered out at the fallen poles. Someone declared it must have been a whirlwind, and everyone else agreed.

The repairer said, 'Look here, Mr Wyatt, I can't mend this line.'

As if to prove the point, he showed Wyatt his repair kit, which consisted of small tools and some splicing wires; nothing that would fix a major break. He asked Wyatt to deliver a message to Melbourne from Euroa. Wyatt said, 'All right.'

Even so, Watt and his colleague planned to inspect the break, then walk to Euroa, which was about three or four miles away, where they would wait for supplies and assistance. Carrying their repair kits, Watt and his assistant stepped off the crawling train, which then picked up pace for the last leg of the trip to Euroa.[1]

As he had promised, Wyatt delivered the message about the broken lines to the Euroa stationmaster, Mr Gorman, and the urgent request for equipment. The courthouse was about half a mile from the platform. On the way there, he walked past the National Bank. It was closed for the afternoon. He saw nothing suspicious.

None of the licence applications were opposed, so the hearings in the little Euroa courthouse took only fifteen minutes. Wyatt walked back to the railway station, again past the bank and again seeing nothing untoward. With time to kill before the next train north, he decided to investigate the broken telegraph line.

He hired a horse and buggy from Mr Hart, the new proprietor of de Boos's hotel. The horse was a slow old carthorse, and the roads were more confusing than he'd anticipated. There was a track north alongside the railway line, which he assumed would take him there, but it veered away unexpectedly. He hit a dead end, and another road that had seemed promising took him in the wrong direction. He tried to turn the buggy around but got stuck in some fallen timber.

A man rode up and asked, 'Is this the way to Faithfulls Creek Station?'[2]

Can't tell you,' replied Wyatt grumpily.

The man swore at him, then rode off.

After returning the horse and buggy, Wyatt visited Gorman in the stationmaster's office for news about the telegraph wires. Remembering Watt's comment that he would walk to Euroa, he asked Gorman if the repairmen had arrived yet, but Gorman said they hadn't.

The answer surprised him. 'How is that?' he asked Gorman. 'It's only three miles and three-quarters, and he couldn't repair the line himself. What could keep him?'[3]

Wyatt was now sure something was terribly wrong. He said, 'There's something up. You must give me express permission to ride upon the engine and stop the train and get down and examine the line. I don't believe it was a whirlwind now, because I recollect there wasn't a single tree or shrub injured anywhere about.'

They decided to keep their concerns a secret, for now.

A grizzled, hairy face leered at them through the ticket window. It was a hawker called Ben Gould, a longstanding friend of the Kelly family. He was aged about 50 and was tall and tough as a tree trunk. When sober, Gould could be calm and reasonable, but he was a hard drinker and prone to bouts of alcohol-fuelled violence. Right now, he was drunk, breathing alcoholic fumes through the aperture at them.

Gould must have mistaken Wyatt for Robert Scott, the manager of Euroa's National Bank branch. He pointed a long finger at the magistrate, and said, 'All right, Mr Scott! I mean to have £500 out of your bank today.'

An annoyed Gorman corrected him. 'That isn't Mr Scott. It's Mr Wyatt, the police magistrate. You'd better clear out of this before you get into trouble.'

Thankfully, Gould left them alone.

A few minutes out of Euroa, the train stopped in the twilight near Faithfulls Creek Station, where no lights were on. Wyatt, who had been travelling with the driver, jumped off the footplate and hurried across to the fallen poles.

This was no whirlwind. He could now see that the poles had been chopped down, and the wires had been cut then tied into Gordian knots to thwart repair. He twisted a piece of knotted wire around until it snapped off, to take as evidence. On the other side of the track, all four government telegraph wires were also destroyed.[4]

He hurried back to the train and climbed into the engine cab, anxious to get to Benalla so he could alert the police. He told the driver and guard not to alarm the public: if anyone asked what happened to the telegraph wires, he suggested, just say it was a whirlwind.

The journey from Euroa to Benalla took about an hour and a quarter. By the time the train stopped at Benalla, Wyatt was jumpy as hell.[5]

He had looked around for blue uniforms but, seeing none, decided to hire a trap (a horse and buggy) to the police station. He then noticed Superintendent Sadleir and Superintendent Nicolson by a carriage door, about to board. They had escaped his attention at first because they were both in plain-clothes.[6]

He had rushed over, breathless and excited. He needed to speak with Nicolson privately. The meeting was very short—too short. Afterwards, he thought of things he should have said, but forgot to say, that might have made them change their mind. The disappearance of the two repairmen, for example.

Sadleir had gone off to confirm the story. He wasn't gone long.

Sadleir had spoken to the guard and driver; but he was wearing plain clothes and to them he was just another member of the public. When he asked if there was a problem with the telegraph lines, they reassured him that they had been brought down by a whirlwind. After all, that's what Mr Wyatt had strictly told them to say, if asked.

Later on, Wyatt tossed and turned in his Benalla hotel room. He couldn't sleep, because he kept thinking about those cut wires. Suddenly he got up, got dressed, picked up his wire bouquet and walked as fast as he could to the local telegraph office, where he met the chief telegraphist, Mr Saxe.

Wyatt asked him, 'You know the line is down?'[7]

Saxe knew it was down, but not that it had been sabotaged. He stared wide-eyed at the cut wires and listened intently to Wyatt's story.

They realised they needed to contact the police commissioner, Captain Standish. Saxe explained that it could be done by sending a message 'around the Sydney side'. That meant sending a message north—as if to Sydney—with instructions for it to be relayed west, and then south to Melbourne on a different line.

They composed a message:

To: Captain Standish, Chief Commissioner of Police, Melbourne.

Going from Violet Town to Euroa, at about 4.40 p.m., by luggage train, was informed telegraph lines out of order. Found both lines (Government and railway) down at 97 miles from Melbourne, Faithfull's Creek Road crossing, by bridge under the railway. On return, at 6.50, from Euroa, rode on engine, stopped train, got down and examined. Found all wires (4 of Government line and 1 of railway line) cut through with powerful nippers, and both lines dismounted, one for 300 yards, and the other for 200. Met Nicolson and Sadleir at Benalla Station, going to Wangaratta. Informed them, and showed them the cut ends of one wire, which I had twisted off and put in my pocket. Nicolson said, I know what it means; it won't alter my plans. They went on. The line cannot be repaired before tomorrow noon.[8]

While Saxe sent the message, Wyatt went across to Benalla police headquarters, 300 yards away, where he met Sergeant Whelan. He told

Whelan everything. He urged Whelan to organise a patrol, requisition a special train and go to Euroa immediately.[9]

Whelan explained it didn't work that way. He didn't have the authority to do such things. He would have to ask either Sadleir or Nicolson. As they were both out of contact, he would have to request permission from Captain Standish personally, and he would have to make a very good case for it.

Wyatt convinced him to try, so Whelan composed a formal request to Standish. As Saxe was busy with the first message, they decided to ask the stationmaster to try to send Whelan's message via the railway system. With two messages using two systems, their chances of getting word through to Melbourne had surely doubled. Whelan's message was sent at 9.45 p.m.

Wyatt returned to his hotel but was even more keyed up than before. He sat, fully dressed, until 11 p.m., then went back to the police station to find out if Sergeant Whelan had heard back. He had.

Standish's telegram said:

Bank at Euroa stuck up. You have now a good case. Go ahead.[10]

Whelan dampened Wyatt's relief with the revelation that there weren't large numbers of police in the Benalla barracks for such an expedition. Wyatt volunteered to join them, if he would be able to make it to Avenel for court the next day.[11]

Whelan said he could go. Wyatt hurried back to his hotel room, grabbed his revolver, went to the railway platform, and waited.

28

Night train to Euroa

At about 10 p.m. on Tuesday, 10 December 1878, Detective Michael Ward was relaxing in the home of some friends in Benalla. A constable arrived with news that the Euroa bank had been robbed, and with instructions for him to report to the railway station to take charge of a contingent of mounted constables bound for Euroa.[1]

Despite having expressed concerns to Wyatt about potential numbers, Sergeant Whelan had managed to assemble several men at the station. Whelan himself, currently the most senior officer at headquarters, could not leave Benalla. Alfred Wyatt, the excitable magistrate, was on the platform, packing a revolver.

The late train from Melbourne arrived at 10.20 p.m. and who should step off? None other than Constable Anderson, the sole police constable in Euroa. They pressed him for news, but he didn't know much. Apparently, after being out of town for the day, he arrived at Euroa Railway Station that evening where he was immediately informed that the bank had been robbed. He had spoken to the stationmaster, Gorman, long enough to learn that the telegraph lines were out, and he reasoned that someone should travel north to alert Benalla police headquarters. He immediately jumped back on the train and departed north. And now, here he was![2]

The obvious rejoinder would surely have been that anyone on the train could have done that. Indeed, Gorman himself had suggested just this to Constable Anderson and made some quite disparaging remarks when Anderson insisted on getting back on the train. So here he was, delivering the very important message that the Euroa bank had been stuck up.

Ward insisted Constable Anderson join them to return to Euroa.

Ward was in charge of the expedition. Accompanying him were eight constables, including Charles Johnston (whose enthusiastic efforts in the Warby Ranges had been thwarted by his superiors) and two police blacktrackers. And, of course, Alfred Wyatt.[3]

Johnston was itching to go. A native of County Tyrone in Ireland, he had a reputation for being zealous, but also at times irascible and insolent. Wyatt recalled later: 'Johnston was very eager, and so positive in his notions of what should be done, that I feared, if Ward should not agree with him, he would not be quite subordinate.'[4]

Sergeant Whelan had arranged a special train for them, which seemed to take forever to get ready.

Finally their horses were loaded and they departed at around half past one in the morning. Wyatt rode up front on the outside of the engine, gripping a railing with one hand and his field glass with the other, so that he could find the fallen wires. The driver understood the urgency and the train reached sixty miles per hour in some places. Wyatt later said he had never travelled so fast in all his life.[5]

The train sped past Violet Town Station without stopping, crashing through a boom gate. As they approached Euroa, the driver slowed it down to give Wyatt a chance to find the location.[6]

Wyatt saw the broken line in the moonlight and signalled the driver. The train came to a stop. Ward stepped off and investigated the fallen poles and cut wires. There were two people running towards him from the Faithfulls Creek Station, dressed in white. They had donned white silk coats to make themselves more visible.

One of them was Bill Macauley, the overseer at the station. He told Ward that the gang had left a few hours ago. They had held a large number of hostages at the homestead the previous day and night and had used it as a staging point for the bank robbery.

Ward swung up onto the engine and conferred with the driver. He wanted to quickly go across to the homestead. The driver said there would be no trains coming down the track. They could wait for him for half an hour or so.

As Ward trudged across the moonlit grass with the two white-clad figures towards the lights of Faithfulls Creek Station, another person appeared beside them. It was Alfred Wyatt, the magistrate.[7]

At the homestead, they found several people who had been hostages. They were told there had been other hostages who had since left.

Apparently, the gang had arrived at Faithfulls Creek Station on Monday afternoon and taken everyone there prisoner. Anyone who passed nearby on the road was taken. The missing line repairers were taken. And when the gang returned from the bank robbery on Tuesday afternoon, they brought with them even more hostages from town.

Having Wyatt on hand turned out to be an unexpected bit of luck, because Ward spoke to others while Wyatt interviewed Macauley. Then he and Wyatt hurried back over the moonlit grass to the train. They had been gone only 25 minutes.

On the train, Ward asked Wyatt to repeat his interview with Macauley. Ward wrote it all down as Wyatt talked.

Macauley had arrived home at about 4.20 p.m. on Monday 9 December to find all the servants gathered together in the kitchen. Someone said, 'The Kellys are here.'[8]

Then Ned Kelly appeared and said, 'Don't be frightened. We won't shoot you if you're quiet.' But then he said, 'If I find out you give information, you will be shot. We have plenty of friends and you will be shot in six months. We have at least four rifles like this.' Kelly was brandishing the Spencer rifle taken from Stringybark Creek.

A hawker named Gloster and his teenaged assistant, Frank Beecroft, arrived with their wagon full of clothing for sale. Macauley knew

Gloster to be a 'plucky fellow', was worried he would resist, which he did at first, earning Kelly's ire, and risking a bullet to the head.[9]

All the men were locked in the storage shed overnight, allowed outside for occasional relief breaks. All the men except Macauley. He slept under the stars next to one of the gang members, who he believed was Joe Byrne, and who was guarding the storage shed.

On Tuesday, Steve Hart cut down the telegraph poles with a tomahawk. A group of four elderly men, returning from a hunting party in the Strathbogie Ranges, rode by in a spring cart. Around the same time four navvies (railway workers) went by on a railway trolley. Kelly shouted joyfully, 'Here's a go! Here's nine traps!' He and Hart rode down, bailed them all up, and brought them back to the homestead.

Ned and Dan took the hawker's wagon and the spring cart into town for the robbery. Ned made Gloster's assistant, Frank Beecroft, drive one of the wagons. Beecroft, it should be noted, was never suspected by the police as being an accomplice. It seems that Kelly had picked him at Faithfulls Creek based on his judgement, accurate in hindsight, that the boy would be compliant. Some have suspected that Gloster was an accomplice, conveniently providing a wagon and clothes for the gang, but that theory makes no sense. The gang could have done the robbery without either his wagon or clothing. Furthermore, Gloster later testified against Kelly. No other Kelly associate did that. This theory downplays Gloster's courage in standing up to the outlaw, and Kelly's aggression in response.[10]

Hart rode one of the Faithfulls Creek horses. Ned took with him a small cheque written by Macauley to provide an excuse to get inside the bank. He and the other three were wearing expensive felt hats stolen from Gloster's wagon. Byrne stayed behind to guard the hostages.

While the three were gone, the telegraph repairers got off the train. Byrne bailed them up and put them in the storage shed with the others.

The Kelly brothers, Steve Hart, and Frank Beecroft returned three hours later with the two wagons, plus another wagon driven by the bank manager's wife, Susy Scott. In the process of robbing the bank, they had made hostages of the bank manager, Robert Scott, and the two clerks, as well as everyone in the Scott residence adjoining the bank: Susy Scott, their children, their maids and Susy's mother, who was visiting.

The women and children hostages from the bank robbery were allowed to wander freely, but Robert Scott and the clerks were put in the storage shed. When the late afternoon train stopped by the fallen poles, Kelly told the hostages not in the shed to hide inside, then he and the other gang members watched Wyatt get out of the train, inspect the wires, and return to the train. They kept watching until the train was out of sight.

Macauley recalled watching the four outlaws count the proceeds of the robbery, 'I saw notes and papers but no gold.'

Before leaving, Kelly instructed that the prisoners in the storeroom were not to be released for three hours. He and his men left at half past eight. Macauley said they were last seen riding south, in the direction of Mansfield.

As soon as they had gone, Macauley took the storeroom key off its hook. Susy Scott said, 'Don't touch that key, for heaven's sake!'

Macauley scoffed, 'Oh, damn Kelly!' He grabbed the key, then hurried out and released all the prisoners.

Supper was soon laid out, and everyone ate and drank. They discussed how to get everyone home once the Kelly's deadline had passed.[11]

Some aspects of Macauley's version of events were suspicious.

First, all the other men were locked in the storeroom, yet he slept outside with Joe Byrne. Slightly odd.

Second, Ned Kelly had taken a cheque signed by Macauley so the clerks would let him in. Macauley claimed he did not write it;

that Kelly found it by ransacking his papers, and maybe that's what happened.

Third, when the gang returned from the heist, and counted their takings, Macauley was in the room with them. By his own admission, they allowed him to stay and watch while they counted their haul. No other prisoners had that privilege.

More than a year later, Macauley made a curious slip in a chance meeting with Wyatt. They were discussing the sale of some stock, and to explain where the sale had occurred, Macauley said, 'Just about where you met Steve Hart.'

Wyatt replied, 'I never said it was Steve Hart.' Furthermore, Wyatt hadn't even known the identity of the horseman until Macauley said that.

Macauley then gave a somewhat unsatisfactory explanation: 'When the party came back with the Scotts from the bank, we were yarning, and Steve Hart said to me, 'Who was that old bugger I met in the lane?' Then someone else remembered that 'Wyatt, the magistrate', was in town that day, so they all agreed it must have been him. According to Macauley, Hart responded, 'By God, if I had known that I would have popped him.'[12]

The police special train from Benalla arrived at Euroa at 3 a.m. The horses were led out of their carriage, huffing and stamping in the night air. The stationmaster, Gorman, was still awake. Wyatt thought he heard Ward say something like, 'I'm to stop,' or 'Mr Nicolson is on his way'.

Sensing uncertainty, Wyatt advised him to stay until the superintendent arrived. He said, 'I think, under the circumstances, you will not do unwisely in waiting for your officer, provided the time isn't too long.'

But Ward was less uncertain than he appeared and didn't heed the magistrate's advice. He and Constable Johnston were both on edge. They both wanted to start the pursuit.[13]

He instructed Wyatt to catch the next train to Benalla, to inform or update Nicolson. Then he mounted his horse and led the other constables down the moonlit road to Faithfulls Creek Station. They did not get lost, because they had Constable Anderson from Euroa with them.

Ward spoke to two employees at Faithfulls Creek, William Fitzgerald and George Stephens, who were there when Kelly first arrived.[14]

Kelly had first appeared in the kitchen doorway at lunchtime, wearing an expensive tweed coat, asking to see Macauley. They told him Macauley wasn't around. Later, George Stephens was in the stables with stable hand John Carson, when station hand William Fitzgerald brought Kelly over as if he was giving him a tour of the property.

Kelly had said, 'Don't you know who I am?'

Joking, Stephens said, 'Perhaps you're Ned Kelly!'

Kelly replied, 'You're a damned good guesser.' He pulled out a revolver and aimed it at Stephens. The other gang members appeared with their horses, which they wanted fed.[15]

As they sat about, while the horses munched on oats, Kelly was in a talkative mood. He told them: 'At the time Fitzpatrick came to take my brother, I was 40 miles away.' He said nobody shot Fitzpatrick, 'as he only had a scratch. It would have broken the bone.'

Kelly's version of the Stringybark Creek murders made it sound like an exciting gunfight. He said only he and Dan were there. Steve Hart and Joe Byrne were back at their own hut. Lonigan took cover behind a log, his gun aimed at them. Ned and Dan also crawled behind a log, their guns pointing right back at Lonigan.

When Kelly fired, he hit Lonigan 'somewhere in the temple'. Lonigan got up and staggered around. Kelly fired again, striking him on the forehead.

When Scanlan and Kennedy returned, McIntyre approached them, then Kelly sang out for them to throw up their hands. Kelly told Stephens, 'Instead of doing so, Scanlan immediately turned the rifle around to the front. It was slung on his back. He couldn't get it off, but he got hold of it and fired at me, the bullet passing close by me. I believe the ball went about a foot away from me. I then fired at Scanlan and he bent forward on the horse's neck. I still kept him covered, thinking he was shamming, till the horse moved, and then I saw he was shot.'

Kelly said that Sergeant Kennedy fled through the forest. And Kelly pursued him. Kennedy turned and fired, the bullet grazing Kelly's chest. Kennedy turned again, with his hands up. Kelly shot him in the chest.

Kelly explained to Stephens that blood had pooled on Sergeant Kennedy's hand, making it look like he was holding a revolver, which is why he mistakenly shot him in the chest.

Ward asked Stephens if he would be willing to make a statement about his interactions with Kelly, and if necessary, testify against him in court. Stephens was willing.

The conversation in the stables had been overheard by Fitzgerald, who recalled something else Kelly had said: 'He was very angry with Hart and Byrne for not catching and preventing McIntyre's escape.'[16]

Kelly had expressed remorse about killing Kennedy, whom he described as a 'brave man', but made it clear he had no regrets about killing Lonigan.[17]

Ward also learned that, before Kelly left to rob the bank, he handed a gun to John Carson, telling him to assist Joe Byrne in guarding

the hostages. Carson was now gone. The police subsequently went to
some effort to find Carson, but he was never found.[18]

The cook, Mrs Fitzgerald (William's wife), had prepared dinner for
the gang. Before he took a mouthful, Kelly made one of the hostages
sample it, in case the food was poisoned.[19]

After talking to these station employees, Ward and the constables
searched Faithfulls Creek Station thoroughly and found some tracks.

Around mid-morning, a southbound train stopped at the same
place where the train had stopped the night before. Superintendent
Nicolson stepped off and walked across to the homestead. Ward gave
him a full briefing on the situation.[20]

Nicolson then instructed Ward to return to Benalla on the next
available train. He was in charge now and Ward was no longer needed.
Ward had hoped to get statements from Stephens, and the hawkers
Gloster and Beecroft, but he would have to follow them up later. He
departed for Euroa township, and there, as ordered, caught the next
northbound train.

Nicolson then went inside and interviewed the cook, Mrs Fitzgerald.
He asked her which direction Kelly and his men had gone. She told him
they rode up the railway line towards Violet Town. On the strength of
that, he despatched the two blacktrackers and some constables up the
railway to search for tracks. They soon returned, having found none.

Later that Wednesday morning, some horse tracks were found on
the other side of the track, heading east, in the direction of the Strathbogie Ranges. It seemed that Mrs Fitzgerald and Bill Macauley were
both mistaken.[21]

29

The hawkers and Kelly

The two hawkers had arrived at Faithfulls Creek Station at seven o'clock on Monday evening. James Gloster was a travelling draper from Seymour. He travelled the district in his wagon, selling clothes. Sitting beside him was his teenaged assistant, Frank Beecroft.

They pulled their horse and wagon to a stop next to the homestead, lit a fire there, and put on some food to cook. Their arrival had not yet been noticed by the four outlaws. Gloster went into the homestead's kitchen to fill his billy can with water to make some tea. As he walked out the door carrying the full billy can, he heard a voice calling out to him to stop. Whoever it was, he ignored them, walked back to his wagon, put the billy on the fire, and climbed up onto the wagon seat to get his pistol.

Ned Kelly and Joe Byrne rushed out from the kitchen to opposite sides of the wagon, their revolvers aimed at Gloster's head. 'Come down or I'll shoot you.'[1]

Gloster was a hard-boiled working-class man who cowered to nobody. He refused.

There was an argument. Kelly pressed the revolver to his face and said if Gloster didn't get down he would blow his brains out.[2]

Gloster got down, muttering curses.

Kelly said, 'I've a great mind to shoot you for not coming back.'[3]

If everyone at Faithfulls Creek had been this stubborn and uncooperative, Kelly's crowd-control efforts would have been challenging. But they weren't: Gloster was the only one who resisted.

Kelly added, 'It's a very easy matter for me to pull the trigger if you don't keep a civil tongue in your head.'[4]

Gloster said, 'Why are you interfering with me? Who and what are you?'

Kelly said, 'I'm Ned Kelly, the son of Red Kelly, and a better man never stood in two shoes.'[5]

Gloster said, 'If you are, I suppose there's no use resisting.'

Kelly said, 'If you keep a civil tongue in your head, you'll take no harm. You were nearer being shot than any man here.' He then asked, 'Have you any firearms in the wagon?'

Gloster said evasively, 'I don't carry firearms for sale.'

Kelly said, 'I know you have a pistol, and if you don't give it me at once, I'll burn the wagon down.'

The overseer Bill Macauley was there now, pleading with Kelly not to shoot Gloster, and likewise pleading with Gloster to comply with Kelly's instructions. Gloster reluctantly handed over his pistol.

Just when Gloster appeared compliant, he sauntered past Kelly to his campfire, sat down, picked up his dinner, and ate. Frank Beecroft later said in a sworn deposition, 'I was astonished that Gloster wasn't shot. He was obstinate.'[6]

Gloster called for Beecroft to join him. The two hawkers sat by the fire and ate while Kelly waited impatiently. When they were finished, he ordered them inside the homestead.

Kelly spent much of the night in the storage shed with his hostages. He was in a talkative mood and made no secret of his plan to rob the Euroa bank. They asked him about the Stringybark Creek killings. Kelly loved talking about that.[7]

He said, 'The people and papers call me a murderer, but I never murdered anyone in my life.'

Gloster asked him, 'How about Sergeant Kennedy?'

Kelly answered, 'I killed him in a fair fight. A fair, stand-up fight.'[8]

He added, 'The police are my natural enemies.' Then he explained that a man killing his enemy wasn't murder. The police were his enemies. Therefore, killing police didn't count as murder.[9]

Kelly retold the story of Kennedy's death to his captive audience.

According to him, Sergeant Kennedy ran from tree to tree, turning to fire at Kelly, while Kelly pursued.

Kelly said that one of the sergeant's shots went through his whiskers, another went through his sleeve! He couldn't help exaggerating a little more with each retelling. Only that afternoon he had told George Stephens that Kennedy's closest shot missed him by a yard. Now the story was that it went through his whiskers.[10]

One detail was the same as before: the sergeant put up his arms in surrender, then Kelly fired, hitting him in the armpit. That much, at least, was true. And incriminating. It was news to the hostages, but not to Detective Ward when he later heard it from Gloster. The police had already inferred that scenario from the post-mortem and inquest.

As Sergeant Kennedy lay wounded, Kelly had a long conversation with him. In the end, they didn't want to leave him there to die alone in the forest, so they decided to put him out of his misery. Sergeant Kennedy asked them to let him live, but they killed him anyway, with a shotgun blast to the chest.[11]

Out of respect, Kelly said, he covered Sergeant Kennedy's body with a cloak. Kelly didn't mention that he had stolen the wedding ring off Kennedy's corpse, or that Joe Byrne stole rings from the bodies of Scanlan and Lonigan, and was now wearing them as trophies. Respect has its limits.

Someone close by in the dark was bold enough to suggest that Kelly 'should have given Kennedy a chance'. Kelly didn't reply to that.

Gloster got the distinct impression that Kelly wanted to take all the blame for the shootings, and to incriminate only himself. Whether it was true or not, he couldn't tell.[12]

As for Fitzpatrick, Kelly said he was at least 200 miles away when Fitzpatrick claimed to have been shot. Therefore, Fitzpatrick's testimony was perjury and his mother was wrongfully convicted.[13]

He told them his mother had seen better days and had struggled to bring up a large family. He was very upset about her going to gaol 'with a baby at her breast', because of the perjured statements by Fitzpatrick.[14]

He claimed that he had been persecuted by the police. Once a man was convicted of a crime, from that day on, the police wouldn't leave him alone. He admitted, 'I've stolen upwards of 200 horses since I commenced business, and if the police had taken me for any of these I wouldn't grumble.'[15]

He was fine with being arrested for the many crimes he had committed, but it was the accusations about crimes he *hadn't* committed that rankled.

Gloster got the impression that the real motivation for the Stringybark Creek murders was revenge for his mother's imprisonment. Kelly told him, 'If my mother doesn't get justice and is released soon, I'll possibly overturn the train.'[16]

Daybreak came, and light filtered in. All morning, and all afternoon, the hostages were kept in that stuffy, smelly shed. They were allowed outside for occasional brief comfort breaks, under the implacable gaze of the men with rifles.

The gang raided Gloster's wagon. They burned their old clothes and dressed themselves in fine suits and felt hats. Gloster wrote an invoice for 17 pounds for the stolen clothes and the pistol, and handed it to Kelly, who ignored it.

Gloster later complained to Detective Ward that Kelly never paid the bill.[17]

The door opened, and more hostages came in. A team of navvies. Some elderly gents who had been on a hunting holiday. Ned came in, summoned John Carson and gave him a revolver. Carson had been promoted from hostage to guard.

They heard the wagons pull out on their way to the bank robbery and three hours later heard the wagons return. More hostages were brought in at gunpoint: two bank clerks, and Robert Scott, the Euroa National Bank manager. The door swung shut again and someone outside turned the key.

Finally, more than 30 hours after the first hostages were put in that horrible little shed, the door was unlocked by Bill Macauley. Kelly and his men had gone, and they were free.

When Detective Ward tracked down Gloster and Beecroft in the township of Avenel, he asked them to write detailed statements of what happened, and mail them to him in Beechworth. They promised to do so, and they did.

Beecroft, whom Ned Kelly had enlisted to help with the bank robbery, had been given £2 when they returned to the homestead. Kelly had also given him a watch, solemnly telling him that it was the dead Sergeant Kennedy's watch.

Ward examined the watch. It wasn't Sergeant Kennedy's watch. It was a cheap, worthless trinket.[18]

30

The Euroa bank robbery

They hit the Euroa bank at five minutes to four on the Tuesday afternoon, right on closing time.

A clerk named Mr Bradley saw a man knocking at the door, waving a cheque. He opened the door a crack and told the man the bank was closed for the day. The man showed him the cheque, which was for £4, written out by William Macauley, the overseer of Faithfulls Creek. The man said he very much wanted to cash the cheque today. He asked to speak to the manager, Mr Scott.

Bradley refused, saying there was no point asking because they had already locked up all the cash for the day.

The man shoved the door open, barged in, and drew a revolver, declaring: 'I'm Ned Kelly!'

Another armed man came in behind him. They aimed their weapons at Mr Bradley and the other clerk, Mr Booth, ordering them back towards the manager's office. Robert Scott was sitting in his office when Ned and Dan Kelly came in, pointing their revolvers at him.[1]

Scott had a revolver nearby. He tried to stall, mumbling, 'There's no hurry, I suppose,' but Kelly was in no mood for prevarication.

'Throw up your hands!' he shouted.

Scott stood and raised his hands.

They searched through drawers, taking all the cash, silver and gold they found, totalling £300. Young Frank Beecroft was in there, stuffing cash into a sack and rushing around as Kelly barked orders at him.[2]

Meanwhile, Steve Hart had gone around the back to the adjoining residence where Robert Scott lived with his family. He entered the kitchen, where he came face to face with a fifteen-year-old girl he knew from school in Wangaratta, Fanny Shaw. She was employed as the Scotts' maid. Fanny was ironing clothes in the kitchen, when she saw a familiar face appear at the back door.[3]

She said, 'Hello Steve Hart! What are you doing here?'

He said, 'Oh, nothing much, Miss Shaw. I have a little business with the boss.' After they had exchanged pleasantries, Hart said, 'I think your missus wants you inside.'

Fanny said, 'No she doesn't. I've just come from the living room.'

Hart was pressing. 'I'm sure she does. You go in and see.'

Fanny left the ironing, went to the living room, and asked Mrs Scott if she needed anything. Mrs Scott said 'No.'

When Fanny turned around to leave, Hart was there behind her. He had shut the living room door and was leaning against it.

While the Kelly brothers looted the bank, everyone next door was taken hostage by Steve Hart.

The safe was locked. Kelly demanded the key, but the bank staff stalled. Kelly said he would go into the adjoining residence to see Mrs Scott.

There must have been something menacing about the way Kelly said it, an implied suggestion or threat, because his words got the bank manager's blood going. According to Robert Scott, he confronted Kelly with the words, 'If you do, I'll strike you, whatever the consequences!'[4]

Dan raised two revolvers in Scott's face, up close. Ned Kelly walked past them, down into the residence. Scott didn't strike him down, and there were no consequences.[5]

Scott's wife, Susy, showed Kelly the key hanging on a hook.

Kelly unlocked the safe. This was the jackpot.

There were piles of bank notes, a small amount of silver and 31 ounces of gold. They took it all, stuffing it into the sack and taking the haul to a whopping £2243.[6]

Steve Hart had several prisoners: Susy Scott, Fanny Shaw, the family nursemaid, and several children. Ned went through the house, conducting a thorough search for others. He found Susy's mother, Mrs Calvert, in a bedroom.

She was visiting from the Bendigo district, and before departing had joked to her friends, 'Goodbye, the next thing you will hear of me will be that I am in the hands of the Kellys.'

Mrs Calvert later recalled that Ned said: 'Don't be frightened: nothing will happen to you. I have a mother of my own.'[7]

The entire family were dressed for church, because they were about to leave to attend the funeral for a local boy who had died in a horse-riding accident. Robert Scott offered Kelly whisky, but Kelly refused.[8]

They wanted water. Susy filled a jug from the waterbag on the back verandah. Before having some, Ned Kelly made Susy drink some of the water, in case it was poisoned.[9]

The nursemaid was hysterical, crying and screaming that they were all going to be shot. Kelly tried to make her drink whisky to stop her from making a racket, but she choked and coughed on the drink, causing the baby in her arms to start crying too.[10]

Kelly told them all that they must leave with him.

Between the Scott family, the two bank clerks and Beecroft, the gang had fourteen hostages at the bank. Kelly instructed Susy to put the children in their family wagon and to drive it. The robbers had arrived at the bank with two wagons, and they left with three: Gloster's wagon, the hunting party's spring cart and the Scotts' buggy. The hawker's wagon, driven by Frank Beecroft, went first with the bank clerks, two older children and Dan Kelly. The second was the Scotts' cart, driven by Susy Scott, and loaded up with the younger children, her mother and the nursemaid. At the rear, Robert Scott and

The four members of the Kelly Gang, clockwise from top left: Ned Kelly; his younger brother Dan; Ned's friend Joe Byrne; and Dan's friend Steve Hart. While in Beechworth Gaol in 1876, Joe Byrne and Aaron Sherritt befriended Ned's younger brother Jim. The criminal network that would eventually morph into the Kelly Gang had its genesis in these gaol friendships. STATE LIBRARY OF VICTORIA

Clockwise from top left: Tom Lloyd, Aaron Sherritt and Wild Wright were all close friends and supporters of the Kelly Gang, and affiliates of a loose criminal network known as the Greta Mob. Tom Lloyd was Ned's cousin; Wild Wright was married to Bridget Lloyd, sister of Tom Lloyd.

Right: the Quinn family's Glenmore Run, which was Ned's mother's family home, was on the stock-smuggling route through the King River valley. Ned's maternal uncles were notorious stock thieves. Ned's uncle, Pat Quinn (below left), was a violent criminal who turned police informer. The bushranger Harry Power (below right) was accompanied in his 1869–1870 crime spree by Ned Kelly.

The real hero of the Kelly Gang story was Detective Michael Ward, who spent years in pursuit of the Kelly Gang. This undated photograph of Ward was published alongside a newspaper interview with him in *The Sun*, 5 September 1911. Trove.

Kelly sympathisers claimed that Constable Alexander Fitzpatrick assaulted Kate Kelly when he went to the family home in Greta in April 1878 to arrest her brother Dan for horse theft, and that this justified the gang's murder of three police at Stringybark Creek. However, the evidence suggests Fitzpatrick behaved professionally.

Superintendent John Sadleir was the district police chief in north-eastern Victoria while the Kelly Gang was at large. After Frank Hare was shot, he took command of the police operation during the Glenrowan siege, where he made the decision to set fire to the hotel. VICTORIA POLICE MUSEUM

Sub-Inspector Henry Pewtress was on duty when Mounted Constable Thomas McIntyre stumbled into Mansfield police station, the only survivor of the ambush at Stringybark Creek. VICTORIA POLICE MUSEUM

Harry Power's hideout, named 'Powers Lookout', is on a craggy outcrop in the Wombat Ranges, overlooking the King River valley. Detective Michael Ward used it as a base camp while searching for the gang. JENNY EDWARDS

Clockwise from top left: Constable Thomas McIntyre, Constable Thomas Lonigan, patrol leader Sergeant Michael Kennedy and Constable Michael Scanlan. The four went into the rugged Wombat Ranges in search of the Kelly Gang. On 26 October 1878, they were ambushed by the gang at their camp near Stringybark Creek. Only McIntyre escaped. The gang murdered the other three. VICTORIA POLICE MUSEUM

The campsite at Stringybark Creek during the police investigation of the murders.
PUBLIC RECORD OFFICE OF VICTORIA

The body of Sergeant Kennedy was discovered five days after the Stringybark Creek murders. He had initially attempted to surrender, but after the gang opened fire, fled on foot. Located a quarter of a mile from the campsite, his body bore multiple bullet wounds. His weapon was gone and his pockets had been emptied. VICTORIA POLICE MUSEUM

Large rewards offered for information and the capture of the Kelly Gang encouraged ordinary citizens to join police in the manhunt. Popular media covered the story with breathless enthusiasm. This engraving of a search party in the Wombat Ranges was published in the *Illustrated Australian News*, 21 February 1879. STATE LIBRARY OF VICTORIA

One of the many *cartes de visite* produced by photographers to capitalise on the huge public interest in the Kelly Gang. This shows one of the many search parties that pursued the elusive outlaws over months. VICTORIA POLICE MUSEUM

THE KELLYS AT EUROA.

Illustrated account of the bank robbery at Euroa published in the *Illustrated Australian News*, 27 December 1878. TROVE

Compass used by police in the Kelly Gang manhunt. STATE LIBRARY OF VICTORIA

Constable Fitzpatrick was armed with a police standard-issue Webley revolver much like this one when he visited the Kelly homestead to arrest Dan Kelly in April 1878.

These seven police were at the siege of Glenrowan on the morning of 28 June 1880: constables Barry, Bracken, Phillips, and Arthur, Senior-Constable Kelly, and constables Canny and Gascoigne. VICTORIA POLICE MUSEUM

Superintendent Frank Hare with a search party of nine other police in 1879, just before they rode into the Strathbogie Ranges in search of the Kelly Gang.
VICTORIA POLICE MUSEUM

The gang robbed the bank in the New South Wales town of Jerilderie in February 1879. They also raided the Jerilderie post office (pictured), where they smashed the telegraph equipment and made the postal workers cut down the telegraph poles to ensure no message for help could be sent.
STATE LIBRARY OF VICTORIA

Hurdle Creek schoolmaster and postmaster James Wallace was a close friend of Joe Byrne and Aaron Sherritt. Detective Ward suspected Wallace of being an important associate of the Kelly Gang. GANNAWARRA LIBRARY

of my mates was near him after he was
shot & I put his cloak over him and left him
as well as I could and were they my
own brothers I could not have been more
sorry for them this cannot be called wil_
ful murder for I was compelled to shoot
them, or lie down and let them shoot
me it would not be wilful murder
if they packed our remains in, shattered
into a mass of Animated gore to Mans_
field, they would have got great praise
and credit as well as promotion but
I am reconed a horrid brute because
I had not been cowardly enough to
lie down for them under such trying
circumstances and insults to my
people certainly their wives and
children are to be pitied but they
must remember those men came
into the bush with the intention

A page from the Jerilderie Letter, which purports to be the story of Ned Kelly's life, and is the source of many false claims that persist today. Circumstantial evidence overwhelmingly points to James Wallace as the author of the letter. STATE LIBRARY OF VICTORIA

Superintendent Charles Nicolson was in charge of the pursuit of the gang after the Stringybark Creek murders until December 1878, when he was replaced due to poor health by Frank Hare. He took charge again from mid-1879 to June 1880, again replaced by Hare. His efforts were sabotaged by the double-agent James Wallace.
STATE LIBRARY OF VICTORIA

Using constables drawn from across the colony, Superintendent Francis 'Frank' Hare undertook months of stakeouts and searches for the Kelly Gang, but to no avail.

Appointed chief commissioner of police in 1858, Frederick Standish oversaw the evolution of the Victorian police force into a functional, respectable institution. However, his hedonistic lifestyle tarnished his reputation, and his inclination to play favourites hampered police efficiency. VICTORIA POLICE MUSEUM

The Hibernian Hotel in Beechworth, where James Wallace taunted Detective Ward with a stolen banknote in 1879, is still trading today. DAVID DUFTY

The location of Sherritt's hut, with a lower ridge of the Pilot Ranges, north of Beechworth, in the background. JENNY EDWARDS

Constable Patrick Gascoigne photographed in his mounted constable uniform. He took part in the hunt for and capture of the Kelly Gang. VICTORIA POLICE MUSEUM

Sub-Inspector Stanhope O'Connor led the contingent of six Native Police from Queensland requested by the Victorian government to assist in the search for the outlaws. VICTORIA POLICE MUSEUM

In this 1879 photo, the Queensland Native Police pose with Queensland and Victorian police officers in the Benalla Police Paddock. Back row (left to right): Senior-Constable Tom King (standing); Troopers Jimmy, Hero and Barney and Victorian Police Superintendent Sadleir. Front row (left to right): Queensland Sub-Inspector Stanhope O'Connor, Troopers Johnny and Jack and Victoria Police Commissioner, Captain Standish. VICTORIA POLICE MUSEUM

Tracks were removed at a bend in the railway line north of Glenrowan in Ned Kelly's plot to derail the police train speeding from Melbourne to Beechworth to investigate Aaron Sherritt's murder. This wood engraving was published in the *Illustrated Australian News* on 3 July 1880. STATE LIBRARY OF VICTORIA

Glenrowan's brave 25-year-old school teacher Tom Curnow defied the outlaws to save the train from derailment. STATE LIBRARY OF NSW

Suspected Kelly sympathiser Ann Jones' Glenrowan Hotel, before it was burnt to the ground in June 1880 during the deadly siege in which the police finally nabbed Ned. STATE LIBRARY OF VICTORIA

A photograph of Glenrowan railway station taken on the day of the siege. Ann Jones' hotel has not yet been burned and can be seen in the background to the left.
STATE LIBRARY OF VICTORIA

BIRD'S EYE VIEW OF GLENROWAN.

1.—Jones's Hotel.   2.—Out House.   3.—Railway Station.   4.—Stationmaster's House.   5.—M'Donald's Hotel.   6.—Platelayers' Tents.
7.—Positions Taken by the Police.   8.—Trench : Lieutenant O'Connor and Black Trackers' Post.   9.—Spot Where Mr. Hare was Shot.   10.—Paddock
where Horses were Shot.   11.—Tree where Ned Kelly was Captured.   12.—Road to Bracken's Station.   13.—Half a Mile from Here the Rails were Taken up.

A bird's eye view of Glenrowan. This map of the town was published in the *Illustrated Australian News* on 17 July 1880. STATE LIBRARY OF VICTORIA

The Wangaratta contingent of police involved in the Glenrowan siege. Sergeant Steele, crouching, is the third from left. BEECHWORTH BURKE MUSEUM

Police in position near Ann Jones' hotel during the Glenrowan siege. STATE LIBRARY OF VICTORIA

'A strange apparition'. This wood engraving by artist James Waltham Curtis shows Ned Kelly appearing through the gun smoke in his armour at the siege of Glenrowan. Its publication in *Illustrated Australian News* on 17 July 1880 contributed to Kelly's growing mystique.
STATE LIBRARY OF VICTORIA

Glenrowan's only police officer, Constable Hugh Bracken, was one of the hostages in Ann Jones' hotel. He escaped, warned the police arriving at Glenrowan railway station, then rode to Wangaratta to alert the police there as well. VICTORIA POLICE MUSEUM

At the siege, Sergeant Arthur Steele of Wangaratta aimed at Ned Kelly's legs, which were not protected by armour. He then ran forward, tackled Kelly, and took him into custody. In the struggle, Kelly in his armour rolled on top of Steele, crushing his leg. VICTORIA POLICE MUSEUM

The burnt remains of Glenrowan Inn after the siege. STATE LIBRARY OF VICTORIA

Ned's Snider Enfield rifle, abandoned at the siege because an injury to his arm prevented him from wielding it. STATE LIBRARY OF VICTORIA

After the siege, Detective Ward found the outlaws' horses at McDonnell's hotel stables on the other side of the railway tracks from Glenrowan Inn. Detective Ward may be the figure to the right of the man holding Joe Byrne's horse.
STATE LIBRARY OF VICTORIA

Seized by police after the siege of Glenrowan were four suits of armour, one for each member of the gang. The armour and one helmet are shown laid out on the grass, along with Ned Kelly's cap and rifle. At least some of the armour—possibly all of it—was manufactured for the gang by blacksmith Tom Straughair.

Ned Kelly's armour is held by the State Library of Victoria.

A buggy loaded with the coffins of Dan Kelly and Steve Hart outside McDonnell's tavern, on the opposite side of the railway tracks from Glenrowan Inn. STATE LIBRARY OF VICTORIA

Ned Kelly's charge sheet from Beechworth Police Station. Kelly returned to Beechworth shortly after the siege at Glenrowan to appear before Police Magistrate William Foster, to answer a charge of murder of Constable Thomas Lonigan at Stringybark Creek two years earlier. He was found guilty and later executed.

STATE LIBRARY OF VICTORIA

The old Beechworth gold treasury (left) and courthouse (right) still stand in the centre of town.

JENNY EDWARDS

Beechworth Gaol. Beechworth Courthouse can also be seen in the foreground to the right. BEECHWORTH BURKE MUSEUM

The door to cell 30 in Beechworth Gaol, where Ned Kelly was held in 1880 during his committal hearing for the murder of Constable Lonigan. JENNY EDWARDS

Prison photographer Charles Nettleton's portrait of Ned Kelly posing defiantly against the bluestone wall of Melbourne Gaol on 10 November 1880, the day before his execution. A photographer's stand props him upright because his bullet-riddled legs could not support him. STATE LIBRARY OF VICTORIA

A monument to the three police murdered at Stringybark Creek was erected in Mansfield in 1880, funded by public donations. An inscription reads, 'To the three brave men who lost their lives while endeavouring to capture a band of armed criminals in the Wombat Ranges near Mansfield, 26 October 1878'.
JENNY EDWARDS

Fanny Shaw travelled in the spring cart with Ned Kelly. The wagons actually passed the funeral attendees, who noted with disapproval that the Scott family were riding about town, having not paid their respects. Susy slowed the horses, but Dan Kelly appeared at the back of the wagon in front of her, gesturing for her to speed up.[11]

When they pulled up at Faithfulls Creek Station, Scott, Beecroft and the two bank clerks were taken to the storage shed at gunpoint and shoved inside with the other men. The women and children were escorted to the homestead, where they were allowed to move around freely.

Ned Kelly, riding with Robert Scott and Fanny Shaw, arrived later than the others. He did not approach until he saw a green flag, hanging on the garden fence, giving the all-clear.[12]

A passing northbound train slowed to a stop. Kelly ordered anyone outside to hide inside. He watched a man in the distance get off the train, walk to the broken wires, and crouch down to study them. He saw the man climb aboard with some broken wires and watched as the train disappeared towards Violet Town.

When interviewing witnesses, the police investigators were particularly interested in anything Kelly said about the Stringybark Creek murders. For that, they wanted an absolutely airtight case. Kelly's confessions to the murders were helpful.

Robert Scott said that he and Kelly had conversed on the way to Faithfulls Creek. Scott had a particular interest in Constable Lonigan, whom he knew, as Lonigan had been stationed at nearby Violet Town. Scott had asked Kelly what happened to Lonigan.

Kelly replied, 'Oh, I shot Lonigan.'[13]

Scott made a sworn statement about Ned Kelly's casual confession, and said that if it ever came to trial, he was willing to testify.

31

Nicolson out

Captain Standish learned about the Euroa bank robbery on the evening of Tuesday 10 December, when he returned to the Melbourne Club from a dinner at Melbourne Town Hall. A messenger was waiting with an urgent telegram from the Euroa railway stationmaster. He hurried to the telegraph office, hoping to contact Superintendent Nicolson in Benalla about the news, but learned the lines north of Euroa were down.[1]

All was not lost: the operator could send the message along the north-western line to New South Wales with relay instructions. It was transmitted to Deniliquin, then Albury, then down to Benalla. Meanwhile, messages from Sergeant Whelan and chief telegraphist Saxe in Benalla arrived via the same circuitous route. Then a reply from Whelan to the first message: Nicolson wasn't there. He was apparently up in Albury. Standish messaged Albury with instructions to locate Nicolson.

Then finally a telegram from Nicolson: messages received. He was in Albury, and he would be on the next southbound train.

Through the night, Standish communicated via telegram with various district headquarters. He left the telegraph office at dawn, grabbed a quick breakfast, then at the start of business hours, he visited the National Bank's head office with some very bad news.

The rest of Wednesday was a haze of ministerial briefings, telegrams, orders, questions and instructions. Premier Graham Berry was furious. He told Standish that long-distance command was not enough: he needed to personally go up and sort this Kelly issue out.

At dawn on the morning of Thursday 11 December, Standish boarded the early northbound train. He had assigned Frank Hare to run the chief commissioner's office in his absence. He arrived at Euroa at 10 a.m. Nicolson was waiting to meet him.

Nicolson looked *terrible*. Puffy eyes, haggard and drained. The man before him did not look like someone who could catch Ned Kelly. Nicolson informed him that according to the latest information, the gang had ridden towards the Strathbogie Ranges. They decided to send a patrol there. Nicolson admitted that he was too sick to go with them.[2]

Standish relieved Nicolson of active duty on the spot.

He instructed Nicolson to return to Melbourne on the next available train and take temporary command of the Police department in his absence, as he would no doubt be in Benalla 'for some time'. Frank Hare, currently filling that administrative position, would replace him by taking charge of the Kelly operation. He immediately sent a telegram to Hare, instructing him to report with 'horse and accoutrements' to Euroa by nightfall.

The zealous, hot-headed Charles Johnston was assigned to lead the patrol into the Strathbogie Ranges with the available mounted constables and a blacktracker named Jemmy.

Nicolson was too sick to work, but Frank Hare's health wasn't exactly in tip-top condition either. Nearing 50, he had gained weight and was being treated for ongoing heart issues. His days of crash-tackling burglars and staring down late-night crowds of drunken miners were well behind him. Even so, Standish was betting that some of that old Hare magic remained.

Hare duly arrived on the Thursday evening train, his horse in a rear stock carriage. As the steam engine idled at the end of the platform, Standish briefed them both. Hare was in charge of the Euroa investigation. Nicolson was temporarily in charge of police headquarters. And he, Standish, was appointing himself in charge of finding the Kelly Gang and would take over Nicolson's office in Benalla. After investigating the Euroa hold-up, Hare was to report to him in Benalla to help him find the Kelly Gang. Everything clear?

Neither of his superintendents was happy. Nicolson was understandably upset at being relieved of the high-profile Kelly operation.

Frank Hare complained that he knew nothing about the bank robbery other than what he'd seen in the newspapers. Besides, two days had elapsed. The robbers could be a hundred miles away by now. As for hunting the Kelly Gang, he just wasn't physically up to it. He was certain that any doctor in the state would declare him unfit for such duty.[3]

Too bad. Those were the orders. Standish boarded the train and departed north for Benalla.

Nicolson caught the next train south. Hare slept at the Euroa barracks, to discover the next morning that he had no constables at his disposal. They had all gone with Johnston, looking for the Kelly Gang in the Strathbogie Ranges.

At district headquarters in Benalla, Standish discovered Detective Ward on desk duty, as if with nothing better to do. He sent Ward back to Euroa to do some investigating.

Given the inexplicable absence of detectives in the days following the robbery, Robert and Susy Scott conducted their own investigation. Susy learned from a man she knew named Healy that on the night after the robbery, the gang had camped at the foot of the Strathbogie Ranges to the east, on a property of the recently deceased R. McClean.[4]

Euroa publican Charles de Boos told Robert that, a few nights before the robbery, a hawker named Ben Gould had come into his hotel with a stranger. He was talking about the Kellys, and also made a comment about 'Scott the banker and his spectacles'. Significantly, Ned Kelly, who had never met Scott, said to Macauley at Faithfulls Creek, 'I will make Scott drink through his spectacles today'. It was a striking coincidence that they both had referred to Scott's glasses.[5]

It was later determined that the stranger with Gould that day was Joe Byrne.[6]

Gorman, the Euroa stationmaster, told Robert that Gould had been doing regular business at the station of late, collecting rail deliveries of German sausages and corned beef, yet never included them among his wares, and that he often 'disappears in a sudden and mysterious way'.[7]

The Scotts' work was much appreciated by Detective Ward. He was particularly pleased to learn that Ben Gould was still in town and had last been seen heading towards the station.

A seedy, shabby Ben Gould huddled on the platform under the pounding sun, waiting for the northbound train. After a four-day bender funded by pocketfuls of unexplained cash, he now had a severe hangover. He should have bailed out of town days ago. Detective Ward strolled up for a friendly chat while he waited.

Ward asked Gould if he perhaps was involved in the Euroa robbery. Gould said no.

Was he in Euroa last Tuesday? Gould said no.

Well that was funny, because Ward had witnesses who said otherwise. Gould muttered that he had been drinking for 'three weeks', and couldn't remember anything.

Ward asked him if he'd told Robert Scott he would 'dine out' at Scott's expense.

Gould said, 'It was a joke'.

Some joke. Ward arrested him under the *Felons Apprehension Act* for providing assistance to the outlaws, remanded him at the Euroa courthouse, then put him in the lock-up.[8]

32

The Cameron Letter

A week after the Euroa bank robbery, the politician Donald Cameron received a letter from Ned Kelly. It is often called 'The Cameron Letter', or sometimes 'The Euroa Letter'. It was sixteen pages long, written in red ink. The letter sat on his desk in parliament house for some hours before he opened it. Before reading it, he disposed of the envelope, tearing it up as he did so. As soon as he realised who the letter was from, he was on his hands and knees, picking up the pieces of the envelope so he could reassemble it. A copy of the letter had also been sent by its writer to Standish, via Sadleir.[1]

The police learned about the Cameron Letter the next day when they read about it in the news. Standish fired an urgent telegram to Premier Graham Berry, advising against the publication of the letter because it 'contains many falsehoods'. He was right about that.[2]

Standish also asked to see the letter to Cameron, both to find out if the one to Sadleir was identical, and so that it could be studied to determine authorship.

No doubt Cameron was chosen as the recipient on the strength of his recent statements in parliament in which he mentioned reports of police culpability and had called for an inquiry. However, Cameron was not sympathetic to Kelly.

In the letter, Kelly justified the Stringybark Creek murders, denied shooting Fitzpatrick, and ranted about various individuals, police and civilians, against whom he had a grudge.

Kelly claimed he was not in Victoria at the time, because he was a famous outlaw (although he wasn't then): 'every schoolboy knows me'.

He claimed that Fitzpatrick threatened to blow Ellen's brains out. Dan played a trick on the stupid policeman:

> To frighten the trooper Dan said, Ned is coming now. The trooper looked around to see if it was true. Dan dropped the knife and fork which showed he had no murderous intention clapped Heenan's Hug on him, took his revolver and threw him and part of the door outside and kept him there until Skillion and Ryan came with horses which Dan sold that night, the trooper left and invented some scheme to say he got shot, which any man can see it was impossible for him to have been shot.[3]

That's not what happened. Ned's own mother later admitted that the version in the letter was a lie. But Ned wasn't finished with Fitzpatrick yet:

> I have been told by Police that he is hardly ever sober, also between him and his father they sold his sister to a Chinaman, but he seems a strapping and genteel looking young man and more fit to be a starcher to Laundry than a trooper, but to a keen observer, he has the wrong appearance to have anything like a clear conscience or a manly heart.

Ned claimed he had to kill the police in Kennedy's patrol at Stringybark Creek or be killed by them:

> This cannot be called wilful murder for I was compelled to shoot them in my own defence or lie down like a cur and die. Certainly their wives and children are to be pitied, but those men came into the bush with the intention of shooting me down like a dog, yet they know and acknowledge I have been wronged.

The letter claimed that Constable Lonigan was hiding behind a log when Ned shot him through the eye. This vivid image was amplified through the newspapers so much that 40 years later, when Superintendent Sadleir wrote his memoir, he mistakenly gave Ned's version of the shooting of Lonigan, rather than McIntyre's. Such is the malleability of human memory.[4]

According to Kelly, Constable Hall, who was 'a great cur', had framed Wild Wright and Alex Gunn, and had then falsely convicted Kelly by paying the police informer James Murdock 'who was hung in Wagga Wagga'. Murdock was in fact alive and well.[5]

Kelly bragged that when, arrested by Hall, it required fourteen police to bring him under control.

Davis Goodman, the owner of the Winton store that Dan and his mates had trashed in a drunken frenzy, 'got 4 years for perjury concerning the same property'. There's no record of that in official records. It seems to be another lie.

James Whitty and Constable Michael Farrell, whose father was a friend of Whitty's, had falsely accused him of theft, Kelly claimed:

> Some time afterward I heard again I was blamed for stealing a mob
> of calves from Whitty and Farrell, which I never had anything to
> do with, and along with this and other talk, I began to think they
> wanted something to talk about.

And he bitterly resented James Whitty and Andrew Byrne having control of the Myrrhee Run:

> Whitty and Burns not being satisfied with all the picked land on King
> River and Boggy Creek, and the run of their stock on the Certificate
> ground free, and no one interfering with them paid heavy rent for
> all the open ground so as a poor man could not keep any stock and
> impounded every beast they could catch even off Government roads,

if a poor man happened to leave his horse or bit of poddy calf outside
his paddock, it would be impounded, I have known over 60 head of
horses to be in one day impounded by Whitty and Burns, all belong-
ing to poor men of the district.

There was a modicum of truth to that: they *had* impounded some
stock found on their land, but not any belonging to Kelly and his
friends; and the accusation that they rounded up random animals in
some vindictive crusade against the 'poor man' was both slanderous
and ridiculous.

Inspector Brooke-Smith and the Wangaratta police were child
abusers, according to Ned Kelly:

. . . they used to repeatedly rush into the house revolver in hand
upset milk dishes, empty the flour out on the ground, break tins
of eggs, and throw the meat out of the cask on to the floor, and
dirty and destroy all the provisions, which can be proved and shove
the girls in front of them into the rooms like dogs and abuse and
insult them.

Likewise, Detective Ward and Constable Hayes:

Detective Ward and Constable Hayes took out their revolvers and
threatened to shoot the girls and children while Mrs Skillion was
absent, the oldest being with her.

He claimed that Cooke and the Baumgartens had nothing to
do with the Whitty raid, that he and his stepfather, George King
(who seemed to have disappeared), were solely responsible for all the
horse thefts:

I consider Whitty ought to do something towards the release of those
innocent men, otherwise there will be a collision between me and
him as I can to his satisfaction prove.

He claimed of his mother's arrest that she wasn't allowed bail:

Next day Skillion, Williamson and Mrs Kelly, with an infant were taken and thrown into prison and were six months awaiting trial and no bail allowed and was convicted on the evidence of the meanest man that ever the sun shone on.

Completely wrong. Ellen was granted bail (admittedly set quite high) at the May hearing, and she subsequently made bail in June. She spent most of the six months awaiting trial at home, not in prison. In his desperation to elicit sympathy for his mother's cause, he had reflexively resorted to exaggeration and lies. If there was one case he knew very well, it was his mother's: if he couldn't tell the truth about the woman he claimed to be most dear to his heart, he could not be trusted about anything.

The letter complained at length that Skillion, in particular, was wrongly convicted of the Fitzpatrick shooting, because he wasn't there; it was someone else, whom Fitzpatrick mistook for Skillion. Probably it was Joe Byrne, but the letter was coy about who. Kelly mistakenly believed that, if he could prove Skillion wasn't there—by getting the testimony of the man Fitzpatrick thought was Skillion—then the whole case would crumble. That was curiously naive.

For sixteen pages, the letter rambled on, slandering, justifying, accusing and lying.

Towards the end of Ned's missive, threats rolled forth like punch-lines:

I have no intention of asking mercy for myself or any mortal man or apologising, but wish to give timely warning that if my people do not get justice and those innocents released from prison and the police wear their uniform, I shall be forced to seek revenge of everything of the human race for the future, I will not take innocent life, if justice is given, but as the police are afraid or ashamed to wear their uniforms, therefore every man's life is in danger.

And there *had better* be a massive search for the man who would clear Skillion's name, and if not, innocent people would be killed:

The witness which can prove Fitzpatrick's falsehood can be found by advertisement and if this is not done immediately horrible disasters shall follow, Fitzpatrick shall be the cause of greater slaughter to the rising generation than St Patrick was to the snakes and frogs in Ireland . . .

Then the ominous sign-off:

For I need no lead or powder to revenge my cause. and if words be louder, I will oppose your laws. With no offence. (Remember your Railroads), and a sweet good bye from
    EDWARD KELLY
    A Forced Outlaw

Remember your railroads was a clear and specific threat.

One week earlier, Ned Kelly had told one of his hostages that if his mother was not released from prison, he might overturn a train. These were not mere words. Ned Kelly was obsessed with a terrible, murderous fantasy.

Despite all the lies, paranoid delusions, half-truths and egomaniacal threats, the letter contained not one word about Kate. The account of the Fitzpatrick shooting not only failed to mention anything about Fitzpatrick seducing or molesting Kate, it contradicted that theory. In the letter, Ned's version of the shooting overlapped with Fitzpatrick's account in all respects but two: he claimed he wasn't there at the time, and that no gun was fired.

Journalists were given access to the letter, but only to summarise it. Some took that opportunity to insert the Kate Kelly angle, which was now well known.

The *Mount Alexander Mail* claimed: 'He alludes to the outrages committed on his sister . . .'[6]

Likewise, the *Weekly Times*:

> **The scoundrel in the letter accuses certain members of the force of having committed grave offences against the chastity of certain female members of his family, and more particularly mentions the name of Trooper Fitzpatrick . . .**[7]

The press was hooked on the Kate Kelly angle. They couldn't let it go, even after it had been debunked by Ned Kelly himself.

The envelope was postmarked Glenrowan, posted on 14 December, two days after the Euroa hold-up.[8] Stories emerged in the press that the gang had the letter with them at Faithfulls Creek.

Joe Byrne had told the cook, Mrs Fitzgerald, to bring him two postage stamps. She said later that she saw 'several pages written in beautiful writing'. Some papers reported that Mrs Fitzgerald posted the letter for the gang. Others reported that she watched Joe Byrne writing it late into the night. There seems to be no substance to these rumours, other than that Joe Byrne took stamps.[9]

As for Mrs Fitzgerald, sometime after the Euroa hold-up she was fired from her job at Faithfulls Creek, after being found with a substantial amount of unexplained cash. The police were confident she was a Kelly accomplice, but did not have a sufficiently strong case to prosecute. She was never charged.[10]

Standish hoped to find out who wrote the Euroa letter. It was a good question. Who did write it?

Not Ned Kelly. He had attended school for only two years and, although he could read, was not capable of this level of literacy. The one surviving piece of writing known to be produced by Kelly is a scrawled note of a few words, but is enough to dispose of any notion that he could create this lengthy document.

Perhaps it was Joe Byrne. He was more educated and more literate (and also more numerate). But that, too, is just a guess. Joe Byrne was a farmer, a larrikin, a bushman and a career criminal. He had more education than Ned, but that was a low hurdle to jump. Yet here, from these bush boys, was a letter that sounded like it was written by a bored bureaucrat on a Friday afternoon:

> *Take no offence if I take the opportunity of writing a few lines to you, wherein I wish to state a few remarks concerning the case of Trooper Fitzpatrick against Mrs Kelly, W. Skillion, and W. Williamson, and to state the facts of the case to you.*

Take no offence . . . wherein I wish . . . remarks concerning the case . . . state the facts of the case . . .

By the end of the first sentence, the letter is already pompous and legalistic. Sure, maybe Ned Kelly and Joe Byrne wrote it themselves. Or maybe they had outside help.

33

Sympathisers

The trail of the robbers from Euroa was cold.

Detective Brown, who had done such great work on the Thompson (i.e., Kelly) crime ring, leading to the arrest of Cooke, the Baumgarten brothers, and others, was assigned to the Euroa robbery case, but he learned little more of importance.

The money trail, on the other hand, was hot. Kelly's sister Maggie Skillion went on a shopping spree in Benalla. Joe Byrne's mother made a large cash payment on a debt. Aaron Sherritt paid outstanding fees on his selection. By the Friday after the robbery, the pubs of Benalla were crowded with a well-known group of disreputables getting drunk.

None of them could be prosecuted. The stolen money was untraceable because the bank had not recorded serial numbers.

After speaking with all the constables at his disposal, Hare picked from them three leaders: Constable Mullane, stationed many years at Beechworth; Constable Flood, who had lately been assisting Detective Ward; and the enthusiastic Constable Johnston, recently thwarted in the Warby Ranges by Inspector Brooke-Smith.[1]

At Hare's request, Mullane, Flood and Johnston were immediately promoted to senior-constable, and given wide latitude. They were empowered to select other constables to accompany them on patrols and were, in Hare's words, 'left unfettered in every possible way to go into the ranges and search'.[2]

However, the three senior-constables soon discovered that they were in fact quite fettered; not by Hare or the police bureaucracy, but

196

by the gang's extensive network of criminal associates, known as Kelly sympathisers.

These were the same types of larrikin seen in the townships flush with money after Euroa; the same ones going on pub crawls and benders funded with stolen money. Once they'd sobered up, they spent their days and nights quite openly watching the police. Scruffy men hung around the railway station, gazing stonily at constables as they unloaded their police horses. They loitered across from the barracks, and when a patrol departed they would tail them. They followed the police everywhere: on foot around the streets of Benalla, Wangaratta, Beechworth and Greta, and on horseback as mounted police searched the district. Wild Wright was the worst. His home away from home was the Benalla police barracks gate. He did not try to hide what he was doing, or disguise himself.[3]

The effect on operations was corrosive. The police had no secrets. And moreover, the overt surveillance by the sympathisers sent a strong public message. It was a power play. It hampered investigations as nobody was willing to talk, given the high likelihood of being punished by the sympathisers. It was almost as if the Kelly sympathisers were daring Standish to do something about it.

Melbourne editors urged him to arrest these miscreants under the provisions of the *Felons Apprehension Act*. For example, *The Argus* said, 'If this were done, it would strike terror into the breasts of those who do not refrain from openly avowing themselves sympathisers with the Kellys.' And *The Herald*: '. . . if the police will take charge of all the Kelly sympathisers, people would not be afraid to open their mouths; but to detain the friends of the Kelly Gang would require very extensive accommodation.'[4]

Standish later described the situation: '. . . if I had determined, without consulting anybody, in the middle of any night to come down to the barracks by myself and to start a party of police, which I could have done in half an hour, I firmly believe that before the men had left the barracks some of those spies would have been galloping off to the outlaws.'[5]

Standish called a special meeting with everyone working the Kelly case in attendance. He wanted to know the names of the miscreants. They weren't hiding or in disguise. They didn't care about being identified. Okay, so identify them.

Names were called out. Frank Hare took notes. By the end of the meeting, he had recorded twenty names. Not all had been monitoring the police; some were simply known associates of the gang.

Standish decided to arrest everyone on the list under the *Felons Apprehension Act*. They were all to be arrested on the same day, in a district-wide sweep, to prevent word getting out from some to the rest.

Warrants were issued on Thursday, 2 January 1879. The arrests were conducted two days later.

There were mistakes. Instead of arresting Tom Lloyd, they brought in his uncle, Tom Lloyd senior. But although the older Lloyd wasn't on Standish's list, perhaps he should have been. He persuaded the gullible constables at Benalla lock-up to allow him to send a telegram. He sent it to someone at the Greta post office. The message was: 'Turn the four bullocks out of the paddock.'[6]

The arrests received positive press coverage. The Beechworth *Advertiser* applauded the move, but cautioned that the sympathisers weren't the gang's only source of information. Journalists were also watching every action taken by the police and broadcasting them far and wide through the colony's newspapers. The gang didn't need sympathisers to spy for them when they could read about police movements in the daily news.[7]

There were multiple unverified reports of sightings near Mansfield of Steve Hart in disguise as a woman. On the weekend after the police sweep, two awkward-looking women, unknown to anyone, passed through Mansfield without stopping or speaking to anyone. Passers-by remarked that one of them matched descriptions of Steve Hart. A farmer on the road out of town later reported that he had seen Steve Hart in a woman's dress, riding side-saddle.[8]

Two men encountered a woman riding on her own towards the Wombat Ranges. Concerned for her welfare, they asked if she was afraid of meeting the Kelly Gang. The woman, whom they now realised was a man, said she was not, and nor of meeting the police. Two revolvers were visible as the mysterious rider galloped away.

Ben Gould appeared at Euroa court on Thursday 2 January charged with withholding information in violation of the *Felons Apprehension Act*, before magistrate Alfred Wyatt, who heard the case with another magistrate, R.H. Graham.[9]

By the principles of modern jurisprudence, Wyatt would never have been allowed to preside, being so involved. He was the man who had discovered the broken wires by the track; who had interviewed a witness on behalf of the police; and whom Ben Gould had mistaken for the bank manager at Euroa Railway Station.

But in a rural colonial district where judges knew criminals, the issue of conflict of interest was not adhered to, and perhaps would not have been considered practicable.

At any rate, Wyatt's conduct was biased *towards*, not against, Ben Gould. On at least one occasion, Wyatt dispensed legal advice to him from the bench, advising him not to say any more, lest he incriminate himself.

Frank Hare prosecuted. He called Detective Michael Ward, who summarised the evidence against Gould, whom he had arrested under the *Felons Apprehension Act*. Hare then called a string of further witnesses. Gorman, the stationmaster, recounted Gould appearing at the window and saying to Wyatt, 'Hello, old Scott, I'll have £500 today.'

Publican Charles de Boos testified that Gould was in his pub prior to the robbery, and on the topic of the Stringybark Creek murders had said, 'Serves the buggers right. There will be more of the buggers knocked over yet before Kelly is caught.' Another witness, George Murray, testified that he saw Gould outside the bank in the late afternoon of the day of the robbery.

Gould called a witness of his own who testified that when informed of the bank robbery, Gould had been astonished.

After conferring, the magistrates remanded Gould for trial by jury on 6 May.

Frank Hare and Michael Ward escorted Gould to the railway station and then on to Beechworth Gaol. He appeared uneasy and agitated, as if expecting something to happen on the way. He repeatedly pulled and tested his handcuffs. As the train neared Benalla cemetery, a shot was fired from the side of the track and a bullet hit the guard's van. The passengers were alarmed, but they arrived at Beechworth without further incident.[10]

That was Thursday. The sympathiser hearings were scheduled for court in Beechworth two days later.

Late on Friday night, or to be more precise, at about 2 a.m. on Saturday morning, Michael Ward left the Beechworth barracks with a telegram he wanted to send to police headquarters. It was a moonless night, but he had walked the short distance to the telegraph office many times before.

The next thing he knew, he was at the bottom of a pit. He had dropped down a nine-foot shaft into a cellar. He lay in agony, sprawled on the cellar floor. He was concussed, with numerous broken bones including several broken ribs, a dislocated hip and a dislocated knee. How he fell down that shaft is a mystery. Perhaps he was drunk; perhaps he lost his way in the dark; perhaps a careless person had accidentally left a trapdoor open overnight. Perhaps he was pushed. Nobody knows. The brief report on the incident sheds no light.[11]

The following morning, Ward did not appear as a witness in the sympathiser hearings. As the principal detective on the Kelly case, he would certainly have testified.

When court opened on the Saturday morning, the prosecutor John Bowman asked for a delay, because the police had no witnesses. He put Superintendent Sadleir on the stand, who explained that they 'could not get the police witnesses at present, as many of them were in pursuit of the Kellys, whilst private citizens . . . required as witnesses were in terror of their lives'.[12]

The defence lawyers, Zinke, Read and Brown, ridiculed him. Read chuckled: 'If what Mr Sadleir said was true then the witnesses who were afraid to come should be in the dock with the prisoner!'

Read cross-examined Sadleir, asking for the names of these fearful citizens. Sadleir refused to divulge their names. Read asked him to divulge the names of the missing police witnesses. Prosecutor Bowman instructed Sadleir: 'Don't tell.'

Read mocked the police: 'Some officers say, "Oh, we can't catch the Kellys!" Is that "reasonable cause"? If the police could give any evidence, and His Worship had been satisfied that due diligence had been exercised, then a remand might be granted, but it's nothing merely to assert they can't get witnesses.'

Bowman reminded the court of the *Felons Apprehension Act*, declaring that the existence of the Act was evidence that it should be used, because it showed 'reasonable cause in the state of public opinion'.

There was heated legal debate about the validity of the *Felons Apprehension Act* and whether it contravened long-standing principles such as requiring evidence to convict. Zinke, for the defence, said, 'It's all nonsense to talk about sympathy with the Kellys. Sympathy is an involuntary action of the mind, and I can sympathise with whoever I please.'

It ended with a partial victory for the police. Magistrate Foster remanded the prisoners for another eight days.

In the interim, Bowman had a dispute with Standish and the attorney-general, and was fired. In his place, Frank Hare was appointed as prosecutor.

When Hare arrived for the next remand hearing, he was shocked to discover that Bowman was now working for the defence. Bowman gleefully told the court about confidential interactions he'd had with Standish and Sadleir before being fired as prosecutor.[13]

The prisoners were again remanded. As he was led out of the dock, Wild Wright said, 'You may as well remand us for life. The police only stick to the main roads.'

At first the sympathiser round-up had widespread support but, over successive hearings and with no strong evidence against them forthcoming, the sympathisers gained some sympathy of their own. Foster released several at hearings in February. Fifteen of them were detained until April.

The sympathisers were affiliates of a loose criminal network known as the Greta Mob. Some were selectors, but made scant attempt at honest farming, choosing properties that backed onto bushland so as to facilitate clandestine movements and livestock trafficking. They were feared and reviled by their neighbours, who were sick of livestock theft and horrified by the Stringybark Creek murders.

There were more sympathisers than those in the round-up. Stoking its readers' prejudices about dangerous, nasty rural folk, *The Age* declared, 'The sympathisers are more numerous than law-loving people in the district, and their relations, who seem to be innumerable, are scattered along the borders of New South Wales and Victoria'. A cooler-headed estimate from a local journalist put their number at 300 across the north-east, a fraction of the population, but enough to be a menace. With most of them at large, nobody was foolish enough to testify against the few behind bars.[14]

34

A bedside visitor

In Beechworth hospital, a most prominent sympathiser made a bedside visit to Michael Ward. Aaron Sherritt had been spared in the sympathiser round-up, probably because Standish was still hopeful that he could be turned.

And now he was sitting next to the immobile Detective Ward, offering to help. Over the past year, Ward had tried several times to get information from Sherritt. The tight-lipped response was understandable given that Ward had sent both Sherritt and Joe Byrne to prison some years earlier. But the young larrikin was expressing a change of heart: he claimed that he wanted to help.[1]

Sherritt told him that he had been in contact with the Kelly Gang very recently. They were heading north, and they wanted him to join them. In fact, he was going to join them at a very specific time and place, and that time was fast approaching. This was Sherritt's offer: Detective Ward could accompany him to that secret meeting place, discover the outlaws, and arrest them all! But there was no time to lose. There was one catch. Sherritt explained, with as serious a face as he could, that he didn't trust any other traps. Only Detective Ward. So if he agreed to this excellent plan, Ward would have to go with him alone—no other police—to find the Kellys.

Nice try.

Ward popped Sherritt's balloon by drawing his attention to his current state of health. He needed assistance just to roll onto his side.[2] But even if in perfect health, he would have been crazy to

203

accept the offer. Going off into the wilderness alone with Aaron Sherritt, who would lead him to the Kelly Gang? Or was the plan instead to lead the Kelly Gang to him? He was, after all, high on the gang's hit list. No thanks.

Ward said he would send someone else. Sherritt wasn't interested in 'someone else'. It was Ward or nobody. Ward said that, in that case, it would be nobody.

He added if Sherritt really wanted to help, he should talk to Captain Standish. Ward wrote a message for him to take by way of introduction. This clearly indicated that Ward had not been informed that Sherritt had previously met Standish and Sadleir.

When Sherritt arrived at Benalla police headquarters, Frank Hare was on duty. Sherritt asked to speak with Captain Standish, saying, 'I have some important information to give him, and I wish to speak to him privately.'[3]

Hare told him Standish was away on business. He asked what it was about. At first, Sherritt wouldn't divulge, but after they had chatted for a while, Sherritt said, 'I think I can trust you.'

Sherritt confided that Joe Byrne and Dan Kelly had visited him at home a day ago. They told him they were going to Goulburn because the Kellys had a cousin there. They asked him to join them as a scout, but he refused. Joe Byrne had responded, 'Well, Aaron, you're perfectly right. Why should you get yourself into this trouble and mix yourself up with us?' Dan and Joe were looking around nervously the whole time.

Hare asked him to describe the horses and brands. His description matched two of the gang's known horses.

Hare warned him, 'Be careful, now you're in Benalla, that you aren't seen here. Don't go into the town, but get some hotel near the railway station.' He gave Sherritt money for a hotel plus a payment for the information received.

Much later, Hare said of Sherritt, 'He was a remarkable-looking man. If he walked down Collins Street, everybody would have stared at him: his walk, his appearance, and everything else were remarkable.'[4]

Hare was impressed. He believed he had won over an important ally.

Support for Sherritt's story arrived that evening, with a report that the gang had been seen riding towards the Murray. Hare issued alerts to the border towns.[5]

The storms and roiling floods of November were long gone. The summer had been hot and dry, and the river was low. There were many easy crossing places.

The most likely crossing point was Gravel Plains Station, a property on the Victorian bank south of Corryong. Friends of the Kellys lived around there. Also, if they crossed the river there, a chain of wild hills would take them all the way to Goulburn. Hare instructed Senior-Constable Mullane to take a patrol to Gravel Plains Station and monitor the crossing points.

A patrol stationed at Eldorado, led by Senior-Constable Strahan, was directed to monitor some other crossing places, but Standish had no confidence in Strahan, whom he described as 'a blathering fellow'.[6]

Hare also liaised with the New South Wales force, which sent patrols along the northern banks. The gang was not detected.

On the morning of Tuesday 11 February, a telegram arrived from Jerilderie, a New South Wales town about 30 miles north of the border:

> Jerilderie Police barracks and bank stuck up by Kellys yesterday horses and arms stolen riding two bays one chestnut and one black horses stolen grey 16 hands JS near shoulder bay JE conjoined near shoulder.[7]

The Kelly Gang had robbed another bank, and they had again taken hostages.

Jerilderie

35

The Jerilderie barracks

The little town of Jerilderie was, and still is, in the middle of nowhere. Thirty miles south of town, across the scrubby plains, drift the sluggish brown waters of the Murray River, the border between New South Wales and Victoria. The town's main waterway is the Billabong Creek. It twists and curls to a place beyond the horizon, where it joins the Edward River, which in turn eventually joins the Murray River.[1]

Only 200 people lived in Jerilderie in 1879, although many more lived and worked on nearby farms and stations. There was a one-teacher school, a courthouse and no fewer than five hotels, which did brisk trade with the large population of farm workers across the scattered outlying properties. Four times a week there was a coach service that travelled each way between Wagga Wagga to the north and Deniliquin to the south-west.[2]

The town also had a branch of the New South Wales Bank, and this was Ned Kelly's next target. The gang was not, as Aaron Sherritt had claimed, going to visit a cousin in Goulburn, which was much further east and closer to Sydney. Jerilderie was the target because Ned Kelly and Steve Hart both knew it well.

The plan was broadly the same: capture a nearby base, take hostages, rob the bank, return to base, then scramble out of town. This time, their chosen base of operations was the police barracks, with the police their hostages. The barracks were beyond the edge of town, isolated and vulnerable.

There were two police in Jerilderie.

George Devine, aged 32, was the senior-constable. His wife, Mary, and their two sons lived with him in the barracks' married quarters. Henry Richards, the junior constable, was 23 and single, and also lived at the barracks.

Richards had previously played a small role in the search for the Kelly Gang and was involved in an incident which at the time seemed harmless and amusing. After the Stringybark Creek murders, Richards had been deployed to Tocumwal, to help monitor the punt crossing there.[3]

They saw four men on the far bank, waiting for the punt. Richards suggested to his superior, Coleman, that as the punt approached, 'we should challenge them, and if they don't give a satisfactory answer, we should fire at them'.

The punt man crossed the river, collected them, and brought them across. The four men were Victorian plain-clothes police.[4]

At 11 p.m. on the evening of Saturday, 8 February 1879, Richards was disturbed by a loud voice outside: 'Devine! Devine! There's a drunken man at Davidson's hotel committing murder. Get up at once, all of you!'[5]

Richards got out of bed. He had to deal with it because earlier that day Devine had had a horseriding accident and was recuperating in bed.[6]

Outside, there was a man on a horse, talking about a brawl underway at Mrs Davidson's Woolshed Inn, just down the road. The man said, 'I've been sent up for the police. There will be murder down there!'[7]

Roused by the commotion, Senior-Constable Devine came outside and asked, 'What's the matter?'

The man moved closer, repeating the story about the brawl. When he was ten yards away, he jumped off his horse and drew two revolvers.

With his guns pointed at the unarmed police in their nightclothes, he said, 'Move and I'll shoot you. Hands up. I'm Kelly.' They put their hands up. He whistled, and three other armed men emerged from the dark.[8]

Kelly demanded that they tell him their names. On hearing Richards' name, Kelly said angrily: 'You're the man who was going to shoot me on the ferry at Tocumwal!' It is unclear how Kelly knew about that.[9]

Richards explained, 'Men were crossing, and I thought they were the Kellys.'

Kelly turned his attention to Devine. 'I'm going to shoot you, Devine, for you have always been tracking me. You're worse than a blacktracker. You've been closer to me than any man.'

Devine's wife, Mary, came out in her night gown. She begged, 'For God's sake, don't shoot my husband!'

Kelly said, 'Don't be afraid, I won't shoot him.'

The three prisoners were taken inside. The gang raided the armoury, taking everything: two rifles, a Colt revolver, Richards' personal revolver, and the ammunition. The prisoners were then taken into the dining room, where Kelly told them, 'I intend to rob the bank of Jerilderie.'[10]

The outlaws smelt of alcohol.

Kelly led Devine and Richards to the lock-up, a small building behind the barracks. He locked them in, then returned to get better acquainted with Mary Devine.

There was no riot at Davidson's Woolshed Inn, but the gang had come from there, and had consumed several drinks there.

On arrival at Davidson's, Kelly had claimed they were poor itinerant workers 'from the back blocks of the Lachlan', and everyone pretended to believe him. As the outlaws relaxed over a drink, Kelly asked the locals what they thought of the Kelly Gang. They answered, perhaps too enthusiastically, that everyone in Jerilderie—and especially everyone here tonight—just *loved* the Kelly Gang, although they 'regretted' the sad events at Stringybark Creek. Of course they said that.[11]

At Davidson's, Kelly asked about the whereabouts of two men, Collier and Maslim, but was told that neither had been seen around town for about four years. Then he asked if a barmaid named 'Larrikin Mary' still worked there. The barmaid at the counter said she didn't know that name, but the owner's daughter, Mary Davidson, appeared and revealed she was once known as Larrikin Mary.[12]

The barmaid tried to sell Kelly a watch, but he declined. As if confused by her offer, he asked, 'How could poor men buy watches?'

She then sang a song for him with the refrain, 'Kellys have made another escape, keep it dark.' He enjoyed her song.[13]

After a pleasant evening of revelry, the gang departed on their mission to terrorise the local constables, Mary Devine and the Devine children.

When morning came, Mary Devine explained that she was supposed to make preparations for the church service, held at 11 a.m. every Sunday in the courthouse. If she didn't go, it might arouse suspicion. Dan Kelly donned a police uniform, escorted her there, watched as she made the preparations, then escorted her home again. Her children stayed behind, guarded by the others.[14]

Later in the morning, Devine and Richards heard the rattle of the lock, and Kelly appeared, bearing good news. He had intended to murder them both, but Mrs Devine had persuaded him otherwise. Even so, Kelly added, if Devine didn't resign from the police within a month, he would return and shoot him dead.[15]

Devine said he couldn't do that, because he had a wife and children to support.[16]

He interrogated Devine at length about Jerilderie. He wanted to know all about the bank, and also, surprisingly, about the printery. Kelly explained that he needed the printer to print some bills, and also the history of his life.

They talked at length. Devine and Richards asked him about the Fitzpatrick shooting and Stringybark Creek murders. Kelly said he didn't shoot Fitzpatrick because he was 'one or two hundred miles distant'. He repeated his version of what happened, which was largely the same as the account given in the Cameron Letter, and to hostages at Faithfulls Creek: that Dan had pointed out the door, said 'Here's Ned coming', then grabbed and disarmed the distracted Fitzpatrick. But in this version, he claimed that Fitzpatrick's gun went off in the struggle with Dan.[17]

As for Stringybark Creek, he told them, 'The reason I shot the sergeant, Lonigan and Scanlan was to get their horses and make a rise. The police were persecuting me and I was resolved to avenge myself.'

He said that Sergeant Kennedy had 'fought to the last, firing with both hands' at himself and Dan. Kennedy was only equipped with one revolver, so it's hard to see how he could have been 'firing with both hands', but for Kelly, facts were secondary in the telling of a good yarn.[18]

He also said that there would be 'more murders yet', and that if he ever got a hold of Constable Flood or Sergeant Steele, he would roast them alive.[19]

He produced a beautiful gold watch, and showed it to them. He said, 'This is the Sergeant's watch. I'll return it to Mrs Kennedy in the course of time.' Then he turned it over so that they could see the initials: M.K.

It was, as Kelly had said, Michael Kennedy's watch.[20]

Devine was made to don his uniform and then give Ned and Dan Kelly, also in uniform, a guided tour of the township. He was then put in the lock-up again.

In the residence, Ned produced a document, which he told Mary was 'the story of his life', and read out parts of it to her. When asked about it later, she could not recall any of it. Understandably, as she probably had other things on her mind.[21]

In the afternoon, the gang cleaned their weapons, extracted the bullets then carefully reloaded them. They were preparing to rob the bank that night.[22]

But Ned's plan was foiled by Joe Byrne, who had enjoyed himself so much at Davidson's hotel on Saturday that he went back there late on Sunday afternoon. He spent the evening in the company of the barmaid and Larrikin Mary, leaving around midnight. He was so drunk that the barmaid had to help him mount his horse. As she did so, she saw revolvers around his belt.[23]

When he arrived at the barracks, he was barely able to stay upright on his horse. Ned was furious.[24]

36

The Jerilderie bank

At 11 a.m. on Monday 11 February, Ned Kelly, Dan Kelly and Constable Richards walked to the Royal Mail Hotel, all three of them in police uniform. Steve Hart and Joe Byrne followed on horseback. The Kelly brothers and Richards entered the hotel, hoping to find the proprietor, Mr Cox, but he wasn't there, so they waited.

Meanwhile, Hart and Byrne rode around to the hotel stables, stuck up the groom and told him to put their horses in the stable, but not to give them any feed.[1]

Hart entered the hotel kitchen, where he encountered a Chinese cook and ordered him into the parlour.[2] The cook asked, 'What for?' Hart replied by raising two revolvers at him. As the cook went through the doorway, Hart struck him on the head with the butt of one of his revolvers.[3]

When Mr Cox arrived, Kelly aimed revolvers at his head and introduced himself. Over the next hour, everyone entering the hotel was taken prisoner and put in the parlour, guarded by Hart.[4]

The hotel was next to the town's only bank. At midday, Joe Byrne crossed the rear courtyard shared by the hotel and the bank and entered the bank through the back door. The only person inside was a teller named Edwin Living. He was separated from the customers' area by a counter partitioning the room.

Hearing someone come through the door behind him, Living turned and saw a man he didn't recognise staggering around as if intoxicated. He thought it was a drunk from the hotel who had lost his way.[5]

He told the drunk to turn around and get out. The drunk suddenly sobered up, raised a revolver and said, 'Hands up!'

The bank's junior clerk, J.T. Mackie, came through the front door. Byrne aimed his revolver at Mackie and ordered him to jump over the counter. Then he took them both out through the back door. Ned Kelly was outside, waiting in the courtyard. They were taken into the hotel billiard room with several other prisoners.[6]

When Kelly learned (probably from Constable Richards) that neither of them was the bank manager, Tarleton, he rushed into the billiard room and demanded of Living: 'Where's Tarleton?'

Living said that Mr Tarleton was in his office. Kelly told Living to show him, but Tarleton wasn't there.

They found him in a bath at the back of the manager's residence. He had returned that hot summer morning on horseback from a nearby town, so was freshening up before work.

Entering the bathroom, Living broke the news: 'The Kellys are here.'[7]

'Nonsense!' Tarleton replied.

Then Ned Kelly and Steve Hart walked in behind Living, each brandishing two revolvers.

Kelly said to Tarleton, 'Come along, I want you.'

Tarleton protested, 'I can't until I've had my bath!'

Kelly left Hart behind to guard Tarleton while he finished his bath. When he was dried and dressed, Hart took him to the hotel billiards room.

Kelly and Byrne returned to the bank with Living, and Kelly asked him how much money there was.[8]

Living said, 'About £900 or £1000.'

'You have more,' Kelly insisted, 'you have £10,000!'

Living said, 'That's all we have.'

In the banking chamber, Kelly searched and found letters and cash. He turned to Living and asked, 'What firearms have you?'

Living replied, 'We have none.'

Kelly said, 'You'll have to produce them. I'll do something if you don't!'

Living pulled open a drawer, took out a revolver, and handed it over.

Kelly and Byrne emptied the drawers of their cash, dumping it into a bag. When that bag was filled, Kelly hurried off to find another.

At 12.30 p.m., Jerilderie's schoolteacher, Mr Elliot, entered the bank on his lunchbreak. Byrne aimed his revolver at Elliot, saying, 'Throw up your hands!'

The shocked schoolteacher stopped, but did not raise his hands.

Byrne said it again, eyeing Elliot from behind his revolver. 'Throw up your hands!'

Living said, 'It's no use, old fellow, these are the Kellys.' Elliot's hands went up.

Byrne ordered, 'Come over the counter.'[9]

Elliot protested that he couldn't, but Byrne insisted, so he clambered over.[10]

Kelly returned with a sack. He told Elliot to hold it open, and ordered Living to pile the cash into it.

So far, the robbers had taken £700, which sat in two bulging bags on the floor.

Kelly said, 'You have more money here.'[11]

Living replied, 'No, we have no more.'

Kelly found the safe. It had two locked drawers. Living opened the top drawer containing jewellery, which Kelly loaded into the sack. He asked what was in the second drawer.

Living said, 'Nothing of value.'

Kelly insisted that it be opened.

Living turned his key in the lock, but it only went halfway around: the drawer would not open. He said, 'There. I've done all I can and I can't unlock it.'

Byrne said, 'Let's get a bloody sledgehammer and burst it open!'

Living told them there was no need to do that. The drawer required two keys to open, and Mr Tarleton had the second key.

Byrne went to the hotel and returned with the bank manager, who provided his key for the bottom drawer. It was the treasury drawer, and was stacked with money. Kelly took it all, amounting to £1450.[12]

Kelly asked Tarleton if there was any more money in the bank. Tarleton said there wasn't.

Kelly said, 'No bloody lies, or I will shoot you!'[13]

He took his time, searching thoroughly. He found a box up high, and asked Tarleton what it was. Tarleton said it was nothing important. Kelly got it down, opened it, and discovered that it contained deeds, stock mortgages, and other securities. He declared he would burn it all. Tarleton and Living told him that there was no point in doing that, because there were duplicates in Sydney. (They were lying.)

Kelly said, 'I will burn all the bloody stock mortgages, as they belong to poor men, and the bank can afford the loss.'

'For God's sake, don't burn my life policy or I'll be ruined,' Living pleaded.

Tarleton said, 'Don't destroy them, Kelly. You will only get me into trouble and they are really of no use to you. I give you my word of honour that you have all the money, and there's nothing else of any value to you.'

'I'm an outlaw and *must* have all I ask for!' Kelly declared.

He asked if there were any deeds of town allotments. 'There may be one or two,' Tarleton replied, 'but it would take hours to pick them out from all these documents.'

Kelly also asked where the bills and promissory notes were, but Tarleton and Living were evasive, then he got distracted and seemed to forget the question. He demanded the manager's revolver. He went into Tarleton's office, couldn't find it, came back, pointed at the papers, said 'I don't have time now, but I'll come back directly and look over them.'

They informed him that the manager's revolver was in the bank's dining room. Kelly made Living go in and get it, all the while covering him with his revolver.

When he wrote of his experience later, Elliot said he was impressed that Tarleton stayed so cool under pressure. Living did not. In fact, Living alarmed the other two prisoners by muttering within earshot of the outlaws that if only he'd known the 'drunk' was Joe Byrne, he would have shot him on the spot.

'I thought once or twice he would get the three of us shot,' Elliot wrote.[14]

Kelly and Byrne escorted Living, Tarleton and Elliot next door to the Royal Mail Hotel, where they already had about twenty or 30 other hostages. Kelly returned to the bank alone to search for deeds of town allotments.

Three more customers entered the bank: J.G. Rankin, a magistrate; a storekeeper named Mr Harkin; and Samuel Gill, the printer, journalist and proprietor of the *Jerilderie and Urana Gazette*.[15] Kelly heard someone entering and rushed out from the back room. As soon as they saw him, they turned and ran. Kelly leapt over the counter in pursuit, sliding across it with a revolver in each hand.[16]

Rankin tripped as he was going out the door and fell. Kelly grabbed him by the collar.

Rankin said, 'Why did you want to shoot me?'[17]

Kelly said, 'Because you wanted to take me.'

Rankin said he was only going to the bank on business.

Kelly told Rankin to help him find the other two, or he'd kill him. Rankin showed him to Harkin's store across the road, where they found the storekeeper hiding. Kelly escorted him into the hotel, where Dan and Steve took him and placed him with the other prisoners.

Then he and Rankin went out, hunting Gill. They didn't find him. Gill had run as fast as he could to Billabong Creek and hidden there.

Kelly was angry that Gill had escaped.

When he and Rankin returned to the hotel, Kelly pushed Rankin against the wall and levelled the revolver at him. He stepped back three paces, aimed the revolver at Rankin, and told him he was about to die. Several people called out, begging Kelly to hold his fire. He lowered the weapon.[18]

Indicating Rankin, Kelly said to Hart, 'Keep this man covered, Revenge, and shoot him if anyone attempts any resistance.'[19]

He turned to Rankin and said, 'If anyone makes a move, you'll be the first to be shot.'[20]

The gang had nicknamed Steve Hart 'Revenge' for this robbery; he knew Jerilderie well, and had a score to settle there. He asked the hostages where Curtain, the auctioneer, could be found, so he could kill him. But Hart was out of luck. Curtain was out of town that day. Hart was frustrated to learn he would not get his revenge.[21]

Hart also told some hostages that they would have murdered the two constables, Devine and Richards, except for Mrs Devine 'pleading for them'.[22]

Kelly returned once more to the bank. He dumped several bank-books in the backyard, then went into the hotel and chose two men to assist him. He made them build a fire in the backyard and burn the books.[23]

One of the books they burned was the vital 'recounter book', containing records of banknote numbers and other details about cash holdings. Without the recounter book, the stolen notes could not be traced.[24]

37

'The Story of My Life' by Edward Kelly

There was one more piece of business that needed attention. Kelly desired the manuscript he called 'The Story of My Life' to be published. Kelly told Constable Richards and Living to accompany him to the printery of the *Jerilderie and Urana Gazette*, owned and operated by Samuel Gill.[1]

They found Gill's wife, Eliza, home, but not Gill himself, who was still in hiding.

Living said to her, 'This is Kelly. Don't be frightened.'

'Don't be frightened,' Kelly repeated. He asked where her husband was. She said she didn't know. He pulled out a roll of paper from his jacket, saying, 'I only want your husband to print this.'[2]

He said, 'This is a bit of my life. I hadn't time to finish it. I'll finish it another time. Will you take it?'

Interpreting Eliza's lack of response as refusal, Living said to Kelly, 'Give me the papers. I'll get them to Mr Gill.'

After some hesitation, Kelly handed the document to the banker, saying, 'I want you to get it printed.'

Living replied, 'I'll see that it's done.' He tucked the document into a pocket.[3]

Kelly then told Living and Richards to come with him to the telegraph office. Bewildered, Eliza Gill watched from her doorway as the three men walked down the road.[4]

Kelly made idle conversation with Living and Richards. He confided to Living, 'I've made a great blunder over this affair. I shouldn't be surprised if we were caught this time.' As they chatted further, Living learned that they had delayed the robbery until Monday because of Joe Byrne's drinking spree and Kelly was worried the delay would ruin everything.[5]

They stopped in at a hotel. Kelly asked the proprietor, McDougall, if he owned a blood mare called Minnie, which he did. Kelly said, 'I want her.' He ordered McDougall to send his groom to the Royal Mail Hotel with Minnie.[6]

At the post office, they met Byrne, who had captured the postmaster, J.D. Jefferson, and his assistant, Rankin (not the magistrate Kelly had earlier tormented). He had cut the telegraph wires and was now reclining in Jefferson's office, reading through all the day's outgoing telegrams, to check if any warnings had been transmitted about the gang. He was pleased to discover that none had been sent.[7]

Kelly smashed the telegraph insulators with a revolver butt. He warned Jefferson that if he mended the wires before tomorrow, or 'offered any resistance' he would be shot. Kelly made Richards, Living, Jefferson and Rankin chop down several telegraph poles, then, with Byrne, took them all back to the Royal Mail Hotel.[8]

Byrne rode out of town with the bags of cash.[9]

The hotel was now packed with hostages. Ned Kelly made a speech, while Dan Kelly and Hart hung back as guards.

Kelly declared: 'It's all very well for people to talk of my shooting those men in cold blood. I did it in self-defence. I've been persecuted by the police ever since I was a lad of fourteen, and have been driven to be an outlaw. This revolver,' (he displayed one) 'was taken from Lonigan after he was shot. I shot him, Scanlan and Sergeant Kennedy.' He also said, 'There were only two of us there, my brother and I. Hart and Byrne were some miles away at their own camp.'[10]

Kelly held up his other gun, announcing that it was the one he shot the police with. It was held together with string. He said it was an old one, but a good one. He said it could shoot around corners.[11]

A drunk swagman created a disturbance at the bar, rendering Kelly's speech inaudible to those further away.[12]

Kelly said that of the police at Stringybark Creek, Constable McIntyre was a braver man than Sergeant Kennedy, 'because he had the presence of mind to realise his situation at once, when called upon to surrender.'[13]

He said bitterly that the Jerilderie police 'were worse than black-trackers'. He told the room that he had planned to murder constables Devine and Richards but Mrs Devine had begged him not to. He confessed that he 'could not resist her entreaties'.[14]

But then he changed his mind again. He *would* kill Richards after all. He pointed at Richards and announced, 'I'm going to shoot him immediately.'

The bank manager, Tarleton, interjected: 'If he has followed you up, he was only doing his duty.'[15]

Kelly replied, 'Suppose you had your revolver ready when I came in to the bank this morning, would you not have shot me?'

Tarleton said, 'Yes.'

Kelly said, 'Well, that's just what I am going to do, I will shoot Richards before he shoots me.'

The crowd pleaded with him not to kill Richards.

Kelly said, 'No, he must die.'

The tension was shattered by raucous interruptions from the drunk swagman, oblivious to all threats and warnings. Perhaps that swagman unintentionally saved Richards' life.

Kelly entered the bank next door one final time, to steal Tarleton's riding trousers and saddle. He found some jewellery and a gold watch belonging to Tarleton, so he stole those while he was at it. He saddled McDougall's blood mare. Dan mounted the horse, went for a test ride, and returned a few minutes later, handing the mare over to Ned.[16]

Dan Kelly and Hart mounted their horses and rode down the street, waving their guns in the air.[17]

Ned instructed everyone in the hotel to remain inside for another three or four hours. Living complained that there were townsfolk outside moving freely. Kelly relented: 'All right, but you mustn't go out of town for four hours.'[18]

Ned left with Minnie the blood mare. He took Richards, Jefferson and Jefferson's assistant, Rankin, to the lock-up, and put them in.[19]

On the way to the barracks, Reverend Gribble approached Kelly and complained that Steve Hart had stolen his watch. Kelly called Hart back and asked if it was true. Hart produced the watch. Kelly examined it, and on finding it to be a cheap watch, told Hart to return it to the reverend, saying that, if he was going to steal a watch, it should be a nice one.[20]

Reverend Gribble saw that they had McDougall's beautiful mare and said they should return it. Kelly agreed. It was wrong to take the blood mare. He told the reverend to deliver a message to McDougall: if he wanted Minnie back, he had to send his daughter Mary to the police barracks to collect it.[21]

At the barracks, the gang locked Richards, Jefferson and Rankin in the watch house with Devine. They burned all their clothes and changed into new.

Mary McDougall arrived to collect Minnie. There is no record of how long she was there. When she was ready to depart, Hart got up to fetch the mare for her, but Kelly stopped him. He said she couldn't have it yet, but he promised to return it later in payment for her visit.[22]

Kelly and Hart went to McDougall's again, where several strangers, unknown to anyone in the small town, had gathered.

Kelly shouted drinks for everyone and paid McDougall for them, with stolen money. He also bought two bottles of brandy . . . with stolen money.

Kelly said, 'Anyone could shoot me, but if a shot was fired, the people of Jerilderie would swim in their own blood.' He said he would never be taken alive, and would take his own life first. He pulled a small revolver from his breast pocket and put it to his head, demonstrating how he would do it.[23]

As Kelly and Hart mounted their horses, they shouted, 'Hurrah for the good old times of Morgan and Ben Hall!' The strangers clapped and cheered.[24]

They departed at around 7 p.m. in the direction of Wannamurra Station.[25]

Twenty minutes after they left the hotel, Living saddled his horse and rode hard for Deniliquin, 40 miles south-west, with Kelly's manuscript in his pocket. He left Jerilderie at 3.30 p.m., while the gang were still there. He knew a shortcut, and arrived in Deniliquin at midnight. He boarded the 5.45 a.m. train to Melbourne.[26]

Tarleton left in the same direction about half an hour later, but did not know the shortcut, and arrived just in time to board the train with Living.[27]

Mary Devine released her husband, Constable Richards, and Jefferson from the cells. Jefferson returned to the post office and immediately began repairing the telegraph equipment, defying Kelly's edict that he leave it broken. He used a nearby fence wire to connect the telegraph machine to an unbroken section of line and transmitted a message to the Sydney telegraph head office at 9 p.m.[28]

The strangers in Jerilderie stayed for another day or two, dressed as swagmen, with revolvers visible in some of the swags.[29]

38

The Jerilderie Letter

On the advice of Captain Standish, the Victorian government suppressed publication of Ned's letter. Its contents were not made available to the public until 1930. Ned referred to it as 'The story of my life', and 'A bit of my life', and it is now known as 'The Jerilderie Letter'.

It is a revised and expanded version of the Cameron Letter, often almost identical to that earlier letter. Again there was the disgusting, racist slander that Constable Fitzpatrick had 'sold his sister to a Chinaman'. Again, 'Detective Ward and Constable Hays took out their revolvers and threatened to shoot the girls and children in Mrs Skillion's absence . . .'

Again, 'Fitzpatrick will be the cause of greater slaughter to the Union Jack than Saint Patrick was to the snakes and toads in Ireland.'

Did he really mean that? Apparently so.

Again, there were longwinded complaints about past legal cases, interactions with police, and run-ins with local rivals.

That time he assaulted the hawker, Jeremiah McCormick? Totally false. 'Mrs McCormick struck my horse with a bullock's shin, it jumped forward and my fist came into contact with McCormick's nose . . .'

We can all relate to that. Who hasn't accidentally punched someone in the face?

That time he gave McCormick's wife a parcel of bullock's testicles and an obscene note? Sure, he did that, but it was Ben Gould's idea.

Constable Flood, Constable Hall, James Whitty and others are castigated.

That time he was arrested for riding a stolen horse? He had innocently found it beside the road.

That time he shot Lonigan? Same as before:

> But when I called on them to throw up their hands, McIntyre
> obeyed and Lonigan ran some six or seven yards to a battery of
> logs instead of dropping behind the one he was sitting on. He
> had just got to the logs and put his head up to take aim when
> I shot him that instant, or he would have shot me as I took him
> to be Strachan, the man who said he would not ask me to stand,
> he would shoot me first like a dog.

That was a new twist. He shot Lonigan because he thought
Lonigan was Constable Strahan. But never mind, because Lonigan
deserved it anyway. He says much later:

> I do not call McIntyre a coward as he is good a man, as wears the
> jacket he had the presence of mind to know his position directly
> he was spoken to, it is only foolishness to disobey an outlaw, it
> was cowardice made Lonigan fight, it is foolhardiness to disobey
> an outlaw as it means a speedy dispatch to kingdom come.

Perhaps he, or whoever it was that wrote this seemingly endless
litany of self-justification, lost track of his earlier version, because
now he was claiming that Lonigan was shot because it is *foolishness to
disobey an outlaw*. In Ned's worldview, police should obey criminals,
not the other way around.

Although proud of his record as a horse and cattle stealer, Kelly
boasts he was never caught: 'I can say I never was convicted of horse or
cattle stealing.' That is immediately followed with: 'My Brother Dan
was never charged with assaulting a woman . . .'

What a curious thing to say. None of the gang had ever been charged
with assaulting a woman. Why was this mentioned right after the boast
about Ned getting away with horse theft? Was this Dan's equivalent?

There were threats, of course:

And yet in every paper that is printed I am called the blackest and coldest blooded murderer ever on record. But if I hear any more of it I will not exactly show them what cold blooded murder is but wholesale and retail slaughter something different to shooting three troopers in self defence and robbing a bank.'[1]

And this:

It will pay Government to give those people who are suffering innocence justice and liberty. If not I will be compelled to show some colonial stratagem which will open the eyes of not only the Victorian police and inhabitants but also the whole British army, and no doubt they will acknowledge their hounds were barking at the wrong stump, and that Fitzpatrick will be the cause of greater slaughter to the Union Jack than Saint Patrick was to the snakes and toads in Ireland.

The reference to the British army is odd, since Ned Kelly had probably never seen British soldiers in his life. In their blue uniforms, Victorian police were styled on London bobbies. Since the publication of the Jerilderie Letter, some historians have wondered at the meaning of the phrase 'colonial stratagem'. The clear, simple interpretation is that he was referring to committing terrorist atrocities on a grand ('colonial') scale, plans for which he subsequently put into motion.

Towards the end, the letter indulges in playful and clever language and metaphors. The police are described, mockingly, as 'a parcel of big ugly, fat necked, wombat headed, big bellied, magpie legged, narrow hipped splaw-footed sons of Irish bailiffs or English landlords which is better known as officers of justice or Victorian police who some calls honest gentlemen.'

He then lambasts them for betraying their roots:

Either ways a policeman is a disgrace to his country and ances-
tors and religion, as they were all Catholics before the Saxons
and Cranmore yoke held sway since then they were persecuted
massacred, thrown into martyrdom and tortured beyond the
ideas of the present generation. What would people say if they
saw a strapping big lump of an Irishman shepparding sheep for
fifteen bob a week or tailing turkeys in Tallarook ranges for a
smile from Julia or even begging his tucker.

They would say he ought to be ashamed of himself and tar
and feather him. But he would be a king to a policeman who
for a lazy loafing cowardly billet left the ash corner, deserted the
Shamrock, the emblem of true wit and beauty to serve under
a flag and nation that has destroyed, massacred and murdered
their forefathers by the greatest of torture as rolling them down
hill in spiked barrels, pulling their toes and finger nails, and on
the wheel and every torture imaginable. More was transported to
Van Dieman's Land to pine their young lives away in starvation
and misery among tyrants worse than the promised hell itself.

Ned's family, on both sides, had come from Ireland. Likewise,
the Victorian police force consisted almost entirely of Irish-born men:
more than 80 per cent. Ned accused them of 'deserting the Shamrock',
effectively attacking them for being Irish. His sentiments were not
held by most Irish residents in north-eastern Victoria, many of whom
were victims of Kelly's crimes, and who wanted police protection from
Kelly and his gang.[2]

As for Catholicism, both Ned's sister, Maggie, and his mother
were married in Anglican churches. And many churchgoing, struggling Irish Catholic selectors had woken to find their horses stolen in
the night by Ned's network of horse thieves.

As with the Cameron Letter, Ned did not write the Jerilderie
Letter, and nor did he claim to have written it. Someone wrote it for

him. How much of it is Ned's work, and how much the work of others, is unknown. Someone involved—not Ned—had a flair for writing well-constructed, powerful prose, and that same person seems to have harboured a deep sectarian grudge against the English.

Four months later, with no publication of the Jerilderie Letter, Ned's sister Maggie Skillion wrote to Samuel Gill, asking for it back.

> *You would oblige me very much if you would send me the statement of Ned Kelly. He is my brother, and I would like to see it to see what he has to say of his life. I would be very thankful to you if you would send me the letter of Ned Kelly.*
> *Mrs. M. Skillion, Greta.*[3]

Gill couldn't publish it, because he didn't have it, and never had.

The day after Maggie Skillion's letter was sent from Greta, Wild Wright and another man arrived in Jerilderie, staying at McDougall's hotel. In a dispute over a bet, Wright attacked another man, then 'danced about like a madman,' punching anyone who came near. Constables Devine and Richards were called. While Devine moved away to interview witnesses, Wright broke free from Richards' grasp and punched a nearby man, giving him a black eye.

He appeared the next day before Magistrate Rankin on a charge of being drunk and disorderly. It was Magistrate Rankin whom Ned Kelly had shoved against a wall and promised to execute. Rankin dismissed Wright with a paltry five-shilling fine. Wild Wright was later seen in the street shouting, 'Hurrah for the Kellys!'[4]

A likely motivation for Wright's visit was to follow up on the Jerilderie Letter, and to visit Samuel Gill. Sometime after the letter from Maggie Skillion and the visit from Wild Wright, Samuel and Eliza Gill sold up and left town. They went north, far away from the Victorian border.

Agents

39

Agent Aaron Sherritt

At midnight on Saturday evening, 15 February 1879, five days after the Jerilderie heist, Michael Ward and Frank Hare visited a nondescript patch of scrubland near Beechworth. Ward had arranged a secret meeting between Hare and their new agent, the Kelly sympathiser Aaron Sherritt.[1]

Sherritt told them that the previous Wednesday, two days after Jerilderie, Dan Kelly had breakfast at Mrs Byrne's house. Apparently, Dan was supposed to meet the rest of the gang there and got worried when they didn't show. Sherritt's news checked out with other reports that Ward and Hare had received. They had been told of a sighting of Dan Kelly that Wednesday, riding towards the Buckland Gap, which wasn't far from Mrs Byrne's property.

Sherritt told them: 'You'd better come tomorrow night. I have good reason to believe they will be at Mrs Byrne's house, the other three men.' The police and their informer arranged to rendezvous at the same place at 8 p.m. the following night.

In the meantime, Hare instructed Senior-Constable Strahan to be on stand-by during this next rendezvous, waiting at a prearranged location in bushland out of town.

Sherritt met the police again on the Sunday evening. He said the gang were not at Mrs Byrne's house, but he knew where they were camped. He said, 'I am confident of them being there tonight.'[2]

They rode out of Beechworth, guided by a bright, almost-full moon. It was four weeks since Ward had fallen into a pit, and his broken ribs were not yet fully healed. Although they rode at walking pace, riding must have been painful. Strahan's patrol was not at the meeting place: they had no backup. Therefore, if they continued, it would be just Ward and Hare versus the four outlaws.

Sherritt urged them to keep going regardless, exclaiming, 'If we don't go at once, you'll lose the chance of getting the gang!'

Hare asked Ward, 'Will you stick to me if we go by ourselves?'

'I will, Mr Hare,' Ward assured him.

Then Hare turned to Sherritt. 'All right, lead the way.'

They rode through thick, wild, stony bushland. After a while, Sherritt pulled up his horse, and Ward and Hare pulled up beside him.

He asked them, 'Do you see anything?' They didn't. He pointed through the trees. 'Do you not see a fire there?'

Yes, they could make out a distant flickering light.

Sherritt said, 'Those are the bushrangers. They've made a fire tonight, and they're camping there. And it's a thing I never knew them do before. They must have some drink in them, otherwise they wouldn't make that fire so foolishly.' He added, 'This is the bush-rangers' country, and no one but them would be out in this country.'

They dismounted and sat on the ground to figure out what to do next.

'I think the best plan to do is to make certain the outlaws are at the fire, because if we know they're at the fire, we know how to act. It may be anybody else.' Hare said. He turned to Sherritt. 'You crawl up to it. Take your boots off, and get as close as you can, and ascertain if you can hear voices or anything else.'

Sherritt slipped off through the scrub, barefoot, then returned ten minutes later, walking casually, making no effort at concealment.

Ward gasped, 'My God, we've been sold!'

As Sherritt approached, Hare asked him, 'What's the matter, Aaron?'

Sherritt pointed again at the flickering light. 'How far do you think that fire is?'

'About 150 yards, I thought.'

Sherritt said, 'It's nothing of the kind, it's three miles away.'

Hare said, 'Nonsense! Aaron, you've sold me. You've gone and warned those fellows to be off.'

Sherritt replied, 'No. Come, get your horses. Where's the fire now? We'll ride up to it.'

They rode again, wending towards the glow of the fire, until they came to the top of a cliff. They could still see the light of the fire. It was on the ridge on the other side of the valley.

An abandoned gold-mining site, the so-called Woolshed Diggings, lay in the valley between. They were vulnerable here, at the top of the cliff: their silhouettes might be seen against the night sky. And it would be suicide to try to sneak uphill to the fire from the diggings.

Sherritt suggested that they go to the Byrne house, which he was sure the gang would visit soon. So they rode towards the Byrne homestead, and at about half past twelve tethered the horses in a quiet spot half a mile away, then approached on foot.

Sherritt crept up to the house, listened under a window, then returned. He had heard nothing. He showed them a nearby clearing in the forest, saying, 'That's where they tether their horses when they come here.' He said that sometimes the outlaws would eat at Mrs Byrne's house, then come out here and sleep under the stars with their horses.

The police had known about this clearing for some time, and another detective had shown it to Hare previously, noting the horse droppings and places where horses had eaten bark off the trees. That Sherritt was revealing this information, which they already knew to be true, increased Hare's confidence that Sherritt could be trusted.

The three men hid near the house and clearing, and waited. Dawn broke, but the outlaws never came. Sherritt reassured them: 'Those men will be here. They've disappointed me tonight, but they will come within a day or two.'

Ward and Hare retrieved their concealed horses and returned to Beechworth.

The two men had very different opinions of Sherritt. Ward didn't trust him at all. Oh, sure, it was worthwhile keeping him on the books, because you never know, but everything Sherritt said needed to be treated with caution and scepticism.

In contrast, Frank Hare admired Sherritt and was convinced he was a valuable asset. He had been wrong about Jack Lloyd all those years ago. Jack Lloyd, whom Hare had dismissed as a conniving ex-con, had been critical in catching Harry Power. Hare probably had that poor judgement in mind now and did not want to make the same mistake again.

Sherritt had said the outlaws would visit the Byrne house 'within a day or two'.

Hare had massive resources at his disposal. He organised a stake-out of the Byrne house. Sherritt assisted, escorting Hare into the hills behind the property, where he showed him a campsite that the outlaws didn't use. It would be perfect for such an operation, all the more because its vantage point made it almost impossible to attack.

Hare set up an observation point in a clearing near the house, and a base at the higher campsite. Senior-Constables Mills and Mayes were his patrol leaders. The watch patrol hid behind rocks during the day and trees during the night. They monitored the Byrne house all the next week, and the following week, and the week after that.

Aaron Sherritt was engaged to Joe Byrne's sister Katie. They would watch him arrive at the Byrne house in the early evening, then leave around midnight. She would walk with him a short way down the road. After they parted company, Sherritt would circle around and visit the police camp.[3]

Sherritt and Hare would chat under the stars. Sherritt told him that his father had been a police constable back in England. He also explained that he was the head scout for the outlaws in the district, and that he knew everything the police did.[4]

Hare told him, 'I don't believe you.'

Sherritt replied, 'Question me. Try me if you like.'

Hare asked him what the police movements were the day before yesterday. Sherritt said, 'Detective Ward and another man rode out from Beechworth, a party of police have come into Eldorado, and some men through near Everton.'

'Now, Aaron, will you tell me how you know?' Hare asked.

Sherritt said, 'No, I won't.'

Hare said, 'Why? Aren't you in my confidence?'

'No,' Sherritt replied. 'There are some things I won't tell. I'll tell nothing against myself to convict me, although I've been in all the crimes with the Kellys for years past.'

One time, as they lay on the hill in the dark, Sherritt told Hare he would never catch Kelly, although 'you will catch Joe, Steve and the others'. Hare asked why and Sherritt replied, 'He's too bloody smart.'[5]

'If he comes here, I'll get him,' Hare vowed.

Sherritt said, 'Do you think Ned ever goes in front? No, he sends the other three a hundred yards ahead.'

Hare asked, 'Why do they obey him?'

'He carries out his orders at the point of his pistol.'

'This must come to an end!' Hare declared.

Sherritt said, 'No. I look upon him as invulnerable. You can do nothing with him.'

The dry summer gave way to a dry autumn. The weather turned suddenly cold, but Aaron Sherritt would get around shoeless, and slept in the open with no cover while the police rugged up and huddled under blankets.

Hare had a reputation as a tough man, or at least, he had in his youth. He was now getting on in years with declining health, but had been a traveller and a goldminer and a cop in some of the roughest towns there were. He was awestruck by Sherritt's resilience.

He asked Sherritt one night, 'Can the outlaws endure as you are doing?'

To Sherritt, the natural way to compare men was by comparing their ability to fight each other. So he replied, 'Ned Kelly would beat me into fits.'

Sherritt explained the physical pecking order, in which a man who could beat another in a fight was a 'better man'. He said, 'I can beat all the others. I'm a better man than Joe Byrne, and I'm a better man than Dan Kelly, and I'm a better man than Steve Hart. I can lick those two youngsters to fits. I've always beaten Joe, but I look upon Ned Kelly as an extraordinary man. There is no man in the world like him. He is superhuman.'[6]

Supplies for the watchers came from the trusted Beechworth storekeeper Paddy Allen via the Sherritts. Aaron's sisters Annie and Julia were seen taking provisions into the bush. Someone assumed they were supplying the Kelly Gang. Hare received an anonymous letter in April: '. . . they won't tell on Kelly they are two of Kellys worst sympathisers they want locking up'. A second letter a few weeks later accused Annie Sherritt and Patsy Byrne of provisioning the outlaws.[7]

Ward visited the camp from time to time. He was openly scornful of Hare's trust in Sherritt. When he'd recruited Sherritt as an informer, he hadn't expected this. He was appalled that a major police operation was based on the whims of Aaron Sherritt.

He told Hare, 'He's only deceiving you, Sir. Please don't trust him. He wouldn't sell his friend Joe Byrne for all the money in the world.'[8]

Hare had promised Sherritt that, if his information led to the capture of the Kelly Gang, he would receive the entire £8000 bounty. Detective Ward believed that Sherritt *would possibly* betray the others for that kind of money, but that even then, he would do anything to protect Joe Byrne. Sherritt had discussions with Ward and with Hare about ways to get the others arrested while saving Joe Byrne.

One day, Ward visited with news that Dan Kelly had been seen near Myrtleford, riding towards Beechworth.

When Sherritt arrived a short time later, Hare told him this news. Sherritt said, 'Then he will call at my mother's place tonight, or else at my hut.'

He urged Hare to take some police to both locations and lie in wait in his parents' barn.

Hare took two men with him to the house of Aaron Sherritt's parents. He talked to Mrs Sherritt, and arranged a signal. If anyone came to the house, she would call out, 'Is that you, Jack or Willie?' (those being the names of her other two sons), so that Hare, hiding in the barn, would hear the response.

Frank Hare had worked the Ballarat goldfields in his youth. He had slept for the past several days on a rocky hill. He had tracked bushrangers through swamps and forests. Yet sleeping in the Sherritt's barn was one of the worst experiences of his life. He described it in his memoir:

> The pigs slept in the straw, and the fleas beat anything I have ever felt in all my life; the mice, also, were running over me; and I really believe a snake went over me also; but there was a chance of the Kellys coming there, and that was enough for us.[9]

They heard footsteps in the night. They heard Mrs Sherritt call out, 'Is that you, Jack?' Then the answer, 'Yes.' It was only Aaron's brother Jack coming home.

When he returned to the outpost on the hill, Hare was overjoyed. He said, 'I . . . took my position under the rock, feeling as if I had got home again; the bare rock was paradise to the abominable place I had just left.'[10]

At around 10 one morning, Hare was keeping watch down near the Byrne house, at the stake-out location near the stockyards. A man approached from behind them, climbed over the rail, and walked up to the house.

Hare remained very still, and so his men, following his lead, stayed still too. It crossed his mind to stand up, blow his cover, and challenge the man. But he let the man pass through because surely, if it was one of the outlaws, Sherritt would give him a signal. No signal came.

Later that evening, Sherritt came to the camp. Hare waited to see if Sherritt would tell him about the visitor, but he made no mention of any visitors to the Byrne house.

Hare asked him directly if any strangers had come to the house.

Sherritt said, 'Yes, a man named Scotty, who lives up the hills, came here.'

That was the first and last time anyone heard of a man named 'Scotty'.

Hare later concluded that the visitor was probably Joe Byrne himself, and he had let the outlaw slip through his fingers.[11]

The police had to get water from a creek about a mile and a half away. A neighbour told Mrs Byrne she saw a man who looked like a constable with a bucket near the creek. Mrs Byrne investigated and found a bar of soap near the creek, and a whittled stick. She also saw a man sitting near the creek who she thought might be a constable. She told

Sherritt there were police about, showed him the stick as proof, and asked him to investigate.[12]

He returned the next day and said to her, 'I've been in every direction, and can't find them at all.'

The following Sunday morning, the sentry ran down to where Hare was sleeping and woke him up.

'What's the matter?' Hare asked.

The sentry told him: 'The old woman is in our camp, and Aaron is lying down at the lowest point, and she has seen him.'

Hare jumped up and hurried over, just in time to see Mrs Byrne's back as she walked out of the camp and over the brow of a hill.

Aaron was lying down, a hat over his face. Hare rushed over, and exclaimed, 'Good heavens! You're discovered. The old woman has seen you.'[13]

Turning pale, Sherritt said, 'Now I am a dead man.'[14]

Hare gave Sherritt his hat and coat, to change how he was dressed, and said, 'Cut away to some place so as to provide an alibi, if you've been seen.'

Sherritt went away, made sure he was seen in another part of the district, and returned in the evening to Mrs Byrne's house. He took a flute, which he later told Hare had broken the ice.[15]

He said that everything was fine: Mrs Byrne had not recognised him. However, after she discovered police in the hills, she had lost faith in him, saying, 'A pretty fellow you are, going to search. I found the men in the mountains today.'

Hare asked Sherritt, 'How did she find us?'

He explained, 'Because one of the men left a sardine tin on the rock.' Apparently (according to Sherritt) Mrs Byrne was walking on the other side of the valley, when she saw something glisten in the sun. It was just luck that a sardine tin had glinted at that moment.

He said Mrs Byrne was going to ask Joe to shoot the police, as long as there were 'under fifteen or twenty.'

Hare thought it was best to pack up the camp immediately, but Sherritt suggested they stay. He explained that it didn't even matter if Mrs Byrne knew they were there, because she had no way to warn the outlaws.

They saw Mrs Byrne again the following morning. She was, in Hare's words, 'crawling along like a rabbit, and only showing her head over the rocks'. She was circling around them, up to the ridge so that she could look down on the camp from above. Hare said to Senior-Constable Mills, 'Go up and give her a fright.'

Mills cut across to intercept her, then hid behind a rock. She passed him on the other side of the rock, so he came around behind her, and jumped out, giving a great roar.[16]

Mrs Byrne got a tremendous shock. She exclaimed, 'What? What? I'm only looking for lost cattle!'

After regaining her composure, she snapped, 'I'll get my son to shoot the whole bloody lot of you.'

A few days later, Hare returned to Benalla, leaving Mills in charge.

The stake-out amounted to nothing. Two weeks after Hare had departed, he ordered Mills to pack up. It was over.[17]

40

Trackers

A team of six Native Police arrived from Queensland, led by two white Queensland policemen, Inspector Stanhope O'Connor and Senior-Constable King. The Native Police were brought for their tracking skills, but, unlike the Victorian blacktrackers, were enlisted, uniformed police who performed a range of other duties.

It was political. The Victorian government had requested them, although Standish didn't ask for them and Hare didn't want them. They already had two talented Victorian blacktrackers, Moses and Spider, on the case. Moses, considered the best blacktracker in the colony, was on standby in Benalla, while Spider was based in Mansfield.[1]

As Frank Hare saw it, the problem with the Queensland trackers was twofold. First, they weren't local. A blacktracker's talent and skill came largely from their deep knowledge of the land. Queensland differed from Victoria in flora, fauna, landscape and climate; he was not convinced their skills would translate. Second, in Hare's experience, blacktrackers operated best on their own or, at most, sometimes in pairs. It wasn't clear that a team of six Queenslanders would be more effective than a team consisting of one Moses.

A third problem arose from tensions between the senior Victorian officers and O'Connor, who believed that *he* was Standish's second-in-command in the hunt for the Kelly Gang.[2]

The Queensland Native Police proved to be far more competent than Hare had expected, although he still preferred his blacktracker Moses. Their leader was Corporal Sambo. Indigenous people in the employment of Europeans were typically given European names, and Sambo was a common name for men of colour in such roles in the nineteenth century. It is now considered derogatory.[3]

O'Connor's team left on their first patrol on 11 March, and were gone for a week. There was an unseasonal cold snap, for which they were unequipped. Corporal Sambo became sick from exposure, and was escorted back to Benalla. He died on the evening of 19 March from congestion of the lungs.[4]

Moses took Sambo's place in O'Connor's blacktracking team. When O'Connor learned that Moses had actually moved to Victoria from Queensland when very young, he enlisted him in the Queensland police. This was the cause, two years later, of an intercolonial dispute, because O'Connor wanted to take Moses back to Queensland (and he claimed that's what Moses wanted), whereas the Victorian police wanted to retain him.[5]

Standish requested that O'Connor's Native Police be assigned to different townships around the district. O'Connor refused on the grounds that he had instructions from the colonial secretary in Queensland 'not to separate yourself from your troops'.[6]

From that moment, the working relationship between O'Connor and the Victorian police was on an inexorable downhill slide.

In late May, while dining with Standish at the house of a Mr O'Leary, Frank Hare received a mail delivery. He looked through it and found a letter from an informer, which he read out to Standish. The informer, a farmer, had seen four men matching the appearance of the gang, riding towards the place of a man named Cleary, near Greta.[7]

Standish told him to leave at first light, and not to say a word to anyone in the meantime.

Hare asked, 'Not even to O'Connor?'

Standish said, 'No, I want this to be kept perfectly quiet.'

Later, at headquarters, O'Connor asked Hare if there was any news. Hare replied, 'Ask Captain Standish.'

O'Connor went into Standish's office and did so. Standish had apparently had a change of heart since his conversation with Hare. He told O'Connor all about the dawn patrol, and requested that black-trackers be deployed.

Irritated that Hare had kept it a secret from him, O'Connor said to Hare, 'What's the meaning of this?' Hare said nothing.

At dawn, in order to mask their destination, they went north from Benalla to Glenrowan, then circled east, then south to Greta. They were all in great spirits. As they rode out of Glenrowan, one of the constables cantered up to Hare, saying, 'Mr Hare, we have just passed that fellow, Nolan.' Nolan was a known associate of the gang, and was likely to report police movements to them.[8]

Following the directions in the letter that Hare had read, they turned left onto a lane running east through a crossroad and up a hill. Cleary's house was on a piece of open ground behind a chock-and-log fence, just as the letter had described.

They reached it at 4 a.m. on Monday morning.

Hare sent a team of four around to the back of the house, while he and three constables approached from the front.

He knocked. Someone said, 'Who is there?'

Hare called, 'All right! Open the door.'

Cleary opened the door.

'Do you have any strangers in the house?' Hare asked him.

Cleary said, 'Yes.'

'Who are they?'

Cleary hesitated, then said, 'A man by the name of Nolan.'

Hare rushed in and signalled for his constables to follow. Nolan, the Kelly Gang associate spotted earlier in Glenrowan, was there.

'Oh, hello Nolan,' Hare said, 'what brought you here?'

Nolan replied, 'I came to warn the people of the district about a funeral that [is] going to take place.'

'Where?' Hare asked him.

Nolan gestured westward. 'Out in that direction. The other side of Glenrowan.'

Hare ordered a thorough search of the property. Moses looked around for tracks, but did not find any. There had been some recent heavy rain; but even so, if the outlaws had been there, some sign, some trace, might be found.

Neither Cleary nor Nolan asked what they were looking for.

There was no sign of the outlaws.

Hare led several patrols through autumn.

They camped without fires for fear of being seen by the outlaws, and they travelled light. Hare would get cold at night under his covering—on some mornings their possum rugs would be frozen stiff around them. They would thaw the blankets at their morning fire so they could fold them.[9]

When Hare returned to Benalla from a winter patrol, he was clearly unwell. O'Connor and Sadleir both told him he was fool for going out in such weather.

O'Connor said, 'Standish ought to be ashamed of himself, sending you out so much.'

Hare defended Standish by deflecting. 'It's a disgrace to us that we can't catch the Kellys.'[10]

But he was suffering. His health was declining. He told Standish the job was killing him, and he could not continue. His last day in charge of the Kelly search was 7 July 1879.[11]

Standish reassigned him to his regular patch, the Bourke district (the towns to the north of Melbourne), then informed Nicolson he was back in charge.[12]

Standish returned to his Melbourne headquarters, which Nicolson had been running in his absence. The office was in disarray. Nicolson had been working hard, and driving the office staff to work long hours, but he had no sense of how to prioritise. There were severe administrative backlogs everywhere.[13]

Meanwhile, a book had been published earlier that year that included shocking revelations about the murder of Sergeant Michael Kennedy. Written and published by the *Mansfield Guardian*'s editor, George Wilson Hall, *The Kelly Gang, or, the Outlaws of the Wombat Ranges* relied in part on interviews conducted with the outlaws. With the aid of intermediaries, a journalist with the pseudonym Mr Blank (possibly Hall himself) had been guided to a rendezvous deep in the ranges, bringing bottles of alcohol in payment for the exclusive interview. The book blended Kelly's version of events with information from other sources. The title page bore a curious quotation:

Be cautious of what you say, of whom, and to whom

The motto may well have been Hall's guiding principle in writing his book: the outlaws would be paying attention. There was a detailed section about the murders at Stringybark Creek.

As related by Hall, after McIntyre escaped on Kennedy's horse, Kennedy commenced shooting at the gang, then fled in the general direction that McIntyre had gone. Kelly pursued him, finally shooting Kennedy with his last bullet. Hart and Byrne departed in pursuit of McIntyre, while the Kelly brothers interrogated the wounded, helpless sergeant for an hour and a half.[14]

Apparently, Kennedy didn't tell them much. He kept changing the subject to his wife and children, and reminisced about his infant son who had recently died. They propped him up, and provided him with a pencil and a notebook from his jacket. He wrote a farewell letter to his wife, describing his current condition, and giving his instructions and wishes for how to proceed after his death. He handed the letter to

Ned Kelly, who promised to deliver it to his wife 'if ever a favourable opportunity should occur'.

By then, it was almost dark, and the gang needed to get moving. Kelly placed the shotgun against Kennedy's chest. At that, Kennedy burst into life, exclaiming, 'Let me alone, for God's sake! Let me live, if I can, for the sake of my poor wife and family. Surely you have shed enough blood already!'[15]

Kelly fired. Sergeant Kennedy died almost instantly.

When Bridget Kennedy learned that, according to a new book, her husband had written her a farewell letter, hope flickered to life that she might one day read it. But no letter came, and Kelly later denied its existence.[16]

41

New agents

The government was burning vast amounts of money on the Kelly search, so in mid-1879, Premier Graham Berry slashed Standish's budget. Most of the redeployed constables returned to their home districts. It was at this time that Standish returned to Melbourne and placed Superintendent Nicolson in charge of the Kelly search.

Nicolson was not bothered by the reduction in police numbers, since he was sceptical of their value, and believed Hare had achieved nothing with his relentless searches of the district. Perhaps recalling his success years ago with the informer Jack Lloyd, who helped catch Harry Power, he intended to take a new approach, one that required brains rather than brawn.

To safeguard the banks, Nicolson made the best of what he had. He stationed small parties of police under competent officers in the towns with banks: Sergeant Harkin at Wodonga, Sergeant Steele at Wangaratta, Senior-Constable Shoebridge at Bright and Sub-Inspector Pewtress at Mansfield. Their bank guard duties were supplemented by local volunteers considered to be trustworthy.[1]

The gang seemed to have many agents around the district. Well, Nicolson could play that game too. Under Nicolson, as the number of constables under him diminished, the number of informers and secret agents multiplied.[2]

Still based in Beechworth, Detective Michael Ward's role now became more important. He was responsible for managing the agents, although Nicolson decided to run a few agents of his own without Ward's knowledge.

Sadleir approved of the change in strategy. He commented later about Nicolson: 'He was not as brilliant in some respects as Hare, but he was an expert in dealing with criminals, an art that Hare knew nothing of.'[3]

Sergeant Whelan introduced Nicolson to a schoolteacher named Daniel Kennedy, who was a pillar of the local community, liked and respected by just about everyone, including acquaintances of the Kelly Gang. Kennedy became a trusted informer. His metaphor for the Kelly Gang was that they were 'diseased stock', so he was given the codename The Diseased Stock Agent. He would write letters to Nicolson laden with coded language and strong, but often vague, suggestions. If the gang was in the area, Kennedy would make a remark such as 'pleuro is about', or 'disease is on the increase'.[4]

Nicolson sifted through old paperwork left behind by Standish. He discovered a letter, several months old, from another local teacher offering his services. Like Daniel Kennedy, James Wallace was also an upstanding member of the community, yet Standish had seemingly ignored his offer.

Nicolson's supposition was wrong. Standish had investigated James Wallace's offer.

Standish had received the letter from Wallace in December 1878, soon after the Euroa bank robbery. At Standish's invitation, Wallace had met him twice in Benalla to discuss a possible role as an agent. He was well-positioned to do so: Wallace was the schoolmaster, and only teacher, at two local schools, each of which he ran part-time. One was in the village of Hurdle Creek, where he lived, and the other a short distance east at a village called Bobinawarrah. Wallace explained that he had plenty of leave available over the Christmas holidays and liked to go out shooting in the ranges: he could use that time scouting for the gang. He added that he was acquainted with Joe Byrne, and Byrne's friend Aaron Sherritt.[5]

Standish was cautious. His policy, as he explained much later was this: 'If you employ a man on duty of this kind, it is necessary to make inquiries. If you place yourself in the hands of men you do not know, it would be unsafe.'[6]

Standish set out from Wangaratta at dawn one morning with a newly employed constable, and made for the Hurdle Creek school-house. They arrived at about a quarter past eight, and found James Wallace outside, surprised to see them.

Wallace exclaimed, 'Oh, Captain Standish! What are you doing here?'

Standish was there to check up on Wallace before employing him. He told a lie: 'It's a perilous job. I came here to meet a man who gave me information.'

Wallace invited him in for breakfast. They chatted for a couple of hours, the conversation drifting onto the topic of the outlaws.

Wallace said, 'You're doing rather a risky thing coming here.'

Standish replied, 'I've got my revolver here, and a constable with me.' Then he changed the topic. 'By-the-bye, have you seen Aaron Sherritt lately? I know he's the man who is in the habit of going to your house often.'

Wallace said, 'No, he has not been here for six weeks.'

Standish thanked him and his wife for breakfast, then departed with his constable—who had waited patiently outside—back to Wangaratta, and then to Benalla.

A message was waiting for him that Aaron Sherritt wanted to see him. He went out into the nearby bushland, where Sherritt was waiting.

He said, 'Well, Aaron, where did you come from?'

Sherritt answered: 'I have just spent two days at Wallace's, and I came away [this] morning early.'[7]

Sherritt had inadvertently revealed to Standish the true character of James Wallace, schoolteacher.[8]

In the course of their first conversation, Wallace had recommended that a local man named Slater be recruited into the police. Standish was not interested in Wallace's services, but he did follow his suggestion of recruiting Slater as a new constable.

James Wallace had visited Standish another time in Benalla with an astonishing new offer. He confided that he had been in contact with Joe Byrne, and that Joe was willing to betray the other members of the gang to spare his own life. He proposed a deal: Byrne would give away the gang's location, and in return, Byrne would be granted his freedom, paid one or two hundred pounds, and be allowed to leave Victoria. Standish said he might be interested and arranged to meet again, but at their next—and final—meeting, Wallace informed him that Byrne was no longer interested.[9]

Standish didn't mind. He didn't trust James Wallace, so wasn't particularly interested in Wallace's deal. It was, ironically, one thing he had in common with Joe Byrne.

Nicolson visited James Wallace at the Hurdle Creek school in July 1879. He was impressed, and offered Wallace payment in return for regular information.

Wallace replied there was no need for payment: he would do it for free! His sense of civic duty would be payment enough. It would be nice if he could be reimbursed for expenses from time to time, however. Nicolson agreed. Wallace was assigned the codename 'Fisher'.

The first report from Wallace arrived by mail in August, in which he revealed that the gang had recently been in the vicinity of Beechworth 'on several occasions'. Referring to his favourite outlaw, Joe Byrne, as 'the Poet':

The Poet seems to have been ill, the exposure and occasional prolonged fasts not agreeing with his naturally delicate constitution. The others are in good fettle and they are all in good spirits.[10]

Then came a warning that there might be a double-agent in the police ranks:

I think it more advisable to communicate details to you personally, as there is a screw loose in your department somewhere. Even the list of places I gave you at our previous interview is in the hands of our friends' friends. And they would like to know 'who the bloody hell gave him that rigmarole'.[11]

The possibility of a mole was alarming. In their numerous private meetings and in his many letters to Nicolson, he repeatedly maligned Detective Ward.[12]

Wallace warned Nicolson of a complex web of intrigue:

There is a beautiful game of cross purposes being played on both sides that is worth the trouble of watching, if there were no other motive.[13]

He did not, of course, reveal that he was at the centre of the game. He also began undermining his other old schoolfriend Aaron Sherritt, whom he sarcastically called 'Hare's protégé'. He told Nicolson that Sherritt had Sergeant Kennedy's stolen watch. On one occasion he reported:

I think I can persuade someone to return the chronometer to the widow per post, but he is avaricious and would rather melt it down. You have frightened his brother a bit. He is shy, and will have to be played with 'finesse'.[14]

All the while, Wallace was in close contact with Sherritt. For his part, Sherritt believed that the two of them were working together with the police and the gang. They had concocted a scheme whereby the three friends—Sherritt, Wallace and Joe Byrne—would collect the reward money by betraying the rest of the gang. But after that plan failed, Wallace began working against Sherritt.

Wallace visited Aaron Sherritt at the house of Sherritt's parents. In a private conversation, he told Sherritt that he knew for a fact that Sergeant Kennedy's watch was at Joe Byrne's mother's house, and that she would be happy to get rid of it. He urged Sherritt to go around there and offer to buy it from her. Perhaps sensing a trap, Sherritt declined.

42

The thief who came
in from the cold

At the beginning of winter 1879, Aaron Sherritt went into hiding.

A warrant had been issued for his arrest on 31 May, following a complaint by Mrs Byrne that he had stolen her horse. The story was more complex than a simple theft. Aaron and Mrs Byrne were no longer on speaking terms. The details of the sorry saga came to light through court documents and later revelations from police.

Mrs Byrne didn't trust Sherritt, so she forbade him from continuing to visit her daughter Kate. She therefore called off their engagement. Banned from seeing his now-former fiancée, Sherritt asked for his engagement present, a filly he had given Kate three years earlier, to be returned. The Byrnes didn't have the filly anymore, because Patsy Byrne had traded her for a horse named Charlie.

That being the case, Sherritt demanded that Mrs Byrne at least pay him for Charlie. She said, 'I want nothing more to do with you. Take Charlie and do what you like with him.' So he did.[1]

He rode Charlie to Eleven Mile Creek, where he met up with Ned's sister Kate, who was at the home of Ned's older sister Maggie. Maggie wasn't home. He enticed Kate to go for a romantic walk with him down to the river. Maggie arrived and discovered that Kate was gone (and possibly realised she was being seduced by Aaron Sherritt). She called the police.

A constable arrived, tracked the pair down, and fired two shots in the dark at Sherritt, who fled on foot to the house of his good friend James Wallace, arriving there shaken and scared. Days passed before he had the courage to confidently visit Maggie Skillion, and to ask her if she would like to purchase the horse that was roaming free in the bush near her house. She paid him £2.

Mrs Byrne made it known that if Charlie wasn't returned she'd prosecute. Aaron visited Maggie Skillion and asked to buy Charlie back from her for the same price she'd paid him, but she refused. They had him. He was trapped.

Mrs Byrne filed a charge against him, but the police couldn't arrest him because they didn't know where he was.[2] After a tip-off, the Eldorado police waited in ambush for him at his parents' place, but arrested his brother Jack by mistake.[3]

A note arrived for Detective Michael Ward on 1 July.

Mr Ward I want to see you immediately. I have some news of great importance.
I remain yours respectively
Mrs A Sherritt Sheepstation Creek
Mr Ward please burn my communications for fear I might be found out.[4]

When he arrived at the Sherritts' home at Sheep Station Creek, Annie showed him a two-page letter which had arrived, addressed to Aaron, from Joe Byrne.

It began:

Dear Aaron I write these few stolen lines to you to let you know that I am still living I am not the least afraid of being captured dear Aaron meet me you and Jack this side of the Puzzel Ranges Neddie and I has come to the conclusion to get you to join us I was advised to turn treater but I said I would die at Ned's side first Dear Aaron it is best for you to join us a short live and a jolly one[5]

If the police believed that Joe had acted as Ned's scribe for the Jerilderie Letter, this letter must surely have given doubt. Joe couldn't spell 'traitor' and misspelled 'life' as 'live', yet both words had been spelled correctly in the Jerilderie Letter.

Joe's letter degenerated into a bloodthirsty rant:

I intend to pay old sandy doig and old Mullane oh that bloody snob where is he I will make a targate of him . . .

I told Hart to call last Thursday evening I would like to know if he obeyed us or not if not I will shoot him . . .

I will riddle that bloody Mullane if I catch him no more from the enforced outlaw till I see yourself

I remain yours truly

You know

The letter went on to claim, 'the Lloyds and Quinns want you shot but I say no you are on our side'. There was no signature, only the words, 'You know . . .'

He showed the letter to Senior-Constable Mullane, who was certain it was Joe Byrne's handwriting.

Ward arranged, probably through Annie, for Sherritt to meet the gang in the Puzzle Ranges. Aaron later made contact with Ward to say that he had gone to the meeting place but nobody was there.[6]

A week later, while adult members of the Sherritt house were absent, Ned Kelly visited and chatted with the two girls, picking up the baby, Hugh, and cooking some bread with dough he found in the kitchen. He told the children he was there to see Aaron, so Aaron could help him with 'a mob of cattle'. He pulled out a bottle of brandy, poured a glass, and told the children to give it to Aaron when they next saw him, with the message that there was a man who wanted Aaron's help with some cattle.[7]

Aaron was arrested for horse stealing on Monday 14 July and allowed bail pending trial, which was set for Tuesday 22 July.[8] Believing that this event might lure Joe Byrne and possibly the other outlaws out of hiding, Ward asked Nicolson to arrange a stake-out of Mrs Byrne's house for the three days leading up to the trial, but Nicolson rejected the plan.

The detective had learned that he was going to be subpoenaed as a witness, which would be a catastrophe. There was a risk he would be interrogated on his relationship with Aaron Sherritt, exposing his informer and police activities broadly. Luckily, there was a prisoner in Beechworth Gaol awaiting escorted transportation to Melbourne; this provided an excuse for Ward to be out of the district for a few days.[9]

In reporting Sherritt's arrest, *The Herald* stated with surprising accuracy, 'The accused has been employed for some time as a private detective or special constable to work in connection with the regular police in catching the Kellys.'[10]

At Sherritt's trial, Mrs Byrne testified she had told Aaron she had heard he was working for the police. He'd asked who told her that, but she'd refused to say. Aaron then threatened to slit the throats of all her horses if she did not answer the question.

In Aaron's defence, a credible witness who had overheard the conversation said that Mrs Byrne told Aaron to take Charlie.

She lost: Aaron Sherritt was acquitted.

The Sherritt–Byrne conflict had multiple fronts. A broken engagement. Suspicion. Accusations of horse theft. Threats to murder horses. And Beechworth storekeeper Paddy Allen, who had been supplying the police surveillance team with provisions, learned of another source of friction. Aaron Sherritt had been promised a £100 cut of the takings from the Jerilderie Bank robbery, which he never received. Joe Byrne swore it was sent via his brother Patsy. Aaron Sherritt swore he never got the cash.[11]

Mrs Byrne was fond of telling people that Detective Ward was behind the dispute over Charlie the horse.

A truant officer visited in November about one of her children not attending school. Over tea, the topic of the outlaws came up. She said of Joe, 'He has made his bed and must lie in it.'[12]

On the topic of Charlie the horse, she said, 'It was a dodge of that bloody Ward. He's using all sorts of dodges to bring Joe back again to have revenge on Sherritt.' She said the dodge wouldn't take, and that the gang would bide their time. She made it clear they intended to kill both Aaron Sherritt and Michael Ward.

After leaving the Byrne property, the truant officer relayed the conversation to Ward. The good news was that, according to Mrs Byrne, they were not planning to kill him or Sherritt any time soon. They would 'bide their time'. It was cold comfort for Ward, who was receiving death threats from Joe Byrne by post. (These letters were placed in police files but have since been lost.)[13]

Some historians have made mileage from the truant officer's recollection of Mrs Byrne's comment as evidence that Ward engineered the horse theft to sow discord between the neighbours. Aside from one man's memory of a conversation he had two years earlier, there is no evidence for that. Charlie the horse was a personal feud. Ward had nothing to do with it.

43

Agent Wallace

Detective Ward found it hard to keep his movements secret. People gossiped about the things he did and the places he went, and sympathisers of the gang kept an eye on him. He bought some greyhounds to give himself an excuse to walk around town every day without attracting attention. Ward liked dogs: when he first moved to Beechworth, he had a pet dog named Jack, but someone had killed Jack with poison (he never found out who).[1]

Ward suspected the schoolteacher James Wallace of being deeply involved with the Kelly Gang. A teacher and postmaster, Wallace was a respectable member of the community, yet was friendly with the disrespectable Sherritt and Byrne families.

On a Saturday evening in mid-August 1879, Ward met Wallace on the outskirts of Beechworth. They stopped and chatted. Wallace was evasive in his reasons for coming to Beechworth. Ward requested that he visit the police station for a chat before leaving town, but although Wallace said he would, he did not.

Ward followed up on his movements.

Wallace had stayed overnight in town and then visited the Sherritt family. He and Aaron Sherritt had left the house together, talking privately as Wallace rode and Aaron walked beside him.

Ward visited the Sherritt house to find out more. They said Wallace had told them that his brother had recently seen Ned Kelly. Wallace had given them a description of Kelly that Ward found surprisingly detailed for a second-hand (and now third-hand) account: 'He wore a brown overcoat, grey hood, trousers, leggings and soft felt hat, and rode Joe Byrne's grey horse.'

Ward asked Aaron Sherritt what he and the schoolteacher had spoken about. That conversation turned out to be very interesting.

Wallace had accused Sherritt of betraying their mutual friend Joe Byrne. Sherritt had made it clear he didn't care about the other three outlaws, and was prepared to sell them for the £8000 reward, but he would *never* sell Joe. Sherritt reassured Wallace that he was making inquiries 'to try and get a pardon for Joe Byrne'.

Wallace told him not to bother, because he had also been trying, but had learned it was off the table. 'I've been to see Mr Graves, member of parliament. He told me there's no reprieve for Joe Byrne. When he is caught, he will be hanged.'

They had arranged to meet again in Beechworth the following weekend.

The next weekend, Wallace was back as promised. Ward tracked him carefully.[2]

This time, he arrived with a horse and buggy, indicating that he was there to do some shopping. He visited the store of Ward's friend Paddy Allen. There, he purchased an entire case of whisky, a bag of bread loaves, six pocket-handkerchiefs, some perfume and a packet of arsenical soap. It was an unusual shopping list for a family man like Wallace.

In the afternoon, Ward intercepted him in a Beechworth street, pretending it was by chance, and invited him to come and have some drinks at the nearby Hibernian Hotel.

Wallace was keen to hear Ward's opinions about the gang. He asked if Ward thought they were still in Victoria. Ward said yes, then followed up with: 'Why don't you catch them?'

There was nothing Ward could say to that.

In the course of conversation, the possibility came up that one of the outlaws might be induced to betray the others in exchange for a pardon, but Wallace said sadly, 'That's worked out. It can't be done.'

Aaron Sherritt arrived. It was Wallace's shout. He pulled out a National Bank note, showed it to Ward, and remarked, 'It is a pity you haven't got the numbers now.'

The banknote serial numbers. The cash taken from both robberies was untraceable. Wallace was taunting him with stolen money.

Ward kept his cool and replied, 'Not at all. You're a friend of mine. I would take no action.'

The conversation broke up. Wallace's attention switched to other patrons. Ward stayed at the hotel for a while, to observe. Wallace was spending cash freely. How strange: the four outlaws had risked everything for those banknotes. Yet the four outlaws were now fugitives, hiding far from sight, while James Wallace and Aaron Sherritt partied on stolen money. Who was really in charge of this gang?

Wallace and Sherritt moved on to the Empire Hotel. Ward went home.

Making inquiries the next day, Ward learned that their binge had ended with them sleeping in a room together at the Imperial. They had checked out around midday and ridden in Wallace's buggy to Sherritt's parents' home. They stayed there for about four hours, then departed, Sherritt riding with Wallace as far as the Golden Ball Hotel. There he had jumped out and walked home; while the schoolteacher returned to Hurdle Creek.

Ward dropped in on Aaron Sherritt for an update. Joe Byrne had visited Wallace the previous Thursday, wanting to know if Aaron Sherritt was 'after him yet'. If so, Wallace was instructed to warn Sherritt of the consequences, which he had done the night before.

Ward asked Sherritt how much cash Wallace had on him. Sherritt said he had about nineteen or twenty banknotes. He had spent more than £8 in the Saturday night spree. That was quite a lot, given that his teacher's salary was about £3 per week.[3]

Also, according to Wallace, Joe Byrne was worried that Ned and Dan were going to betray Byrne and Hart through one of Ned's contacts.

And the gang were planning to stick up the bank at Oxley because 'there is whip of money there'.[4]

Wallace had told Sherritt to shoot Detective Ward 'and it would be left on the Byrnes'.

Sherritt reassured Ward that he had no intention of doing it.

Finally, Wallace had given Aaron instructions to visit his (Wallace's) home the following Friday, because the gang needed Aaron's help in selling some gold.

All of this went into a report from Ward to his superior down the mountain track in Benalla, Superintendent Nicolson.

Meanwhile, Wallace, in his capacity as Nicolson's private detective, wrote Nicolson a very different account of the evening. Referring to Aaron Sherritt as 'Mr Hare's protégé', he said:

> He has National Bank notes—at least he had two on Saturday evening, but whether they came from Euroa or not is not easy to determine. He said they were 'square' and he had obtained them in payment for service rendered to the police. I changed one of them for him and cashed it purposely in Ward's presence at Wertheim's [Hibernian Hotel in] Beechworth. I jocularly drew his attention to it being a 'National' and asked what he would give to be told where it came from.[5]

That was a complete inversion of Ward's version of events. He was sure that Wallace, not Sherritt, had stolen banknotes. Then came an admission in Wallace's account:

> . . . towards morning—for we slept together—he asked me if I could imitate Byrne's handwriting. I replied in the affirmative. He wanted a threatening letter written to Mr A Crawford of Beechworth purporting to come from Byrne and warning him to prepare for his latter end as they were informed that he had informed on G. Baumgarten for supplying them with sugar etc.[6]

In his verbose attempt to incriminate Aaron Sherritt, Wallace had incriminated himself: he had admitted that he could forge Joe Byrne's handwriting, and that he had done so on at least one occasion on behalf of the outlaws. Wallace's willingness and ability to produce written material on behalf of Joe Byrne might provide a solution to the mystery of the authorship of the Cameron and Jerilderie letters.

Wallace's belief in his ability to imitate handwriting was perhaps overblown, but the fact that he thought he could successfully do it is the salient point. He was also an activist for selectors' rights, which might explain the tone and content of some passages in the Jerilderie Letter.[7]

In another report, Wallace warned Nicolson not to trust Sherritt:

You'll have to do something with Aaron soon—he is sweating horses right and left. If he don't get into some steady billet where he could make an honest living he'll develop into another outlaw before long.[8]

Sherritt departed for Hurdle Creek the following Friday. He was not back by Monday, so Ward searched for him. He finally reappeared on Thursday.[9]

Ward demanded to know where he had been all week. Sherritt said he stayed at Wallace's house, hoping that 'Joe would call there', but Byrne had not shown up. However, he had learned that Wallace knew where the outlaws were hiding.

Ward reported his conversation with Sherritt to Nicolson on 4 September, referring to Sherritt by his codename 'Tommy':

I have seen Tommy this morning, and he has very little news. He gives his reasons for stopping so long at Wallace's, as to try [to see] if Joe would call there as he was expected, but he did not call, but he states that he is certain Wallace knows their whereabouts and can find them when he likes, but will not sell Joe Byrne.

Wallace and Tommy have made an arrangement to go to Chiltern on Friday evening to try to meet a person who knows where he can be seen. I asked him if he would have any objection for me to be in Chiltern to see if Wallace would be there. He said no, you can come, and you might then get the gold which we are in the act of selling.

Tommy states that the gang told Wallace that they would not try the Oxley bank now, as there is too many police there. Four troopers every morning when the bank opens. And another drawback is the pound is too soft. They are not going to do anything until the pound gets harder. They are frightened by the black boys.[10]

How interesting that the gang's decision about the timing of the next bank robbery was influenced by fluctuations in the value of gold. Another striking piece of information was that Ned was scared of the blacktrackers. Ward believed that Sherritt was lying to him about hearing all this second-hand through Wallace. He added, towards the end of the report:

I am not at all satisfied by Tommy's tale.

I am of the opinion that he saw Joe Byrne himself . . .

Sherritt had arranged to go to Chiltern the following week to meet up with Wallace and then to sell some of the stolen Euroa gold. Despite his misgivings, Ward gave Sherritt some cash to pay for a day-trip to Chiltern.[11]

On the morning of the arranged meeting, Ward arrived in Chiltern, found a convenient hidden location to observe the main street, and settled in. He watched Sherritt arrive in town and go about some business. The schoolteacher did not come.

In the following weeks, Ward learned a strange thing. James Wallace was going about the district buying up scrap iron. He was collecting mouldboards (the curved iron plates of farming ploughs), telling people that they were for his father, whom he claimed was a blacksmith. (Wallace's father was a storekeeper, not a blacksmith.) The detective was perplexed: what on earth was Wallace, a schoolteacher, planning to do with all that iron?[12]

Meanwhile, as Detective Ward spied on Wallace, he was unaware that Wallace was spying on *him* on behalf of Superintendent Nicolson.

At Benalla headquarters, Nicolson was irritated by Wallace's lengthy missives, and the escalating expenses he was incurring—and being reimbursed for—as he travelled the district as Nicolson's secret agent. Yet, even as he doubted Wallace's value, Nicolson seems not to have questioned his loyalty, despite the arrival of some alarming news.

The police in outlying stations in the King River valley were frustrated by postal delays. All police correspondence travelled in parallel to the standard mail, relayed through post offices. An investigation determined that the bottleneck was occurring at the Bobinawarrah post office, which was run on a part-time basis by James Wallace and his wife. Confidential memos and reports would seemingly sit idle at Bobinawarrah for more than a week, before resuming their journey to their destination.

Nicolson demanded an explanation. Wallace blamed his wife. There had been an extended delay, he explained, when he was away in Melbourne with his sick brother, and his wife was left to run things. Even so, he informed Nicolson, the main problem was 'the defective postal arrangements which now pertain on this line'. For example, letters were transited through too many post offices, and this caused delays all around.[13]

Wallace was almost certainly intercepting mail. No wonder the police searches never amounted to anything! The outlaws had access to all police correspondence and could anticipate their every move.

As Michael Ward said years later of the hunt for the gang: 'They knew too much for us. The information they obtained throughout the country was such as to let them know exactly what we were doing.'[14]

44

Jack, Aaron and the Cave Party

While Aaron became entangled in his dealings with the outlaws, his friend James Wallace and the police, his brother Jack had also been cultivated as an informant. James Wallace set up the connection, introducing him to Superintendent Nicolson at the Wangaratta show. Nicolson didn't handle Jack personally; he became one of Detective Ward's agents.

Unfortunately, there was ongoing tension between Detective Ward and Jack. Ward believed that the information he received from Jack was valid as far as it went, but that it was never the whole truth.

Aaron Sherritt's younger sister Annie returned one day from a visit to Mrs Byrne's house with a 'short written quick' note for Jack. It instructed him to meet Joe at Thompson's farmhouse, near Sandy Creek. Jack showed it to Ward. He was scared that the outlaws had discovered his role as a double agent and would murder him.

There was no time to gather a police patrol, and Ward had no intention of going on his own. He advised Jack to attend the appointment.

Named after its most recent occupant, the Thompson farm was an abandoned selection. Jack waited at the empty run-down farmhouse, but nobody came. He stayed overnight, and probably did not sleep easily.

In the morning, as he rode home, Joe Byrne stepped onto the road. His boots and spurs were bloody, as if he had been riding hard, using the spurs to urge his horse to keep going.

Byrne talked about Hare and Nicolson. Of Hare, he said, 'That's the old buck that caught Power,' and said, 'He's a smart old cove.'

He asked Jack if he knew Nicolson. He did! But Jack told Byrne he knew nobody.

Jack asked him, 'Where are your mates?'[1]

'Not very far off.'

Byrne tasked him with scouting the Yackandandah bank for a potential hold-up, and to look for plain-clothes policemen.

Byrne appeared at the Sherritt house some time later, to tell Jack that the Yackandandah robbery had been called off.

On another occasion, Byrne assigned Jack the task of surveilling the Eldorado bank. Ward instructed him to tell Byrne that 'there would never be more than ten, twenty or thirty pounds found in that bank'.[2]

In his dealings, Jack fed lies supplied by Ward to the outlaws. One bank had so little money it wasn't worth robbing; another bank was too well guarded. This ploy seems to have succeeded, confusing and thwarting the gang in their efforts to plan another heist.

Ward could not take timely action on intelligence. He had to notify Superintendent Nicolson of everything because, if the outlaws were caught, Nicolson wanted to be there. He *insisted* on being there.

It was a slow, clunky system. Ward would get a tip-off. He would send it to Nicolson. Nicolson would eventually read it and make a decision. He would send his decision to Ward. The risk was huge. If they acted on information from a member of the Sherritt family, but failed to catch the outlaws, they would expose and endanger their informers.

Red tape, and Nicolson's vanity, looked as though it was going to get one or more members of the Sherritt family killed.

Ward complained that the response time from tip-offs was unworkable. Nicolson saw his point. The sensible thing to do would have been to give Ward more latitude. However, that wouldn't have done at all: Ward might have caught the outlaws and got all the glory. Instead, Nicolson came up with a very expensive alternative solution: another stake-out of Mrs Byrne's house.

Nicolson and O'Connor went to Beechworth with Ward and Senior-Constable Mullane to brief the two teams to be involved. Each of the eight were called into the office one at a time and given their instructions in writing. Nicholson told them that the work was secret, and that they must speak to nobody about it.[3]

Again, Ward was responsible for logistics and personnel management. Storekeeper Paddy Allen would provide supplies, and Aaron Sherritt was the guide.

Ward had another grievance. Despite being the only full-time detective assigned to the Kelly case, he was still a third class detective, the lowest rank. Standish had made airy promises of promotion but had then returned to Melbourne. Nicolson, since his return to Benalla headquarters, had promoted two other detectives in preference to him. Ward wrote to Frank Hare, who spoke to Standish, who promised Ward a promotion within three months. It was done against Nicolson's wishes.[4]

Aaron was unenthusiastic because he was now a newlywed. There were other things he would rather be doing with his evenings.

Sometime towards the end of 1879, Aaron had a romantic fling with a local Catholic girl named Ellen Barry, known as 'Belle' Barry. Belle became pregnant, and Aaron married her on Boxing Day at the Beechworth Catholic church, 'behind the altar', Aaron being a Protestant.

The Sherritt family did not approve of Belle. They said it was because she was a Catholic, yet Aaron's former fiancée, Joe Byrne's sister Kate, was also a Catholic, as was Jack's sweetheart. Whatever the reason, they never visited Aaron's selection again. Jack in particular did not like the new state of affairs, and there was tension between the brothers. In contrast, Belle's mother embraced her new son-in-law, visiting regularly.

Aaron had purchased a saddle as a present for his new wife, and had left it hanging on a fence at his parents' house. That evening, Aaron snuck away to assist with the police watch, but in the early morning, when he went to collect the saddle, it was gone.

He reported the theft to Detective Ward, and furiously blamed Jack. A merry-go-round had arrived at The Woolshed that summer. On the day of the theft, Aaron and Belle were taking rides on the merry-go-round. Jack was there too, but he had left early, and Aaron now believed he had gone to steal the saddle.

But Jack told Ward that he had nothing to do with it, and he believed it had been taken by Patsy Byrne. Ward obtained a search warrant for Mrs Byrne's selection, found the saddle, and charged Patsy Byrne and Mrs Byrne with theft.[5]

Aaron didn't believe it. He was sure it was Jack.

A necktie with Detective Ward's name on it was found on the ground near where the saddle had been taken. This did not incriminate Ward, as it might first appear, but Jack. Detective Ward had given clothes to both Aaron and Jack, including ties and jackets. In Aaron's mind, the discovery of an old Ward tie—which had been given to Jack—proved Jack's guilt. (It did nothing of the sort, of course, Jack could have dropped it when simply going about his business on his parents' property.)

Ward believed that Patsy Byrne had taken the saddle. That theory at least made sense: it was payback for breaking Katie Byrne's heart.

His temper up, Aaron stormed off to Sheep Station Creek. Seeing him, Jack jumped on a horse and galloped away. Aaron pursued him, caught him and dragged him off his horse. They fought. Aaron grabbed a stick and hit Jack on the head. Jack fell and lay still.[6]

Aaron rode into Beechworth, where he went into Paddy Allen's store and cried, 'I'm after murdering Jack! I've come to see Mr Ward and give myself up.'

But Jack wasn't dead. He came into town, found Aaron, and said, 'You bloody wretch. You thought you'd murdered me.' They eventually made up, in a manner, with whisky, but the bond was broken.

The new stake-out, the so-called 'Cave Party', seemed a waste of time to Ward. But it was Nicolson's idea and there was no point arguing. Ward hired one of his agents in Benalla to travel to the Beechworth district and make inquiries about what the police were up to. The agent was not told about the Cave Party, or why they were doing this, but merely to ask around. The agent heard nothing about the Cave Party.[7]

Ward learned that Aaron Sherritt himself had sabotaged the operation. Jack Sherritt explained to the detective that there was a mining run from the Chinese mining camp on the adjacent property into the Byrne selection which provided excellent cover for anyone coming to or going from the Byrnes.

Aaron had positioned the police watch party in a place where the end of this run was not visible. Joe could sneak in and out right under their noses if he wanted to. Informers in the Chinese camp confirmed that Joe had in fact done so. There were also reports of Ned and Joe purchasing alcohol at the Chinese camp.

Standish believed the operation was 'useless'. He was right. Nicolson's brilliant idea was an expensive failure. On 1 April, Nicolson instructed Ward to wrap it up.[8]

It had been a dreary, hard three months for the constables assigned to the watch. None of them were locals. Here they were, far from home on rotating night shifts, camping out in boring yet stressful conditions and eating cold camp food.

The operation was secret, and Ward suspected that these constables would be redeployed to their own districts without any acknowledgement on their records of the duty they had performed. His attempts to help those poor men backfired farcically, proving the adage that no good deed goes unpunished.

The Cave Party constables had returned and were at Beechworth barracks. Ward was required in Benalla to discuss the termination of the Cave Party. Before catching the train, he told Constable Haggard (whom he mistakenly judged to be brighter than the others) that they should all make a record of the duties they had performed.[9]

In Benalla, Ward told Nicolson what he was doing, and why: 'The men that have been engaged on that Cave Party have had very severe duty to perform.'

Nicolson replied that he was willing to make favourable entries on their personnel files, but the constables would all be leaving for their districts that day at noon, so the descriptions needed to be done immediately.[10]

Before he caught the train back to Beechworth, Ward telegraphed Mullane:

> Call on the special duty men for separate reports as to the nature
> of their duty. Hagger knows what to say.[11]

The men just wanted to go home, and resented being told by Ward and Mullane to write these reports. Here's an example of what they wrote:

> I am at a loss to know what to report about, as I am under the
> impression the Superintendent is well aware of the duty I have
> been engaged on, and how it was carried on.[12]

One of the constables reported that in his opinion, the outlaws knew all about their Cave Party. Ward told him that wasn't the point of this report, and their opinions on what the outlaws knew was not wanted. The constable tore up his report, and wrote a new report, stating that the outlaws did *not* know about the Cave Party. He later complained that Ward had told him to lie in his report.[13]

No good deed . . .

Ward asked Aaron Sherritt's parents to clean up the cave where the Cave Party had camped. They did so in the moonlight, loading everything into a nearby dray. There was detritus scattered all around. Some of the constables had even left oil coats behind.[14]

On a visit to his parents' selection, Aaron met his old friend James Wallace, who confided that he was writing a book about the Kelly Gang, which he hoped would be published after they were captured. He asked Aaron to tell him everything he knew about the police operations, and his role in that. When the book was published, if it became a bestseller, he and Aaron could share the profits. Aaron told him everything.[15]

45

The Graves Letter

At the end of April 1880, local parliamentarian Henry Graves received a letter signed 'M. Connor'. Some cursory inquiries convinced him that Connor was a pseudonym. Written by someone with inside knowledge, it provided a lengthy, detailed commentary on police activities. It included this passage:

> There has been a secret party of police in charge of Detective Ward of Beechworth for the last four months watching Mrs Burns house this party of police were going to succeed at once the gang who were supposed to be always visiting Mrs Burns were to be sold by Aaron Sherritt who is engaged at a very high salary by the police department and as it is well known that Sherritt did assist these outlaws when they first turned out, and will assist them again.
>
> And I would not be the least surprised if he carries all the information about the police movements to the Kellys yet this is the man that the Assistant Commissioner of Police places his confidence in this party is now withdrawn on account of the outlaws friends knowing what the police were up to, and it seems that the party was nothing but a complete farce as the Burns and Sherritts are great friends and know as much as the police about this secret party. In fact Detective Ward has expressed himself on several occasions to some of his friends in Beechworth, previous to the party going out, that he knew there was nothing in it but he must do something to curry favour with Nicolson . . .[1]

Nicolson was shown the letter by Graves. He had by now seen enough longwinded letters from James Wallace to recognise the handwriting. If the penny had not dropped before, it did now, but the revelation came too late. With a stroke of a pen, James Wallace had embarrassed and damaged Superintendent Nicolson, the highest-ranking officer in the district.[2]

In Melbourne, Graves circulated the letter around parliament. It was discussed in cabinet. The new police minister, Robert Ramsay, told Captain Standish that he wanted Nicolson out of the job. Standish telegrammed Nicolson about the decision.

In a panic, Nicolson caught the next train to Melbourne and hurried to parliament as soon as he arrived, looking for Ramsay. Standish was in the lobby. They argued. Nicolson asked who would replace him, to which Standish replied, Frank Hare.

Nicolson lost it. In recalling the incident, he later said, 'That's when my indignation broke forth'.[3]

Ramsay entered the building and tried to slip past the rowing officers without being noticed, but Nicolson saw Ramsay disappear up a flight of stairs, broke off with Standish, and ran after him. Standish hurried up the stairs after them.

Nicolson barged into Ramsay's office. Turning, he saw Standish behind him, glowering. He later publicly accused Standish of 'looking at me in an insulting manner'.[4]

Ramsay tried to calm him down. It wasn't personal. It did not reflect poorly on him. Ramsay said: 'It was just a change, like a game of cricket. A change of bowlers.'[5]

Nicolson retorted that there was very little analogy between the Kelly business and a game of cricket. He begged to be given one more month, because he was on the verge of catching the Kelly Gang. With a sigh, Ramsay conceded. One more month. But after that, he was off the Kelly case.[6]

Having won a reprieve, Nicolson returned to Benalla on the afternoon train.

Ramsay and Standish met with Frank Hare, instructing him to
replace Nicolson in a month. Hare complained that the job had nearly
killed him and his health wasn't up to it, but it made no difference.
They weren't asking.

In Standish's mind, the Graves Letter busted Aaron Sherritt's
credibility: whoever had written it must have learned about the cave
party from Sherritt. He forbade Nicolson from employing Sherritt as
an agent. In defiance of the order, Nicolson continued to do so, paying
Sherritt out of his own pocket.[7]

Some time in early 1880, a rumour reached the ears of the inspector-
general of education, Tom Bolam, that a teacher in the north-east
district had been a schoolfriend of the outlaw Joe Byrne. In the stuffy
departmental offices, Bolam launched his own bureaucratic investigation into James Wallace. Sifting through old records confirmed that
Byrne and Wallace had not only attended the same school, they had
been in the same class together.

Bolam said later, 'I saw that he had very great facilities for
assisting the outlaws.' He learned that Wallace was responsible
for two part-time schools, one near Greta and one near Beechworth,
requiring him to travel through the district, a perfect cover. He also
learned that Wallace and his wife ran a post office, giving them
access to confidential police records. The deeper he dug, the more
convinced he became that James Wallace, schoolteacher, was either
a fifth member of the Kelly Gang, or was providing assistance to
the gang.

Bolam took his concerns to the chief of police, Captain Standish,
who assured Bolam that his theory was 'well founded'. Bolam then

spoke to the minister of education, recommending that Wallace be transferred to another district. Wheels went into motion.[8]

On 24 May, Aaron's mother, Mrs Sherritt, visited the Byrne house on her way home. Joe Byrne and Dan Kelly rode up. Someone whistled, and then Ned Kelly and Steve Hart appeared. Patsy Byrne gave them some bread, bacon and something in a bottle. Then Patsy asked them, 'Which way did you come?'

Joe replied, 'The way we always come. We came down the steepest part of Wall's Gully.'

The next day, Mrs Sherritt encountered Joe at the edge of her property, where it joined Murphy's property, on Sheep Station Creek. Joe declared he had come to take the life of Aaron and Detective Ward.

He said, 'Those two had us starved to death!'[9]

She begged him not to murder Aaron. 'He has no harm, he wouldn't murder you.'

Joe replied, 'You need not try to impress that on my mind, because I tell you now that there was Ward and him, and Mr Hare, very nearly twice catching us, and that tells you whether they will hurt me or not.'

Mrs Sherritt hurried into Beechworth and told Detective Ward everything.

Ward arranged to meet with Aaron that night, to search for tracks that Byrne might have left. At the edge of Murphy's selection they picked up the trail, followed it into the Byrne selection, then out again, but it was raining hard, and the trail disappeared on a muddy road churned with other tracks.

Five days later, an informer codenamed Renwick told Detective Ward that he saw Joe Byrne with a greyhound on Crawford's farm, near the Byrne selection, going up the gully.

Ward said, 'I don't think you can be correct. It'll be Patsy Byrne, for he has a dog of that description.'

Renwick replied, 'I know it's one of the outlaws. You're frightened to follow them to catch them. I'll never work another rap if you don't take this opportunity.'[10]

When Nicolson read Ward's report of the exchange, he was excited. He only had three more days to catch the Kelly Gang, before he was removed. This was his last chance. He took the blacktrackers and some mounted constables by train to Beechworth and insisted that Aaron Sherritt act as their guide. According to O'Connor, Aaron Sherritt 'begged and prayed of Mr Nicolson not to go out' as his life was in danger. Nicolson consulted with O'Connor, Sadleir and Detective Ward, about whether to pursue Renwick's lead. They all advised against it. Nonetheless, Nicolson decided to go.[11]

It was worse than a false alarm. It was a trap. The trackers found not Joe Byrne, but his brother Patsy Byrne with a cow. He was dressed in clothes just like his brother; his facial hair was like his brother's; his boots were identical to Joe Byrne's boots, leaving the trackers to believe they were closing in on the outlaw. And, when Renwick had passed by, he had play-acted hiding behind rocks, as if trying to conceal himself. All to make it appear to Renwick as if he was his brother, Joe. As they searched, a well-known sympathiser of the gang named Batchelor appeared in front of them, coming face to face with Aaron.

Patsy Byrne had exposed two police informers—Renwick and Aaron Sherritt—in one swoop.

Detective Ward's strategy was simple and brutal at its core. By monitoring their families and friends, and by tracking their movements, to cut off the gang's supply lines. To pull the net slowly ever tighter.

A cat hunting a mouse patiently waits until the mouse becomes careless.

The properties of the families of all four gang members were surveilled, on and off, over the course of the year and a half to June 1880. A sympathiser codenamed Lord Byron was known to be supplying the gang with food; his activities were watched by informers.[12]

Constable Bracken was placed in Glenrowan, his true role being to monitor comings and goings at nearby Eleven Mile Creek.

Given that overarching strategy, it didn't even matter particularly if the gang knew they were being watched. It didn't matter if they suspected Aaron or Jack or any of their other friends of spying for the police. The very knowledge, indeed the mere suspicion, was enough to hamper them. They could not move freely. They could trust nobody. Even their efforts to purchase groceries were fraught with danger.

There were signs that the strategy was working.

Agent Smith of Lake Rowan reported on 24 April: '. . . gang said to be reduced to the last straits, and without means of carrying on longer. Movements circumscribed, and unable to find an unguarded bank to rob.' In May, an informer reported that the gang 'were miserable and ragged, and in want of food'.[13] Another informer, codenamed Denny, reported, 'They are very short of money, and becoming suspicious of their friends.'[14]

There had been signs the gang was planning something. It was not clear exactly what.

In March, mouldboards of ploughs had been stolen from Mr Sinclair of Glenrowan. More were subsequently stolen. When the thieves stole the mouldboards of a selector named Carney, they also stole two sides of bacon from him.[15]

Horses were stolen from a drover in Greta.[16] On 21 April, Agent Denny reported that the stolen mouldboards had been made into suits of armour for the outlaws to wear.[17]

The next day, Agent Smith reported that a man who had been provisioning the gang, McAuliffe, had told Ned Kelly that he could not help any further without money. McAuliffe told Kelly, 'he must do another bank'.[18]

There were reports that Ned's sister Maggie Skillion and known sympathisers like the Kellys' cousin Tom Lloyd, who was especially close to the gang, were becoming more active. There were suspicious comings and goings through the little town of Glenrowan, the railway town between Benalla and Wangaratta, and particularly at Mrs Jones' hotel in Glenrowan.

Superintendent Nicolson's spy, the Diseased Stock Agent, wrote to him in May:

> *Missing portions of cultivators described as jackets are now being worked, and fit splendidly. Tested previous to using, and proof at 10 yards.*[19]

The letter further said:

> *A break-out may be anticipated, as feed is getting very scarce. Five are now bad. I will post a note giving any bad symptoms I may perceive from Wangaratta on Monday or Tuesday at latest, and will wait on you for news how to proceed on a day which I shall then state, before end of the week. Other animals are, I fear, diseased.*

'Five are now bad.' Not four, but *five* outlaws, according to the Diseased Stock Agent. And due to scarce feed, a 'break-out' was imminent.

46

The Hut Party

Frank Hare arrived in Benalla on 2 June 1880. The changeover meeting with Nicolson was short and tense. O'Connor, the Queenslander in charge of the blacktrackers who believed he was second-in-command, was there. So too was Superintendent John Sadleir, officer in charge of the north-east district.

Nicolson said nothing about stolen mouldboards, or intelligence that the gang had made suits of bulletproof armour, or that another bank robbery was in the wind. With an airy gesture at the paperwork, he invited Hare to peruse the files to familiarise himself with the case, then left to catch the next train to Melbourne. At the railway station, he sent one last telegram to Constable Mullane in Beechworth, instructing him to fire all Ward's agents including Sherritt (codenamed Tommy).

> No more money for Tommy or his friends, Ward already instructed.[1]

Ward had not been instructed. When he learned of Nicolson's message, Ward caught the next train to Benalla, informed Hare, and had the agents reinstated.

Hare wanted three standing patrols ready to go, and wanted to resume surveillance of the Byrne property. Ward suggested they could resume surveillance by having the watch party reside in Sherritt's hut. 'They could stay in Aaron's place in the daytime . . . and leave at night, go down to Mrs Byrne's and watch all night.'

Ward's other motivation for suggesting the hut was that the watch party would provide police protection for Aaron Sherritt. Ward believed that posting a sentry outside the hut would advertise their presence, as the hut was on open land, next to the road.[2]

It was called the Hut Party. Ward bought calico and hung it on the doorway between the main room and the bedroom of the two-room hut, so that the four constables could remain hidden if visitors came. He also passed by the hut on his horse sometimes during daylight hours to check that there were no telltale signs that police were inside.[3]

The constables did not take the duty particularly seriously. They did not possess expert knowledge of the district (one was a Melbourne foot constable); did not have outstanding records; knew little about the Kelly Gang other than what they read in the papers; and were in the dark about their own operation. They differed in their opinions of Aaron Sherritt. For example, Constable Armstrong later testified that he trusted Sherritt, whereas Constable Alexander thought he was 'true sometimes and sometimes not'.[4]

Their incompetence was laid bare on Saturday 19 June, when Frank Hare arrived in Beechworth to personally inspect the Hut Party. Ward travelled with him, hiding in the boot of a buggy so he would not be seen approaching Sherritt's house. Ward entered first, and met constables Duross and Alexander. Belle Sherritt was there, but not Aaron.[5]

He asked Duross, 'Where are the other men?'

'Out the back chopping wood.' *Chopping wood?*

He said to Belle, 'Run out the back and tell them to come down as quick as they can and go to Byrne's!'[6]

Hare entered the hut, and asked Duross where constables Dowling and Armstrong were. He said, 'Watching the Byrne house.'

Frank Hare had performed this duty himself more than a year ago. He wanted to see the police watch. He told Alexander to lead him to the stake-out position near the Byrne house.

Constable Alexander pretended to get lost on the way, leading Hare on a very circuitous route, giving the others time to reach the observation point ahead of them. (Or maybe, without Aaron Sherritt to guide him, Alexander really did get lost as he claimed.)[7]

They arrived at the observation point, just 50 yards from the Byrne house. Hare asked Armstrong how he found his way there, since Constable Alexander did not seem to know the way.

Armstrong spilled the beans. 'The fact of it is—I'll tell the truth, no matter what's the result—Dowling and I were helping Sherritt to cut wood." His reason for not going out on watch: "We were seen by Chinamen last night, and we had arranged not to go down till ten o'clock tonight, and remain out a little longer in the morning.'

Hare said, as if to himself, 'That man has told me a lie.'[8] Then he told the constables they should be ashamed of themselves. He turned to Sherritt, who was now with them. 'What sort of men have you got with you here?'

Sherritt said, 'The man in charge is an excellent man, Armstrong. You couldn't get a better man in the world.'

Hare asked Armstrong if he believed the operation was worthwhile. Armstrong said it was. Hare asked him, 'Suppose you saw them come into the house, what would you do? What is your plan of operations?'

Armstrong said, 'I'd shoot them dead if I was certain they were the outlaws, if Aaron told me they were the outlaws.'

On the return to Beechworth, Hare was irritated with Detective Ward, who, he made it clear, had deceived him in an act of gross insubordination.

The very next night, at about 2 a.m. Monday morning, Aaron peered out the window and told the police to be quiet. They all looked out through gaps in the boards. Patsy Byrne was sitting on his grey mare, in the moonlight, on the road. He was staring at the hut.[9]

On Tuesday 22 June at Benalla headquarters, Frank Hare received a letter from Aaron's brother Jack, expressing grave concerns for his brother. He revealed that Joe Byrne would sometimes sleep in the haystack of a gang sympathiser in Sebastopol, and that Mrs Byrne had a large stash of clothes—enough for six families—stored in her house.[10]

Jack warned that the Hut Party would be discovered eventually and should be terminated. He also said that that Joe Byrne's brother Patsy was acting suspiciously. John wrote that Patsy was 'out all night and sleeps all day':

> Sir, I don't want to dictate to a gentleman of your ability, but the plan I would suggest is this—for Patrick Byrne to be watched minutely day and night, as this is a particular time.[11]

At the end of the letter, Jack warned that a new outrage was imminent:

> I am certain before long they are going to make another raid; I have not heard yet what it is. I am very busy now, but if you don't succeed, sir, I have a grand plan made up that I think will carry through.

Distrusting Jack Sherritt, Hare placed no great importance on the letter.

On the night of Tuesday 22 June, the Hut Party police saw Patsy Byrne ride into the ranges. When Detective Ward was informed, he and Aaron tried to follow Patsy's trail, but were unsuccessful. The blacktrackers came up by train from Benalla, but it had started raining and the tracks were gone.

On Wednesday 23 June, the Hut Party police saw Patsy Byrne sneaking around the back of Aaron Sherritt's hut.[12] They did not report the incident to Detective Ward.[13]

On Thursday 24 June, Hare met with the agent known as Diseased Stock Agent (or DSA) in Benalla. In an agitated state, DSA told him, 'There is no doubt that they are going to make a raid very shortly on some bank.'[14]

'How do you know?'

'I know it from various sources.'

Superintendent Sadleir, who was present, interjected: 'But haven't you been telling us this for the last six or seven months?'

DSA admitted that he had thought the gang would rob a bank long before now. He was not aware that the gang had been thwarted by Detective Ward's protracted campaign of misinformation against them.

Hare said, 'I hear they're going to appear in armour.'

DSA said, 'Yes, no doubt about it.'

Hare asked, 'How is it to be used?'

'They will wear it when they're robbing the bank.'

'Is it bulletproof?'

'Yes, at ten yards.'

Hare retorted, 'I don't believe that any armour ever made, that man could carry, would stand a Martini Henry bullet at ten yards.'

DSA said, 'Well, this is proof.'

These were extraordinary revelations. Afterwards, when the two officers were alone, Hare sought Sadleir's opinion, commenting, 'This looks black to me.'

Sadleir laughed off Hare's concerns. 'Oh, that man has been giving us this information for months,' he said dismissively. 'He's the most sanguine and tantalising man I know.' He told Hare about this man's previously unfulfilled promises to provide important revelations (without stopping to ponder that perhaps, today, DSA was actually fulfilling those promises).

Sadleir acknowledged that the man was sincere. He meant well, and was doing his best, and probably even believed that the things he said were true. But that didn't mean they *were* true.[15]

Relieved, Hare said, 'If this is the sort of person you've been depending on, it's no wonder you haven't caught the Kellys.'[16]

With Sadleir's reassurances that DSA's information was groundless, Hare let it slide.

That same Thursday, schoolteacher James Wallace answered a knock at the door. It was a representative of the Education department informing him that he was no longer the teacher at the Hurdle Creek and Bobinawarrah schools. He had been transferred to a school in the township of Yea, eighty miles south, effective immediately.[17]

A pillar of support for the gang was gone.

Also on that same Thursday, O'Connor and the Queensland Native Police departed. Having spent fifteen months assisting in the search for the Kelly Gang, they had been recalled by the Queensland government. They boarded the train to Melbourne, where they were to travel by sailing ship to Brisbane.

Their departure occurred two days in advance of the lapsing of the *Felons Apprehension Act*. Always intended to be a temporary measure, the Act had a built-in sunset clause, continuing in force 'until the end of the next session of parliament'. There had been continuances since then, but an election had been held in March, and the colonial government led by Premier James Service had not extended the Act. It expired on Saturday, 26 June 1880.

From that day forward, the four members of the Kelly Gang were no longer outlaws. That was the day they murdered Aaron Sherritt.

47

The murder of Aaron Sherritt

At 6.30 p.m. on Saturday evening, there was a knock at the back door of Aaron Sherritt's hut.[1]

Inside the hut, on that cold winter's night, the fireplace was crackling, and the air smelt of cooked food. Aaron was home with his pregnant wife, Belle, and his mother-in-law, Mrs Barry. They were eating dinner with Constable Duross. The other three constables—Armstrong, Dowling and Alexander—were in the bedroom trying to get some rest in advance of their night-time watch duties.

When they heard the knock, Duross hurried into the bedroom to hide. The doorway to the bedroom was covered by the calico sheet provided by Detective Ward.[2]

Aaron answered the knock at the back door. It was only Anton Wicks, a local farmer, who had lost his way in the dark. Wicks lived only a few hundred yards away, so he must have been drunk to be lost this close to home. Wicks asked for directions.

Aaron said, 'Do you see that sapling over there?' It was the first line of an old joke.

Belle said, 'Go outside and show him the way.'

Aaron stepped outside. They heard him say, 'Who's that?' Then he stepped back in.

A gunshot blasted through the open doorway.

Aaron staggered backwards, wounded in the chest.

Joe Byrne appeared in the doorway, holding a shotgun. He fired it a second time.

Aaron fell to the floor. Mrs Barry ran to him and knelt down by his head.

Belle cried, 'Oh, Joe, Joe! What have you done, what did you shoot poor Aaron for?'[3]

Byrne said, 'They will never put me away again.'[4] He moved out of the doorway, beyond the threshold.

Mrs Barry asked that she and Belle be allowed out of the house. From out of the darkness, Byrne said he allowed it, but he ordered her to first open the front door. When she did so, she came face to face with Dan Kelly pointing a gun at her.[5]

When they went outside, they saw a miserable Anton Wicks standing there by the chimney in handcuffs. Wicks had, sometime before, filed a complaint that Joe Byrne had stolen his horse, so Byrne had little sympathy for him.[6]

Byrne asked Belle, 'Who's that man along in the room? That man who went into the room? I'll put a ball through you and your daughter if you don't tell me.'[7]

'That's a man by the name of Duross,' Belle replied.

Byrne asked, 'What is he?'

Belle said, 'He is looking for work about here.'

Byrne told her to go inside and make Duross come out. He kept her mother close in front of him while Belle went inside.[8]

When she went into the bedroom, the police were scrambling around, looking for their weapons in the dark. They gestured for her to leave. Duross said he was not going out. She returned, and told Byrne that Duross wouldn't come.[9]

He said to Mrs Barry, 'Go and bring him out or I'll shoot you, too.'

When she entered the bedroom, the four constables had moved into defensive positions. Armstrong and Alexander were on either side of the doorway, Duross was near the window, and Dowling was facing the doorway. Duross asked her who was outside. She answered: Joe Byrne, Dan Kelly and Anton Wicks.

Mrs Barry went outside and informed Byrne that Duross still wouldn't come. Byrne had heard whispering and the clicking of weapons. He asked her how many people were in there. She dare not say 'one', so she said, 'two'.

He asked if there were more than two. She said no.

He asked, 'What are their names?'

'I don't know,' Mrs Barry replied.

'How green you are,' Byrne said to her. 'If you be telling me lies, I will murder both of you.'[10]

He called to someone hidden in the scrub nearby that there were 'bloody dogs' inside that wouldn't come out. He walked around to the outside of the bedroom, then fired at the wall.

Mrs Barry broke down and begged him not to kill them. Byrne said he wouldn't, but he insisted that whoever was in the house must come out, making it clear that he intended to shoot those currently inside.[11]

He sent Belle inside, keeping Mrs Barry as a hostage at the end of his gun. When she returned alone, he asked her how many men were in the room. Her mother nudged her as a signal for her not to answer. She said nothing.

He fired into the wall again, and declared that he would 'riddle the bloody house!'

Byrne sent Belle in again. Dan Kelly had previously been inside the main room, by the table, but he was gone when she returned.[12]

Byrne called to the police to show themselves or he would shoot them down like dogs. He called out, 'Come out here, out of the house!' Then he called to someone, 'I'll make them come out.' They heard Byrne whistling outside. It seemed to Mrs Barry that his whistle was a signal to someone, not Dan, hidden further away in the shadow of the forest.[13]

Meanwhile, Dan Kelly had begun collecting sticks, piling them against the side of the house, and talking to Byrne about setting fire to the house.[14]

Mrs Barry called through the door, 'Come out, they're going to burn the house down.'

Byrne sent Belle in again. Dowling grabbed her and tried to pull her down under the bed with him. She struggled and resisted, so Armstrong helped. The two of them dragged her under the bed with them, and held her in place by putting their feet on her.[15]

Mrs Barry cried to Byrne, 'My daughter will be burned!'

He replied, 'Well, call her out.'

She called to Belle to come out. Belle called back that that she was not allowed.[16]

The fire was ready. Dan struck a match, but the wind blew it out.

Mrs Barry declared: 'If you set fire to the house, and the girl gets shot or burned, you can just kill me along with them.'[17]

Byrne asked her if there was any kerosene on the property. She said, 'No, we burn candles.'[18]

Byrne fired in through the door towards the bedroom, then sent Mrs Barry in to find out if he had hit anyone, telling her, 'Go and see, did that shot go in through the boards?'[19]

She said, 'If I go in, they might shoot me.'

Byrne replied, 'If you don't go, *I* will shoot you.'[20]

Mrs Barry went into the bedroom, Alexander was sitting near a wall on the far side of the room, Armstrong was at the foot of the bed, and Duross and Dowling were under it with her daughter. She tried to pull Belle out from under the bed, but Duross and Dowling grabbed her, pulled her down onto the floor, and would not let her go.[21]

As she struggled, Dowling told her, 'You had better stop in, Mrs Barry, and if you stop in the outlaws won't set fire to the place while there are women in the place.'[22]

They could hear the outlaws outside, talking to each other. They could not get the fire to start. It had been raining, and all the wood was too wet.

They heard one of the outlaws call to the other, 'Look out for the window in the bedroom.' A short time later, a shot fired into the bedroom.

They heard Byrne shout, 'Who fired that?'

Then Dan Kelly shouted a response: 'It was me.' He added, 'All right, look out for the window in the front of the house.'

Boom. The front window shattered.

Five more shots were fired into the bedroom in rapid succession. Constable Dowling, who was covering the door, had taken cover behind a large sack of flour. One of the bullets hit the sack, splitting it open.[23]

Constable Armstrong whispered, 'Well, boys, I'll go out, if you'll come with me.'[24]

Duross and Dowling refused, because they reasonably believed they would all be killed the moment they exited the hut. They argued that it was better to wait until morning.

They heard discussion about releasing Anton Wicks. Neither Byrne nor Dan Kelly had the key to the handcuffs. One of them went away, presumably to the third, hidden accomplice, and returned with the key.

They heard Wicks leave. They heard voices from time to time, but there were no more demands for them to come out.

Aaron's dog barked, then whimpered, then howled.

The moon rose, improving their situation, because it would be harder for the outlaws to remain hidden outside.

By midnight, the fire had burned down, reducing visibility inside and thus giving some protection, and they had not heard any voices for a while. Dowling and Armstrong crept out and closed the front and back doors.[25]

They heard voices outside throughout the night. They could not tell whose voices, or how many. Eventually they allowed Belle and Mrs Barry to move around inside the house, but the four constables remained hidden in the bedroom.

Aaron's dog howled all night.

Constable Armstrong went outside at dawn, followed by Constable Alexander. A search of the perimeter confirmed that the outlaws had gone. Only then, after the all-clear had been given, did Duross and Dowling emerge.[26]

They moved Aaron's body to the side of the hut and covered it with a blanket. Armstrong then wrote three copies of a letter to be delivered to Detective Ward seven miles away at Beechworth.[27]

A schoolteacher named O'Donaghue walked past along the road. Armstrong stopped him and asked him to deliver the message for them. He agreed, but returned a short time later, explaining that given the circumstances, his wife would not let him, because the outlaws might kill him for helping the police. He said he knew another man who might help and would send him along shortly. But the friend never came.[28]

Armstrong eventually delivered the message to Beechworth himself, reporting to Mullane at half past one in the afternoon. Mullane fetched Detective Ward, who was eating lunch.[29]

Ward was shocked by the news of Aaron's death and appalled that it had taken so long to be notified. 'Why didn't you let us know before?' he asked Armstrong. 'You just sat there over the body, and never went for help?'[30]

Ward rushed to the telegraph office to inform Superintendent Hare, but Hare could not be contacted, so he then sent a message to Captain Standish in Melbourne. By the time he arrived at Sherritt's hut, inquisitive locals had heard about it and were walking around, destroying footprints and ruining the crime scene.

As for Aaron himself, he died dressed head to foot in clothes given to him by Detective Ward.

The telegraph operator found Hare at the railway station and told him to come quickly: there was a very urgent message. Hare was disgusted by what he saw as cowardice. He said later, 'My view is that those men ought to have either died, or shot the Kellys. One or the other.'[31]

The following year, the Police Royal Commission issued an even blunter assessment:

> The conduct of those constables throughout the night was characterised by shameful poltroonery, which, in the army, would have been punished by summary expulsion from the service with every accompanying mark of contempt and degradation.[32]

Standish saw it differently, telling the commissioners, 'My firm belief is that if they had left the house every one would have been shot dead.' And Ellen Barry, who witnessed it all, concurred: 'I do not think the men would have had any chance of doing anything by rushing out. I think they would have been shot.'[33]

Hare fired off a telegram to Standish, informing him of the murder. He requested that the Queensland Native Police, currently in Melbourne waiting for their ship, return to the district immediately.[34]

The messages from Ward and Hare reached the Melbourne Club at 2.30 p.m., but Standish didn't see them until 4.30 p.m., as he had gone out for a late lunch. He immediately sent a letter by hansom cab to O'Connor, the head of the blacktracking team currently staying in Essendon, and another message to Mr Ramsay, the police minister. He telegrammed a reply to Hare that O'Connor had been asked to return to Benalla on Monday.

Hare fired back:

> If Mr O'Connor does not come up tonight, it is no use his coming at all, and I will take my two blacks with my party, and start off tonight.[35]

Standish arrived back at the Melbourne Club just as Ramsay was arriving there to see him.[36] Together, they met with the minister for railways, Mr Gillies. Standish explained the need to send search parties to Beechworth immediately, or the outlaws' trail would be lost. Gillies approved the departure of a special train to Beechworth, writing a signed order to that effect. Standish pocketed the order. He returned to the Melbourne Club just as O'Connor was arriving there.

According to Standish, O'Connor was surprisingly flippant. Standish recalled that, 'He, in a rather haw-haw way, said he did not see any objection, and said he would go.'[37]

Standish took Gillies' order for the special train and delivered it to Spencer Street Station. It was to depart at 10 p.m.[38]

He also sent couriers across town to four journalists, informing them of the imminent departure of the special. They were George Allen from the Melbourne *Daily Telegraph*, Thomas Carrington from *The Australasian Sketcher*, Joe Melvin from *The Argus* and John McWhirter from *The Age*. All four hurried to Spencer Street Station and took their seats.[39]

The special departed at 9.57 p.m. It stopped at Essendon at 10.15 p.m. to collect O'Connor and the Queensland trackers.

Travelling at high speed, the train crashed through a boom gate at Craigieburn, which tore off the engine brake and the footbridge of the carriage and destroyed the light on the guard's van. The guard was looking out from the side of the train at the time and 'had a narrow escape'. The train came to a halt for a few minutes, then restarted, relying on the brake in the guard's van as a substitute for the engine brake.[40]

Glenrowan

48

The Curnow family's day trip

Late on Sunday morning 27 June 1880, Glenrowan's 25-year-old schoolteacher, Tom Curnow, took his family for a pleasant country ride in their horse and buggy. Tom's wife, Jean, sat beside him, cradling their eleven-month-old baby girl, Muriel, and Tom's sister Cathy climbed in, too. Jean's brother David Mortimer joined them, but as there wasn't room in the buggy, he rode alongside on his horse.[1]

Tom Curnow had been born in England, but had come to Victoria with his parents at the age of two. His early childhood memories were of growing up near the goldfields of Ballarat. He had been the Glenrowan schoolteacher for four years, and had been married to Jean (who was sometimes known by her middle name, Isobel) for two years.

As they set out on that crisp wintry morning, they had no idea that Aaron Sherritt's body lay on the cold dirt floor of his hut in the hills twenty miles east, while four constables near the body fretted about what to do. They couldn't know that the railway workers camped on the edge of Glenrowan had been taken hostage overnight. And they certainly had no inkling that, in the next 24 hours, Tom would play a critical role in bringing down Ned Kelly.

Around midnight the previous night, Ned Kelly and Steve Hart had entered the quarry workers' camp, rousing the sleeping men. The foreman, Louis Piazzi, was in the tent at the end with a woman. When he heard someone outside shouting orders, Piazzi rolled out of bed and grabbed his shotgun.

Kelly ripped open the tent cover; he was holding a rifle. Seeing Piazzi's gun, Kelly shouted, 'You bastard! You lift a gun to me?'[2]

Kelly fired his rifle as Piazzi knocked it aside. It fired into the bed. The woman screamed.

Kelly backed out of the tent. He had brought one of the railway workers, J.C. Lowe, with him to rouse the quarrymen, and now berated Lowe for not telling him there was a woman in that tent.[3]

Kelly then marched several of the workers at gunpoint to a bend in the railway line along the gully north of town, near the 'Sydney Crossing', where he ordered them to remove a length of track, telling them he intended to derail the next train that passed through Glenrowan.[4]

There were no regular passenger trains on that line on Sundays. Kelly knew that the only train passing through that Sunday would be a police special train speeding up to Beechworth to investigate Aaron Sherritt's murder.[5]

One of the railway workers later testified that Kelly said, 'There are a lot of police and blacktrackers coming up from Benalla, and I want you to take up the rails, and break their bloody necks.'[6]

Ahead, the Curnow family saw people gathered near Mrs Jones' hotel. Tom Curnow wondered if the hotel's proprietor, Ann Jones, had died, as she had been very sick recently.[7]

On the road was Mr Stanistreet, the local stationmaster, signalling for them to stop. Tom Curnow asked, 'What's the matter?'

Stanistreet said, 'The Kellys are here. You can't go through.'

They realised now that the gate in front of them was blocked by a stranger on horseback with two revolvers in his belt, talking to a young man named John Delaney.

The stranger wheeled his horse, came up and asked, 'Who are you?'

Curnow told him.

'And who are those?'

Curnow introduced his family to the stranger, who was Ned Kelly. Kelly said, 'I'm sorry, but I must detain you.'

They tethered the horses to a nearby fence and joined the other townspeople, who were listening intently to Kelly's conversation with Delaney. It wasn't a conversation as much as an aggressive interrogation. Kelly had learned that Delaney had recently shown kindness to a constable, and he was displeased.

While riding their spring wagon to Wangaratta, Delaney and his sister had passed a constable walking in the same direction. The constable's horse had been injured in a fall, and he had to walk everywhere until it healed. They had given him a ride into Wangaratta in their wagon.[8]

Pointing his revolver, Kelly ranted at Delaney, loudly accused him of doing favours for police, and of being 'sympathetic' to police. He accused Delaney of wishing to *join* the police, all because he gave a constable a ride.[9]

White as a sheet, Delaney denied the accusations.[10]

Kelly turned to the onlookers, and said that since the government had made it a crime to assist his gang, he now declared it a crime against the Kelly Gang to assist the police. He warned that he would take the life of *anyone* who helped the police, in *any* manner. In fact, he would kill anyone who even showed so much as friendly feelings towards the police. Waving his revolver, he glared at the onlookers and snarled, 'I can, and will, find you out!'[11]

He then announced that he and Delaney would settle their differences with a duel to the death. He made Delaney stand against a fence post, then handed him a revolver.

Delaney took it with a trembling hand. Kelly went to an opposite fence post, faced Delaney in readiness, then called out to him to fire the first shot.[12]

Delaney started crying.

Some of the onlookers pleaded with Kelly to spare the poor man's life.

Kelly demanded that Delaney promise never to apply to join the police force. Delaney agreed. Kelly said, 'I forgive you this time, but mind you be careful for the future.'

Joe Byrne was calmly watching nearby, having ridden the 25 miles from the Sherritt hut to Glenrowan with Dan Kelly overnight. Byrne produced a bottle of brandy, filled a tumbler, and offered it to people in the crowd. Some took a drink. He took the tumbler, two-thirds full, to Delaney, who drank it all.[13]

Kelly did not partake. He ordered everyone to move across to Jones' hotel, where there were more hostages. He ordered some boys in the crowd to take the Curnows' horse and buggy across.

There were, by now, around 50 hostages, including all the railway workers who had been captured the night before. The hostages were allowed to move freely around the hotel grounds and inside the hotel, with the exception of one locked room, to which only the outlaws had the key. Constable Bracken, Glenrowan's only policeman, was not among the hostages, because he had not been outside that day: he was convalescing in bed after a severe illness.

Inside the hotel, Dan Kelly invited Tom Curnow to join him for a drink at the bar. Over a brandy, Curnow asked Dan about the rumours. Dan replied that they had been near Beechworth overnight, that they had 'done some shooting', and that they had 'burned the bastards out'. That was a lie, but in all likelihood, Dan and Joe believed their hail of gunfire had killed at least some of the police and the two women inside Sherritt's hut.[14]

Joe Byrne entered and, gesturing at Dan's glass, said, 'Be careful, old man.'

'All right,' said Dan, and added water to his brandy.[15]

Curnow expressed surprise that the outlaws had stuck up Glenrowan of all places. Byrne and Dan Kelly told him that they had come there in order to derail a special train full of inspectors, police and blacktrackers that would be passing through Glenrowan to Beechworth to look for them there. They said they had ridden hard across country, sometimes 'up to the saddle girths in water', to reach Glenrowan, and that they had sabotaged the railway line at a particularly dangerous section; and that they were 'going to send the train and its occupants to hell'.[16]

The gang declared that they would shoot any survivors from the train wreck. They said that if any civilians were on the train, they would suffer the same fate, and deserve it, because they were accompanying the police. Once all the police were dead, they planned to rob the Benalla banks.[17]

Horrified by the planned mass murder, Curnow recalled later that he resolved to do whatever he could to stop them:

> About one o'clock I was standing in the yard of Jones' hotel, thinking of the intentions of the gang, and I keenly felt that it was my duty to do anything that I could to prevent the outrage which the outlaws had planned from being accomplished, and I determined that I would try to do so.[18]

As Curnow stood pondering, Dan Kelly came out, and invited him back inside to dance. Curnow refused, saying that he couldn't dance in the boots he was wearing. Ned Kelly came out, overheard Curnow's excuse, and said, 'Come on. Never mind your boots.'

Curnow said he was lame and couldn't dance barefoot, and he did not want to dance in the heavy boots he was wearing, but if he was allowed to fetch his dancing shoes from the school (where he lived), he would gladly dance with Dan.

Ned Kelly said he would escort Curnow there to get his dancing shoes. Dan, who was partly drunk, complained that *he* wanted to escort Curnow home. Someone nearby—Curnow didn't see who—mentioned that they would have to pass the police barracks on the way to the school. As far as everyone knew, Constable Bracken was still there, bedridden.

Kelly demanded to know if it was true. Curnow answered, 'Yes, we shall have to pass the barracks. I had forgotten that.'[19]

Dan Kelly accompanied Curnow into the hotel, and they danced together.

When they finished, Kelly said that he should go and capture Constable Bracken, and the postmaster Reynolds, too. Curnow laughed approvingly, and said that he'd rather see that happen than be given a hundred pounds. He asked if he could come along and watch. Kelly didn't reply.

In the mid-afternoon, Kelly was fiddling with the revolver he had taken from the foreman, Piazzi, the night before. It exploded, hitting a nearby labourer named George Metcalf in the face. Blood was streaming down Metcalf's face. Mr Stanistreet got his son to bathe and treat Metcalf's injury.

Kelly said, 'I didn't mean to fire. It went off accidentally.'[20]

Metcalf died from the injury several months later.

Ned Kelly organised another round of dancing, making the hostages do the *jump*, and the *bop, step and jump* with them. When the dancing finished, the exhausted, sleep-deprived outlaws rested.[21]

Curnow crossed to Stanistreet's house, which was inside the allowed confinement zone, and where his family was being held. They saw him coming and came outside to meet him. His sister was wearing a red llama wool scarf. An idea surfaced: could her red scarf be used as a warning signal?

When they went into the house, Curnow saw Steve Hart lying on the sofa with three guns beside him. Hart complained that his feet hurt. He said he had been wearing the same boots for several days and nights. Curnow suggested soaking them. While the others tended to

Hart's sore feet, Curnow moved out to the back of the house, where he had a hushed conversation with Mr and Mrs Stanistreet.

The Stanistreets wanted to raise the alarm. Curnow knew that Mr Stanistreet had a revolver. He asked if the outlaws had confiscated it. Mr Stanistreet said no, he still had it with him. They returned inside.

Dan Kelly came across from the hotel, looking for a parcel; he seemed distraught about not locating it. Thinking it might be at McDonnell's hotel (the other hotel in town), he went there but came back without luck. Curnow offered to go back to Jones' hotel and help him keep searching there. Dan accepted his offer.

As they crossed back to Jones' hotel, Curnow told Dan that he wanted to talk to Ned Kelly privately. Dan disappeared and returned with Ned.

Curnow told him that Stanistreet possessed a revolver at his home that had been issued by the Railway department and advised Ned to confiscate it, 'as someone might get it and do them an injury'.

Kelly thanked him, and stormed across to the Stanistreet residence.

Curnow said later, 'I perceived that I had, in great measure, obtained their confidence by telling them this.'[22]

At dusk—probably around the time that the special police train was sliding out of Spencer Street Station—Curnow overheard a conversation between Ned Kelly and the hotel proprietor, Ann Jones. Kelly told Jones he needed to go and capture Constable Bracken. He wanted Jones' daughter Jane to come along, so she could call out from the street, luring Bracken outside. Jones asked him not to take her daughter. It would be fine, Kelly reassured her, because he had no intention of killing Bracken, only kidnapping him.

Curnow interjected, suggesting that, instead of Jane, Kelly could take Curnow's brother-in-law David Mortimer, a friend of Bracken's. Bracken would trust him. Kelly liked the idea.

Curnow followed him to the stable, and asked if, when they went to capture Bracken, he could take his family home. He assured Kelly, 'I'm with you heart and soul.'

Kelly said, 'I know that, and can see it.' He agreed to the suggestion.

Curnow hurried across to the postmaster's office, told his family they were going home imminently, and brought them to Jones' hotel. Meanwhile, Ned and the other outlaws had started playing cards with some of their prisoners. Curnow and his family waited in the kitchen for two hours.

The card game eventually finished, and Ned told Curnow to get his buggy ready. Curnow hitched his horse and took the buggy to the front of the hotel, where his family climbed in. They sat in the buggy and waited . . . for another hour.

Eventually, Ned Kelly and Byrne joined them on horseback. Both carried a mysterious bundle, and both wore oilskin overcoats that looked surprisingly bulky. They were going to collect the postmaster, Reynolds, on the same trip, and brought with them Reynolds' brother and son, and another boy who lived with Reynolds. The two boys climbed up and squeezed into the Curnow buggy.

Constable Bracken wasn't there. Kelly took cover at the corner of a nearby building and Byrne guarded the hostages while Mortimer knocked and called out, to no reply. Kelly took the other three hostages to Reynolds' house, and soon returned with both Reynolds and Bracken in custody. Constable Bracken said defiantly that they would never have captured him if he wasn't bedridden at Reynolds' house.

Kelly told Curnow to take the women and the baby home, but not Mortimer.

He told them, 'Go quietly to bed, and don't dream too loud.' Then he said that someone would check on them later, and if they weren't in bed asleep, they would be killed.[23]

When the outlaws were out of earshot, Curnow told his wife and sister that he had no intention of going to sleep, but instead planned to go to Benalla to warn the police that the railway line had been sabotaged. The horse and buggy would be too dangerous, so he would have to go on foot.

They thought he was mad. It would take him all night to cover the 18 miles from their house to Benalla, and that at a constant brisk pace. And he wouldn't make it anyway, they said, because he would be discovered and shot. Or the outlaws would go to the house, discover him missing, and shoot the women. Curnow reminded them what would happen if he did not try: a train would derail, and the outlaws would murder any survivors.

Jean was in a state of fear and dread. She was so agitated that Curnow soothed her by telling her that he had changed his mind. He wouldn't do it after all. It was just a crazy, reckless idea. They put her to bed, then Curnow asked to borrow his sister's red scarf to use as a red stop signal. He also took a candle and matches to illuminate it. Then he left.

He hurried through the undergrowth, still wet from the recent rainfall, towards the railway line.[24] Before long, as he ran along the line in the dark, he heard a train approaching. When he reached a long, straight stretch—long enough to give the driver a chance to halt the train—he stopped, lit the candle, and held the red scarf in front of it, hoping that when the train came around the corner onto the stretch, the driver would see it.

Sometimes, history turns on the smallest things: a scarf; a candle; an opportunity seized.

Incredibly, Curnow's crazy plan worked.

49

The night special

On Sunday evening, in the brisk night air, Frank Hare waited on the railway platform at Benalla. With him were Senior-Constable Kelly and seven other constables. Not Superintendent Sadleir, however. Hare had told Sadleir to stay home in Benalla, 'in case anything occurred' in his absence.[1]

The special train bringing O'Connor and his Native Police was on its way from Melbourne. From Benalla, they would travel north to Wangaratta, and then east up the mountain to Beechworth. This was not a passenger train and they wouldn't be stopping at places on the way, like Everton or Glenrowan. Hare figured they would arrive in Beechworth shortly before dawn, ride directly to Sherritt's hut, and try to pick up the trail of the outlaws. Given his health, he had tried to snatch a bit of sleep earlier in the evening. It was going to be a long night.

The train arrived at Benalla at 1.30 a.m. Sub-Inspector O'Connor disembarked with his five trackers. Hare noted with disapproval that O'Connor's wife and sister-in-law had joined him as passengers. There were also four journalists on board.[2]

A local man named Charles Rawlins arrived, asking if he could catch the special to Beechworth with them. Rawlins was an entrepreneur who had introduced cattle trucks to the Victorian railways. Due to his commercial relationship with Victorian Railways, he was allowed to travel anywhere in the colony for free. Since there were already several civilians on the train, Hare allowed him on board, sending him to sit with the reporters.[3]

Earlier that day, before Standish had arranged the special from Melbourne, Hare had arranged his own special train from Benalla to Beechworth as a precaution. It was no longer needed, but as he now had a spare engine at his disposal, he decided to use it as a 'pilot' engine, to travel ahead of the train as a safety measure. Without any carriages, the pilot could stop more quickly than the main train. If danger arose, the pilot engine could brake, and signal the train behind to do the same. It seemed prudent, given that Kelly had threatened to derail a train on more than one occasion.[4]

The police loaded their horses into a carriage in a siding, which was then rolled out and attached to the end. While the horse carriage was being attached, one of the engineers for the pilot engine asked Hare if a policeman could be posted in the pilot engine as a lookout.

Hare liked the idea. He took Constable Barry to the engine and showed him the narrow platform alongside the boiler. He told Barry to ride there, on that platform, and to keep a sharp eye out. Hare tied some straps to the boiler for Barry to hold onto.

When they learned that the special train's brakes had been destroyed at Craigieburn, making it quite unsafe, Hare and the stationmaster decided to switch engines. The Benalla engine, which was intended to be the pilot, would pull the train, while the engine that had brought it from Melbourne, having no brakes, would be the pilot.

The drivers argued against the change, but the swap was made. The special's engine was detached and brought forward on the tracks. A brake van was attached to it, as a makeshift brake system. The Benalla engine was then slowly backed out, and attached to the front of the special.[5]

Hare brought Constable Barry and some straps to the pilot engine, but the driver refused to let Barry aboard, saying it would be too dangerous. That might have been a valid point, except that the same driver, for all his safety concerns, had driven the special at reckless speed, crashed through a boom gate and was miffed at not being allowed to continue without a functioning brake system. Barry rode in the carriages with the others.

Before they departed, on a hunch, or some sense of foreboding, Hare asked the stationmaster for the key to the carriage, and was given it. Typically the carriage doors were locked and only the driver or stationmaster could open them.

The pilot engine started down the line at 2 a.m., and the special started five minutes after that. The drivers were instructed to take them directly to Beechworth without any further stops.

Just before Glenrowan, the pilot engine driver saw a red light ahead. As he brought the engine to a halt, Curnow stepped onto the tracks. The train guard, Archibald McPhee, shouted, 'What's the matter?'

Curnow said simply, 'The Kellys.'

McPhee jumped down. Curnow told him that the Kelly Gang had captured Glenrowan, the line was torn up on the other side of town, and that they planned to ambush the train after it was derailed.[6] McPhee told Curnow that a special police train was coming behind, and was only a few minutes away. He said that, given this news, they would stop the pilot engine at Glenrowan Station and signal the special train to stop there too.

Curnow cried, 'No, no! Don't you do that, or you will get shot!'

While they talked, the driver sounded the whistle several times.

Curnow said later, 'Every second I stood there I expected a bullet.'[7]

He invited Curnow to jump aboard, but Curnow declined, saying that his wife and sister were without protection, and that he needed to get back to them. He turned and ran off down the line, back towards Glenrowan.[8]

The passengers on the special heard the whistle of the pilot engine. The train stopped. Hare stuck his head out of the window and peered forward. He could see the three red lights of the pilot engine, also stopped on the tracks ahead. He grabbed his shotgun from the luggage rack, loaded some cartridges into it, slung more cartridges around his neck, unlocked the carriage door and climbed down onto the tracks.

He walked along the line towards the three red lights of the pilot engine. He met McPhee, the pilot engine guard, who told him that a man on the track had made a stop signal with a scarf and a candle. The man had told him that the gang had sabotaged the line, but McPhee couldn't remember whether the break was on this side, or the other side, or Glenrowan. The man had also told McPhee that the Kelly Gang 'had taken possession of the town'.

Hare told the pilot driver, 'I think the best plan will be for you to go quietly along to Glenrowan and we'll follow close up to you in the train.'

The stoker looked out into the darkness ahead, and said that he didn't like the idea of arriving in Glenrowan without police protection. Hare relented. They shunted the pilot back down the line to the special and hitched the two engines together.

Back inside the special, Hare addressed all the passengers, explaining the situation. He instructed Senior-Constable Kelly, his second-in-command, to ride up front on the pilot engine with two other constables.

They briefly considered getting the horses out immediately, but decided against it. The carriage lights were extinguished. The train started again, and slowly brought them into the station.

When Curnow arrived home, his wife and sister were both wide awake. His wife was almost insane with fear. The train whistle had woken her up, and she had realised he was missing. She told him that the outlaws had suits of armour. If only he had known that earlier, he could have told the engine driver![9]

They hid the scarf and his wet clothes, blew out the lights, and went to bed. They lay awake, expecting the gang or their agents to come and murder them. Surely the gang had heard the engine whistle; had realised that someone had given a warning; and had realised who had done it.

They waited in their beds for the outlaws, but the outlaws did not come.

50

Gunfight at Jones' hotel

As the train slid to a halt at the Glenrowan platform, everyone inside was silent. It was 2.30 a.m. The driver came back to warn Superintendent Hare that he had seen someone on the platform. They waited for a moment, then Hare signalled for the police to exit the train.[1]

Senior-Constable Kelly supervised the unloading of the horses from the rear carriage.

Glenrowan was a small village and Hare was not familiar with it. The businessman, Mr Rawlins, seeing Hare's confusion, gave him a quick description of the town's layout. He pointed to a nearby house where a light was on and said that was the residence of Stanistreet, the stationmaster, adding, 'I know the stationmaster'. He led Hare across to Stanistreet's house at a quick pace. On the way, he said, 'I'm not armed. Can any of your men lend me a rifle?'

Hare replied, 'I don't think so, but I'll give you my revolver and I'll stick to the double-barrelled gun.'

Rawlins asked if he could have the shotgun instead, but Hare replied, 'No, I'll stick to the gun myself.'

Hare produced his revolver, and began to explain how to operate it. Rawlins interrupted: 'If it's a Webley revolver, I know how it's worked.'

Through a window, they saw a woman and some children inside. Hare tapped on the glass. When the woman looked up, they could see she was crying. They went inside.

The woman was Mrs Stanistreet.

'Where is your husband?' Hare asked her.

She didn't answer, but continued to cry.

Hare said, 'Oh, oh, my good woman, do be calm for a minute!'

She stopped crying. Hare asked her again where her husband was. She said, 'They've taken him away.'

'Who has taken him away?'

She paused, then said, 'The Kellys.'

He asked where. She gave a vague answer and motioned to the west, in the direction of the Warby Ranges. Hare did not know that it was also the direction of Jones' hotel.

They hurried back to the railway station. There were police, reporters and others on the platform, and half a dozen horses had already been brought out of their carriage. Hare announced that there was a change of plan. He confirmed that the Kellys had been in Glenrowan, and therefore they would not continue to Beechworth. The search would begin here and now.

As they prepared for the search, Constable Bracken appeared, having slipped from the hotel without Kelly noticing. He said, 'Mr Hare, the outlaws are in Jones' hotel. I've just escaped from them. They have a number of people in the hotel. Go quickly or they will escape.'[2]

Bracken then disappeared into the night. His breathless message was confusing and ambiguous. There were others in the hotel, but how many? And were they hostages, or accomplices?

It seemed to take forever to get the men organised. Frustrated, Hare shouted, 'Oh, come on! We've got them in the house and if we don't be quick, they'll escape from us!'

Someone called out, 'What will we do with the horses, sir?'

Hare called back, 'Let the horses go, and come along as quickly as you can.'

The horses still in the carriage were dashed down the ramp, and they were all released, and scampered away. Hare was not concerned. They wouldn't go far and could be rounded up later.

Hare ran towards Jones' hotel, closely followed by constables Gascoigne, Phillips and Canny; Sub-Inspector O'Connor; some of the Native Police; and Mr Rawlins.

There was a fence around the hotel grounds and they entered through an iron gate. Hare made to the left of the building, running in a low, crouched position, his shotgun held in front of him.

A flash of gunfire came from the hotel. The shooter, briefly illuminated by the flash, was a man standing about ten yards from the corner of the verandah.[3]

Hare's left arm dropped to his side, limp. He felt no pain, but knew that he had been hit. He raised the shotgun with his right arm and returned fire.

The sound of the rifle was still echoing in their ears when a line of four flashes simultaneously burst from the verandah. The moon was behind the hotel, throwing shadow and obscuring the shooters.

Hare returned fire.

Hare called out, 'Don't be foolhardy!' then called out that he wanted to speak a few words with the shooter.[4]

The man replied, 'I don't want to speak to you.' Then he fired again, the flash of his gun momentarily illuminating him near the corner of the hotel.

Someone called, 'Look out!'

A moment later, a row of flashes burst simultaneously from under the verandah of the hotel. Constable Gascoigne and others returned fire.

The police took cover wherever they could find it: behind the fence; behind trees. Sub-Inspector O'Connor found a ditch further away and led his Native Police team into it. Gascoigne took cover behind a small sapling post. Two men had climbed into trees behind Gascoigne, and were firing over his head, putting him at risk from friendly fire. He shouted at them to cease firing, which they did.[5]

Both Hare's cartridges were spent. He held the gun between his knees and touched the action, so that both barrels fell forward.

With his one good hand, he emptied the old cartridges and dropped in two new cartridges.[6]

Hare's injury was serious. He said later:

> The effect that the shot had on me was just as if I had looked at the sun. Immediately I was struck my eyesight was affected, my eyes became dim. I kept firing from time to time. The two shots, I recollect most distinctly, were the two I fired immediately my hand dropped beside me, and I know I fired several after, how many I would not like to swear. I think six.[7]

The gunman who had shot Hare called out, 'Fire away! You can do us no harm.'

Constable Gascoigne called, 'That's Ned Kelly's voice!'[8]

Gascoigne later said he heard Ned Kelly say, 'You bloody cocktails, you can't hurt me!'[9]

Gascoigne, armed with a Martini-Henry rifle, fired at Kelly, hitting him in the foot.[10]

Hare said later: 'I had but one thought, to keep firing as long as those men kept firing at us.'[11]

Hare's shotgun posed no danger to anyone inside the hotel (unless they were at a window, which nobody was). A shotgun blast could not have penetrated the wall even from close range. The police armed with rifles did pose a risk to those inside, because rifle bullets could penetrate the weatherboard walls.

They heard shrieks from inside the hotel. Gascoigne called out for everyone to stop firing. After firing his shotgun again, Hare also gave the order to stop firing.

The shooting from the hotel ceased.[12]

The air was thick with gunfire smoke. The initial exchange had lasted fifteen minutes. The police had fired around 80 rounds, and the outlaws had fired about 100 rounds.

Hare instructed Senior-Constable Kelly, 'Surround the house! And for God's sake take care those fellows don't escape. I'm going to have my arm tied up.'[13]

He went back through the gate to the railway station.

On the way, he passed O'Connor, running in a low crouch towards the hotel. He said, 'O'Connor, the buggers have got me in the arm.'

At the station, the journalists were gathered on the platform. Blood was spurting from Hare's arm 'as if out of a spout' so Thomas Carrington, artist for *The Australasian Sketcher*, applied a tourniquet made from his handkerchief.

The Argus reporter Joseph Melvin patted Hare on the back. 'Well done, Hare. You've managed this affair as you have everything else you've undertaken.'

But Melvin's congratulations were premature. Hare picked up his shotgun with his good arm and returned to the siege. On the grounds of the hotel, Senior-Constable Kelly told him, 'We're short of ammunition.'

Mr Rawlins overheard, and offered, 'I'll take it around to them if you like.'

Hare accepted the offer, and told Rawlins that extra ammunition could be found in the guard's van.

Hare started moving around the perimeter to instruct and post sentries in strategic positions, but as he was crossing an open space, he felt weak. He began to stagger. His heart was pounding like a drum. Thinking he saw Rawlings again, he called out, 'For God's sake, Rawlings, go and get me a horse, or anything that will carry me to Benalla, where I can have my wound dressed properly.'[14]

Coming to a fence with a top wooden rail and wires, he tried to climb through, to go back to the platform, but got stuck with his body halfway through. His right hand held his gun, while his left hand hung limply.

He dropped back down and propped himself into a sitting position under a nearby tree, perhaps for ten minutes. He wasn't sure.

He looked at his left arm. Blood was streaming out from beneath the handkerchief. He had to get back to the railway station. He staggered back, barely able to walk.[15]

Near the station he heard someone say, 'There goes Hare, as drunk as possible.'[16]

When he reached the station verandah, he said, 'Catch me, please,' and fell onto a pile of sacks. Then he blacked out completely.[17]

About ten minutes after the first exchange of fire, Constable Phillips, who had crept around to the back of the hotel, heard Ned Kelly and Joe Byrne talking.[18]

Kelly said, 'Is that you, Joe?'

Joe replied, 'Yes. Is that you, Ned? Come here.'

Ned: '*Come here* be damned. What are you doing there? Come with me and load my rifle. I'm cooked.'

Joe: 'So am I. I think my leg is broke.'

Ned: 'Leg be damned; you got the use of your arms. Come on, load for me. I'll pink the buggers.'

Joe: 'Don't be so excited; the boys will hear us, and it will dishearten them. I am afraid it's a case with us this time.'

Ned: 'Well, it's your fault. I always said this bloody armour would bring us to grief.'

Joe: 'Don't you believe it. Old Hare is cooked, and we will soon finish the rest.'

Inexplicably, historical accounts of this conversation invariably have Joe (not Ned) saying, 'I always said this bloody armour would bring us to grief', but the account in the proceedings of the Police Royal Commission clearly has *Ned* complaining about the armour, saying to Joe, 'it's your fault'. A transcript of Constable Phillip's statement was provided to several newspapers, which all reproduced it with the same wording and punctuation, and in every version, Ned complained that the armour was Joe's fault.[19]

Behind them, out of sight past the railway station, the two steam locomotives sat motionless and black, the engines still sizzling hot from the journey, the coal furnaces still glowing. A burst of sparks broke free from one of the locomotives, perhaps as the engineer opened the door or stoked the coals with a shovel. Constable Arthur looked back over his shoulder and, like a marvelling school-boy, thought he saw fireworks. It must be Kelly's sympathisers, he thought, letting the outlaws know the police had arrived. Yet there were drivers, guards and four prominent journalists down there, who all saw nothing. Arthur's fireworks rockets were just a flurry of sparks from one of the locomotives.[20]

Some women and children escaped from the hotel, dashing from the far side of the building through the moonlit haze of gun smoke. One man came out holding a crying boy. During the second exchange of gunfire, a bullet had struck Jack Jones, the son of proprietor Ann Jones, in the hip. He was rushed to Wangaratta hospital, where he died twelve hours later.

Ann Jones came out in the moonlight, abusing the police, calling them murderers. She said, 'Ned Kelly is man enough for any of you. Why don't you come up and take them out?'[21] Then she went back inside, and could be heard abusing the outlaws, telling them to shoot the police. She went in and out multiple times before leaving the scene entirely.

When Hare regained consciousness, he was in the passenger carriage of the train. It was moving. O'Connor's wife and sister-in-law were there with refreshments for him. They told him that the train was taking him to Benalla.[22]

Hare uneasily made his way forward to the engine, and asked the driver how long it would take to go to Benalla, then go back to Glenrowan. The driver told him that from Benalla, they could get back within half an hour.

He suddenly felt cold. They both looked down and saw blood pooling on the engine room floor. It was coming from Hare's arm. He staggered back to the carriage.[23]

When they arrived in Benalla sometime between 3 and 4 a.m. Mr Lewis, the inspector of schools, was on the platform. Hare said, 'I feel very weak. I've been shot by the Kellys.' He asked Mr Lewis to take him by the arm, and to help him walk to Dr Nicholson's home, and from there to the telegraph office.[24]

Lewis took him to the doctor's house, where they woke Dr Nicholson up. Hare showed him his wounded arm, but explained that he had to get to the telegraph office urgently; could Dr Nicholson come with them and treat him there? Nicholson said he would follow soon.[25]

Meanwhile, a messenger woke Superintendent Sadleir, telling him to meet Superintendent Hare at the telegraph office. The messenger said that the outlaws were surrounded in Glenrowan, that Hare was wounded and in need of medical attention, and that nine police had been 'knocked over' (that last detail was untrue: of the police, only Hare was wounded).

Sadleir wrote of the moment in his memoir:

> Serious as this piece of news was, my first impulse was to kneel down beside my bed and thank God that He had given the enemy into our hands. It was not that I thought less of those police, but rather that I thought more of the prospect at any cost of ending the horrid uncertainty that had oppressed us all so long.[26]

His prayers may have been about more than the deliverance of the enemy into his hands. He was about to take command at Glenrowan, and when the gang was caught, he would get the glory.

By the time Hare and Lewis got to the telegraph office, Hare was agitated. His mind was foggy. He dictated a message to Standish, which Mr Saxe, the telegraph master, transmitted. He then sent a message to Detective Ward, in Beechworth awaiting the arrival of the train.

> Ward, all is right. We have them safe. Muster all hands and take them to Glenrowan.[27]

There was a mattress nearby that Saxe slept on when doing night shift. They persuaded Hare to lie down on it.

Superintendent Sadleir arrived. Hare said, 'Sadleir, I'm shot in the arm, but I don't think it's anything of any consequence. I'll return with you to the ground. To Glenrowan.'[28]

Sadleir said, 'Don't be such a fool. You're a regular glutton. You've got one shot through you, and you want to get some more, I suppose.'

Dr Nicholson arrived. He cut away the handkerchief tourniquet, commenting on the poor technique used. Blood was flowing freely from Hare's wrist. Dr Nicholson said that he'd been shot in an artery, and that the blood from his heart could not get to his veins. He made a splint from a book, and fastened it to Hare's hand.

Hare lost consciousness.

Before leaving the telegraph office, while Hare lay comatose on the floor, Sadleir requested Saxe to transmit one more message. It was to Detective Ward in Beechworth, countermanding Superintendent Hare's instructions. All the other police in Beechworth were still to go to Glenrowan immediately, but under Sadleir's new instructions, Detective Ward was ordered to remain in Beechworth.[29]

After spending two years engaged in the pursuit of Ned Kelly and his gang, Michael Ward was the only policeman in the entire colony who was specifically instructed *not* to go to Glenrowan that night. The putative reason was that someone had to stay behind and deal with the Sherritt murder, but given the siege situation and Ward's deep knowledge of the gang, that was a strange decision. Superintendent Nicolson—who was tight with Sadleir—had stymied Ward and denied him promotion. It is hard to escape the conclusion that both superintendents saw the detective as a threat to their chance of receiving acclaim for catching the Kelly Gang, and of getting the reward money for doing so. Before passing out, Frank Hare had told Sadleir that the gang were surrounded. Perhaps his motives were pure, but it certainly looks as if Sadleir did not want Detective Ward to steal his glory.

51

Glenrowan by moonlight

Sergeant Steele had gone to Wangaratta Railway Station around 2 a.m. to wait for the police special. He would not be boarding it to join the search in Beechworth, but the train was scheduled to stop there on the way through, and he had been asked to deliver a last-minute message to Frank Hare when it did. He clutched that message as he waited in the cold night air. He was not in uniform; the Irish soldier's son was instead dressed in the style of an English gent: tweed jacket and waterproof leggings.[1]

He had been waiting about half an hour when he heard a volley of gunfire to the south, followed by a second volley. The sound was unmistakeable. It seemed to be coming from the tiny village of Glenrowan, about eight miles down the line, between Wangaratta and Benalla.

What to do? Superintendent Sadleir at Benalla headquarters needed to be told, but he could not leave the station in case Hare's special train arrived while he was gone.

He quickly found the railway's telegraph operator and asked him to hurry over to the main telegraph office and transmit an urgent message to Superintendent Sadleir about gunfire in Glenrowan. Then the stationmaster, Mr Mangan, found him and said he could hear a horseman approaching along the railway line from Glenrowan.[2]

Steele jumped down onto the tracks and ran down the line. The rider appeared. It was Constable Bracken of Glenrowan. He told Steele about the Kelly Gang, the arrival of the police and the siege. Steele borrowed his horse, told Bracken to go to the barracks and wait for further orders, then rode to the telegraph office, where he delivered a more detailed update for Sadleir.

He returned to the barracks, where he woke all the constables up, telling them to get armed and saddled. No time for uniforms: they had to leave immediately. Bracken joined them. Steele divided them into two groups, one to ride with him to Glenrowan, and the other to go down on a special train that the stationmaster was arranging. With a small party of mounted troopers, he saddled up and galloped out of town, arriving at the edge of Glenrowan around 5 a.m.[3] They dismounted about 400 yards from the hotel and approached on foot. Senior-Constable Kelly challenged them, calling out for them to identify themselves.

Steele responded with, 'Wangaratta police!'[4]

Senior-Constable Kelly briefed Steele on the situation. They did not yet have the numbers to surround the hotel, and in particular, had no coverage of the western side, which backed onto bushland, so they could not be sure the outlaws were still in the hotel.

About an hour earlier, near the stockyard fence north of the hotel, Senior-Constable Kelly and Constable Arthur had discovered a blood-stained six-chambered rifle and a bloodstained cap. The blood was fresh. Senior-Constable Kelly believed that the items belonged to one of the outlaws who had escaped from the hotel. They sensed they were being watched. The night was cold, and Senior-Constable Kelly had dropped his own hat somewhere, so he wore the bloodied cap to keep his head warm.[5]

Sergeant Steele took position behind a tree near the back door, and his men positioned themselves to cover the far boundary, but the cordon was still incomplete.[6]

Supposedly, Sub-Inspector O'Connor, the Queensland officer in charge of the Native Police, was the highest ranking officer on site. Frank Hare had assumed he would take charge, but none of Steele's party saw O'Connor. He was still sheltering in the ditch, far away from the hotel, instructing the Native Police to keep up a steady rate of gunfire. The ditch was too deep for them to see the hotel, so they were firing into the air, creating the illusion that the gunfight was more sustained throughout the night than it was. Thus, the Native Police, who had served with dedication, verve and enthusiasm while in Victoria, were ordered to behave in an embarrassing and cowardly way by their officer. One of the Native Police, Hero, climbed out and joined the other police around the hotel. One constable admiringly said of Hero, 'He was as plucky and cool as any man could be'.[7]

The leadership vacuum was filled by Senior-Constable Kelly, who visited everyone at their posts, doing his best to maintain discipline and morale. However, soon after the start of the siege he made a terrible mistake. He noticed some horses at the back of the hotel, saddled and bridled, ready to ride at a moment's notice. He assumed they belonged to the gang. He could not approach them due to the heavy gunfire, so he ordered another constable to shoot them, to prevent the outlaws' getaway. He was wrong: the horses in the yard did not belong to the gang. Some horses were killed by gunfire that night, quite likely due to Senior-Constable Kelly's instructions.[8]

It was a bright moonlit night, almost as bright as day. Nonetheless, the police had the advantage until sunrise. The outlaws maintained sporadic gunfire with a seemingly unlimited supply of ammunition, but were unable to hit their hidden targets around the perimeter.[9]

They heard the special train approach from the south, bringing Sadleir up from Benalla headquarters, and the special that Steele had organised coming from Wangaratta to the north. The Wangaratta special stopped a considerable distance north of the town, to avoid being derailed on the broken track.

Sadleir disembarked with nine additional police. Senior-Constable Kelly went over to meet him and brief him. He showed Sadleir the bloodstained rifle he had found on the north side, then removed the bloodstained cap from his head and handed it over too. Sadleir asked where Sub-Inspector O'Connor was. Senior-Constable Kelly replied, 'He's quite safe. He's in the drain in front of the hotel.'[10]

As the police conferred, the outlaws in the hotel launched a barrage of gunfire. The railway station and the train were both hit by bullets.[11]

Sergeant Steele saw a woman appear at the door, and heard her say, 'For God's sake, let me go.' He called on her to come on, quick. She retreated into the house. Then he heard her say, 'For God's sake, let me and my child go out.' Steele called out to her, 'Come!' She was Martha Reardon, wife of one of the platelayers who, under Kelly's instructions, had sabotaged the line.[12]

She ran, passing close by Steele, with a baby in her arms. The outlaws appeared on the verandah and opened fire. The police returned fire. O'Connor's men in the ditch launched a deafening round. Martha Reardon was convinced that Steele himself was firing at her; but, as he later explained, if he had fired his shotgun at such close range he would have killed her.[13]

A witness later said that Steele did fire two shots, but not until she was well past him, out of the line of fire. To a terrified woman fleeing a hostage situation, even that would have been traumatic; but he was not aiming at her. He was censured the following year by the Police Royal Commission, but a later inquiry, established specifically to investigate his behaviour at Glenrowan, reversed those conclusions and found that he had acted bravely and professionally . . . despite what happened next.[14]

Steele saw another figure emerge from the hotel. It was a man, crouching on his hands and knees. The sound of gunshots was deafening. The outlaws were again firing from the verandah; the police— especially those in the ditch—were firing. It was around sunrise, the moon was sinking, and the house was cast in dark shadows. Steele called for him to put his hands up. The man kept going.

Steele thought the man was trying to flank him. Twice more, Steele called to the man to stop and put up his hands. Then he did something that would haunt him forever. He fired.

The figure cried 'Oh, my God!' and darted back into the hotel. Steele had made a mistake. He had shot Martha Reardon's teenaged son, Michael.

The slug lodged in Michael's chest, but didn't kill him. He outlived almost everyone else there that night, and when he died at the age of 79, Sergeant Steele's slug was still embedded in his ribcage.

52

Reverie

The bloodstained rifle and cap discovered by Constable Arthur and Senior-Constable Kelly belonged to Ned Kelly, who watched them pick up the items. Wounded, he staggered away into the scrub. He had abandoned his rifle because an injury to his arm prevented him from wielding it. He tried to mount his horse to ride away, but the armour and his injuries prevented him, and he fell over. He lay down in the grass and dozed until dawn, with the popping and cracking of gunfire in the distance like a psychotic lullaby.[1]

There is a bizarre theory that Kelly mounted his horse, rode to a prearranged meeting place, and addressed a secret army awaiting his command. The army, so the theory goes, was part of an underground revolutionary movement of which Ned Kelly was the leader. To them, he is supposed to have made a speech in which he said, 'This is our fight', and 'Now is not the time'. He then dismissed the disappointed soldiers, and rode back to the hotel to resume the fight.[2]

None of that happened.

It was a fantasy proposed and promoted from the 1960s onwards by the late historian Ian Jones. He claimed that in Kelly's pocket that night was a manifesto for the Republic of North-Eastern Victoria. Entranced by Jones' remarkable theory, a journalist claimed that he had once seen the document with his own eyes on display in the British National Archives, more than 80 years after the Glenrowan siege. Yet according to the British National Archives, no such document exists. There was no mention of a secret army in the days following

Glenrowan. There was no revolutionary mood or republican push in North-Eastern Victoria. There was no sectarian conflict between Irish and English, or between Catholics and Protestants, in the district. The selectors were not an angry, organised political movement: most succeeded financially and the wealthiest were indistinguishable from squatters. Ned Kelly did not have a political bone in his body, but rather was motived by revenge and greed. He represented nobody but himself and his associates in the criminal underworld.

Even there, at the siege of Glenrowan, he had tried to flee, leaving his friends to their fate, he could not get away, because he was wounded, and dressed in heavy armour that was fastened onto his body with bolts and nuts. Although he lay undiscovered in the grass, he was utterly trapped.[3]

Ned Kelly was seriously wounded by bullets in his right foot, upper and lower left arm, and right hand. With those injuries, and with 95 pounds' weight of iron, he could neither mount a horse nor flee on foot. Escape was impossible.[4]

The imaginary document, the Manifesto for a Republic of North-Eastern Victoria, was a phantom, like the non-existent selector army waiting nearby to charge to the gang's rescue. Yet the manifesto is central to the modern fantasy of Ned Kelly as a revolutionary hero, rather than the psychopathic murderer that he was.

53

The man in the iron mask

Seven a.m. Monday.

The smoke of gunfire hung over the ground like a fog. Distant gum trees were silhouetted by the pre-dawn sheen. The police watched the hotel, waiting for the next attack from the outlaws, the next burst of gunfire. They hunched over their weapons, shivered in the chill, and tried to stay awake and alert.[1]

Someone said, 'Who's that fellow?'

They looked to the west. A strange, hulking figure crunched towards them through the twilight scrub. It wore a long grey hooded cloak that in the smoke and moonlight looked angel-white. 'What is this coming?' someone called.[2]

Sergeant Steele, the closest to the back of the hotel, turned and looked behind him. At first glance, he saw nothing alarming: 'He looked like a tall black man, an Aboriginal about Wangaratta, and I thought curiosity had brought him down there at daylight to see what was the matter.'[3]

The figure then threw back the cloak. It was monstrous. Its head was a bizarre dark cylinder. To Jesse Dowsett, a railway guard, the figure looked nine feet high as it came through the gloom, and he sincerely thought it was the devil.

Someone cried out, 'Keep back, keep back!'

Some believed they were looking at a ghost. Others saw a lunatic.[4]

It was Ned Kelly, in his suit of armour.

He raised a revolver and fired at Constable Arthur, who got up and ran as fast as he could, not stopping until he reached the railway station. Kelly fired at the other constables. They broke cover and ran away, hiding on the far side of the hotel.[5]

He beat his revolver against his breastplate, like a war drum. Like a signal.

Kelly came past the rear of the hotel. Steele had moved around his tree to hide from the advancing form, but was now exposed to the hotel's back door. He fired at Kelly, but his shots had no effect.

One bullet appeared to strike Kelly's hand, causing him to recoil.

Kelly called out to the hotel, 'Come out, and we will whip the lot of the bloody police!'[6]

If Joe Byrne had been alive, he would have joined with Kelly in his own suit of armour, with Dan Kelly and Steve Hart following close behind. Four armoured juggernauts, lumbering across the hotel grounds, killing all and sundry in a festival of slaughter.

Joe Byrne would have done it. After all, he was the co-author of the entire grotesque master plan; and if the conversation heard by Constable Phillips was right, the suits of armour were his idea. He had spent months preparing for this moment, and fantasising about it, and he wouldn't have backed out now for all the gold in Victoria.

But Joe Byrne did not come, because Joe Byrne was dead.

A short time earlier, around 5 a.m., some hostages inside the hotel saw Joe Byrne serve himself a drink at the bar. He had lifted his armour up to allow his arm the range of motion needed to down the glass. He said, 'Many more years in the bush for the Kelly Gang!' A bullet pierced the wall and struck him in the groin. He spun around and dropped to the floor. Dan Kelly had then turned to Steve Hart, and said, 'What do we do now?'[7]

But right now, hearing Ned's metallic war drum, Dan and Steve went out onto the back verandah of the hotel with their rifles and commenced firing at the police.

Sergeant Steele was now trapped, with Kelly before him on the hotel grounds, and the other two outlaws behind him on the verandah, also in armour. But luckily for Steele, Kelly was now moving past him, shooting at the railway station.[8]

After firing six shots, Kelly sat down in a clump of trees, seemingly to reload. Steele sprinted forward to get close enough to shoot him, but he was too late. Kelly stood and lifted a revolver. Steele dived to the ground to take cover. A bullet from behind him kicked up dirt, temporarily blinding him. Kelly fired at him but missed, then continued his cumbersome march towards the railway station.

Only three others held firm, although much further back. They were Constable Montiford, Dowsett (the railway guard who had joined the siege, armed only with his personal revolver) and Senior-Constable Kelly.[9] Taking cover behind a large fallen tree with Dowsett, Senior-Constable Kelly fired with his Martini-Henry rifle. Dowsett advised him: 'That was a little to the right.'

A bullet struck Kelly. Dowsett called out, 'How did you like that?' Kelly cursed and swore retaliation.[10] Senior-Constable Kelly shouted, 'Look out, he's bullet-proof!'[11]

Steele's vision cleared. He recalled hearing rumours that the outlaws had made body armour. Kelly was wearing a long coat, and Steele now wondered if that was to conceal the fact that the armour didn't cover the legs. He reloaded his shotgun, planning to aim low.

He shouted, 'Rush him, boys!' Then he charged.[12]

Nobody else rushed at Kelly. It was a one-man charge.

Kelly swung his enormous, lumbering body to face Steele and fired the revolver, but missed. Steele fired his shotgun, aiming low. He hit Kelly in the knee. Kelly staggered, and his right arm dropped. He raised it again, ready to fire, but before he could, Steele fired his second barrel. The outlaw staggered and fell. He shouted, 'I'm done! I'm done!'

Steele dived onto Kelly, and tried to grab his revolver. They wrestled for it. It discharged, the bullet passing through Steele's tweed hat, but missing his head. Kelly's finger was stuck in the trigger guard trapped by Steele's grip. He cried out 'Don't break my fingers!'[13]

Steele pinned Kelly by the throat with one hand, and by the wrist with another.[14]

Dowsett, Montiford and Senior-Constable Kelly rushed up to help bring the outlaw under control. In the tussle, Kelly in his armour, with the three men on top of him, rolled onto Sergeant Steele, crushing his leg and causing injury, yet he felt no pain until several minutes later.[15]

In Steele's recollection, the helmet came off as he hit the ground, rolling away. But Senior-Constable Kelly recalled pulling the helmet off during the tussle, then exclaiming, 'By God, it's Ned!'[16]

Others arrived. Soon there was a crowd around the men in the dirt. Steele asked for a knife. When someone handed him one, he cut Kelly's armour straps. Someone took Kelly's revolver. It was then handed to someone else, then someone else, and later proved difficult to locate.[17]

A constable named Dwyer kicked Kelly.[18]

Kelly called to nearby Constable Bracken, who had 'escaped' the hotel the night before, 'Save me! I saved you.'

Senior-Constable Kelly who was nearby, retorted, 'Ned, you showed very little mercy to poor Kennedy and Scanlan.'

Ned replied, 'I couldn't help it. I had to shoot them for my own safety.'[19]

Bracken told the others to back off. He said he had been treated well as a hostage, and would not allow any harm to come to the outlaw.[20]

Two bullets whizzed over their heads. The reporter Joe Melvin called, 'Keep watch, keep watch!'

Dwyer, the constable who had kicked Kelly, hurried to the railway station to inform Sadleir. On his way, he saw an outlaw standing at the hotel's kitchen door and levelling his gun at them. Dwyer levelled his in reply. The outlaw then withdrew, calling out, 'Fire away, you bastards, you cannot kill me!'[21]

Steele and Bracken walked Kelly down to the platform and put him in the guard's carriage. Superintendent Sadleir entered the carriage. It was the first time that Steele had laid eyes on Sadleir since he had arrived in Glenrowan. Sadleir was worried about gunfire from the hotel, so he told them to relocate the prisoner to the railway station house.

There, Kelly was placed on a mattress, and his wounds were treated by Dr Nicholson of Benalla, the same doctor who had treated Frank Hare during the night; indeed, the same doctor who had treated Constable Fitzpatrick when he had been shot by Kelly. Unable to rejoin the siege due to the searing pain in his leg, Steele stayed and guarded Kelly for the rest of the day.[22]

A travelling priest named Father Gibney visited the station house. Kelly said, 'Lord Jesus have mercy on me.' Then told the priest, 'It's not today that I began to say that.' Steele moved away while Gibney listened to Kelly's confession and administered last rites. However, Kelly was not dying. His spiritual needs accounted for, Doctor Nicholson resumed care of the physical.[23]

Constable Dwyer came in, having been sent to ask Sadleir for provisions. Kelly recognised him and said, 'You cowardly dog, you kicked me when I was down.'[24]

Dwyer replied, 'No, *you're* the cowardly dog, you killed my poor comrade.'

'Who was your comrade?'

'Poor Lonigan.'

Kelly said, 'Look here, old man, when you were out there, didn't you try to shoot me?'

Dwyer said, 'No,' ruining Kelly's punchline, which would, no doubt, have been an accusation of moral equivalence.

Deflated, Kelly said dismissively, 'Then you had no business there.'

Sadleir apologised to Kelly for Dwyer kicking him, explaining that Dwyer had lost his temper and was very sorry. Dwyer listened in silence to Sadleir's apology on his behalf.

At 9 a.m. a train came from the north, delivering all the Beechworth police, except for Detective Ward. Again, the train pulled up some distance before the town. Jack Sherritt was with them, brandishing a police rifle, hoping for vengeance.[25]

Two Beechworth telegraph operators also arrived on the train. There was no telegraph office in Glenrowan, although the lines ran alongside the railway track through the town. One of the operators climbed up a telegraph pole, rigged a connection, and ran a wire to the railway station, where a makeshift telegraph office was established.

The journalists wasted no time. Thousands of words were transmitted to Melbourne, causing an unprecedented surge of demand for newspapers. People clamoured in the streets for the latest copy, and printing presses churned out editions as fast as they could.

At 10 a.m., a white handkerchief appeared at the front door of the hotel.

Sadleir ordered all firing to cease, then called for the hostages to come out. Nobody came, because his voice wasn't loud enough. Mr Rawlins—the businessman who had assisted Hare the previous night—offered to call out to them, saying, 'I've got a voice like a bull.'[26]

He stepped forward and bellowed loudly, calling the hostages to come forth. He had barely finished when the first of them appeared. As they streamed out of the building, the police ordered them to put their hands on their heads. When they were clear of the hotel, they were ordered to lie flat on the ground. Two known sympathisers, the McAuliffe brothers, were taken away for further questioning.[27]

More police arrived.

There were, by now, more than 50 police at the siege. Crowds of spectators had gathered. Sadleir had no idea what to do, so he did nothing at all.

In the hunt for the Kelly Gang, Superintendent John Sadleir had made a few mistakes. A year and a half earlier, as Kennedy's patrol headed to Stringybark Creek, Sadleir had doubted Detective Ward's contention that the Kelly Gang were near. He had released the notorious Kelly associate Wild Wright based on empty promises of assistance. He had led Superintendent Nicolson on what proved to be a wild goose chase north while the gang were looting the Euroa bank to the south. He had led Nicolson and Standish into the public relations disaster that was the Great Sebastopol Raid, while the gang hid far away in the Warby Ranges. He had persuaded Superintendent Hare to ignore the tip-off from the Diseased Stock Agent that the gang had made suits of armour and were about to strike. All were understandable mistakes in isolation, but given his track record, perhaps indecision was for the best.[28]

He dithered, and fretted and smoked his pipe on the railway platform. He consulted with Sub-Inspector O'Connor on the railway platform. He read the newspaper, and smoked his pipe some more.[29]

Senior-Constable Kelly informed Sadleir that several of the police wanted to storm the hotel. Sadleir was opposed, replying that 'he did not see why he should sacrifice any man's life for the two ruffians inside.' The Royal Commission, held the following year, noted drily in its report, 'Of course, if an attack were made, as suggested, the officer in charge was in honour bound to take the lead . . .' But this was unfair. They believed (wrongly) that there were no longer any hostages inside, so the risk was not justified by urgency.[30] Then Sadleir had a brilliant idea: an artillery cannon! With no risk to himself or others, he could blow Jones' hotel and the outlaws inside to smithereens!

He sent a telegram to the chief secretary in Melbourne, requesting the urgent delivery of an artillery cannon to Glenrowan. Because the

eyes of the government—and indeed of the population of Victoria—
were transfixed on Glenrowan, they acquiesced. An Armstrong gun
was rolled onto a railway carriage at Spencer Street Station, and
despatched north. However, due to line delays, it did not arrive in
time to end the siege.[31]

After 1 p.m., no more shots were fired from the hotel, although
glimpses of the outlaws were seen.[32]

However, another deadline was looming. Captain Standish was on
his way by train from Melbourne and due to arrive that afternoon. As
the chief commissioner of police, Standish would then be the ranking
officer on location, and Standish would receive the credit when the
gang were captured or killed. Surely this played in Sadleir's mind. In
the rift between Nicolson on one side, and Standish and Hare on the
other, he aligned with Nicolson. Even if he was not concerned with
personal acclaim, he must have blanched at the thought of those two
immoral gamblers and drinkers, Standish and Hare, being vindicated
so soon after Nicolson's humiliation. We cannot know what went
on inside his head. But surely that must have passed through it. The
zealous Constable Johnston—who had actively searched the Warby
Ranges, and who had gone to Euroa with Detective Ward—proposed
burning the hotel. He believed that a fire would drive the outlaws
from the hotel, and they could then be arrested. The only catch was
that someone would have to put themselves in danger by setting the
building alight. Johnston volunteered.[33]

Sadleir approved the plan.

Johnston gathered straw and kerosene, then reported back to
Sadleir on the platform, announcing, 'All ready'.

Sadleir gave the order for others to open fire on the hotel, to provide
cover for Johnston. He crept up, piled the straw, and lit it.

It was 3 p.m.

Ned's sister Maggie Skillion arrived, elegantly dressed in a black
riding habit, red underskirt and an expensive white hat. She said she

would talk the outlaws into surrendering, then went through the cordon, towards the hotel. There was a clamour of shouts and orders.[34]

She turned and complained to the crowd that some police were telling her to stop and some were telling her to continue. Flames were flickering now near the hotel wall. Maggie retreated back behind the cordon.

The straw burned out. It seemed that Johnston's arson attempt had failed. But then, a few minutes later, smoke billowed out of the roof. Through the window, they could see flames dancing inside.

A priest named Father Gibney had joined the onlookers. When the flames appeared, he walked resolutely towards the hotel door. Sadleir commanded him to stop.

Father Gibney paused, turned to Sadleir, and told him, 'I am not in the police service. I am going on my duty, and there is no time to lose.' Then he hurried towards the burning hotel.[35]

Some constables rushed forward, initially to prevent him from entering, but he moved too quickly, so they followed him in.[36]

The priest found Joe Byrne first. Byrne's body was lying at the entrance to the bar. His face was black from smoke. Rigor mortis had set his elbows at bizarre right angles. *The Argus* reporter noted later that Byrne was dressed in 'a blue sac coat, tweed striped trousers, Crimean shirt, and very ill-fitting boots. Like Ned Kelly, Byrne wore a bushy beard.'

The passage beyond was blazing. Father Gibney tried to find a detour through an adjoining room, but it was a dead end, so he blessed himself and ran through. As he moved through the smoke, he called out that he was a Catholic priest. There was no reply. Near the back of the hotel he found the bodies of Dan Kelly and Steve Hart. They were lying side by side, their armour removed, their heads resting on pillows of rolled-up bags. He touched them. They were cold.[37]

Entering soon afterwards, two constables also found Joe Byrne's body, and hauled it outside. In the kitchen behind the main building, some police found Martin Cherry, too wounded to have left with the others. He had been shot in the groin. They carried Cherry a short distance away and laid him on the ground.

Father Gibney emerged from the hotel as the flames licked at the roof. He knelt by Martin Cherry and administered the last sacrament. Cherry was an Irishman, born in Limerick, and about 60 years old; he had worked as a platelayer on the railway. He was described as a 'quiet, harmless old man'. He died within minutes.

Flames soared into the sky. Explosions were heard inside the hotel. The building collapsed.

When the fire burned lower, and the heat was no longer so intense, some men went in and retrieved the bodies of Dan Kelly and Steve Hart. They were unrecognisable. Nothing left of them but two charred torsos and blackened heads.[38]

There were four bodies now at the railway station: Joe Byrne, Dan Kelly, Steve Hart and Martin Cherry. Wild Wright took Mrs Skillion to view the body of her brother Dan. *The Argus* reporter said:

She bent over it, raised a dirge-like cry and wept bitterly.[39]

Steve Hart's brother Dick demanded that the family members be allowed to take possession of the bodies of Steve and Dan. Standish had sent strict instructions *not* to hand over the bodies to the relatives, as inquests were pending, but Sadleir did so to preserve the peace.

In the late afternoon, Captain Standish arrived by train from Melbourne. Constable McIntyre, the only survivor of the Stringybark Creek massacre, accompanied him. Sadleir explained that he had promised the bodies of Hart and Dan Kelly to their families, who loitered nearby. Standish reluctantly conceded to release them. The bodies were loaded onto a cart and taken to Maggie Skillion's residence at Eleven Mile Creek, where friends and sympathisers of the gang commenced a bitter, drunken wake.[40]

A telegram arrived from the governor, praising Superintendent Hare (then convalescing in Benalla) for his service. Standish instructed Sadleir to release the telegram as an official police announcement. Sadleir was incensed: he replied that such an announcement should include himself and Sub-Inspector O'Connor, not just Frank Hare! Standish remarked, 'You, Nicolson and O'Connor are so damned jealous of Hare that you'd do something . . .' Curiously, Sadleir neglected to suggest Sergeant Arthur Steele—the man who actually captured and arrested Ned Kelly—as someone worthy of the governor's praise.[41]

Nobody asked for Joe Byrne's body, so it was transported to the Benalla morgue. His mother had meant it when she said, 'He has made his bed, and must lie in it.'[42]

Ned was transported to Benalla, where he was placed in the lock-up. Joe Byrne's body was stored in the neighbouring cell.

The flames burned lower in the dying afternoon light until there was nothing but smouldering ashes. All that remained of the hotel were the two brick chimneys, a lamppost and a sign that said:

THE GLENROWAN INN.
ANN JONES.
BEST ACCOMMODATION.[43]

54

The morning after

Wracked with pain, Ned Kelly had broken sleep in the Benalla lock-up on Monday night, and on one occasion asked to see Constable McIntyre during the night. At dawn, Senior-Constable Kelly who was in charge of the lock-up, escorted McIntyre to Ned Kelly's cell.[1]

Senior-Constable Kelly said, 'Ned, do you know this man?'

Ned asked if it was Flood.

McIntyre said, 'No, you took me for Flood last time we met.'

'Oh yes, it's McIntyre.'

McIntyre asked him, 'Was my statement correct?' Referring to his version of events at Stringybark Creek.

Kelly said it was, but they soon argued about Lonigan's death.

Kelly said, 'No, Lonigan got behind some logs and pointed a revolver at me.'

McIntyre retorted, 'No, that's only nonsense!'

McIntyre asked, 'Why did you come near us at all? You could have kept out of our way when you knew where we were.'

Ned replied, 'You would have soon found us out, and if we didn't shoot you, you would have shot us.'

It was a total, damning confession. The Stringybark Creek killings were not an unfortunate mistake, but premeditated murder. Yet McIntyre did not reveal this conversation at the trial, and even at the subsequent Royal Commission purported not to know if the gang had intended to murder the police.[2]

After McIntyre had departed, Senior-Constable Kelly asked Ned Kelly if he had shot Fitzpatrick in the wrist. Kelly said that he had shot Fitzpatrick. He told the senior-constable that he had had an opportunity to shoot him too, but had refrained. Regarding Glenrowan, Ned said that after they had killed all the police and blacktrackers on the train, they planned to ride down to Benalla to rob a bank.[3]

The official government photographer, J. Burman, arrived, asking to take a picture of Byrne's body. He had come with Standish from Melbourne, charged with capturing important scenes with the new technology of photography. Some constables helpfully carried Byrne's body outside and propped it up against the wall for him. The body, now in public, attracted other journalists, Thomas Carrington, artist for *The Australasian Sketcher*, and a German-born Melbourne photographer named Walter Lindt, who had the innovative idea of, rather than photographing Byrne, capturing the other photographer doing so. The macabre picture is believed to be Australia's first instance of a press photo. After the moment was captured, the body was carefully carried back inside to its cell. Burman's photography session took place without the knowledge or approval of Captain Standish.[4]

At about 8 a.m. Senior-Constable Kelly and seven other constables escorted Ned Kelly to the Benalla railway station, where they loaded him into the guard's van of the southbound train. Then the train departed and Ned Kelly was on his way to Melbourne Gaol.

Detective Ward caught the morning train to Glenrowan. There, crowds wandered about the grounds and ruins of the hotel, fossicking for souvenirs. He learned that Wild Wright had stayed in McDonnell's hotel, on the other side of the railway tracks, and had been there during the entire siege. Following a tip-off from a journalist, he discovered the outlaws' horses in the McDonnell's hotel stables. There were saddles with the horses, two of which were police saddles taken from Stringybark Creek. There was also a saddle that previously belonged to the Sherritts. He learned from Jack Sherritt that it had been borrowed by the schoolteacher James Wallace the previous year. This was strong evidence linking James Wallace to the Kelly Gang.[5]

Ward left instructions at the police station for Constable Bracken to take custody of the horses and then to transport them to Benalla, before heading to Benalla. Bracken was unavailable, so two other constables took them. On the way to Benalla, one horse escaped and was later recaptured, breaking the evidentiary chain of custody. None of the saddles were marked or documented, but instead they were placed in general storage, rendering them useless as evidence.[6]

At the Benalla lock-up, Ward inspected Joe Byrne's body. A short time earlier, an inquest had been held by magistrate Robert McBean, the squatter whom Ned Kelly and Harry Power had bailed up ten years earlier. McBean ruled: 'A verdict was given that Byrne met his death at the hands of the police while the latter were in the discharge of their duty, and that therefore the act was justifiable homicide.'[7]

Nobody had come to claim the body. In a few hours it would be buried in an unmarked pauper's grave in the Benalla cemetery.[8]

He noticed that Byrne was wearing the rings of two of the police murdered at Stringybark Creek: Byrne had Michael Scanlan's ring on his right hand, and Thomas Lonigan's wedding ring on his left hand. Kill trophies. Ward pulled the rings off Byrne's cold fingers. He placed Scanlan's ring in police storage, but he put Lonigan's ring in his pocket. It didn't belong to Byrne. It belonged to Lonigan's wife, and he intended to return it to her.[9]

Which he later did.[10]

About a month later, Ward visited Kelly, in a cell awaiting a court hearing. They had a brief conversation.[11]

Ned looked at him critically and said, 'You've had some luck.'

'What does that mean?'

Ned said, 'That you're not shot.'

Ward replied, 'You never could have shot me.'

Ned said, 'Oh, yes we could. We could have shot you easy between Beechworth and Eldorado.'

Ward said, 'It would have done you no good.'

Ned said, 'No, it wouldn't, but for all that, the boys would have shot you but for me. I had a terrible job to keep Joe Byrne from shooting you many a time. You were always very kind to my sisters when travelling, Ward, and you must have had the prayers of all the women in the country, so you can put down your escape to that.'[12]

How merciful. But that's not what Kelly told Constable Bracken in Jones' hotel before the siege. He had told Bracken, 'We're just after shooting one traitor,'—Aaron Sherritt—'and we now want that bloody Detective Ward, but he isn't game to show up.'[13]

Ward replied, 'Thank ye kindly, Ned, but I can't do as much for you. You're past hope, but maybe I'll see you off.'

Ward investigated James Wallace's role with a view to prosecuting him as an accessory. He and another detective travelled the district, gathering evidence. They established that while the gang were at large Wallace had frequently made large purchases of alcohol and food; that he had purchased men's clothes that were too big for him, but that would have fitted Ned Kelly; that his son had told a friend about meeting Ned Kelly at the Wallace household; that he had attempted to send a messenger to urgently warn the gang about police activity. They learned that Wallace's father was not a blacksmith, yet he had given this as a reason for purchasing scrap iron prior to the Glenrowan siege. But it was circumstantial, and the primary evidence was tainted: Ward could not reconstruct the chain of custody for the saddle found at Glenrowan after the siege. Ward learned of the existence of a hut in the bush behind Wallace's schoolhouse but by the time he found it, the hut had burned to the ground.[14]

55

The trial

The colony was electrified by the events at Glenrowan. Newspapers were unanimous in celebrating the end of the Kelly Gang. There were criticisms, certainly. Had unscrupulous police abused Kelly's sisters? Why did his mother get a prison sentence merely for being present during a crime? (She had been a participant, not a mere witness, but this fact was lost on many.) Did the hotel really need to be burned? But whatever the circumstances, Ned Kelly's actions, and his planned actions, were horrific, and nobody praised them.

An ambitious lawyer and politician named David Gaunson acted for Ned Kelly. Gaunson jealously guarded access to his client. When Kelly was transported to Beechworth for a committal hearing, Gaunson conducted a gaol cell interview with him on behalf of a journalist for *The Age*.

According to Gaunson, he asked Kelly: 'You have said you were harshly and unjustly treated by the police, and that you were hounded down by them. Can you explain what you mean?' This was Kelly's answer, supposedly:

Yes. I do not pretend that I have led a blameless life, or that one fault justifies another, but the public, in judging a case like mine, should remember that the darkest life may have a bright side, and that after the worst has been said against a man, he may, if he is heard, tell a story in his own rough way that will perhaps lead them to intimate the harshness of their thoughts against him, and find as many excuses for him as he would plead for himself. For my own part, I do not care one straw about my life now for the result of the trial. I know very well, from the stories I have been told, of how I am spoken of, that the public at large execrate my name; the newspapers cannot speak of me with that patient toleration generally extended to men awaiting trial, and who are assumed according to the boast of British justice, to be innocent until they are proved to be guilty; but I do not mind, for I have outlived that care that curried public favour or dreads the public frown. Let the hand of the law strike me down if it will, but I ask that my story might be heard and considered; not that I wish to avert any decree the law may deem necessary to vindicate justice, or win a word of pity from anyone. If my life teaches the public that men are made mad by bad treatment, and if the police are taught that they may not exasperate to madness men they perse-cute and ill-treat, my life will not be entirely thrown away. People who live in large towns have no idea of the tyrannical conduct of the police in country places far removed from court, and they have no idea of the harsh and overbearing manner in which they execute their duty, or how they neglect their duty and abuse their powers.[1]

It was beautiful. But those were not Kelly's words. They were Gaunson's. Only the most gullible fool could believe that Kelly made that speech, sitting on a gaol cell mattress, in reply to the question, 'Can you explain what you mean?'

The 'interview' also included this question and answer, which, although also penned by Gaunson, was true:

'Now, Kelly, what is the real history of Fitzpatrick's business; did he ever try to take liberties with your sister Kate?'

Kelly: 'No, that is a foolish story; if he or any other policeman tried to take liberties with my sister, Victoria would not hold him.'

Gaunson, and his brother William, also a lawyer, tried everything: lobbying politicians, briefing journalists, advocating for petitions in support of Kelly, and making grand speeches. They hired the barrister Henry Bindon to represent Kelly at trial.

Ned Kelly was tried by jury for the murder of Thomas Lonigan on 28 and 29 October 1880. The trial was presided over by Justice Redmond Barry, the man who had freed the Eureka Stockade protestors . . . and the man who had sent Kelly's mother to prison.

The jury found Kelly guilty of the murder of Thomas Lonigan.[2]

His lawyers had made a valiant effort, but it was a lost cause, because had he been acquitted of Lonigan's murder, he would have been tried for Scanlan's murder, then perhaps Kennedy's . . .

Justice Barry sentenced him to death by hanging. Ned disrupted Barry's summation with repeated interruptions. He claimed he could have done a better job of defending himself than his lawyers had done, but his performance now, at the very end of it all, showed otherwise. Kelly had longed to interrogate McIntyre. He wanted to accuse McIntyre of perjury. He wanted to bully McIntyre on the stand into agreeing with him. But even if, as Kelly deceitfully claimed, Lonigan was hiding behind a log when Kelly shot him, and not running away, as claimed by McIntyre, it was still murder. Whether his victim was running, hiding or returning fire in self-defence, it changed nothing.[3]

That Kelly thought it mattered reveals his utter absence of remorse, and lack of comprehension of the magnitude of his crimes. It also shows that he understood neither the law, nor the principles of justice.

Justice Barry's health had been declining. He probably knew he did not have long to live, and his last act as a judge was to take Kelly with him.

When Barry sentenced him to death, Kelly retorted, 'I'll see you there, where I go.'

There was a last-minute flurry of activity. Gaunson organised petitions and rallies that he knew were doomed to fail. Kelly's siblings, and friends such as Wild Wright and Tom Lloyd, appeared at rallies and collected signatures. The public, curious to see these notorious celebrities and excited by anything Kelly-related, attended in swarms.[4]

The cogs in the machinery of death began to turn. On 11 November 1880, Kelly was led out quietly to the scaffold. Journalists and others close by either didn't hear him say anything, or perhaps a quiet, 'Ah well.' One reporter spiced up his report by putting words into Kelly's mouth, moments before the scaffold dropped: 'Such is life.'[5]

But he didn't say that.

Like so much else about him, it was a lie.

Epilogue: Two mysteries and their possible solutions

Mystery 1

Who made the armour?

A week after the Glenrowan siege, Detective Wilson was despatched from Melbourne to investigate the making of the Kelly Gang's armour. After six weeks in north-eastern Victoria—some of that time lodging as a guest on Robert McBean's Kilfera estate, some of it with another welcoming squatter, and some of it roaming around the district—he learned nothing.[1]

This city detective reported on his time spent roughing it up north:

> I made myself acquainted with relatives, sympathisers and friends of the outlaws, and found that they either 'did not know' or would not disclose who was the guilty person or persons who manufactured the coats of iron for the outlaws.
>
> I watched the trial of Edward Kelly at Beechworth, but could not gain anything of importance referring to the matter in question.[2]

The 'trial' referred to was Ned Kelly's hearing in Beechworth. Kelly was held in Beechworth Gaol for the duration, before being returned to Pentridge Prison to await trial.

Despite his failure, Detective Wilson did not return empty-handed. He submitted a substantial list of expenses incurred for travel, accommodation and 'refreshments' during his investigation. Wilson's worthless report has been gleefully used to portray the making of the armour as an unsolvable mystery.

There was no chance of the Kellys, Quinns and Lloyds confiding anything in this inquisitive stranger who preferred the company of local squatters. Therefore, the two suspects named in his report—blacksmiths Patrick Delaney and Charles Culph—can be safely ruled out as having had anything to do with the armour.

In March the following year, Detective Michael Ward visited Ann Jones, the former proprietor of the Glenrowan Inn (now a pile of ashes), and her son Thomas. Ward asked them if they knew who made the armour. They both replied that it was made by the Greta blacksmith John Delaney, the son of Patrick Delaney (whom Detective Wilson had named as a suspect). John and Patrick had both been hostages in the Glenrowan siege. Ann Jones described an incident that she claimed happened prior to the siege.

Jones claimed that Dan Kelly placed a mysterious bag 'containing iron' in her bedroom. Seeing it, she said to John Delaney, 'I would like to know what it's for. They've brought enough revolvers to kill the police without killing them with iron.'[3]

John Delaney replied to her, 'I know what's in the bag, and if the special train comes, you'll know as well as me.'

She said, 'I would like to know now.' But Delaney just walked away, laughing. At least, that's what Ann Jones claimed.

Her son Thomas was in New South Wales at the time of the Glenrowan siege, yet he also told the detective, 'I believe Delaney has made the armour, but I have no proof of it.'

Ward didn't believe them. He concluded that they had no idea who made the armour.

Ann Jones's story did not ring true given John Delaney's experience on the Sunday before the siege. He had been the victim of sustained abuse and death threats from Ned Kelly, who suspected him of being friendly with police. The emotional torment of having a revolver repeatedly aimed at his head, and of being told he was about to die, had reduced the youth to a quivering, tearful wreck. It defies belief that, soon afterwards, he rudely walked away from Ann Jones with an ominous laugh.

Ann Jones had reason to hate John Delaney. In November 1880, only days after Ned Kelly's trial and execution, she was charged with aiding and abetting the Kelly Gang. At her hearing in Beechworth, several witnesses testified to her sympathy with the gang, and to the many ways she had assisted them during the siege. John Delaney was one of those who testified against her. She was granted bail at 200 pounds pending a trial by jury.

John Delaney had testified that when he was taken hostage, Ann Jones seemed to be 'a boss', so he asked her to let him go. She replied, 'No bloody fear, revenge is sweet.' He testified that in the evening, when Dan gave some hostages permission to leave, she rushed to the door, blocked their exit, and told them they had to stay, saying, 'Ned will be here shortly to give you all a lecture.' Then, when the train pulled up, she and her daughter went around extinguishing all the lights, and when the police arrived at the hotel perimeter, she informed the gang, 'Here comes the police.' During the siege she swore at the gang members, telling them they 'promised to fight the police man-to-man and now are bloody cowards'. Several other witnesses gave similar testimony of Ann Jones' complicity and allegiance with the gang.[4]

As the trial date neared, Superintendent Sadleir instructed Detective Ward to visit Ann Jones to convey an offer to drop the case if she revealed who made the armour. She was therefore motivated to provide a name, any name at all. Her son blatantly admitted to Ward that he hoped to see John Delaney prosecuted 'on account of the evidence he gave against my mother'. It is no wonder that Ward did not believe them.[5]

Despite a strong prosecution case, Ann Jones was acquitted by the jury. Sadleir was rebuked for sending Ward to offer to drop the case, which was done without the knowledge of the crown prosecutors.[6]

Several months later, Ward reported that he knew 'with very little doubt' who made the armour. A rumour circulated around the

Woolshed district that a local blacksmith named Tom Straughair made it.

Born in Durham, England in 1838, Tom came to Victoria in 1856 with his brothers Mark and George. Mark, the oldest, co-owned a large, successful foundry in Beechworth, where Tom worked.[7]

Tom Straughair was more than twenty years older than the Byrne and Sherritt brothers, yet he came to befriend the young men. Indeed, when Aaron Sherritt visited Maggie Skillion in 1879 to try to get Charlie the horse back, Straughair accompanied him, either as peace-maker or as backup.

On 13 January 1881, Michael Ward and his partner, Detective William Considine, had a breakthrough, establishing a link between Straughair and the schoolteacher James Wallace. In 1879, Wallace had travelled about collecting scrap iron on the false pretext that his father was a metal dealer.[8] Straughair was connected both to the gang itself—through Byrne—and to a key agent of the gang who collected materials for the making of the armour. Furthermore, he had been engaged in a mysterious late-night project at the time that the armour for the gang was being constructed.

> Friday we had an interview with a confidential person at the Woolshed re the connection between Wallace and Straughair, a blacksmith [from] Woolshed, relative to the making of Byrne's armour. We ascertained that Wallace was very intimate with Straughair and used to leave his horse there when visiting the Sherritts or Byrnes, and also that Straughair used to work late at night. We have very little doubt that Straughair made Joe Byrne's armour, but given the length of time that has elapsed, there is no possible means of obtaining any proof against him.[9]

Tom Straughair was never charged.

The source of the inspiration may have arrived in 1873, when the armour of a German cuirasseer (an armoured cavalry soldier) was displayed at the annual Beechworth carnival. Samurai armour was exhibited at the carnival the following year. The German armour is lost, but the samurai suit can still be seen at the Beechworth Museum.[10]

While spectators marvelled, a blacksmith in the crowd might have reacted to the exhibits in a different way, thinking: *I wonder if I could do that?*

The making of the gang's armour has been the subject of speculation and investigation for decades. In 2004 a team of physicists conducted a metallurgical analysis of one of the suits of armour and concluded that 'the side plates had been cold-worked (beaten without being heated), which was not consistent with blacksmithing techniques at the time'. They found that some components had been heated, but at lower heats than commonly used in foundries. They concluded that it was therefore made in a bush forge by 'amateurs'.[11]

The analysis was no doubt sound, but the conclusion is a leap. If the armour was made from scrap metal, applying the heat needed for many blacksmithing tasks may not have been required, and even if desirable, may not have been possible if the blacksmith was an apprentice or an employee.

The question of the work's status as 'amateur' is beyond the realm of metallurgy, encompassing issues of design and craftmanship. The suits of armour are of elegant design and skilled craftsmanship and are Ned Kelly's most enduring and iconic legacy.

Modern-day blacksmith Nick Hawtin observed that hot chisel cuts were required for the helmet eye slits, and hot riveting was used in constructing Ned's armour. These techniques required temperatures above 750 degrees Celsius and required a blacksmithing forge and an anvil (a foundry). However, Hawtin believes that while a foundry was needed for some tasks, the 'finessing, adjusting, and final design' was done in a bush forge.[12]

And indeed, in 2003 an amateur historian discovered the remains of a bush forge near the Byrne homestead, including scraps of iron that he believed might be offcuts. The evidence that one or more suits of the gang's armour were made there is mixed.[13] It is commonly believed that the construction of the suits of armour required multiple blacksmiths, given the variety of techniques and the sheer amount of labour that would have been required. But that belief rests on the assumption that all the suits were made in the months leading up to Glenrowan. What if the project began several years earlier? What if it started as one man's hobby, using leftover scraps from his brother's foundry?

The notion of an underground blacksmith fraternity contributing to a secret project doesn't ring true. It only makes sense in the context of the discredited theory that Ned Kelly was leader of a republican movement. It is hard to imagine why blacksmiths of the north-east would band together for a common cause, when they had no common cause. It's equally hard to imagine how such activity would be co-ordinated across different towns, given that the gang were fugitives and the homes of their allies under constant surveillance. Therefore, it is more likely that a single blacksmith made the armour, perhaps with assistance from the gang.

For these reasons, since Tom Straughair is known to have probably made at least one suit of armour, I believe that he made all four, and that he started making armour before the Kelly gang existed.

Expertise is born from practise. The first suit would naturally have been the roughest, and indeed, Steve Hart's suit is considered to have been inferior to the other three. Perhaps over drinks, the prototype armour's worth was tested with a shot from a revolver, and the notion was born of using it in real combat.

The gang tasked James Wallace with collecting scrap iron, but Wallace did not provide enough to complete the project, so the gang roamed moonlit fields, stealing farm equipment from their neighbours.

That is one possible scenario for the inception of Kelly's murderous, doomed plan. Other scenarios are possible, but it is clear that Ned

Kelly did not make the armour, as he possessed neither the expertise nor the resources. The investigating detectives did not even entertain that possibility. Nor, if the concept originated in Byrne's circle of friends, was it Ned's idea. When German armour was first exhibited in Beechworth in 1873, Ned was locked up in Pentridge Prison. And on that fateful winter's night in Glenrowan in 1880, Ned was heard saying to Joe, 'Well it's your fault. I always said this bloody armour would bring us to grief.'[14]

The origin of the Kelly gang's armour need not remain shrouded in mystery. Thanks largely to the work of detectives Ward and Considine, we know that in all likelihood, at least some of the armour, and (in my view) probably all of it, was made by the blacksmith Tom Straughair.

Mystery 2

Who wrote the Jerilderie Letter?

In February 1879, after robbing the bank in Jerilderie, Ned Kelly handed a 56-page letter to bank teller Edwin Living, telling him that he wanted it published, and explaining that it was 'a bit of my life'. Long and rambling, it is mostly about his criminal career. It is by turns vivid, passionate, witty, chilling, deranged and tedious, depending on which page you are reading. Here's one passage:

> I would have scattered their blood and brains like rain I would manure the Eleven mile with their bloated carcasses and yet remember there is not one drop of murderous blood in my Veins[1]

There are flashes of paranoia, such as when he justifies murdering the three policemen at Stringybark Creek:

> certainly their wives and children are to be pitied but they must remember those men came into the bush with the intention of scattering pieces of me and my brother all over the bush and yet they know and acknowledge I have been wronged[2]

That was a lie, by the way. Sergeant Kennedy's patrol had no intention of killing the Kelly brothers, and nor did they 'know and acknowledge' he had been wronged.

Some people are entertained by a passage mocking the police:

> who has no alternative only to put up with the brutal and cowardly conduct of a parcel of big ugly fat-necked wombat headed big bellied magpie legged narrow hipped splaw-footed

> sons of Irish Bailiffs or english landlords which is better known
> as Officers of Justice or Victorian Police who some calls honest
> gentlemen[3]

Out of context, it's quirky and funny, but in context, he was mocking his murder victims.

But who wrote it? Ned dropped out of school after less than two years of primary education. That's why not even his most ardent and deluded fans pretend to believe that he physically wrote it. According to Kelly mythology, Ned dictated the letter to Joe Byrne, his partner in crime. After all, Byrne had received six years of primary education, rather than Ned's two.

There are other reasons why people think Joe Byrne wrote it. Later that year, Byrne sent his friend Aaron Sherritt a two-page letter inviting him to join the gang. The 'Sherritt letter' proves that Byrne could at least produce legible writing.

And two months before the Jerilderie robbery, Ned sent the politician Donald Cameron a letter (the Cameron Letter) that seems to have been an early draft of the Jerilderie Letter. Byrne is widely believed to have written the Cameron Letter, which leads people to conclude that he therefore also wrote the Jerilderie Letter. However, there is no proof, or even particularly compelling evidence, that he wrote either.[4]

Furthermore, Byrne's letter to Aaron Sherritt actually counts against him as the writer. It has spelling and grammar mistakes that aren't replicated in the Jerilderie Letter.[5]

For example, Joe wrote to Aaron, 'I was advised to turn treater', misspelling 'traitor'. By contrast, in the Jerilderie Letter, the word *traitor* is spelled correctly in the phrase: 'he is traitor to his country'. Did Joe forget how to spell the word a few months later?

Joe wrote *'has'* instead of *'have'*: 'Neddie and I has come to the conclusion . . .'

The writer of the Jerilderie Letter used '*have*': '. . . I have been wronged . . .'

Joe wrote '*live*' instead of '*life*': '. . . a short live and a jolly one . . .'

The Jerilderie Letter: '. . . his life was insured . . .'

These discrepancies eliminate Joe as the writer. Moreover, a graphological analysis in 2014 found significant stylistic differences. But if Joe didn't write it, who did?[6]

The schoolteacher James Wallace had the motive, the means and the opportunity.

He was a prolific writer on behalf of the Kelly gang. He penned multiple anonymous articles for regional newspapers attacking the police, including a satirical piece, '*Christmas in Kelly Land*'. In 1880 he wrote a letter to the politician Henry Graves under the pseudonym 'Connor'. And as a police spy, he wrote voluminous confidential reports for Superintendent Nicolson, under the pseudonym 'Connor'. Nobody else involved in the events of the Kelly outbreak produced as much written work as James Wallace. He had a proven record of producing long handwritten documents as substantial as the Jerilderie Letter. Therefore, he is the only person connected to the gang who we can be certain had the ability to do it. Furthermore, the circumstantial evidence overwhelmingly points to James Wallace as the writer.[7]

Wallace was in contact with the gang while they were fugitives. He was a close friend of Joe Byrne's and visited Joe's mother regularly. Wallace's son told a friend that Ned Kelly had been at the Wallace household. An investigation by detectives Considine and Ward revealed that he had been supplying the gang with provisions and even harbouring them in a remote bushland hut.

If the Kelly gang decided that they wanted to compose some lengthy documents, it makes sense that they would seek help from the most educated person they knew and trusted. That person was James Wallace.

Sure, the content was Ned's, but as the confidante and resident scholar, Wallace probably influenced it. The letter would have taken many hours and multiple drafts (particularly given the neatness of the writing, and the almost complete absence of mistakes and corrections), in a hideaway somewhere. There would have been multiple sessions, re-readings and conversations about it.

A graphological analysis conducted in 2014 of the handwriting in the Sherritt letter (by Joe Byrne) and the Jerilderie Letter (believed by many to have been written by Byrne) was inconclusive, for multiple reasons: the Sherritt letter is only two pages long; many pages of the Jerilderie Letter are faded and therefore unusable for comparison; and because the originals, held in archives, were not available.[8]

James Wallace's letters to Nicolson, as agent Fisher, run to more than 7000 words across 42 pages. It is interesting to compare those letters to the Jerilderie Letter.

A striking feature of the Fisher letters is that Wallace's writing style varies a lot.

Some stylistic features seem, at first blush, to rule Wallace out. But the Fisher letters were written casually and privately, whereas the penmanship of the Jerilderie Letter is neat and clear. Whoever wrote it was doing their very best cursive and concentrating hard.

Look at the word 'glad' in the first sample of Wallace's handwriting above, and especially the 'g', which is a sort of lopsided figure 8. By contrast, the 'g's in the Jerilderie Letter have a standard cursive form. However, Wallace sometimes did use a standard g. Here are all seven instances of the word give and given from the Fisher letters:

The three instances on the left are standard cursive, whereas the others are of the figure 8 form. Here are some instances of the word 'give' from the Jerilderie Letter.

The absence of lopsided figure 8s in the Jerilderie Letter might seem to rule Wallace out. But their absence might just be the result of trying very hard to produce neat, standard script.

When the author's attention flagged, old habits could emerge. There are precious few mistakes and corrections in the Jerilderie letter, but the ones that occur are instructive. The only place that words are crossed out and rewritten is on page 50. That must have been a momentary lapse of concentration. The corrected word was 'give' and look how it was written: as a sloping figure 8, in the style of James Wallace.

Then there are the loops on the 'y's.
Here are some Jerilderie words ending in y.

And here are some Wallace/Fisher words ending in y.

Unlike most of the Jerilderie Letter script, the anticlockwise loop is not standard cursive. The final stroke of a word should carry the pen forward, putting it in position for the next word. Perhaps it was supposed to look fancy. At any rate, it would have required considerable concentration and, again, the pattern was broken in a revealing way when the writer made an error. This occurred on page 35, when the writer accidentally omitted two words before writing 'by'. In that moment of weakness, the loop went clockwise, in the style of James Wallace.

Despite these discrepancies, there are also strong similarities.

I reconstructed a small segment of the Jerilderie Letter in Wallace's handwriting. For each word, I found the closest match in the Fisher letters. If the word did not occur in the Fisher letters, then I constructed one out of multiple words. This isn't a formal scientific test; it is an exploration.

Here is the top of page 42 from the Jerilderie Letter:

Here is a reconstruction of those lines using Wallace's handwriting from the Fisher letters.

They are not identical, but there is an undeniable resemblance.

If Wallace wrote the Jerilderie Letter, then he also wrote the Cameron Letter. The Victorian Public Record Office holds a copy of the Cameron Letter, but nobody knows if it is the original or a transcription, so it cannot be used for handwriting analysis.

And what about the so-called Sherritt Letter of mid-1879? Maybe that, too, was written by James Wallace. After all, Wallace claimed he could forge Joe's handwriting. Furthermore, he admitted to writing a death threat in Joe's handwriting to a Beechworth resident who had cooperated with the police. Again, he had the motive, the means and the opportunity.[9]

The authorship of that letter clearly bothered Detective Michael Ward, because when he forwarded it to his superior, he did not simply describe it as a letter from Joe Byrne. Instead, he went to some trouble to document what was known about its origins, mentioning for example that Mrs Sherritt and his colleague Constable Mullane believed it was written in Joe's handwriting. Rather than explicitly expressing doubts, he obtained a letter smuggled by Joe and Aaron from prison, which he included for handwriting comparison. That letter looks quite different and is barely literate. Ward believed that prison letter was written by Joe, but it was signed '*Joe and Aaron*'. It might have been written by Aaron.[10]

The only known fragment of Kelly's writing is a letter received by Sergeant Babington in 1870, known as the Babington Letter. Near the end is this:

> answer this leter as soon as posabel direct your letter Daniel Kelly
> Gretta post office that is my name no more at present

Why would Ned write 'direct your letter Daniel Kelly Gretta post office that is my name'?

The obvious reason is that Dan wrote the letter on Ned's behalf. But if so, then Ned Kelly didn't write the Babington Letter, and therefore there are no examples of his handwriting in existence. Likewise, if Joe didn't write the Sherritt letter or the Beechworth Gaol letter, there are no surviving examples of his handwriting either.

The literary and rhetorical powers of Ned Kelly and Joe Byrne have been eulogised for almost a century and a half. Yet it is entirely possible that, apart from classroom exercises, neither of them ever wrote anything at all.

Notes

I have used the following abbreviations and notations:

Police Commission refers to *Minutes of Evidence taken before the Royal Commission into the Police Force in Victoria, together with Appendices*. The document is large and unwieldy, so where applicable I have provided either the name of the witness and the page number, or a title for the relevant section.

Police Commission, 2nd Progress Report refers, obviously, to the *Second Progress Report of the Police Royal Commission*.

VPRS stands for Victorian Public Record Series, held by the Public Records office of Victoria. These can be found at the website prov.vic.gov.au.

SLV is the State Library of Victoria.

Most of the newspaper articles can be found with the National Library of Australia's excellent trove service, at trove.nla.gov.au.

Chapter 1. Magistrate McBean's heirloom watch

1 'Bushranging', *Ovens & Murray Advertiser*, 17 Mar 1870, p. 2; 'More bushranging', *Benalla Ensign & Farmer's & Squatter's Journal*, 18 Mar 1870, p. 2; 'Highway robbery under arms', *Portland Guardian & Normanby General Advertiser*, 21 Mar 1870, p. 2.

2 For McBean's relations with the Lloyds and others, see Francis Hare, *The Last of the Bushrangers*, p. 50; 'The Benalla Ensign', *Benalla Ensign & Farmer's & Squatter's Journal*, 10 Jun 1870, p. 2; for the tactic of arson against those who defy or displease the criminals, see, e.g., 'The Benalla Ensign', *Benalla Ensign & Farmer's & Squatter's Journal*, 13 May 1870, p. 2; for judicial corruption, see, e.g., 'The unpaid magistracy', *Ovens & Murray Advertiser*, 15 Oct 1870, p. 2.

3 Description of Power in 'Bushranging in the Ovens District', *Ovens & Murray Advertiser*, 31 Aug 1869, p. 3; and *NSW Police Gazette*, 11 May 1870, p. 131.

4 For examples of Power's criminal activities see: 'Yackandandah', *Ovens & Murray Advertiser*, 13 Apr 1869, p. 2; 'Bushranging at Middle Creek', *The Argus*, 13 May 1869, p. 6; 'Bushranging near Beechworth,' *Leader*, 4 Sep 1869, p. 19; 'Committal of Power, the bushranger', *Leader*, 18 Jun 1870, p. 19; 'Encounter with a bushranger', *Geelong Advertiser*, 20 Oct 1869, p. 3; 'Sydney, Saturday', *Mercury*, 25 Sep 1869, p. 2.

5 For 'Lake', see 'The Bushranger Power', *Ovens & Murray Advertiser*, 29 May 1869, p. 2.

6 'Benalla police court', *Ovens & Murray Advertiser*, 19 Jun 1869, p. 2.

7   Some claim he was born in November 1854, but June 1855 is more likely, based on the age he gave on his father's death certificate and the age given on his school report.
8   Morrissey, *Ned Kelly: Selectors, squatters and stock thieves*, p. 119.

Chapter 2. The Melbourne Club

1   It has recently been criticised for its male-exclusive membership policy.
2   A detailed history of the Melbourne Club is given by Ronald McNicoll, *Number 36 Collins Street*, from which are derived the descriptions here of the club, the servants' attire, and so on.
3   The Standish–McBean meeting is mentioned twice in the Police Royal Commission (Frederick Standish, Police Commission, p. 578, Q 15906, and also Charles Nicolson, Police Commission, p. 624, Q 16861), and by John Sadleir, *Recollections of a Victorian Police Officer*, pp. 159–60.
4   Standish's life story is told in Paul de Serville, *Pounds and Pedigrees*, pp. 42–76; a summary of his career as chief commissioner of police can be found in Haldane, *The People's Force*, pp. 54–74.
5   'Ballaarat', *The Argus*, 7 May 1855, p. 6; 'Chinese marriages,' *The Age*, 8 Oct 1857, p. 6.
6   Early issues in Victoria police are described in Haldane, *The People's Force*, pp. 5–54.
7   The fiz-gig system is discussed in *Royal Commission, Police Special Report on the Detective Force*, pp. 9–10. See also Haldane, *The People's Force*, pp. 96–7.

Chapter 3. The fiz-gig

1   'The recent arrest of John Lloyd', *Ovens & Murray Advertiser*, 26 Apr 1870, p. 3. Local police were out of the loop: Charles Nicolson, Police Commission, p. 632, Q 16899.
2   *New South Wales Police Gazette*, 11 May 1870, p. 131.
3   Frederick Standish, Police Commission, p. 578, Q 15910.
4   Frederick Standish, Police Commission, p. 578, Q 15911.
5   'Bushranging days', *The Argus*, 1 Aug 1908, p. 6.
6   Date estimated from the phrase 'fortnight afterwards', Charles Nicolson, Police Commission, p. 624, Q 16861.
7   'Benalla Police Court', *Benalla Ensign & Farmer's & Squatter's Journal*, 13 May 1870, p. 3; Kelly's arrest reported in 'Arrest of a bushranger', *Bendigo Advertiser*, 5 May 1870, p. 2, and 'The Benalla Ensign', *Benalla Ensign & Farmer's & Squatter's Journal*, 6 May 1870 p. 2. Superintendent William Nicolas may be confused with Superintendent Charles Nicholson, the latter playing a more prominent role in events around the Kelly gang.
8   'Benalla Police Court', *Benalla Ensign & Farmer's & Squatter's Journal*, 13 May 1870, p. 3; Kelly's arrest reported in 'Arrest of a bushranger', *Bendigo Advertiser*, 5 May 1870, p. 2, and 'The Benalla Ensign', *Benalla Ensign & Farmer's & Squatter's Journal*, 6 May 1870, p. 2.
9   Hare, *The Last of the Bushrangers*, p. 93.
10 'News and Notes', *Ballarat Star*, 23 Apr 1870, p. 2.
11 'Benalla', *Bendigo Advertiser*, 13 May 1870, p. 2; 'Benalla police court', *Benalla Ensign & Farmer's & Squatter's Journal*, 13 May 1870, p. 3.
12 Robberies near Kyneton were reported in 'Alleged outrage by Power', *Weekly Times*, 30 Apr 1870, p. 9; Murray's financial hardship mentioned in an untitled article,

Kyneton Observer, 5 May 1870, p. 2; Further information about the Kyneton case in 'Police', *Kyneton Observer*, 21 May 1870, p. 2; 'Police', *Kyneton Observer*, 28 May 1870, p. 2; Untitled, *Kyneton Observer*, 4 Jun 1870, p. 2; 'News and notes', *Ballarat Star*, 4 Jun 1870, p. 2.

13 'The capture of Power: an interesting narrative, by C.H. Nicolson', *The Age*, 6 Feb 1892, p. 14. Since Hare explicitly said that Kelly was of no assistance, it can be inferred that Nicolson paid Kelly a second visit alone. See 'Nicolson to CCP, 24 Oct 1870', VPRS 937/P, Item 272 (not online).

14 Indigenous Australians were often employed by colonial police as expert guides and trackers, known as blacktrackers. Their skill in finding criminals, stolen property, and missing persons in the bush was undisputed.

15 William Montfort, Police Commission, p. 172, Q 3394.

Chapter 4. It takes a thief to catch a thief

1 Hare, *The Last of the Bushrangers*, p. 71.
2 Hare, *The Last of the Bushrangers*, p. 73.
3 Hare, *The Last of the Bushrangers*, p. 73.
4 'Power and his adventures', *The Argus*, 11 Jun 1870, p. 2.
5 See, for example, 'A notorious bushranger', *Evening News* (NSW), 13 Feb 1885, p. 3; 'Nicolson to CCP, 24 Oct 1870', VPRS 937/P, Item 272.
6 'Letter to Sergeant James Babington', VPRS 937/P, Item 272.
7 'Detectives and general police', *Ovens & Murray Advertiser*, 12 Sep 1874, p. 4.
8 Sadleir, *Recollections of a Victorian Police Officer*, p. 163.

Chapter 5. Constable Ward

1 Sources differ on whether he was born in Ballinasloe or Roscommon, about 30 miles apart. I have relied in part on the family history (entitled 'Michael Edward Ward') provided by a relation of Ward's, Michael Dolan.
2 'Sub-Inspector Ward, *Wodonga and Towong Sentinel*, 29 Dec 1905, p. 4.
3 'Sub-Inspector Ward', *Wodonga and Towong Sentinel*, 29 Dec 1905, p. 4.
4 'Beechworth police court', *Ovens & Murray Advertiser*, 2 Nov 1872, p. 2; 'Sub-Inspector Ward', *Wodonga and Towong Sentinel*, 29 Dec 1905, p. 4.
5 'Another sunstroke', *Ovens & Murray Advertiser*, 15 Dec 1874, p. 2.
6 See Haldane, *The People's Force*, for a discussion of Irish police.
7 Michael Ward, Record of conduct and service, Victoria Police Museum.
8 See Michael Ward, Record of Conduct and Service, Victoria Police Museum; for arrest of child molester: 'Wangaratta police court', *Ovens & Murray Advertiser*, 12 Sep 1876, p. 2; Chickens: 'Beechworth county court', *Ovens & Murray Advertiser*, 19 Jul 1871, p. 4; clothes thief: 'South Australia', *Ovens & Murray Advertiser*, 10 Nov 1873, p. 2; body parts: 'Late fatal railway accident at Wangaratta', *Ovens & Murray Advertiser*, 3 Aug 1875, p. 3.
9 'Beechworth general sessions', *Ovens & Murray Advertiser*, 3 Aug 1871, p. 3.
10 'A sad case', *Ovens & Murray Advertiser*, 25 Jan 1872, p. 2.
11 'The boy lost at Stanley', *Ovens & Murray Advertiser*, 5 Nov 1873, p. 2; 'Accident at Deep Creek', *Ovens & Murray Advertiser*, 27 Nov 1873, p. 2.
12 'Capture of the Wild Man of the Woods', *Ovens & Murray Advertiser*, 17 May 1872, p. 2.

13 Michael Ward, Record of Conduct and Service, Victoria Police Museum; 'The floods', *The Argus*, 29 June 1875, p. 6.
14 'A gallant act', *Ovens & Murray Advertiser*, 20 Sep 1873, p. 4.
15 'Play Michael Wiggins once again', *Ovens & Murray Advertiser*, 14 Oct 1873, p. 2; 'Mounted Constable Ward', *Ovens & Murray Advertiser*, 20 Dec 1873, p. 4.
16 Michael Ward, Police Commission, p. 160, Q 3024–3027.
17 'The Kelly gang', *The Argus*, 7 Aug 1880, p. 8; Brian Cookson, 'The Kelly gang from within: Detective reminiscences', *Sun* (NSW), 5 Sep 1911, p. 9.

Chapter 6. Kelly and the cops

1 Corfield, *The Ned Kelly Encyclopaedia*, p. 284; Macfarlane, *The Kelly Gang Unmasked*, pp. 30–31.
2 'Avenel petty sessions', *Kilmore Free Press*, 6 Jun 1867, p. 3.
3 Morrissey, *Ned Kelly: Selectors, squatters and stock thieves*, p. 121.
4 'About the Kellys', *Ovens & Murray Advertiser*, 11 Jan 1879, p. 8.
5 'Benalla police court', *Ovens & Murray Advertiser*, 30 Oct 1869, p. 3. The newspaper erroneously reported it as Fifteen Mile, a nearby locality.
6 'Benalla police court', *Benalla Ensign & Farmer's & Squatter's Journal*, 29 Oct 1869, p. 2.
7 'Benalla police court', *Ovens & Murray Advertiser*, 30 Oct 1869, p. 4.
8 A letter and related editorial comment earlier accused Wills of placing undue reliance on untrustworthy witness testimony: see 'A Bright magistrate', *Ovens & Murray Advertiser*, 7 Apr 1863, p. 3.
9 'Police magistrate book of cases', VPRS 1503, Item 5, 10 Nov 1870.
10 'The town', *Leader*, 3 Dec 1870, p. 9.
11 'Wangaratta Police Court', *Ovens & Murray Advertiser*, 12 Nov 1870, p. 3; 'Report: re conviction of Edward Kelly for assault', VPRS 4969 P0, Item 88.
12 'Beechworth general sessions', *Ovens & Murray Advertiser*, 5 Aug 1871, p. 3.
13 Hall makes clear in his official report that the stolen horse had not yet been gazetted, however he had been already informed of the theft by Mansfield police. Therefore he had valid reason to arrest Kelly. The *Advertiser*'s report of the trial seems to have muddled Hall's testimony, leading modern historians to claim that he committed perjury. See Hall's report, VPRS 937, 22 Apr 1871. See also 'Wangaratta police court', *Ovens & Murray Advertiser*, 2 May 1871, p. 4.
14 'Wangaratta police court', *Ovens & Murray Advertiser*, 2 May 1871, p. 4.
15 Untitled, *The Argus*, 2 May 1871, p. 7.
16 'Wangaratta police court', *Ovens & Murray Advertiser*, 27 Apr 1871, p. 3.
17 'Beechworth general sessions', *Ovens & Murray Advertiser*, 5 Aug 1871 p. 3.
18 'Copy of statement handed by defendant to Mr. Living', VPRS 4966 P0, Item 5.
19 Untitled, *The Argus*, 2 May 1871, p. 7.
20 VPRS 937, 413, for dates 20 Apr 1871; 22 Apr 1871; 15 May 1871; 14 Aug 1871.
21 'Beechworth general sessions', *Ovens & Murray Advertiser*, 5 Aug 1871, p. 3.
22 'Wangaratta police court', *Ovens & Murray Advertiser*, 2 May 1871, p. 4.
23 'A candidate for the gallows', *Ovens & Murray Advertiser*, 3 May 1871, p. 2.
24 'Beechworth general sessions', *Ovens & Murray Advertiser*, 5 Aug 1871, p. 3; 'Country news', *The Argus*, 8 May 1871, p. 6.
25 'Beechworth general sessions', *Ovens & Murray Advertiser*, 5 Aug 1871, p. 3.
26 There was media speculation that Hall was transferred for being overweight, but the Prentice inquiry and the Kelly arrest seem to be the true catalyst. Hall was also

subjected to scrutiny over his expenditure on paid informers. The Prentice inquiry and related correspondence are in a series of documents from Jan–Apr 1871, in VPRS 937, Item 413. For Hall's transfer request, see Inspector Bookey's memo, 11 June 1871, VPRS 937, Item 413; and a memo from Hall himself requesting transfer: 20 June 1871, VPRS 937, Item 413. The community gift to him on departure is mentioned in: Untitled, *Benalla Ensign & Farmer's & Squatter's Journal*, 12 Aug 1871, p. 2.

Chapter 7. Constable Flood

1 He was two years old when the potato blight arrived in Ireland, devastating the crops and causing mass starvation and suffering.
2 Flood and Mary Burne married on 2 Oct 1870 in the Beechworth Catholic church, and Ernest Junior was born on 11 Jul 1871, according to documents from Births Deaths and Marriages Victoria, www.bdm.vic.gov.au.
3 'Wangaratta police court', *Ovens & Murray Advertiser*, 14 Sep 1871, p. 2.
4 'Benalla police court', *Ovens & Murray Advertiser*, 21 Sep 1871, p. 3.
5 'Benalla police court', *Ovens & Murray Advertiser*, 26 Oct 1871, p. 2.
6 Jones, *Ned Kelly: A short life*, pp. 69, 352.
7 de Looper, 'Death registration and mortality trends in Australia 1856–1906', p. 65; Lewis & McCloud, 'A workingman's paradise? Reflections on urban mortality in colonial Australia, 1860–1900'.
8 The Gunn-Flood issue can be found in a series of papers in VPRS 937, Item 414, particularly a report by Inspector Brooke-Smith (10 Feb 1872); a memo by Inspector Barclay (11 Feb 1872); and a summary by Captain Standish (21 Feb 1872).
9 'Births', *Ovens & Murray Advertiser*, 17 Mar 1873, p. 2.
10 Jane Graham was a prostitute, revealed in MacFarlane, *The Kelly Gang Unmasked*, p. 41, citing police logbook.
11 'Benalla police court', *Ovens & Murray Advertiser*, 22 Nov 1872, p. 3.
12 'Changes in the police department', *North Eastern Ensign*, 18 Nov 1873, p. 2; Ernest Flood, Police Commission, p. 456, Q 12620; Ernest Flood, Record of conduct and service, Victoria Police Museum, p. 4.
13 James Graves, Police Commission, p. 560, Q 15490.
14 Police Commission, 2nd Progress Report, p. 4.

Chapter 8. A tale of two Irishmen

1 Senyard, 'Glass, Hugh (1817–1871)'.
2 McQuilton, *The Kelly Outbreak*, pp. 49–50. Morrissey, in *Ned Kelly: Selectors, squatters and stock thieves: A social history of Kelly Country*, 1987, p. 27, says: 'Selectors and squatters generally received a fair and impartial hearing before the district's Land Boards'.
3 See for example, Alfred Wyatt's testimony that most citizens were 'terrorised' and 'thoroughly horrified' by the gang. See: Alfred Wyatt, Police Commission, p. 134, Q 2353–2354.
4 See for example, Police Commission, 2nd Progress Report, p. 9, that 'the Quins [sic], the Lloyds, and the Kellys ... constituted a "ring" that became a standing menace to the respectable and law-abiding people of the district'. Also, Flood stated that most residents of Greta were 'law abiding and honest people', Ernest Flood, Police Commission, p. 454, Q 12571; the 'Greta Mob' is described in the article

'The Greta Mob', *Ovens & Murray Advertiser*, 30 May 1878, p. 2. According to Morrissey (1978), p 294, 'Outside the clan and the Greta Mob, a small group of sympathetic selectors supported the outlaws.' See also Morrissey (1995) for an investigation of the extent of involvement of the Kellys, Quinns and Lloyds in stock theft.

5   Some sources claim he arrived in 1842, rather than 1840. I rely here on Doug Morrissey, *Ned Kelly: Selectors, squatters and stock thieves*, p. 116.
6   Morrissey, *Ned Kelly: Selectors, squatters and stock thieves*, p. 113.
7   Ned's hatred is evidenced by his disparagement of Whitty, Byrne and Farrell in the Cameron and Jerilderie Letters (described later).

Chapter 9. Michael Ward joins the detective force

1   This incident is described in 'Beechworth Police Court', *Ovens & Murray Advertiser*, 1 Jun 1876, p. 4; Police Commission, 2nd Progress Report, p. 8, incorrectly stated that the stolen meat was horsemeat.
2   Ward was accompanied by Constable Michael Twomey to the Byrne selection, and by Constable Patrick Mullane to the Sherritt selection.
3   The charge of 'possessing stolen meat' had been introduced to combat exactly this type of crime, where it was usually difficult to prove theft as the evidence was easily destroyed.
4   'Sub-Inspector Ward', *Wodonga and Towong Sentinel*, 29 Dec 1905, p. 4; Brian Cookson, 'The Kelly gang from within', *Sun* (NSW), 5 Sep 1911, p. 9; 'The Kelly Gang', *The Age*, 13 May 1911, p. 16.
5   'Beechworth police court', *Ovens & Murray Advertiser*, 13 Jan 1877, p. 4.
6   'Beechworth general sessions', *Ovens & Murray Advertiser*, 3 Mar 1877, p. 1.
7   'Beechworth general sessions', *Ovens & Murray Advertiser*, 1 Mar 1877, p. 2.
8   Michael Ward, Police Commission, p. 160, Q 3033–3036; Michael Dolan, 'Michael Edward Ward'.
9   'Presentation', *Ovens & Murray Advertiser*, 3 Jul 1877, p. 2.
10 'Presentation,' *Ovens & Murray Advertiser*, 3 Jul 1877, p. 2.
11 Michael Ward, Police Commission, p. 160, Q 3034, 3036. Ward's promotion into the detective force was approved in 1876, but he seems not to have taken up the role until sometime in the first half of 1877. He told the Royal Commission that he turned down his initial offer to join the detective force, but a Ward family historian asserts that he applied twice before. It's possible that both are correct.

Chapter 10. The Whitty Raid

1   The term 'officer' is now used to mean any member of a police force, whereas in colonial times it referred to someone with a rank that placed them in charge of others. See for example, McIntyre, *A True Narrative of the Kelly Gang*, p. 75, 'constables . . . who have since advanced to the position of officers'.
2   Almost a third of horse thefts occurred within a 60-mile radius of Greta. I calculated that figure by collating the reported horse thefts in the *Police Gazette*, and using google maps to determine the distance from Greta. There were 96 horse thefts within 60 miles of Greta, 313 overall, with missing location data for two; resulting in 31 per cent of horse thefts within the Greta radius. This is all the more significant given that only 6 per cent of Victoria's population lived in the north-east. John McQuilton, in *The Kelly Outbreak*, p. 60, presents a chart that tells a different story but he provides no explanation or citation for it. It's possible he was using jurisdictional boundaries rather

than actual distance, but regardless, without any explanation of his source, McQuilton's chart must be taken with a grain of salt. For cattle thefts, see Police Commission, 2nd Progress Report, p. 9, which clearly shows a two-year spike, in keeping with the temporary activity of a prolific group of organised criminals.

3 Brian Cookson, 'The Kelly Gang from Within: Michael Ward', *Sun* (NSW), 5 Sep 1911, p. 9.

4 *Victorian Police Gazette*, 18 Apr 1877, 25 Apr 1877, 8 Aug 1877; for indicative miners' wages see, for example, 'Reduction of miners' wages at Sandhurst', *Mount Alexander Mail*, 26 Aug 1879.

5 *Victorian Police Gazette*, 26 Sep 1877, p. 277.

6 Charles Nicolson, Police Commission, p. 46, Q 1020.

7 Charles Nicolson, Police Commission, p. 47, Q 1024–1028.

8 Charles Nicolson, Police Commission, p. 47, Q 1035–1036.

9 Charles Nicolson, Police Commission, p. 47, Q 1036.

10 Charles Nicolson, Police Commission, p. 47, Q 1040.

11 McIntyre, *A True Narrative of the Kelly Gang*, p. 5.

12 'Barnawartha and Howlong horse stealing case', *Corowa Free Press*, 30 Nov 1877, p. 3.

13 'Barnawartha and Howlong horse stealing case', *Corowa Free Press*, 30 Nov 1877, p. 3.

Chapter 11. Sergeant Steele

1 Steele's personnel record states that he was born on 1 Aug 1836 in Ireland (Arthur Steele Record of conduct and service, Victoria Police Museum), and ancestry sites reveal that his parents were also both Irish. An obituary of Steele claimed that he was born in France when his father was on active duty there, but the claim does not accord with official records, and may be simply a piece of fanciful family lore. He is sometimes described in Kelly literature as an Englishman, but that is incorrect.

2 Sergeant Steele, Record of Conduct and Service, Victoria Police Museum.

3 'Barnawartha and Howlong horse stealing case', *Corowa Free Press*, 30 Nov 1877, p. 3.

4 Detective Joseph Brown (police no. 1891) was not the same as Constable Joseph Brown (police no. 2876), who was later engaged in the search for the Kelly gang.

5 'Wangaratta police court', *Ovens & Murray Advertiser*, 22 Dec 1877, p. 1.

6 'Mutilating horses', *Ovens & Murray Advertiser*, 27 Nov 1877, p. 3, 'Horse stealing', *Ovens & Murray Advertiser*, 4 Dec 1877, p. 4; 'The Stolen Horses', *Ovens & Murray Advertiser*, 17 Jan 1878, p. 2.

Chapter 12. Constable Fitzpatrick

1 Haldane, *The People's Force*, p. 84.

2 Dawson, 'Redeeming Fitzpatrick: Ned Kelly and the Fitzpatrick Incident'.

3 Brian Cookson, 'The Kelly Gang from within: The genesis of the trouble', *Sun* (NSW), 23 Sep 1911, p. 4. (The existing digitised copy of that article is barely legible; a more legible version that can be found on NLA Trove is the syndicated reprint, 'The Kelly Gang', *Advertiser* (SA), 4 Nov 1911, p. 8.

4 Sergeant Whelan confirmed that Kelly was fined on 18 Sep 1877 for drunkenness, resisting arrest, assaulting a police officer and damaging a uniform; all the other details of this incident come from Kelly himself via his letters, his lawyer and

the 1879 George W. Hall book, and are therefore untrustworthy. See 'Report re prisoner Kelly, sentenced to death', VPRS 4969, Item 29, p. 5.

5   'Facts and scraps', *The Australasian Sketcher with Pen and Pencil*, 27 Oct 1877, p. 123; 'Bushranging and burglary', *Ovens & Murray Advertiser*, 2 Oct 1877, p. 2; 'Beechworth general sessions', *Ovens & Murray Advertiser*, 2 Mar 1878, p. 8.

6   Fitzpatrick's involvement in the arrest is confirmed by Sergeant Whelan in Police Commission, p. 236, Q 5950.

7   Fitzpatrick believed he was responsible, according to his testimony in Police Commission, p. 465, Q 12873. See also *Victorian Police Gazette*, 17 Oct 1877, p. 275, & Victorian Police Gazette, 19 Dec, p. 339.

8   'Beechworth general sessions', *Ovens & Murray Advertiser*, 2 Mar 1878, p. 8.

9   'Wangaratta police court', *Ovens & Murray Advertiser*, 27 Nov 1877, p. 2.

10 Alexander Fitzpatrick, Record of Conduct and Service, Victoria Police Museum; 'Lonigan murder prosecution brief', VPRS 4966, Item 6, p. 16.

11 'Queen vs Ellen Kelly', VPRS 4966, Item 4, p. 31; Alexander Fitzpatrick, Police Commission, p. 464, Q 12837.

12 James Whelan, Police Commission, p. 236, Q 5951.

Chapter 13. The Fitzpatrick Incident

1   Dawson, 'Redeeming Fitzpatrick: Ned Kelly and the Fitzpatrick incident'. Dawson's article provides excellent analysis and insights, which have influenced my understanding of the Fitzpatrick incident. My main primary source for this chapter is 'Queen vs Ellen Kelly', VPRS 4966, Item 4, pp. 24–31, which provides the testimony of Fitzpatrick, Dr Nicholson, Sergeant Whelan, Constable Flood and Sergeant Steele.

2   Alexander Fitzpatrick, Police Commission, p. 463, Q 12822.

3   'Queen vs Ellen Kelly', VPRS 4966, Item 4, p. 25.

4   'Queen vs Ellen Kelly', VPRS 4966, Item 4, p. 10. In his official telegram about the event, Sergeant Whelan stated, 'In throwing up his arms he received the ball'.

5   'Queen vs Ellen Kelly', VPRS 4966, Item 4, p. 31.

6   'Queen vs Ellen Kelly', VPRS 4966, Item 4, p. 26.

7   'The Greta shooting case', *Ovens & Murray Advertiser*, 10 Oct 1878, p. 4.

8   'Queen vs Ellen Kelly', VPRS 4966, Item 4, p. 26.

9   Dawson, 'Redeeming Fitzpatrick', p. 80, footnote 163; But as seen in Williamson, statement, 29 October 1878, VPRS 4965 Unit 5, Item 353. The police believed that Billy King was an alias for Wild Wright.

10 'Queen vs Ellen Kelly', VPRS 4966, Item 4, p. 27.

11 'Queen vs Ellen Kelly', VPRS 4966, Item 4, p. 59.

12 'Queen vs Ellen Kelly', VPRS 4966, Item 4, p. 27.

13 'Queen vs Ellen Kelly', VPRS 4966, Item 4, p. 28.

14 'Beechworth court of assize', *Ovens & Murray Advertiser*, 10 Oct 1878, p. 5; also 'Weather', *Ovens & Murray Advertiser*, 23 Apr 1878, p. 3.

15 'Queen vs Ellen Kelly', VPRS 4966, Item 4, p. 28.

16 'Queen vs Ellen Kelly', VPRS 4966, Item 4, p. 29.

17 'Queen vs Ellen Kelly', VPRS 4966, Item 4, p. 34.

18 James Whelan, Police Commission, p. 236, Q 5947.

19 'Queen vs Ellen Kelly', VPRS 4966, Item 4, p. 6.

Chapter 14. The arrest of Ellen Kelly

1 Arthur Steele, Police Commission, p. 319, Q 8818.
2 'Queen vs Ellen Kelly', VPRS 4966, Item 4, pp. 8–10.
3 Arthur Steele, Police Commission, p. 319, Q 8819.
4 Arthur Steele, Police Commission, p. 319, Q 8817.
5 'Queen vs Ellen Kelly', VPRS 4966, Item 4, pp. 61–2.
6 'Queen vs Ellen Kelly', VPRS 4966, Item 4, p. 36.
7 Arthur Steele, Police Commission, p. 334, Q 9214.
8 'Queen vs Ellen Kelly', VPRS 4966, Item 4, p. 35; 'Beechworth court of assize', *Ovens & Murray Advertiser*, 10 Oct 1878, p. 5.
9 Arthur Steele, Police Commission, p. 334, Q 9215.
10 'Murderous attack on a constable', *Morning Bulletin*, 1 May 1878, p. 3.
11 *Victorian Police Gazette*, 8 May 1878.

Chapter 15. Ward undercover

1 Michael Ward, Police Commission, p. 160, Q 3040.
2 Michael Ward, Police Commission, p. 160, Q 3037–3040.
3 Michael Ward, Police Commission, p. 160, Q 3039.
4 Michael Ward, Police Commission, p. 160, Q 3042–3046. Ward said in testimony that the patrol departed on 7 May, but this is clearly a mistake, because he earlier said it happened in June, and furthermore, he arrived in the district on 17 May. It is obvious he meant 7 June but erred on the stand.
5 'Queen vs Ellen Kelly', VPRS 4966, Item 4, p. 37.
6 See Dawson, 'Redeeming Fitzpatrick' for detailed discussion of this point.
7 Michael Ward, Police Commission, pp. 162–3, Q 3109.
8 Michael Ward, Police Commission, p. 63, Q 3116.
9 Michael Ward, Police Commission, p. 60, Q 3056–3062, and p. 62 (Ward), Q 3110–3116.
10 Example of a wealthy swagman: 'General news', *Gippsland Times*, 27 Jun 1877, p. 3; a swagman dies of exposure: 'Omeo', *Ovens & Murray Advertiser*, 5 Jul 1879, p. 6.
11 Ward's base was in the upper King Valley, although he visited Beechworth vicinity while undercover.
12 John Sadleir, Police Commission, p. 104, Q 1722.
13 His 'lack of smarts' is evident by a range of decisions described throughout this book.
14 John Sadleir, Police Commission, p. 104, Q 1724, Q 1727.
15 John Sadleir, Police Commission, p. 104, Q 1724, Q 1727. I have drawn the reasonable conclusion that the Ward operation was Standish's idea, because given Secretan's scepticism it clearly wasn't his, so he must have been instructed to deploy Ward to the district. The only person who could have instructed him thus was Standish.
16 John Sadleir, Police Commission, p. 105, Q 1738.
17 John Sadleir, Police Commission, p. 105, Q 1745.
18 McIntyre stated in his autobiography that multiple patrols were conducted; Sadleir neglected to mention this at the Royal Commission or in his own memoir. Instead, he cherrypicked the correspondence with Kennedy to make it appear (misleadingly) that the patrol they were planning was the same one that ended up happening in

Oct. In fact, Sadleir explicitly stated that to the RC. He obviously contended that the two of them cooked up the idea for the Oct Stringybark patrol on their own. They didn't. It was Ward's idea all along.

19 McIntyre, *A True Narrative of the Kelly Gang*, p. 7 states that there were 'many patrols', implicitly exposing Sadleir's deception at the Royal Commission.

Chapter 16. The trial of Ellen Kelly

1 'The Greta shooting case', *Ovens & Murray Advertiser*, 21 May 1878, p. 2.
2 'Queen vs Ellen Kelly,' VPRS 4966, Item 4, p. 32.
3 'Queen vs Ellen Kelly', VPRS 4966, Item 4, p. 33.
4 'Mrs. Kelly', *Ovens & Murray Advertiser*, 6 Jun 1878, p. 2.
5 No baby at time of arrest, according to Arthur Steele, Police Commission, p. 319, Q 8824; infant in gaol, see 'Mrs Kelly', *Ovens & Murray Advertiser*, 6 Jun 1878, p. 2, and also prison record 'Kelly, Ellen', VPRS 516 Con 2, Item 7, p. 197; see Brickey Williamson's claim to have fathered the household's youngest child: 'William-son's suggestions re: trap for Kelly Gang', VPRS 4965 P0, Item 34, p. 2, and a media report that Kate and Brickey were in a relationship: 'The bushranging outrage', *Ovens & Murray Advertiser*, 31 Oct 1878, p. 3. There are no birth records for a baby born in the family at that time. In researching her historical novel, *Kate Kelly*, the author Rebecca Wilson concluded that the baby in question was Kate's, rather than Ellen's. At face value, her theory is plausible. Lack of relevant records prevents a definitive answer.
6 'Beechworth court of assize', *Ovens & Murray Advertiser*, 10 Oct 1878, p. 5.
7 Her lawyer William Zinke assisted, but only barristers could argue a case before a Supreme Court judge.
8 David MacFarlane, 'The Fitzpatrick Conspiracy Part IV', notes that Fitzpatrick's death certificate in 1924 lists the cause as sarcoma of the liver, an aggressive cancer that, unlike cirrhosis, is not closely associated with alcoholism.
9 'Beechworth assize court', *The Age*, 14 Oct 1878, p. 3.
10 'Application & associated reports for remission of sentence of prisoner Williamson', VPRS 4969 P0, Item 52, pp. 23–5. Standish's support of remission (which was granted): VPRS 4969 P0, Item 52, pp. 23–4. Williamson never admitted to being an accessory or accomplice in the crime.
11 Indirect speech changed to direct speech, from Prisoner Williamson's statement, Police Commission, p. 702 & 'Statement of prisoner Williamson, VPRS 4965 P0, Item 353; another report says she said, 'By God, they'll get it for this', see 'The Kelly Gang', *The Argus*, 10 Aug 1880, p. 7.

Chapter 17. Border crossings

1 John Sadleir, Police Commission, p. 104, Q 1727.
2 Michael Ward, Police Commission, p. 63, Q 3118; 'Inspector Ward's reminiscences', *Mount Alexander Mail*, 7 Dec 1905, p. 4; The Moyhu connection is mentioned in Michael Ward, Police Commission, p. 164, Q 3135.
3 John Sadleir, Police Commission, p. 104, Q 1727.
4 John Sadleir, Police Commission, p. 104, Q 1727.
5 Michael Ward, Police Commission, p. 63, Q 3126–3131.
6 'The police murders', *Geelong Advertiser*, 12 Nov 1878, p. 3.
7 Michael Ward, Police Commission, p. 63, Q 3126–3131.

Chapter 18. Into the Ranges

1 McIntyre, *A True Narrative of the Kelly Gang*, p. 4.

2 McIntyre, *A True Narrative of the Kelly Gang*, p. 10; John Sadleir, Police Commission, p. 106, Q 1742. The telegram tabled at the Royal Commission contained two errors. First, the Greta patrol was led by Sergeant Shoebridge, not Sergeant Steele. Second, Constable Baird's inclusion was erroneous.

3 McIntyre, *A True Narrative of the Kelly Gang*, p. 11

4 McIntyre, *A True Narrative of the Kelly Gang*, p. 12

5 McIntyre, *A True Narrative of the Kelly Gang*, p. 7.

6 McIntyre, *A True Narrative of the Kelly Gang*, p. 11.

7 McIntyre, *A True Narrative of the Kelly Gang*, p. 11, his reaction to equipping the Spencer rifle was 'I expressed some surprise at this as it was most unusual', and then on p. 12 'the pitiful manner in which Kelly begged Fitzpatrick not to get him into trouble . . . did not proclaim Kelly to be the murderous man he turned out to be'.

8 McIntyre, *A True Narrative of the Kelly Gang*, p. 12.

9 McIntyre, *A True Narrative of the Kelly Gang*, p. 43.

10 McIntyre, *A True Narrative of the Kelly Gang*, p. 12. McIntyre did not recognise the stranger, who was never identified.

11 'Constable McIntyre's first report of police murders by Kellys', VPRS 4965 P0, Item 317; McIntyre, *A True Narrative of the Kelly Gang*, p. 4.

12 'Constable McIntyre's first report of police murders by Kellys', VPRS 4965 P0, Item 317, p. 8; McIntyre, *A True Narrative of the Kelly Gang*, pp. 12–13.

13 McIntyre, *A True Narrative of the Kelly Gang*, p. 13.

14 McIntyre, *A True Narrative of the Kelly Gang*, p. 13.

15 McIntyre, *A True Narrative of the Kelly Gang*, p. 16.

16 McIntyre, *A True Narrative of the Kelly Gang*, p. 15.

17 McIntyre, *A True Narrative of the Kelly Gang*, p. 15.

18 A Vagabond, 'A month in Pentridge II', *The Argus*, 3 Mar 1877, p. 9.

19 A Vagabond, 'A month in Pentridge III', *The Argus*, 10 Mar 1877, p. 4.

20 McIntyre, *A True Narrative of the Kelly Gang*, p. 15.

Chapter 19. Stringybark Creek

1 McIntyre, *A True Narrative of the Kelly Gang*, p. 17.

2 'Constable McIntyre's first report of police murders by Kellys', VPRS 4965 P0, Item 317.

3 McIntyre, *A True Narrative of the Kelly Gang*, p. 17.

4 'Constable McIntyre's first report of police murders by Kellys', VPRS 4965 P0, Item 317; McIntyre, *A True Narrative of the Kelly Gang*, pp. 17–19.

5 In his unpublished memoir, McIntyre said, 'I took a hasty look around when Kelly fired and saw Lonigan fall heavily', McIntyre, *A True Narrative of the Kelly Gang*, p. 17; see also 'Constable McIntyre's first report of police murders by Kellys', VPRS 4965 P0, Item 317; and 'Lonigan murder prosecution brief', VPRS 4966 P0, Item 6, p. 3.

6 McIntyre, *A True Narrative of the Kelly Gang*, p. 17.

7 McIntyre, *A True Narrative of the Kelly Gang*, p. 17.

8 McIntyre, *A True Narrative of the Kelly Gang*, p. 17.

9 McIntyre, *A True Narrative of the Kelly Gang*, p. 23.

10 'Depositions taken at Mansfield into inquiry re death of Sergeant Kennedy', VPRS
    4969 P0, Item 24, p. 6; McIntyre, *A True Narrative of the Kelly Gang*, p. 18.

11 McIntyre, *A True Narrative of the Kelly Gang*, p. 18.

12 McIntyre, *A True Narrative of the Kelly Gang*, p. 17.

13 'Lonigan murder prosecution brief', VPRS 4966 Item 6, p. 26.

14 McIntyre, *A True Narrative of the Kelly Gang*, p. 18.

15 McIntyre, *A True Narrative of the Kelly Gang*, p. 18.

16 'Depositions taken at Mansfield into inquiry re death of Sergeant Kennedy', VPRS
    4969 P0, Item 24, p. 6; McIntyre, *A True Narrative of the Kelly Gang*, p. 18.

17 'Depositions taken at Mansfield into inquiry re death of Sergeant Kennedy', VPRS 4969
    P0, Item 24, p. 6; McIntyre, *A True Narrative of the Kelly Gang*, pp. 18–19

18 This scene, including the dialogue, comes from 'Depositions taken at Mansfield
    into inquiry re death of Sergeant Kennedy', VPRS 4969 P0, Item 24, p. 6; and
    McIntyre, *A True Narrative of the Kelly Gang*, p. 18.

19 McIntyre, *A True Narrative of the Kelly Gang*, p. 19.

20 McIntyre, *A True Narrative of the Kelly Gang*, p. 19.

21 See The Cameron Letter (VPRS 4966, Item 3), Jerilderie Letter (VPRS 4966 P0,
    Item 5), and 'Interview with Ned Kelly', *The Age*, 9 Aug 1880, p. 3.

22 McIntyre, *A True Narrative of the Kelly Gang*, p. 19.

23 McIntyre, *A True Narrative of the Kelly Gang*, p. 19.

24 'Constable McIntyre's first report of police murders by Kellys', VPRS 4965 P0,
    Item 317.

25 'Constable McIntyre's first report of police murders by Kellys', VPRS 4965 P0,
    Item 317.

26 'Depositions taken at Mansfield into inquiry re death of Sergeant Kennedy',
    VPRS 4969 P0, Item 24, p. 8.

27 McIntyre, *A True Narrative of the Kelly Gang*, p. 43.

28 'Lonigan murder prosecution brief', VPRS 4966 P0, Item 6, p. 8.

29 'The shooting of Sergeant Wallings', *Illawarra Mercury*, 1 Oct 1878, p. 4.

30 'The murderer of Senior-Sergeant Wallings killed', *Maryborough Chronicle, Wide
    Bay and Burnett Advertiser*, 26 Oct 1878, p. 6.

31 'Lonigan murder prosecution brief', VPRS 4966 P0, Item 6, p. 8.

32 'Constable McIntyre's first report of police murders by Kellys', VPRS 4965 P0, Item
    317; 'Depositions taken at Mansfield into inquiry re death of Sergeant Kennedy',
    VPRS 4969 P0, Item 24, p. 10.

33 McIntyre, *A True Narrative of the Kelly Gang*, p. 18.

34 'Constable McIntyre's first report of police murders by Kellys', VPRS 4965 P0,
    Item 317.

35 'Depositions taken at Mansfield into inquiry re death of Sergeant Kennedy', VPRS
    4965 P0, Item 317; 'Depositions taken at Mansfield into inquiry re death of
    Sergeant Kennedy', VPRS 4969 P0, Item 24, p. 11.

36 'Constable McIntyre's first report of police murders by Kellys', VPRS 4965 P0, Item
    317; 'Depositions taken at Mansfield into inquiry re death of Sergeant Kennedy',
    VPRS 4969 P0, Item 24, p. 11.

37 McIntyre, *A True Narrative of the Kelly Gang*, p. 23.

38 McIntyre, *A True Narrative of the Kelly Gang*, p. 19.

39 McIntyre, *A True Narrative of the Kelly Gang*, p. 20.

40 McIntyre, *A True Narrative of the Kelly Gang*, p. 20.
41 'Constable McIntyre's first report of police murders by Kellys', VPRS 4965 P0, Item 317; 'Depositions taken at Mansfield into inquiry re death of Sergeant Kennedy', VPRS 4969 P0, Item 24, p. 13.
42 McIntyre, *A True Narrative of the Kelly Gang*, p. 30; he was remarkably consistent, but one of the few variations in McIntyre's many reports and testimonies on the incident is whether he managed to say anything to Kennedy before Kelly opened fire (e.g., in VPRS 4965 P0, Item 317 he said he spoke before the firing commenced).
43 'Constable McIntyre's first report of police murders by Kellys', VPRS 4965 P0, Item 317.
44 'Constable McIntyre's first report of police murders by Kellys', VPRS 4965 P0, Item 317.
45 Scanlan tried to run: 'Constable McIntyre's first report of police murders by Kellys', VPRS 4965 P0, Item 317, p. 5.
46 'Constable McIntyre's first report of police murders by Kellys', VPRS 4965 P0, Item 317; 'Depositions taken at Mansfield into inquiry re death of Sergeant Kennedy', VPRS 4969 P0, Item 24, p. 15; McIntyre, *A True Narrative of the Kelly Gang*, p. 25.
47 'Constable McIntyre's first report of police murders by Kellys', VPRS 4965 P0, Item 317.

Chapter 20. McIntyre's flight

1 'Depositions taken at Mansfield into inquiry re death of Sergeant Kennedy', VPRS 4969 P0, Item 24, p. 15; McIntyre, *A True Narrative of the Kelly Gang*, p. 26.
2 McIntyre, *A True Narrative of the Kelly Gang*, p. 26.
3 'The Mansfield tragedy—McIntyre's narrative', *Leader*, 9 Nov 1878, p. 21.
4 'Constable McIntyre's first report of police murders by Kellys', VPRS 4965 P0, Item 317; 'Depositions taken at Mansfield into inquiry re death of Sergeant Kennedy', VPRS 4969 P0, Item 24, p. 16; McIntyre, *A True Narrative of the Kelly Gang*, pp. 27–8.
5 McIntyre, *A True Narrative of the Kelly Gang*, p. 28.
6 McIntyre, *A True Narrative of the Kelly Gang*, p. 28.
7 'The Mansfield tragedy—McIntyre's narrative', *Leader*, 9 Nov 1878, p. 21.
8 Kennedy & Looby, *Black Snake*, p. 115.
9 'Constable McIntyre's first report of police murders by Kellys', VPRS 4965 P0, Item 317.
10 'Inspector Ward's reminiscences', *Mount Alexander Mail*, 7 Dec 1905, p. 4.
11 'Inspector Ward's reminiscences', *Mount Alexander Mail*, 7 Dec 1905, p. 4; Michael Ward, Police Commission, p. 164, Q 3142–3148.

Chapter 21. Three inquests

1 'Constable McIntyre's first report of police murders by Kellys', VPRS 4965 P0, Item 317, p. 7.
2 'Constable McIntyre's first report of police murders by Kellys', VPRS 4965 P0, Item 317, p. 9.

3 'Constable McIntyre's first report of police murders by Kellys', VPRS 4965 P0, Item 317, p. 8; 'Depositions taken at magisterial inquiry at Mansfield', VPRS 4969 P0, Item 23, p. 8; 'Queen vs Edward Kelly: Murder file', VPRS 4966 P0, Item 2, p. 22.

4 McIntyre, *A True Narrative of the Kelly Gang*, p. 35.

5 McIntyre, *A True Narrative of the Kelly Gang*, p. 36.

6 McIntyre, *A True Narrative of the Kelly Gang*, p. 36.

7 McIntyre, *A True Narrative of the Kelly Gang*, p. 37.

8 'Depositions taken at magisterial inquiry at Mansfield', VPRS 4969 P0, Item 23, p. 20.

9 MacFarlane, 'The Actual True Story of Ned Kelly: Part VI—Stringybark Creek Police Murders.'

10 'Depositions taken at magisterial inquiry at Mansfield', VPRS 4969 P0, Item 23, p. 2.

11 McIntyre, *A True Narrative of the Kelly Gang*, p. 37.

12 Kennedy & Looby, *Black Snake*, p. 120.

13 McIntyre, *A True Narrative of the Kelly Gang*, p. 37.

14 John Sadleir, Police Commission, p. 115, Q 1733.

15 'Depositions taken at Mansfield into inquiry re death of Sergeant Kennedy', VPRS 4969 P0, Item 24, pp. 8–9.

16 'Depositions taken at Mansfield into inquiry re death of Sergeant Kennedy', VPRS 4969 P0, Item 24, pp. 4–9.

17 Kennedy & Looby, *Black Snake*, pp. 122–3.

18 Kennedy & Looby, *Black Snake*, reports that according to Kennedy family lore, the visit was from Sadleir. Sadleir did visit, but to console her while the search was being conducted. Sadleir had left town by the time Kennedy's body was discovered; so it must have been Pewtress who delivered the terrible news.

19 'Depositions taken at Mansfield into inquiry re death of Sergeant Kennedy', VPRS 4969 P0, Item 24, pp. 10–11.

20 'Depositions taken at Mansfield into inquiry re death of Sergeant Kennedy', VPRS 4969 P0, Item 24, p. 12.

Chapter 22. Riders on the storm

1 'Struck by lightning', *Ovens & Murray Advertiser*, 31 Oct 1878, p. 3.

2 Charles Nicolson, Police Commission, p. 15, Q 336; Michael Ward, Police Commission, p. 164, Q 3148.

3 'Letter from Inspector Pewtress re: Mr James' discoveries,' VPRS 4965 P0, Item 177; 'The Kelly haunts', *The Argus*, 13 Nov 1880, p. 9.

4 J. Martain may have been John Martin, a boundary rider for nearby squatter Ewan Tolmie, but details are sparse. See Bill Denheld, 'Two huts at Stringybark Creek.'

5 Sadleir, *Recollections of a Victorian Police Officer*, pp. 192–3; 'The Kelly haunts', *The Argus*, 13 Nov 1880, p. 9.

6 'The Mansfield tragedy', *The Age*, 7 Nov 1878, p. 3.

7 Michael Ward, Police Commission, p. 499, Q 3162–3165.

8 Michael Ward, Police Commission, p. 500, Q 3167.

9 Michael Ward, Police Commission, p. 500, Q 3167.
10 Arthur Steele, Police Commission, pp. 320–21, Q 8856.
11 Henry Laing, Police Commission, pp. 508–9, Q 13961.
12 Arthur Steele, Police Commission, p. 320, Q 8856.
13 Arthur Steele, Police Commission, p. 318, Q 8811, p. 321, Q 8856, p 331, Q 9133;'Wangaratta police court,' *Ovens & Murray Advertiser*, 31 Jul 1877, p. 3; Corfield, *The Ned Kelly Encyclopaedia*, p. 220–21.
14 Alexander Brooke-Smith, Police Commission, p. 652, Q 17291.
15 This was Steele's reasoning as he described it in Police Commission, p. 321, Q 8862.
16 Michael Twomey, Police Commission, p. 657, Q 17450.
17 'The police murders', *The Argus*, 4 Nov 1878, p. 6.
18 Bark stripper informer mentioned in John Sadleir, Police Commission, p. 111, Q 1859; p. 114 (Sadleir) Q 1947; face blackened from Arthur Steele, Police Commission, p. 321, Q 8872.
19 Charles Nicolson, Police Commission, p. 16, Q 361; also Nicolson explicitly states that Sadleir didn't tell them the destination until they arrived at the Sherritt hut— Charles Nicolson, Police Commission, p. 17, Q 392–394.
20 Charles Nicolson, Police Commission, p. 17, Q 389.
21 Frederick Standish, Police Commission, p. 573, Q 15775.
22 Arthur Steele, Police Commission, p. 321, Q 8872.

Chapter 23. The Warby Ranges

1 Charles Johnston, Police Commission, p. 444, Q 12359–12861.
2 Charles Johnston, Police Commission, p. 448, Q 12498–12502.
3 Patrick Quinn, Police Commission, p. 669, Q 17691.
4 Patrick Quinn, Police Commission, p. 669, Q 17694; I'm making the reasonable assumption that whatever Quinn told the Royal Commission, he'd already told Ward.
5 Patrick Quinn, Police Commission, p. 669, Q 17694.
6 'Code names of informers', VPRS 4969 P0, Item 81.
7 Michael Ward, Police Commission, p. 500, Q 13843; 'Memo: police horses recovered', VPRS 4969 P0, Item 44.

Chapter 24. Uproar

1 *Hansard* (Victoria), 30 Oct 1878, p. 1562 (can be found at https://www.parliament.vic.gov.au/hansard/historical-hansard).
2 *Felons Apprehension Act 1878*, <http://www.austlii.edu.au/cgi-bin/viewdb//au/legis/vic/hist_act/faa1878214/>.
3 *Hansard* (Victoria), 30 Oct 1878, p. 1589.
4 *Hansard* (Victoria), 30 Oct 1878, p. 1588.
5 *Hansard* (Victoria), 30 Oct 1878, p. 1594, 1626.
6 Statement of William Williamson, 7 Feb 1879, Police Commission, p. 702.
7 *Victoria Government Gazette*, 'Gazette 115', 6 Nov 1878, pp. 2829–30 (can be found at gazette.slv.vic.gov.au); 'Outlawry of felons', *Ovens & Murray Advertiser*, 7 Nov 1878, p. 2.
8 'The Mansfield tragedy', *The Age*, 11 Nov 1878, p. 3.

9 'The Mansfield tragedy', *Ballarat Courier*, 11 Nov 1878, p. 3.
10 'The police murders', *The Argus*, 18 November 1878, page 5.
11 'By electric telegraph—from our own correspondents', *The Herald*, 18 Nov 1878, p. 3.
12 'The Mansfield tragedy', *The Age*, 7 Nov 1878, p. 3.
13 'By electric telegraph—from our own correspondents', *The Herald*, 17 Dec 1878, p. 3.
14 'The murders by the bushrangers', *The Herald*, 7 Nov 1878, p. 3.
15 'By Herr Scalper', *Ovens & Murray Advertiser*, 16 Nov 1878, p. 3.
16 'The murders by the bushrangers', *The Herald*, 8 Nov 1878, p. 3.
17 *Hansard* (Victoria), 13 Nov 1878, p. 1793.
18 *The Herald* doubled down on its pernicious claims, with a second-hand anonymous source in February ('The Kelly Gang', *The Herald*, 7 Feb 1879, p. 3). Now it is claimed that Ned came to the door 'and caught Fitzpatrick in the act of attempting an outrage'. Fitzpatrick then held up the arrest warrant, saying 'I've got this for you', just as Ned fired his gun, hitting Fitzpatrick in the wrist. Fitzpatrick did not have a warrant, and besides that, the whole story is ridiculously implausible.
19 For detailed analysis of the unwarranted destruction of Fitzpatrick's character, see Dawson, 'Redeeming Fitzpatrick', and also MacFarlane, 'The Fitzpatrick Conspiracy: Part VI—What we actually know about Fitzpatrick'. In short, the media propagated claims of malfeasance by Fitzpatrick, which caused him to be treated with mistrust and hostility elsewhere, resulting in further complaints and trouble and ultimately his dismissal. Standish and Hare both later made negative comments about him, but they seem not to have followed his case closely and were relying on the word of junior officers about him.

Chapter 25. Agent McIntyre

1 McIntyre, *A True Narrative of the Kelly Gang*, p. 40.
2 McIntyre, *A True Narrative of the Kelly Gang*, p. 40.
3 'McIntyre Interviewed', *The Herald*, 2 Nov 1878, p. 3; McIntyre, *A True Narrative of the Kelly Gang*, p. 40.
4 McIntyre, *A True Narrative of the Kelly Gang*, p. 40.
5 McIntyre, *A True Narrative of the Kelly Gang*, p. 27.
6 McIntyre, *A True Narrative of the Kelly Gang*, p. 40.
7 McIntyre, *A True Narrative of the Kelly Gang*, p. 41.
8 McIntyre, *A True Narrative of the Kelly Gang*, p. 41.
9 McIntyre, *A True Narrative of the Kelly Gang*, p. 41.
10 McIntyre, *A True Narrative of the Kelly Gang*, p. 42.
11 McIntyre, *A True Narrative of the Kelly Gang*, p. 42.
12 Prisoner Williamson's statement, Police Commission, p. 702, Appendix 13.
13 Francis Hare, Police Commission, p. 61, Q 1245.
14 Francis Hare, Police Commission, p. 61, Q 1245.
15 Charles Nicolson, Police Commission, p. 19, Q 439.
16 Charles Nicolson, Police Commission, p. 19, Q 437.

Chapter 26. Tip-off

1 John Sadleir, Police Commission, p. 115, Q 1972.
2 John Sadleir, Police Commission, p. 115, Q 1972–1973.

3   John Sadleir, Police Commission, p. 612, Q 16691.
4   Charles Nicolson, Police Commission, p. 632, Q 16901; James Whelan, Police Commission, p. 249, Q 6149.
5   'The men who fought the Kelly Gang', *Advertiser* (SA), 11 May 1912, p. 22.
6   Charles Nicolson, Police Commission, p. 21, Q 487, described it as 'like a bouquet of flowers'.
7   Sadleir, *Recollections of a Victorian Police Officer*, p. 205; John Sadleir, Police Commission, p. 117, Q 1999.
8   Charles Nicolson, Police Commission, p. 21, Q 489.
9   John Sadleir, Police Commission, p. 613, Q 16693–16694.

Chapter 27. Wyatt's day trip

1   Alfred Wyatt, Police Commission, p. 123, Q 2127.
2   Alfred Wyatt, Police Commission, pp. 123–4, Q 2135–2144.
3   Alfred Wyatt, Police Commission, p. 124, Q 2146–2147.
4   Alfred Wyatt, Police Commission, p. 124, Q 2152.
5   James Whelan, Police Commission, p. 236, Q 6220.
6   Alfred Wyatt, Police Commission, p. 126, Q 2176.
7   Alfred Wyatt, Police Commission, p. 126, Q 2182.
8   Alfred Wyatt, Police Commission, p. 126, Q 2182, 2190.
9   Alfred Wyatt, Police Commission, p. 126, Q 2182–2184.
10 Alfred Wyatt, Police Commission, p. 127, Q 2196–2197.
11 Alfred Wyatt, Police Commission, p. 127, Q 2193.

Chapter 28. Night train to Euroa

1   Michael Ward, Police Commission, p. 500, Q 13843.
2   James Graves, Police Commission, p. 561 Q 15954; James Whelan, Police Commission, p. 236, Q 5962, Anderson boarded the 9.50 train from Euroa; the journey was 90 minutes.
3   James Whelan, Police Commission, p. 237, Q 5964.
4   Charles Johnston, Record of Conduct and Service, Victoria Police Museum; Alfred Wyatt, Police Commission, p. 128, Q 2217.
5   Alfred Wyatt, Police Commission, p. 128, Q 2211.
6   Alfred Wyatt, Police Commission, p. 128, Q 2209–2214.
7   'Report re: Young husband's station stuck up', VPRS 4965 P0, Item 379, p. 4; Alfred Wyatt, Police Commission, p. 128, Q 2214–2216.
8   Macauley's story is taken mostly from 'Report re: Young husband's station stuck up', VPRS 4965 P0, Item 379, supplemented with some details from other sources.
9   'The bushrangers', *Kyneton Guardian*, 14 Dec 1878, p. 2.
10 A local constable later reported hearing a rumour that Gloster (not Beecroft) had been assisting the gang, and that he was flush with money after the Euroa robbery (see VPRS 4965, P0, Item 256, 'Report: James Gloster'). Standish's brusque dismissal, written in the report's margin, suggested that he possessed information— perhaps from Detective Ward—that contradicted the hearsay report.
11 Scott, 'The Kelly Gang at Euroa'.
12 Alfred Wyatt, Police Commission, p. 135, Q 2363–2367.
13 Alfred Wyatt, Police Commission, p. 128, Q 2223–2224.

14 Ward interviewed Stephens, as mentioned in 'Lonigan murder prosecution brief', VPRS 4966 P0, Item 6, p. 83. Fitzgerald was there, as mentioned in 'Memos: re the whereabouts of William Fitzgerald of Younghusband's Station', VPRS 4969 P0, Item 17 p. 10.

15 'Queen vs Edward Kelly, Depositions of John Kelly and others', VPRS 4966 P0, Item 7, p. 107.

16 'Memos', VPRS 4969 P0, Item 17, p. 10.

17 'Memos', VPRS 4969 P0, Item 17, p. 10.

18 'Queen vs Edward Kelly: Murder file', VPRS 4966 P0, Item 2, p. 14; 'Kelly Gang at Euroa', *The Argus*, 20 Feb 1923, p. 7. Police tried unsuccessfully to locate Carson (or 'Carson'), see for example: 'Memos', VPRS 4969 P0, Item 17, p. 16.

19 'The Kelly outrages', *The Age*, 12 Dec 1878, p. 3. Mrs Fitzgerald's first name is unknown.

20 Charles Nicolson, Police Commission, p. 23, Q 548.

21 Charles Nicolson, Police Commission, p. 23, Q 551.

Chapter 29. The hawkers and Kelly

1   'Ned Kelly Capital Case File', VPRS 4966 P0, Item 10, p. 215.

2   'The bushrangers', *Kyneton Guardian*, 14 Dec 1878, p. 2.

3   'Ned Kelly Capital Case File', VPRS 4966 P0, Item 10, p. 215.

4   'Queen vs Edward Kelly, Depositions of John Kelly and others', VPRS 4966 P0, Item 7, p. 135.

5   'Queen vs Edward Kelly, Depositions of John Kelly and others', VPRS 4966 P0, Item 7, p. 136; 'Lonigan murder prosecution brief', VPRS 4966 P0, Item 6, pp. 52–8.

6   'Queen vs Edward Kelly, Depositions of McIntyre and others', VPRS 4966 P0, Item 8, p. 87.

7   'Queen vs Edward Kelly, Depositions of John Kelly and others', VPRS 4966 P0, Item 7, p. 139.

8   'Lonigan murder prosecution brief', VPRS 4966 P0, Item 6, pp. 52–8.

9   'Lonigan murder prosecution brief', VPRS 4966 P0, Item 6, pp. 52–8.

10 'Lonigan murder prosecution brief', VPRS 4966 P0, Item 6, p. 53.

11 'Lonigan murder prosecution brief', VPRS 4966 P0, Item 6, p. 64.

12 'Lonigan murder prosecution brief', VPRS 4966 P0, Item 6, p. 56.

13 'Lonigan murder prosecution brief', VPRS 4966 P0, Item 6, p. 57.

14 'Lonigan murder prosecution brief', VPRS 4966 P0, Item 6, p. 57.

15 'Lonigan murder prosecution brief', VPRS 4966 P0, Item 6, pp. 54, 57.

16 'Lonigan murder prosecution brief', VPRS 4966 P0, Item 6, p. 58; indirect speech changed to direct speech and tense altered accordingly.

17 The value of the clothes stolen from Gloster comes from 'Ned Kelly Capital Case File', VPRS 4966 P0, Item 10, p. 222.

18 'Lonigan murder prosecution brief', VPRS 4966 P0, Item 6, pp. 60–1.

Chapter 30. The Euroa bank robbery

1   'Queen vs Edward Kelly: Murder file', VPRS 4966 P0, Item 2, p. 30, 'Queen vs Edward Kelly, Depositions of John Kelly and others', VPRS 4966 P0, Item 7, pp. 166–8; 'Ned Kelly Capital Case File', VPRS 4966 P0, Item 10, pp. 222–24, Scott's statements. Scott thought Dan Kelly was Steve Hart.

2 'The narrative of Mr Scott, the bank manager', *Ovens & Murray Advertiser*, 14 Dec 1878, p. 8. The *Advertiser* seems to be the only source of exact numbers for the Euroa bank robbery.
3 Scott, 'The Kelly Gang at Euroa'.
4 'Ned Kelly Capital Case File', VPRS 4966 P0, Item 10, pp. 222–24. Robert Scott deposition.
5 'The Kelly Gang', *Gippsland Times*, 13 Dec 1878, p. 3.
6 'The narrative of Mr Scott, the bank Manager', *Ovens & Murray Advertiser*, 14 Dec 1878, p. 8.
7 Scott, 'The Kelly Gang at Euroa'.
8 For Susy's version of events see Scott, 'The Kelly Gang at Euroa'. 'They were too cute,' Susy Scott remarked when recalling the offer of whisky. Some news reports claimed that Kelly and Scott had drunk whisky together. However, none of Scott's written accounts or court depositions mentioned this detail, and his wife explicitly said they refused the whisky, so those newspaper reports seem wrong.
9 Scott, 'The Kelly Gang at Euroa'.
10 Scott, 'The Kelly Gang at Euroa'.
11 Scott, 'The Kelly Gang at Euroa'.
12 Scott, 'The Kelly Gang at Euroa'.
13 'Queen vs Edward Kelly: Murder file', VPRS 4966 P0, Item 2, p. 30; 'Lonigan murder prosecution brief', VPRS 4966 P0, Item 6, p. 62; 'Queen vs Edward Kelly, Depositions of John Kelly and others', VPRS 4966 P0, Item 7, pp. 166–8; 'Ned Kelly Capital Case File', VPRS 4966 P0, Item 10, pp. 222–24, Robert Scott statements.

Chapter 31. Nicolson out

1 Frederick Standish, Police Commission, p. 2, Q 21–25.
2 Charles Nicolson, Police Commission, p. 24, Q 553.
3 This section is largely based on Francis Hare, Police Commission, p. 62, Q 1254.
4 'Mr. Scott's information on Euroa Robbery', VPRS 4965 P0, Item 165, pp. 1–3.
5 'Mr. Scott's information on Euroa Robbery', VPRS 4965 P0, Item 165, pp. 1–3.
6 Alfred Wyatt, Police Commission, p. 566, Q 1544–1545.
7 'Mr. Scott's information on Euroa Robbery', VPRS 4965 P0, Item 165, pp. 1–3.
8 'The Mansfield Murderers', *The Argus*, 16 Dec 1878, p. 6.

Chapter 32. The Cameron Letter

1 'Various', VPRS 4969 P0, Item 18, p. 5.
2 'Various', VPRS 4969 P0, Item 18, p. 5.
3 VPRS 4966 P0, Item 3, Ned Kelly's Cameron Letter.
4 Sadleir got other things wrong, such as the description of the armed men near the Glenrowan siege, discussed by Dawson, *Ned Kelly and the Myth of a Republic of North-Eastern Victoria*, p. 51.
5 Morrissey, *Ned Kelly: A lawless life*, pp. 167–70.
6 'Kelly's letter', *Mount Alexander Mail*, 20 Dec 1878, p. 2.
7 'Kelly's letter claiming a free pardon', *Weekly Times*, 21 Dec 1878, p. 15.
8 Copies of the Cameron Letter, also known as the 'Euroa Letter', can be found in 'Edward Kelly gives statement of his murders of Sgt Kennedy and others', VPRS 4966 P0, Item 3, and in 'Various', VPRS 4969 P0, Item 18.

9 'Further station incidents', *The Argus*, 12 Dec 1878, p. 5; 'The Kelly Gang', *Bendigo Advertiser*, 13 Dec 1878, p. 2. Reports that said that Mrs Fitzgerald saw a gang member write the letter are written in such a way that they sound like they are referring to earlier reports; they are not presented in a way to suggest they are providing breaking news, or new information. I conclude therefore that this is just a case of careless reporting.

10 'Mrs. Fitzgerald supposed in the pay of the Kellys', VPRS 4965 P0, Item 351.

Chapter 33. Sympathisers

1 Francis Hare, Police Commission p. 62, Q 1256–1257. The transcript says 'Hood' but the commissioner asks a follow up question about 'Flood' so 'Hood' is clearly a typo.

2 Francis Hare, Police Commission p. 62, Q 1262–1263.

3 Francis Hare, Police Commission, p. 63, Q 1268.

4 'The Mansfield Murderers', *The Argus*, 16 Dec 1878, p. 6; 'The Kelly Gang', *The Herald*, 20 Dec 1878, p. 3.

5 Frederick Standish, Police Commission, p. 3, Q 47.

6 Francis Hare, Police Commission, p. 90, Q 1522.

7 'A right step', *Ovens & Murray Advertiser*, 7 Jan 1879, p. 3.

8 'The Mansfield Murders', *The Argus*, 31 Dec 1878, p. 5; 'The Kellys', *Ovens & Murray Advertiser*, 4 Jan 1879, p. 5; 'The Mansfield Murderers', *The Sydney Morning Herald* (NSW), 7 Jan 1879, p. 6.

9 'The trial of Ben Gould', *Leader*, 18 Jan 1879, p. 23; 'Euroa police court', *Ovens & Murray Advertiser*, 18 Jan 1879, p. 4; 'The Kellys associates', *The Age*, 17 Jan 1879, p. 3. One news report listed a third presiding magistrate named Clark.

10 'The trial of Ben Gould', *Leader*, 18 Jan 1879, p. 23; 'The Kellys associates', *The Age*, 17 Jan 1879, p. 3.

11 'Det Ward hurt', VPRS 4965 P2, Item 72; Untitled, *Ballarat Courier*, 25 Jan 1879, p. 2.

12 'Det Ward hurt', VPRS 4965 P2, Item 72; 'The Kelly Gang', *The Herald*, 18 Jan 1879, p. 3; 'Beechworth police court', *Ovens & Murray Advertiser*, 21 Jan 1879, p. 3.

13 'The Mansfield murderers', *The Argus*, 27 January 1879, p. 6.

14 'By electric telegraph', *The Age*, 12 February 1879, p. 3. 'The Kellys and the police', *Ovens & Murray Advertiser*, 14 Dec 1878, p. 4, estimates 300 sympathisers. Nicolson, a classist snob, also believed that 'the greater portion' of citizens were sympathisers (Police Commission p. 32, Q 743), a rather self-serving claim that perhaps was intended to explain his failure to catch the outlaws. However, see Alfred Wyatt, Police Commission, p. 134, Q 2353, the district was 'considerably terrorized', and Q2354, that 'the general inhabitants of that district were thoroughly horrified at the murders, and would, as far as they could, give the police assistance in making them amenable to justice'. It is not the case that Kelly ever had widespread support in north-eastern Victoria, and particularly not Beechworth (see, e.g., William Foster, Police Commission, p. 482, Q 13360). Sadleir, Police Commission, p. 120, Q 2054, claims that the sympathisers were 'blood relations and intimate friends'—given that Kelly had about 70 adult blood relations in the district, that would accord with the *Advertiser*'s estimate. Senior-Constable John Kelly stated that there were 'nearly 100 families who would render every possible aid to the outlaws' (McIntyre, *A True Narrative of the Kelly Gang*, p. 89).

Chapter 34. A bedside visitor

1 'Michael Ward claim for Kelly Reward', VPRS 4968 P0, Item 41, pp. 5–6.
2 Having suffered multiple broken ribs myself, I can attest that Ward needed help just to roll over.
3 Francis Hare, Police Commission, p. 63, Q 1270.
4 Francis Hare, Police Commission, p. 63, Q 1270.
5 Francis Hare, Police Commission, p. 63, Q 1275.
6 Francis Hare, Police Commission, p. 64, Q 1275 (Hare); Frederick Standish, Police Commission, p. 11, Q 235.
7 'Jerilderie stick up (telegram)', VPRS 4965 P2, Item 75.

Chapter 35. The Jerilderie barracks

1 'The Kelly Gang at Jerilderie', *The Herald*, 11 Feb 1879, p. 2.
2 *The Australian handbook and almanac and shippers' and importers' directory for 1880*, p. 148.
3 'Ned Kelly Capital Case File', VPRS 4966 P0, Item 10, pp. 224–60.
4 'Ned Kelly Capital Case File', VPRS 4966 P0, Item 10, pp. 224–60. Coleman is named on p. 229; and 'they crossed' mentioned on p. 230.
5 'Further particulars of the sticking-up at Jerilderie', *Evening News*, 12 Feb 1879, p. 2.
6 Devine's riding accident mentioned in 'The Kellys' gang at Jerilderie', *Leader*, 22 Feb 1879, p. 2; 'The Kelly Gang', *The Herald*, 13 Feb 1879, p. 3.
7 'Ned Kelly Capital Case File', VPRS 4966 P0, Item 10, pp. 224–30.
8 'The Kellys at Jerilderie', *The Herald*, 18 Feb 1879, p. 3. Jones, *Ned Kelly: A short life*, p. 182, citing the Jerilderie police logbook.
9 'Ned Kelly Capital Case File', VPRS 4966 P0, Item 10, pp. 224–30.
10 'Ned Kelly Capital Case File', VPRS 4966 P0, Item 10, pp. 224–30, p. 226. Some reports said that Kelly made Mary Devine collect the weapons in her nightgown, after the men were locked up, but Richards' depositions gave the impression he was present when the weapons were taken.
11 'By electric telegraph', *The Herald*, 14 Feb 1879, p. 3.
12 'By electric telegraph', *The Herald*, 14 Feb 1879, p. 3; 'The Kellys at Jerilderie', *The Herald*, 18 Feb 1879, p. 3.
13 'By electric telegraph', *The Herald*, 14 Feb 1879, p. 3.
14 'The Kellys at Jerilderie', *The Herald*, 18 Feb 1879, p. 3.
15 'The Kellys at Jerilderie', *The Herald*, 18 Feb 1879, p. 3.
16 'The Kellys' gang at Jerilderie', *Leader*, 22 Feb 1879, p. 2.
17 'Ned Kelly Capital Case File', VPRS 4966 P0, Item 10, pp. 224–30.
18 'The Kellys' gang at Jerilderie', *Leader*, 22 Feb 1879, p. 2.
19 'Lonigan murder prosecution brief', VPRS 4966 P0, Item 6, pp. 81–2.
20 'Lonigan murder prosecution brief', VPRS 4966 P0, Item 6, pp. 81–2.
21 'The Kellys at Jerilderie', *The Herald*, 18 Feb 1879, p. 3.
22 'The Kellys at Jerilderie', *The Herald*, 18 Feb 1879, p. 3.
23 'By electric telegraph', *The Herald*, 14 Feb 1879, p. 3; 'The Kellys at Jerilderie', *The Herald*, 18 Feb 1879, p. 3; 'The Kellys' gang at Jerilderie', *Leader*, 22 Feb 1879, p. 2. The *Leader* says it was Byrne, while *The Herald* says Kelly. There are several reasons to believe the *Leader*'s account. First, it accords with Kelly complaining to Edwin

Living that they had bungled the robbery; second, it explains why the robbery itself was so disorganised; third, the account of Byrne at Davidson's (in the *Leader*) is quite detailed, while *The Herald*'s mention of the visit by a gang member is made in passing; fourth, the *Leader*'s account emerged some days after *The Herald*'s account, and therefore is likely to have comprised more up-to-date, revised information.

24 'The Kellys' gang at Jerilderie', *Leader*, 22 Feb 1879, p. 2.

Chapter 36. The Jerilderie bank

1 'The Kelly Gang at Jerilderie (by electric telegraph)', *The Argus*, 12 Feb 1879, p. 6.
2 'The Kelly Gang at Jerilderie (by electric telegraph)', *The Argus*, 12 Feb 1879, p. 6.
3 'The Kellys' gang at Jerilderie', *Leader*, 22 Feb 1879, p. 2; 'The Kelly Gang at Jerilderie, *The Herald*, 11 Feb 1879, p. 2.
4 'The Kelly Gang at Jerilderie', *The Herald*, 11 Feb 1879, p. 2; 'The Kellys' gang at Jerilderie', *Leader*, 22 Feb 1879, p. 2.
5 'Queen vs Edward Kelly, Depositions of John Kelly and others', VPRS 4966 P0, Item 7, pp. 189–99, Living deposition.
6 'Lonigan murder prosecution brief', VPRS 4966 P0, Item 6, Living deposition pp. 69–71: first met Kelly in the back yard, then was taken into the hotel. Also, 'The Kellys' gang in New South Wales', *The Age*, 12 Feb 1879, p. 3.
7 'Ned Kelly Capital Case File', VPRS 4966 P0, Item 10, pp. 233–6, Tarleton deposition.
8 This scene, including the dialogue, comes from 'Ned Kelly Capital Case File', VPRS 4966 P0, Item 10, pp. 230–233, Living deposition.
9 'The Kellys' gang at Jerilderie', *Leader*, 22 Feb 1879, p. 2. Other versions say that Elliot was bailed up by Kelly, but the *Leader* reproduced Elliot's own written account of the affair, which takes priority over second-hand accounts.
10 'The Kelly Gang: Mr Living's version', *The Herald*, 12 Feb 1879, p. 3; 'Mr Lyving's narrative', *The Age*, 12 Feb 1879, p. 3; 'The Kellys' gang at Jerilderie', *Leader*, 22 Feb 1879, p. 2.
11 This scene and its dialogue come from 'The Kelly Gang: Mr Living's version', *The Herald*, 12 Feb 1879, p. 3.
12 'Interview with messrs Tarleton and Living', *The Australasian*, 15 Feb 1879, p. 19.
13 This scene, including the dialogue, comes from 'The Kellys' gang at Jerilderie', *Leader*, 22 Feb 1879, p. 2.
14 'The Kellys' gang at Jerilderie', *Leader*, 22 Feb 1879, p. 2.
15 'By electric telegraph—Jerilderie, Wednesday', *The Australasian*, 15 Feb 1879, p. 19; 'The Kelly Gang at Jerilderie', *The Argus*, 13 Feb 1879, p. 5. Some accounts say it was only Rankin and Gill, see for example, 'The Kelly Gang at Jerilderie: interview with messrs Tarleton and Living' *The Argus*, 12 Feb 1879, p. 6; 'The Kelly Gang: Mr Living's version', *The Herald*, 12 Feb 1879, p. 3.
16 'The Kelly Gang at Jerilderie', *The Argus*, 13 Feb 1879, p. 5; 'The Kelly Gang at Jerilderie: additional particulars', *The Argus*, 12 Feb 1879, p. 6.
17 'By electric telegraph—Jerilderie, Wednesday', *The Australasian*, 15 Feb 1879, p. 19.
18 'Queen vs Edward Kelly: Murder file', VPRS 4966 P0, Item 2, pp. 3–5, Living statement.
19 'The Kellys' gang in New South Wales', *The Age*, 12 Feb 1879, p. 3.

20 'Interview with messrs Tarleton and Living', *The Australasian*, 15 Feb 1879, p. 19; 'By electric telegraph—Jerilderie, Wednesday', *The Australasian*, 15 Feb 1879, p. 19.
21 'By electric telegraph—Jerilderie, Wednesday', *The Australasian*, 15 Feb 1879, p. 19.
22 'Further particulars of the sticking-up at Jerilderie', *Evening News*, 12 Feb 1879, p. 2.
23 'Interview with messrs Tarleton and Living', *The Australasian*, 15 Feb 1879, p. 19; 'The Kellys' gang in New South Wales', *The Age*, 12 Feb 1879, p. 3.
24 'The Kelly Gang: Mr Living's version', *The Herald*, 12 Feb 1879, p. 3.

Chapter 37. 'The Story of My Life' by Edward Kelly

1 'Statement of E. Living', VPRS 4969 28; 'Queen vs Edward Kelly: Murder file', VPRS 4966 P0, Item 2, pp. 3–5, Living statement.
2 VPRS 4969 P0, Item 16, Various Reports, pp. 11–12, Mrs Gill statement; 'Statement of E. Living', VPRS 4969 P0, Item 28. Living said she refused, whereas she said she wasn't given a chance to respond. The narrative here presents is my own interpretation of that discrepancy.
3 'Statement of E. Living', VPRS 4969 28; 'Queen vs Edward Kelly: Murder file', VPRS 4966 P0, Item 2, pp. 3–5, Living statement.
4 A more detailed dialogue at the printery was reported in *The Argus*, but I haven't included it because it reads to me like a journalistic invention. If you're curious, it's 'The Kelly Gang at Jerilderie: additional particulars', *The Argus*, 12 Feb 1879, p. 6.
5 'The Kellys' gang in New South Wales', *The Age*, 12 Feb 1879, p. 3
6 'The Kellys at Jerilderie', *The Herald*, 18 Feb 1879, p. 3.
7 'The Kelly Gang at Jerilderie, *The Herald*, 11 Feb 1879, p. 2.
8 'Interview with messrs Tarleton and Living', *The Australasian*, 15 Feb 1879, p. 19.
9 'Interview with messrs Tarleton and Living', *The Australasian*, 15 Feb 1879, p. 19; 'The Kellys' gang in New South Wales', *The Age*, 12 Feb 1879, p. 3.
10 'Ned Kelly Capital Case File', VPRS 4966 P0, Item 10, pp. 233–6, Tarleton deposition.
11 'Queen vs Edward Kelly: Murder file', VPRS 4966 P0, Item 2, pp. 3–5, Living statement.
12 'Memos', VPRS 4969 P0, Item 17, pp. 3–6, Tarleton answers.
13 'Memos', VPRS 4969 P0, Item 17, pp. 3–6, Tarleton answers.
14 'The Kelly Gang at Jerilderie, *The Herald*, 11 Feb 1879, p. 2.
15 This exchange between Tarleton and Kelly: 'The Kelly Gang: Mr Tarleton's version', *The Herald*, 12 Feb 1879, p. 3.
16 'Interview with messrs Tarleton and Living', *The Australasian*, 15 Feb 1879, p. 19.
17 'By electric telegraph—Jerilderie, Wednesday', *The Australasian*, 15 Feb 1879, p. 19.
18 'The Kellys' gang in New South Wales', *The Age*, 12 Feb 1879, p. 3.
19 'The Kelly Gang: Mr Tarleton's version', *The Herald*, 12 Feb 1879, p. 3.
20 'By electric telegraph—Jerilderie, Wednesday', *The Australasian*, 15 Feb 1879, p. 19; 'The Kelly Gang at Jerilderie: By electric telegraph—Jerilderie, Wednesday', *The Argus*, 13 Feb 1879, p. 5.
21 'The Kelly Gang at Jerilderie: By electric telegraph—Jerilderie, Wednesday', *The Argus*, 13 Feb 1879, p. 5.
22 'The Kellys at Jerilderie', *The Herald*, 18 Feb 1879, p. 3.
23 'The Kellys at Jerilderie', *The Herald*, 18 Feb 1879, p. 3.
24 'The Kelly Gang at Jerilderie: By electric telegraph—Jerilderie, Wednesday', *The Argus*, 13 Feb 1879, p. 5.

25 'The Kelly Gang at Jerilderie: By electric telegraph—Jerilderie, Wednesday', *The Argus*, 13 Feb 1879, p. 5; 'The Kelly Gang at Jerilderie, *The Herald*, 11 Feb 1879, p. 2.
26 'The Kellys' gang in New South Wales', *The Age*, 12 Feb 1879, p. 3
27 'Interview with messrs Tarleton and Living', *The Australasian*, 15 Feb 1879, p. 19; 'Mr Tarleton's narrative', *The Age*, 12 Feb 1879, p. 3. (Living spelt Lyving in that article).
28 'The Kelly Gang: sticking up a bank at Jerilderie', *The Argus*, 11 Feb 1879, p. 5.
29 'The Kelly Gang at Jerilderie: additional particulars', *The Argus*, 12 Feb 1879, p. 6.

Chapter 38. The Jerilderie Letter

1 Jerilderie Letter, SLV, MS 13361, <http://handle.slv.vic.gov.au/10381/211066>, p. 24.
2 For a detailed exploration of the Irish attitude to crime in north-eastern Victoria, see Morrissey, *Ned Kelly: Selectors, squatters and stock thieves*. The role of Irishness in policing is discussed in Haldane, *The People's Force*, Chapter 3, pp. 75–128.
3 'Local intelligence', *Wagga Wagga Express*, 9 Jul 1879, p. 2.
4 'Local intelligence', *Wagga Wagga Express*, 9 Jul 1879, p. 2; 'Town talk', *Geelong Advertiser*, 5 Jul 1879, p. 2.

Chapter 39. Agent Aaron Sherritt

1 This section is based largely on Francis Hare, Police Commission, p. 64, Q 1277. Ward recruited Sherritt, as stated by Ward himself and also Sadleir, Police Commission, p. 146, Q 2729.
2 According to Hare, Sherritt actually said, 'I am confident of *their* being there tonight', but this felt clunky, so I made a minor tweak for readability.
3 Hare, *The Last of the Bushrangers*, p. 166.
4 Francis Hare, Police Commission, p. 65, Q 1281.
5 Francis Hare, Police Commission, p. 65, Q 1282.
6 Francis Hare, Police Commission, p. 65, Q 1282.
7 Jones, *Fatal Friendship*, p. 126; 'Letter: anonymous information for Police', VPRS 4965 P0, Item 284; Patrick Allen, Police Commission, p. 486, Q 13460.
8 Hare, *The Last of the Bushrangers*, p. 158.
9 Hare, *The Last of the Bushrangers*, p. 184.
10 Hare, *The Last of the Bushrangers*, p. 185.
11 Hare, *The Last of the Bushrangers*, p. 192.
12 Francis Hare, Police Commission, p. 66, Q 1284.
13 Francis Hare, Police Commission, p. 66, Q 1284.
14 Hare, *The Last of the Bushrangers*, p. 187.
15 Francis Hare, Police Commission, p. 66, Q 1284.
16 Hare, *The Last of the Bushrangers*, p. 189.
17 Francis Hare, Police Commission, p. 66, Q 1285.

Chapter 40. Trackers

1 Francis Hare, Police Commission, p. 84, Q 1499.
2 Stanhope O'Connor, Police Commission, p. 49, Q 1075 and p. 419, Q 11810.
3 Francis Hare, Police Commission, p. 66, Q 1285; Stanhope O'Connor, Police Commission, p. 49, Q 1073.

Notes   385

4   Stanhope O'Connor, Police Commission, p. 49, Q 1073–1078.
5   Stanhope O'Connor, Police Commission, p. 51, Q 1100; p. 407, Q 11478.
6   Stanhope O'Connor, Police Commission, p. 50, Q 1092.
7   Francis Hare, Police Commission, pp. 66–7, Q 1285.
8   This episode comes from Francis Hare, Police Commission, p. 67, Q1285.
9   Francis Hare, Police Commission, p. 73, Q 1358–1359.
10 Francis Hare, Police Commission, p. 73, Q 1358–1359.
11 Francis Hare, Police Commission, p. 71, Q 1302.
12 Francis Hare, Police Commission, p. 597, Q 16321.
13 Frederick Standish, Police Commission p. 4, Q 52.
14 Hall, *The Kelly Gang*, pp. 48–50.
15 Hall, *The Kelly Gang*, pp. 50–51. I have altered the punctuation in the dialogue for readability.
16 See Kennedy & Looby, *Black Snake*, pp. 208–9; and Kelly's conversation with Senior-Constable Kelly in 'Destruction of the Kelly Gang—further particulars', *The Argus*, 30 June 1880, p. 6.

Chapter 41. New agents

1   Charles Nicolson, Police Commission, p. 30, Q 713.
2   Sadleir, *Recollections of a Victorian Police Officer*, p. 216.
3   Sadleir, *Recollections of a Victorian Police Officer*, p. 216.
4   Charles Nicolson, Police Commission, p. 642, Q 17065-17067; Sadleir, *Recollections of a Victorian Police Officer*, p. 217.
5   Frederick Standish, Police Commission, p. 583, Q 16033.
6   Frederick Standish, Police Commission, p. 583, Q 16033.
7   Frederick Standish, Police Commission, p. 583, Q 16034.
8   Frederick Standish, Police Commission, p. 583, Q 16034.
9   Frederick Standish, Police Commission, p. 583, Q 16034.
10 'Fisher alias Bruce', VPRS 4965 P2 267, pp. 3–5. Fisher and Bruce were both code-names for Wallace. The passage about the 'beautiful game of cross purposes' was read out at the Police Royal Commission, and Wallace was asked what he had meant by that.
11 James Wallace, Police Commission, p. 528, Q 14523.
12 Charles Nicolson, Police Commission, p. 651, Q 17425.
13 James Wallace, Police Commission, p. 529, Q 14528.
14 'Fisher alias Bruce', VPRS 4965 P2, Item 267, p. 5.

Chapter 42. The thief who came in from the cold

1   'Aaron Sherritt's charge of horse stealing from Mrs. Byrne', VPRS 4965 P0, Item 508, p. 10.
2   Sherritt lived in the Beechworth district, yet see Mullane's comment to Benalla when the warrant was issued: 'the defendant supposed to be in that neighbourhood'. PRs 4965 P0, Item 508, p. 11.
3   'Foiled', *Ovens & Murray Advertiser*, 28 Jun 1879, p. 4.
4   'Letter from Sheepstation Creek', VPRS 4965 P0, Item 285.
5   'Various', VPRS 4969 P0, Item 18, p. 36. 'North Eastern—copy of letter to Aaron' supposed from Joe Byrne, VPRS 4965 P2, Item 215.

6 Michael Ward, Police Commission, p. 501, Q 13850. Jones, *Fatal Friendship*, also concluded the note was a forgery.
7 Mrs Sherritt Snr., Police Commission, p. 474, Q 13166–13168.
8 *Victoria Police Gazettes*, 21 Jul 1879, p. 189.
9 'Memo from Detective Ward', VPRS 4965 P0, Item 403.
10 'Telegramatta, rural', *The Herald*, 15 Jul 1879, p. 3.
11 Brian Cookson, 'The Kelly Gang from within: Patrick Allen storekeeper', *Sun* (NSW), 4 Sep 1911, p. 10.
12 Enoch Downes, Police Commission, pp. 487–8, Q 13490–13496.
13 Threatening letters to Ward mentioned in Michael Ward, Police Commission, p. 501, Q 13849–13850.

Chapter 43. Agent Wallace

1 Michael Ward, Police Commission, p. 505, Q 13884; 'Dog poisoning', *Ovens & Murray Advertiser*, 5 Jun 1873, p. 2.
2 Much of this chapter is derived from a report from Detective Ward on 26 August 1879, tabled in the Royal Commission during the testimony of James Wallace. It can be found in Police Commission, p. 535, Q14773.
3 Thomas Bolam, Police Commission, p. 545, Q 15049.
4 Report of Detective Ward, Police Commission, p. 535, Q14773.
5 'Fisher alias Bruce', VPRS 4965 P2, Item 257, p. 11.
6 'Fisher alias Bruce', VPRS 4965 P2, Item 257, p. 12.
7 See Hall & Stevens, *James Wallace*, p. 13. From 1877 onwards, Wallace was an active member of the Upper Murray Free Selectors Association. 'This took up a great deal of James Wallace's free time and in the years that followed, he began writing articles for numerous newspapers, such as the *Wangaratta Dispatch*, *Yea Advocate*, *Ovens & Murray Advertiser*, and *Kerang Times*.'
8 'Fisher alias Bruce', VPRS 4965 P2, Item 257, p. 16.
9 'Memo from Detective Ward', VPRS 4965 P0, Item 418; 'Ward's report re "Tommy"', VPRS 4965 P2, Item 251.
10 'Ward's report re "Tommy"', VPRS 4965 P2, Item 251.
11 'Ward's report re "Tommy"', VPRS 4965 P0, Item 251.
12 'Ned Kelly capital case file', VPRS 4966, Item 10, pp. 113–14.
13 'Letter from Bobinawarrah Post Office re delay in delivery of letters', VPRS 4965 P0, Item 435.
14 'Detective reminiscences', *Sun* (NSW), 11 Feb 1906, p. 5.

Chapter 44. Jack, Aaron and the Cave Party

1 Jack Sherritt, Police Commission, pp. 540–42, Q 14904–14957; Michael Ward, Police Commission, p. 501, Q 13855.
2 Michael Ward, Police Commission, Q 13855, p. 501; Detective Ward handled Jack Sherritt (alias John Jones) directly, as seen in 'Payment by police to civilians', VPRS 4969 P0, Item 74.
3 Frederick Standish, Police Commission, p. 501, Q 13855.
4 Ward's letter to Hare is archived at 'Francis Hare papers (no. 10): Detective M. Ward to Hare', <https://digitised-collections.unimelb.edu.au/handle/11343/21271>.
5 Ellen Barry, Police Commission, pp. 485–6, Q 13447.

6 Brian Cookson, 'The Kelly Gang from within: Patrick Allen storekeeper', *Sun* (NSW), 4 Sep 1911, p. 10.
7 Michael Ward, Police Commission, p. 514, Q 14110.
8 Michael Ward, Police Commission, p. 502, Q 13855, 13856; Standish's opinion is provided by Henry Moors, Police Commission, p. 102, Q 1665.
9 Michael Ward, Police Commission, p. 502, Q 13855.
10 Michael Ward, Police Commission, p. 502, Q 13857.
11 Patrick Mullane, Police Commission, p. 490, Q 13567.
12 Patrick Mullane, Police Commission, p. 490, Q 13571.
13 Henry Armstrong, Police Commission, p. 431, Q 1207. Armstrong's version was refuted by Ward himself as well as three other Police Commission witnesses: Daniel Barry, p. 288, Q 7535; Alfred Faulkner, p. 234, Q 5913; and Patrick Mullane, p. 490, Q 13568.
14 Mrs Sherritt snr, Police Commission, p. 476, Q 13206.
15 Mrs Sherritt snr, Police Commission, p. 476, Q 13176.

Chapter 45. The Graves Letter

1 'Letter to Mr. Graves', VPRS 4965 P0, Item 37.
2 This was known to the royal commission and Education department at least by April 1881: see the exchange between the commission and Henry Moors, p. 102, Q 1671–1679; see also Wallace's own testimony in which he admits that the letter is in his handwriting, but absurdly claims that it's because the letter in the commission's possession is a copy, a transcription that he made himself, and replaced with the original. Nicolson and Standish both were sure that Wallace wrote it. See Frederick Standish, Police Commission, p. 578, Q 15894–15898.
3 Charles Nicolson, Police Commission, p. 28, Q 671.
4 Charles Nicolson, Police Commission, p. 42, Q 930.
5 Charles Nicolson, Police Commission, p. 42, Q 930.
6 Charles Nicolson, Police Commission, p. 42, Q 931.
7 Standish's instruction, Charles Nicolson, Police Commission, p. 625, Q 16862. Sherritt told Hare that Nicolson no longer trusted him.
8 Thomas Bolam, Police Commission, p. 545, Q 15057–15058.
9 Mrs Sherritt snr, Police Commission, p. 476, Q 13184.
10 Michael Ward, Police Commission, p. 503, Q 13860.
11 Stanhope O'Connor, Police Commission, p. 52, Q 1110.
12 Lord Byron's identity is unknown.
13 Michael Ward, Police Commission, p. 503, Q 13858.
14 'Reported appearances of the Kelly Outlaws', Police Commission, p. 694, entry for 21 April 1880.
15 Charles Nicolson, Police Commission, pp. 32–3, Q 745–753.
16 'Reported appearances of the Kelly Outlaws', Police Commission, p. 694, entry for 21 Feb 1880.
17 'Reported appearances of the Kelly Outlaws', Police Commission, p. 695, entry for 21 May 1880.
18 'Reported appearances of the Kelly Outlaws', Police Commission, p. 695, entry for 22 May 1880.
19 Charles Nicolson, Police Commission, p. 33, Q 755.

Chapter 46. The Hut Party

1 Michael Ward, Police Commission, p. 503, Q 13860; John Sadleir (Nicolson comment during testimony), Police Commission, p. 145, Q 2700.

2 Michael Ward, Police Commission, p. 503, Q 13860. I interpret his comment on the hut that 'I could see it secure' as implying protection for Sherritt.

3 Michael Ward, Police Commission, p. 516, Q 14160.

4 Robert Alexander, Police Commission, p. 471, Q 13045.

5 Michael Ward, Police Commission, p. 516, Q 14163.

6 Ellen Sherritt, Police Commission, p. 480, Q 13325. I've changed 'could' to present tense 'can'.

7 Robert Alexander, Police Commission, p. 471, Q 13045; Hare believed Alexander got lost on purpose, to stall for time: see Francis Hare, Police Commission, p. 83, Q 1483.

8 Henry Armstrong, Police Commission, p. 433, Q 12136.

9 Henry Armstrong, Police Commission, p. 433, Q 12137; Thomas Dowling, Police Commission, p. 205, Q 4715–4721 & p. 213, Q 5099.

10 John Sherritt, Police Commission, p. 213, p. 550, Q 15192.

11 John Sherritt, Police Commission, p. 213, p. 550, Q 15192.

12 Thomas Dowling, Police Commission, p. 213, Q 5095.

13 Thomas Dowling, Police Commission, p. 213, Q 5098.

14 Francis Hare, Police Commission, pp. 89–90, Q 1516.

15 Francis Hare, Police Commission, p. 90, Q 1518.

16 Sadleir, *Recollections of a Victorian Police Officer*, p. 222.

17 Thomas Bolam, Police Commission, p. 545, Q 15058.

Chapter 47. The murder of Aaron Sherritt

1 Byrne went to the back door (not the front): Ellen Barry, Police Commission, p. 483, Q 13390; Ellen Barry, Police Commission, p. 498, Q 13796.

2 William Duross, Police Commission, p. 180, Q 3638.

3 William Duross, Police Commission, p. 180, Q 3657. Duross heard one of the women say this. It must have been Belle, because Mrs Barry did not until then know Joe Byrne; she was asked this twice at the royal commission and replied both times that she did not: see Ellen Barry, Police Commission, p. 483, Q 13388, 13389.

4 William Duross, Police Commission, p. 180, Q 3657.

5 Ellen Barry, Police Commission, p. 483, Q 13389.

6 Ellen Barry, Police Commission, p. 483, Q 13391; p. 485, Q 13416.

7 William Duross, Police Commission, p. 180, Q 3658; Ellen Barry, Police Commission, p. 483, Q 13389. I have synthesised two accounts of Byrne's words, and have converted Mrs Barry's paraphrase into a portion of direct speech.

8 Ellen Barry, Police Commission, p. 484, Q 13400.

9 Ellen Barry, Police Commission, p. 484, Q 13394–13395.

10 Ellen Barry, Police Commission, p. 484, Q 13394.

11 Ellen Sherritt, Police Commission, p. 478, Q 13244.

12 Ellen Sherritt, Police Commission, p. 499, Q 13806.

13 William Duross, Police Commission, p. 181, Q 3679–3680.

14 Ellen Sherritt, Police Commission, p. 499, Q 13806.

15 Ellen Sherritt, Police Commission, p. 478, Q 13251, 13257–13258; p. 498 (Ellen Barry), Q 13803; Ellen Sherritt, Police Commission, p. 478, Q 13257–13258.

16 Ellen Barry, Police Commission, p. 484, Q 13429.

17 Ellen Barry, Police Commission, p. 484, Q 13407.

18 Ellen Barry, Police Commission, p. 484, Q 13408.

19 William Duross, Police Commission, p. 180, Q 3660.

20 William Duross, Police Commission, p. 180, Q 3661.

21 Mrs Sherritt jnr, Police Commission, p. 478, Q 13261; Ellen Barry, Police Commission, p. 499, Q 13784, 13789.

22 Ellen Barry, Police Commission, p. 499, Q 13789. She also claimed that Dowling said that if she was not quiet, they would have to shoot her. But this seems inconsistent with her other Dowling quote and I suspect she misspoke, misremembered or was inaccurately recorded, and that Dowling said something to the effect that if she was not quiet, the outlaws, not he, would shoot her. Surely that makes far more sense. Given the seriousness of the accusation, the fact that it seems to have been said in passing, and that Dowling was never even questioned about it, suggests that the RC transcript is either wrong or misleading.

23 William Duross, Police Commission, pp. 180–81, Q 3669–3671.

24 Ellen Barry, Police Commission, p. 484, Q 13409.

25 Ellen Barry, Police Commission, p. 498, Q 13792.

26 William Duross, Police Commission, p. 181, Q 3731.

27 Ellen Barry, Police Commission, p. 498, Q 13795.

28 Henry Armstrong, Police Commission, p. 435, Q 12162; William Duross, Police Commission, p. 181, Q 3681.

29 Henry Armstrong, Police Commission, p. 435, Q 12162.

30 Brian Cookson, 'The Kelly Gang from within: A detective's reminiscences', *Sun* (NSW), 5 Sep 1911, p. 9.

31 Francis Hare, Police Commission, p. 82, Q 1479.

32 Police Commission, 2nd Progress Report, p. 24.

33 Frederick Standish, Police Commission, p. 9, Q 146; Ellen Barry, Police Commission, p. 484, Q 13412.

34 Francis Hare, Police Commission, p. 82, Q 1500.

35 Francis Hare, Police Commission, p. 84, Q 1501.

36 Frederick Standish, Police Commission, p. 6, Q 77.

37 Frederick Standish, Police Commission, p. 6, Q 77.

38 Frederick Standish, Police Commission, p. 6, Q 77.

39 'Railways', <https://kellygang.asn.au/wiki/Railways>, accessed 19 Jan 2021.

40 'Destruction of the Kelly Gang', *The Argus*, 29 Jun 1880, p. 5.

Chapter 48. The Curnow family's day trip

1 Thomas Curnow, Police Commission, p. 667, Q 17597; Corfield, *The Ned Kelly Encyclopaedia*, pp. 118–20. Intriguingly, Curnow may have been involved in the firing of Wallace, see, e.g., 'News and notes', *Ballarat Star*, 2 Jul 1880, p. 2: 'I have learned from the best authority that Curnow knew all about the Kellys, and gave important information to an officer of the Education department, and this was the cause of the late sudden move by the police'.

2 J.C. Lowe, 'I saw the Kelly Gang wiped out', *ABC Weekly*, 31 Aug 1940, pp. 41–3; Lowe gives the spelling as Piazzi, but the inquest report on Byrne gave his name as Louis Piatza: 'Inquest on Byrne', *Weekly Times*, 3 Jul 1880, p. 20.

3 J.C. Lowe, 'I saw the Kelly Gang wiped out', *ABC Weekly*, 31 Aug 1940, pp. 41–3.

4 J.C. Lowe, 'I saw the Kelly Gang wiped out', *ABC Weekly*, 31 Aug 1940, pp. 41–3; 'Archibald McPhee's claim', VPRS 4968 P0, Item 117, p. 5.

5 Police Commission, 2nd Progress Report, p. 24.

6 'Prosecution of Mrs Jones', *Mount Alexander Mail*, 26 Nov 1880, p. 3.

7 The bulk of this chapter comes from Thomas Curnow, Police Commission, p. 667, Q 17597.

8 J.C. Lowe, 'I saw the Kelly Gang wiped out', *ABC Weekly*, 31 Aug 1940, pp. 41–3.

9 Curnow told the Royal Commission that he believed Kelly's accusation about applying for the police was 'a ruse', but that Delaney thought Kelly was serious. See Thomas Curnow, Police Commission, p. 667, Q 17635.

10 Thomas Curnow, Police Commission, p. 667, Q 17632.

11 Thomas Curnow, Police Commission, p. 664, Q 17597.

12 J.C. Lowe, 'I saw the Kelly Gang wiped out', *ABC Weekly*, 31 Aug 1940, pp. 41–3.

13 Twenty-five miles distance from Sherritt's hut is obtained from Mullane's testimony, Patrick Mullane, Police Commission, p. 492, Q 13639.

14 Thomas Curnow, Police Commission, p. 664, Q 17597; Thomas Curnow, Police Commission, p. 667, Q 17618.

15 Thomas Curnow, Police Commission, p. 664, Q 17597.

16 Thomas Curnow, Police Commission, p. 664, Q 17597.

17 'Thomas Curnow', VPRS 4965 P0, Item 1.

18 Thomas Curnow, Police Commission, p. 664, Q 17597.

19 Thomas Curnow, Police Commission, p. 664, Q 17597.

20 After the siege, Metcalf told Sadleir that he had been hit by police gunfire, and was initially believed. Injury caused by police action entitled him to compensation, whereas being shot by Ned Kelly would not. Metcalf was a poor labourer, unable to afford health care. Detective Alexander Eason subsequently investigated and learned from multiple witnesses that Metcalf had lied (see: 'CCP file concerning the evidence taken', VPRS 4967, Item 60, pp. 241–42). Standish allowed the truth to remain hidden, so that Metcalf could continue receiving medical treatment at government expense, writing in a memo that 'the patient referred to, who is utterly without means, is a fit case for this charity'. ('CCP submits account for expenses incurred on behalf of George Metcalfe', VPRS 4967, Item 53, p. 5). Superintendent Nicolson arranged for all of Metcalf's living expenses to be paid for at the Rose of Melbourne Hotel for the remaining few months of his life ('Metcalfe injured at Glenrowan', VPRS 4965, Item 146). For a detailed discussion of the Metcalf shooting and the cover-up, see Dawson, 2017, 'Ned Kelly's shooting of George Metcalf, labourer', *Eras Journal*, vol. 19, no. 1, pp. 79–93.

21 Thomas Curnow, Police Commission, p. 664, Q 17597.

22 Thomas Curnow, Police Commission, p. 664, Q 17597.

23 Thomas Curnow, Police Commission, p. 664, Q 17597. Indirect speech changed to direct speech.

24 The weather conditions are analysed by Dick Whitaker, 'The Siege of Glenrowan: Ned Kelly's Last Stand', <passingparade-2009.blogspot.com/2021/06/the-siege-of-glenrowan-ned-kellys-last.html>, accessed November 2021.

Chapter 49. The night special

1 This chapter makes extensive use of Frank Hare's testimony, in Francis Hare, Police Commission, p. 85, Q 1501.

2 Francis Hare, Police Commission, p. 85, Q 1501; time of arrival in Benalla given by 'Destruction of the Kelly Gang', *The Argus*, 29 Jun 1880, p. 5.

3 Charles Rawlins, Reward Board, p. 4, Witness statement and Q 48–49. It is unclear how Rawlins knew about the police special train.

4 Francis Hare, Police Commission, p. 84, Q 1501. Sadleir claimed that the pilot engine was his idea. Hare had no recollection of that, but politely said that if Sadleir claimed it, 'I do not contradict it'. (Francis Hare, Police Commission, Q 1501.) Hare acknowledged others' contributions and ideas, including Sadleir (e.g., Sadleir's suggestion to contact Standish first); so Sadleir's claim to have thought of the pilot engine is doubtful.

5 Francis Hare, Police Commission, p. 85, Q 1501.

6 'Archibald McPhee claim', VPRS 4968 P0, Item 117, p. 5.

7 Thomas Curnow, Police Commission, p. 666, Q 17608.

8 Thomas Curnow, Police Commission, p. 666, Q 17597.

9 Thomas Curnow, Police Commission, p. 666, Q 17597.

Chapter 50. Gunfight at Jones' Hotel

1 Much of the material for this chapter, including most of the dialogue, comes from Frank Hare's testimony to the Police Royal Commission, found in Francis Hare, Police Commission, pp. 84–9, Q 1503–1515.

2 Francis Hare, Police Commission, p. 86, Q 1503; 'Claim lodged by Constable Hugh Bracken', VPRS 4968 P0, Item 1, p. 2.

3 Francis Hare, Police Commission, p. 86, Q 1505; Charles Gascoigne, Police Commission, p. 349, Q 9674.

4 Charles Gascoigne, Police Commission, p. 349, Q 9674; 'Patrick Charles Gascoigne', VPRS 4968 21, p. 2.

5 Charles Gascoigne, Police Commission, p. 350, Q 9674.

6 Francis Hare, Police Commission, p. 87, Q 1505. Hare said of his shotgun, 'It is a breech-loader, with action between the hammers, and in touching this action the barrels drop forward . . .'

7 Francis Hare, Police Commission, p. 87, Q 1505.

8 Francis Hare, Police Commission, p. 87, Q 1506.

9 Charles Gascoigne, Police Commission, p. 350, Q 9677. While other accounts support the dialogue recalled by Gascoigne, they don't include the surprising and revealing line, 'I'm in iron'. Gascoigne may have erred in his memory about that, which is why I omitted that line from the narrative here.

10 Charles Rawlins, Reward Board, p. 5, Q 55, 62.

11 Francis Hare, Police Commission, p. 87, Q 1506.

12 Francis Hare, Police Commission, p. 87, Q 1507.

13 Francis Hare, Police Commission, p. 87, Q 1507.

14 Police Commission, 2nd Progress Report, p. 26.

15 Francis Hare, Police Commission, p. 87, Q 1508.

16 Francis Hare, Police Commission, p. 89, Q 1514.

17 Francis Hare, Police Commission, p. 87, Q 1509.

18 Statement of Constable Phillips, Police Commission, p. 674.

19 Statement of Constable Phillips, Police Commission, p. 674; see also, 'Police commission', *The Argus*, 21 Sep 1881, p. 7; 'The Police Commission', *Ovens & Murray Advertiser*, 27 Sep 1881, p. 7; 'The Police Commission', *The Age*, 21 Sep 1881, p. 4. The text, if read aloud, gives no indication of the punctuation breaks indicating change of speaker. Since the news reports have identical punctuation to the printed version in the Police Commission minutes, it is clear that the journalists were provided with some kind of printed version. This may well be incorrect, but it seems that the historical consensus that the armour was Ned's invention comes largely from this transcript, and more specifically, from a misreading of it.

20 James Arthur, Police Commission, p. 399, Q 11190–11191.

21 John McWhirter, Police Commission, p. 371, Q 10319–10327.

22 Francis Hare, Police Commission, p. 87, Q 1509.

23 Francis Hare, Police Commission, p. 88, Q 1508.

24 Francis Hare, Police Commission, p. 88, Q 1511.

25 Francis Hare, Police Commission, p. 88, Q 1511.

26 Sadleir, *Recollections of a Victorian Police Officer*, p. 224.

27 Michael Ward, Police Commission, p. 504, Q 13862.

28 Francis Hare, Police Commission, p. 88, Q 1511.

29 Michael Ward, Police Commission, p. 504, Q 13861.

Chapter 51. Glenrowan by moonlight

1 'Sergeant Steele's report', VPRS 4968 P0, Item 114, p. 1.

2 'Sergeant Steele's report', VPRS 4968 P0, Item 114, p. 1.

3 'Sergeant Steele's report', VPRS 4968 P0, Item 114, p. 1. The time of Steele's arrival comes from: Arthur Steele, Police Commission, p. 512, Q 14065, and Senior-Constable Kelly's testimony, John Kelly, Police Commission, p. 312, Q 8533.

4 Arthur Steele, Police Commission, p. 512, Q 14065.

5 John Kelly, Police Commission, p. 303, Q 81659–8166.

6 Arthur Steele, Police Commission, p. 512, Q 14065.

7 See, for example, Daniel Barry, Police Commission, p. 295, Q 7859, and William Phillips, Police Commission, p. 403, Q 11351. Gascoigne never saw O'Connor again (Patrick Gascoigne, p. 352, Q 9749), also Mr Reardon testified he was afraid of the gunfire coming from the drain. Barry's comments on Hero are in Police Commission, p. 295, Q 7850.

8 Arthur Steele, Police Commission, p. 327, Q 9018, 'CCP submits claims for horses destroyed by police at Glenrowan', VPRS 4967 P0, Item 47 80/R8953; see also McIntyre, *A True Narrative of the Kelly Gang*, p. 91.

9 John Kelly, Police Commission, p. 303, Q 8170.

10 Jesse Dowsett, Police Commission, p. 391, Q 10980.

11 'Destruction of the Kelly Gang', *The Argus*, 29 Jun 1880, p. 5.

12 Arthur Steele, Police Commission, p. 327, Q 9008–9010.

13 Arthur Steele, Police Commission, p. 327, Q 9011. Constables William Phillips (Police Commission, p. 402, Q 11320) and James Arthur (Police Commission, p. 397, Q 11125–6) both claimed that Steele fired at Mrs Reardon. Phillips implausibly

said that he shouted at her, 'Throw up your hands, or I will shoot you like a bloody dog', before firing. They both claimed that he then said, 'I've shot Mother Jones in the tits'. The inquiry concluded that they were lying. Steele privately and publicly accused Arthur of cowardice, so he invented this story to retaliate, and Arthur's mate Phillips backed him up. See 'The Steele board report', *The Age*, 30 Mar 1882, p. 1.

14 'The charges against Sergeant Steele', *The Argus*, 29 Mar 1882, p. 4; 'Is Sergeant Steele to be promoted?', *The Ovens & Murray Advertiser*, 1 Apr 1882, p. 4; 'The Steele board report', *The Age*, 30 Mar 1882, p. 1.

Chapter 52. Reverie

1 Kelly failed to mount his horse, and lay until dawn: see Charles Rawlins, Reward Board, p. 5, Q 49–54.

2 Jones, 'A new view of Ned Kelly', in Cave (ed.), *Ned Kelly: Man & Myth*, pp. 172–3; and Jones, *Ned Kelly: A short life*, pp. 309–10. For a comprehensive rejection of the republic hypothesis, see Dawson's excellent book, *Ned Kelly and the Myth of a Republic of North-Eastern Victoria*.

3 As Frank Hare explained, 'I would point out that Ned Kelly was seriously wounded in the first engagement by a bullet in the foot and through the upper arm and lower arm—and with 95 lbs weight of iron, it was impossible for him to escape, besides being shot in the thumb.' Frank Hare, Police Commission, p. 595, Q 16317. The armour fastenings of bolts, nuts and straps mentioned by John Kelly, Police Commission, p. 305, Q 8252–8253.

4 See Blau & Briggs, 'Anthropology: Identifying the skeleton by its injuries' for a forensic analysis of Kelly's wounds.

Chapter 53. The man in the iron mask

1 Jesse Dowsett, Police Commission, p. 389, Q 10911.

2 Dowsett believed it was 'Old Nick' (the devil), see Jesse Dowsett, Police Commission, p. 389, Q 10964.

3 Arthur Steele, Police Commission, p. 327, Q 9034.

4 Arthur Steele Police Commission, pp. 327–28, Q 9034.

5 Arthur Steele, Police Commission, p. 327, Q 9034.

6 'Reports and correspondence, statistics and expenses', VPRS 4965 P0, Item 394, p. 53; Arthur Steele, Police Commission, p. 328, Q 9036.

7 McIntyre, *A True Narrative of the Kelly Gang*, p. 92.

8 Arthur Steele, Police Commission, p. 328, Q 9036.

9 John Kelly, Police Commission, p. 305, Q 8235–8236.

10 'Sergeant Steele's report', VPRS 4968 P0, Item 114, p. 1. Reported speech changed to direct speech.

11 John Kelly, Police Commission, p. 305, Q 8234.

12 'Sergeant Steele's report', VPRS 4968 P0, Item 114, p. 1.

13 'Queen vs Edward Kelly: Murder file', VPRS 4966 P0, Item 2, p. 1; 'Sergeant Steele's report', VPRS 4968 P0, Item 394, p. 54.

14 'Sergeant Steele's report', VPRS 4968 P0, Item 114, p. 2.

15 'Sergeant Steele's report', VPRS 4968 P0, Item 114, p. 2; John Kelly, Police Commission, p. 305, Q 8248–8250.

16 'Queen vs Edward Kelly: Murder file', VPRS 4966 P0, Item 2, p. 1; 'Sergeant Steele's report', VPRS 4968 P0, Item 114, p. 2; John Kelly, Police Commission, p. 305, Q 8247.

17 'Sergeant Steele's report', VPRS 4968 P0, Item 114, p. 2; 'Reports and correspondence, statistics & expenses', VPRS 4965 P0, Item 394, p. 54.

18 Jesse Dowsett, Police Commission, p. 390, Q 10942.

19 'Queen vs Edward Kelly: Murder file', VPRS 4966 P0, Item 2, p. 28, Senior-Constable Kelly's statement.

20 'Sergeant Steele's report', VPRS 4968 P0, Item 114, p. 2.

21 James Dwyer, Police Commission, p. 342, Q 9473.

22 'Sergeant Steele's report', VPRS 4968 P0, Item 114, p. 2; Sadleir, *Recollections of a Victorian Police Officer*, p. 232.

23 'Destruction of the Kelly Gang', *The Argus*, 29 Jun 1880, p. 5.

24 Jesse Dowsett, Police Commission, p. 390, Q 10942.

25 'Sadleir's first report', VPRS 4968 P0, Item 50, pp. 17–18.

26 Sadleir, *Recollections of a Victorian Police Officer*, p. 235.

27 'Destruction of the Kelly Gang', *The Argus*, 29 Jun 1880, p. 5; William Canny, Police Commission, p. 274, Q 7498.

28 See, for example, journalist Harrington's letter to Hare, in Frank Hare, Police Commission, p. 98, Q 1604; and Senior-Constable Kelly's assertion that Sadleir should have gone around and inspected the police at their posts; John Kelly, Police Commission, p. 312, Q 8565–8566.

29 The Police Commission, 2nd Progress Report was scathing and sarcastic about his leadership at Glenrowan, although to be fair, they were unjustly critical of others including Hare and Ward, and Sadleir was right in his later (albeit self-serving) assessment that they were out 'for scalps'.

30 Police Commission, 2nd Progress Report, p. 28; see testimony endorsing the decision not to go in from Senior-Constable John Kelly, Police Commission, p. 310, Q 3463.

31 'Extermination of the Kelly Gang', *Illustrated Australian News*, 3 Jul 1880, pp. 106-110.

32 Charles Johnston, Police Commission, p. 266, Q 7143.

33 Charles Johnston, Police Commission, p. 266, Q 7159–7161.

34 'Destruction of the Kelly Gang', *The Argus*, 29 Jun 1880, p. 5.

35 Matthew Gibney, Police Commission, p. 442, Q 12312.

36 John Sadleir, Police Commission, p. 153, Q 2880.

37 Matthew Gibney, Police Commission, p. 442, Q 12318.

38 'Destruction of the Kelly Gang', *The Argus*, 29 Jun 1880, p. 5.

39 'Destruction of the Kelly Gang', *The Argus*, 29 Jun 1880, p. 5.

40 'By electric telegraph', *The Age*, 1 Jul 1880, p. 3.

41 John Sadleir, Police Commission, p. 425, Q 11965. At the Police Royal Commission the following year, Sadleir alleged that when a police parade was called at Glenrowan the day after the siege, Captain Standish forbade the Queensland Native Police from participating (John Sadleir, Police Commission, p. 426, Q 11975-11979). Standish denied the accusation (Frederick Standish, Police Commission, p. 591–92, Q 16243–16269). Either Standish or Sadleir was lying. I am inclined to believe Standish's version, despite his wavering at one point that

he was only 'almost certain' he didn't do it, for the following reasons: first, Standish
had, on Hare's advice, personally lobbied for the blacktrackers to go north, so they
were there solely because he had requested them, so it would be bizarre for him
to object to their presence; second, Standish had a history of campaigning for the
rights of racial minorities (see Chapter 2); third, Sadleir admitted to committing
perjury before the commission on at least one other occasion (Sadleir, *Recollections
of a Victorian Police Officer*, pp. 241–42, c.f. Police Commission, p. 178, Q 3569);
fourth, Sadleir could be vindictive (e.g., Sergeant Steele, Senior-Constable Kelly and
Constable Johnston all complained about unfair treatment by him), and there was
considerable acrimony between the senior police during the commission proceedings. Another possibility is that Standish, having learned of O'Connor's appalling
lack of both leadership and courage during the siege, banished O'Connor and his
Native Police from the parade as a slight against O'Connor, rather than, as Sadleir
implied, against the Native Police themselves. If that's the case, then they both
misled the commission.
42 'Inquest on Byrne', *Weekly Times*, 3 Jul 1880, p. 20.
43 'Destruction of the Kelly Gang', *The Argus*, 29 Jun 1880, p. 5; 'Destruction of the
Kelly Gang: Further particulars', *The Argus*, 30 Jun 1880, p. 6. An interesting account
of the archaeological dig at the siege site is given in Terry's book, *The True Story
of Ned Kelly's Last Stand*.

Chapter 54. The morning after

1 McIntyre, *A True Narrative of the Kelly Gang*. McIntyre is sometimes said to have
slept in the cell next to Kelly. This is untrue, but the confusion comes because on
5 August, around the time of Kelly's hearing there, he slept one night in Beechworth Gaol. This is mentioned in 'Lonigan murder prosecution brief', VPRS
4966, Item 6, p. 13. That page in that source also reveals that McIntyre reported
a summary of the meeting to Sub-Inspector Kennedy.
2 McIntyre, *A True Narrative of the Kelly Gang*, p. 97.
3 'Destruction of the Kelly Gang: Further particulars', *The Argus*, 30 Jun 1880, p. 6;
'Ned Kelly's conversation', *Australian Town & Country Journal* (NSW), 3 Jul 1880,
p. 9.
4 Frederick Standish, Police Commission, p. 6, Q 77.
5 'The horses of the gang', *The Age*, 29 Jun 1880, p. 3; 'Destruction of the Kelly
Gang: Further particulars', *The Argus*, 30 June 1880, p. 6. For more detail about
the Sherritt–Wallace saddle, see 'Ned Kelly capital case file', VPRS 4966, Item 10,
pp. 93–124.
6 'Ned Kelly capital case file', VPRS 4966, Item 10, pp. 93–124.
7 'Inquest on Byrne', *Weekly Times*, 3 Jul 1880, p. 20. I removed a stray occurrence of
the word 'that' in the newspaper summary.
8 'Final report re capture of the Kelly Gang', VPRS 4967 P0 59, p. 12; Frederick
Standish, Police Commission, p. 6, Q 77.
9 'Reports: Ring taken from Byrne's finger originally belonging to Constable Lonigan',
4965 P0, Item 327.
10 'Ned Kelly capital case file', VPRS 4966 Item 10, p. 127.
11 'The Kelly Gang', *The Argus*, 7 Aug 1880, p. 8.

12 A blend of two accounts: 'Detective reminiscences', *Sunday Sun* (NSW), 11 Feb 1906, p. 5; and 'The Kelly Gang', *The Age*, 13 May 1911, p. 16.
13 'Statement of Constable Hugh Bracken', *The Australasian*, 3 Jul 1880, p. 22.
14 'Ned Kelly capital case file', BPRS 4966, Item 10, pp. 93–124. For more about the hut, see the article by Denheld, 'The hut behind the school'.

Chapter 55. The trial

1 'Interview with Ned Kelly', *The Age*, 9 Aug 1880, p. 3.
2 For an exploration of the trial and its legal intricacies, see Castles & Castles, *Ned Kelly's Last Days*, a book co-written by a professor emeritus of law and his daughter. Castles and Castles revealed that, contrary to the mythology, Ned Kelly's defence team worked hard and did a great job in a virtually unwinnable case.
3 'The trial and conviction of Edward Kelly', *The Argus*, 30 Oct 1880, p. 6; also see 'Argus', *The Argus*, 30 Oct 1880, p. 8, which says 'the prisoner interrupted him frequently'.
4 The petition to grant a reprieve can be found at 'Petitions for reprieve', VPRS 4966 P0, Item 11. Many of its pages were filled out in the same handwriting, as was noticed at the time.
5 For an extensive discussion of what Ned Kelly did, or did not, say at the scaffold, see Dawson, 'Ned Kelly's last words: "Ah, well, I suppose"'. The 'Such is life' quote originated in *The Herald*, a lowbrow rag with an emphasis on sport, possibly the least trustworthy of the major Victorian newspapers in 1880. Castles & Castles, in *Ned Kelly's Last Days*, p. 217, describe the quote as 'one of the most famous and potent inaccuracies of the Kelly myth'. Kelly was not asked to speak, and even if he had spoken, the journalists were too far away to hear him.

Mystery 1: Who made the armour?

1 'Making of Kelly armour', VPRS 4965 P0, Item 29. A civilian secret agent code-named Patrick Meade arrived in Benalla to assist him, see 'Ned Kelly capital case file', VPRS 4966, Item 10, p. 73.
2 'Making of Kelly armour: reports from Detective Wilson and Expenses incurred by Detective Wilson whilst on Special duty', VPRS 4965 P0 29.
3 'Promise to Mr Sadleir in case of Mrs. Jones', VPRS 4965 P0, Item 84, pp. 1–2.
4 VPRS 4965 P0, Item 138, pp. 16–18, p. 22.
5 'Promise to Mr Sadleir in case of Mrs. Jones', VPRS 4965 P0, Item 84, pp. 1–2.
6 'Promise to Mr Sadleir in case of Mrs. Jones', VPRS 4965 P0, Item 84, p. 11.
7 Corfield, *The Ned Kelly Encyclopaedia*, p. 459; Woods, *Beechworth: A titan's field*, p. 121.
8 'Ned Kelly capital case file', VPRS 4966, Item 10, pp. 94–95.
9 'Ned Kelly capital case file', VPRS 4966, Item 10, p. 96.
10 'The carnival', *Ovens & Murray Advertiser*, 15 Nov 1873, p. 5. The armour was still in possession of the Beechworth carnival committee in 1879, when it was loaned elsewhere: 'Hamilton carnival', *Hamilton Spectator*, 8 Nov 1879, p. 3; see also, 'Was Ned Kelly the real last samurai?' *Daily Mail*, 20 Sept 2020, <www.dailymail.co.uk/news/article-8704601/Was-Ned-Kelly-samurai-Japanese-warriors-costume-inspired-bushrangers-armour.html>, accessed 16 October 2021.

11 Thorogood, 'The science of the Kelly Gang's armour: Distilling fact from fiction', p. 138; Creagh et al., 'Diffraction and fluorescence studies of bushranger armour'.

12 Hawtin, 'Forging the Kelly Gang armour'.

13 The *prima facie* case that some of the gang's armour was made at the site seems strong. Against that, metallurgical analysis determined that the iron scraps there did not match Byrne's armour. However, given that the scraps had been subjected to bushfires as they lay undiscovered for more than a century, such an analysis is surely inconclusive. The forge investigation is described in Terry, *The True Story of Ned Kelly's Last Stand*, pp. 190–94.

14 As mentioned earlier, the common belief that Joe said, 'It's your fault' to Ned is not consistent with the transcript of the Police Commission, nor with contemporary news reports.

Mystery 2: Who wrote the Jerilderie Letter?

1 Jerilderie Letter, SLV, MS 13361, <http://handle.slv.vic.gov.au/10381/211066>, p. 27. This passage appears at the front of Macfarlane's excellent Kelly mythbusting book, *The Kelly Gang Unmasked*. The passage is so striking and colourful, and so revealing of Kelly's state of mind, that I followed Macfarlane's lead in using it.

2 Jerilderie Letter, SLV, MS 13361, pp. 46–47.

3 Jerilderie Letter, SLV, MS 13361, p. 47.

4 'Euroa Letter', VPRS 4966, Item 3 (Euroa Letter being the other name for the Cameron Letter).

5 The Sherritt letter can be seen in VPRS 4965 P0, Item 18, pp. 36–37.

6 Dewhurst, 'Analysing the handwriting'. The handwriting was also analysed in A.N. Baron's *Blood in the Dust*, but this was more of a psychological profile than an attempt to discern identity.

7 Wallace's letters to Nicolson can be found in the document 'Fisher alias Bruce', VPRS 4965 P0 002 267. The first page contains a note that Wallace confessed to writing a news item titled 'On the police and the outlaws'. Wallace's involvement with the gang is detailed by Detective Ward's reports in 'Ned Kelly Capital Case File', VPRS 4966, Item 10, pp. 93–102, and VPRS 4965 P0, Item 409, and in James Wallace, Police Commission, p. 535, Q 14773, and p. 536, Q 14791. Wallace confessed to writing 'Christmas in Kelly Land' in James Wallace, Police Commission, p. 534, Q 14744.

8 Dewhurst, 'Analysing the handwriting.'

9 Wallace's claim to be able to forge handwriting can be found in 'Fisher alias Bruce', VPRS 4965 P2, Item 267, p 12: 'In the night or rather towards morning—for we slept together—he asked me if I could imitate Byrne's handwriting. I replied in the affirmative.'

10 The Beechworth Gaol letter is in VPRS 4965 P0, Item 18, p. 35 and pp. 38–39.

References

Archives

Francis Hare papers, held by the University of Melbourne and available online at: https://digitised-collections.unimelb.edu.au/handle/11343/36

Public Record Office Victoria, VPRS Series 1503, 937/413, 937/414, 4965, 4966, 4967, 4968, 4969

State Library Victoria, Records of Conduct and Service

Victoria Police Museum, Records of Conduct and Service

Trove, National Library of Australia. All newspaper articles more than 30 years old; the 1880 *Australian handbook and almanac*; and the 1881 Royal Commission documents were all obtained via trove's online resource at trove.nla.gov.au.

Articles

Blau, Soren & Briggs, Chris, 2014, 'Anthropology: Identifying the skeleton by its injuries' in Craig Cormick (ed.), *Ned Kelly: Under the microscope*, Collingwood: CSIRO, pp. 53–62

Creagh, D.C., Thorogood, G. James, M. & Hallam, D.L., 2004, 'Diffraction and fluorescence studies of bushranger armour', *Radiation Physics and Chemistry*, 71(3), pp. 839–40

Dawson, Stuart E., 2015, 'Redeeming Fitzpatrick: Ned Kelly and the Fitzpatrick incident', *Eras Journal*, vol. 17, no. 1, pp. 60–91

Dawson, Stuart E., 2016, 'Ned Kelly's last words: "Ah well, I suppose"', *Eras Journal*, vol. 18, no. 1, pp 38–50

Dawson, Stuart E., 2017, 'Ned Kelly's shooting of George Metcalf, labourer', *Eras Journal*, vol. 19, no. 1, pp. 79–93

de Looper, William, 2014, 'Death registration and mortality trends in Australia 1856–1906', PhD thesis, Australian National University, Canberra

Denheld, Bill, 2006, 'The hut behind the school', <www.denheldid.com/twohuts/bobinawarrahut.htm>, accessed 16 November 2021

Denheld, Bill, 'Two huts at Stringybark Creek', <www.denheldid.com/twohuts/story.html>, accessed 30 November 2021

Dewhurst, Tahnee N., 2014, 'Analysing the handwriting', in Craig Cormick (ed.), *Ned Kelly: Under the microscope*, Collingwood: CSIRO, pp. 213–24

Hawtin, Nick, 2019, 'Forging the Kelly Gang armour', <www.ironoutlaw.com/writings/forging-the-kelly-gang-armour/>, accessed 16 October 2021

Jones, Ian, 'A new view of Ned Kelly', in Colin Cave (ed.), *Ned Kelly: Man and Myth*, Wangaratta: Wangaratta Adult Education Centre, pp. 172–73

Lewis, Milton & McCloud, Roy, 1987, 'A workingman's paradise? Reflections on urban mortality in colonial Australia, 1860–1900', *Medical History*, vol. 31, pp. 387–402

MacFarlane, David, 2018, 'The Fitzpatrick Conspiracy: Part VI—What we actually know about Fitzpatrick', <https://nedkellyunmasked.com/2018/09/part-vi-what-we-actually-know-about-fitzpatrick/>

MacFarlane, David, 2018, 'The Fitzpatrick Conspiracy: Part IV' <https://nedkelly unmasked.com/2018/08/the-fitzpatrick-conspiracy-part-four/>, accessed 16 November 2021

MacFarlane, David, 2020, 'The Actual True Story of Ned Kelly: Part VI: Stringybark Creek Police Murders', <https://nedkellyunmasked.com/2020/05/lonigansdeath/>, accessed 16 November 2021

Marsden, Elizabeth, 2014, 'The police perspective', in Craig Cormick (ed.), *Ned Kelly: Under the microscope*, Collingwood: CSIRO, pp. 187–98

Morrissey, Doug, 1995, 'Ned Kelly and horse and cattle stealing', *Victorian Historical Journal*, vol. 66, no. 1, 1995, pp. 29–48

Scott, Susy, 1980, 'The Kelly Gang at Euroa', in John Meredith & Bill Scott (eds), *Ned Kelly: After a century of acrimony*, Sydney: Lansdowne Press

Senyard, J.E., 1972, 'Glass, Hugh (1817–1871)', *Australian Dictionary of Biography*, <https://adb.anu.edu.au/biography/glass-hugh-3620>, accessed 16 November 2021

Thorogood, Gordon J., 2014, 'The science of the Kelly Gang's armour: Distilling fact from fiction', in Craig Cormick (ed.), *Ned Kelly: Under the microscope*, Collingwood: CSIRO, pp. 131–44

Books

Baron, A.N., *Blood in the Dust: Inside the minds of Ned Kelly and Joe Byrne*, Greensborough, Victoria: Network Creative Services. 2004

Castles, Alex C., & Castles, Jennifer, 2005, *Ned Kelly's Last Days: Setting the record straight on the death of an outlaw*, Sydney: Allen & Unwin

Corfield, Justin, 2003, *The Ned Kelly Encyclopaedia*, South Melbourne: Lothian

Dawson, Stuart, 2018, *Ned Kelly and the Myth of a Republic of North-Eastern Victoria*, Clayton (Vic): Dawson

de Serville, Paul, 1991, *Pounds and Pedigrees: The upper class in Victoria 1850–1880*, South Melbourne: Oxford University Press Australia

Haldane, Robert, 2017, *The People's Force: A history of Victoria Police (3rd ed.)*, Carlton: Melbourne University Press

Hall, Arthur & Stevens, Julie, 2005, *James Wallace, 1854–1910: The headmaster of Hurdle Creek*, Victoria: Arthur W. Hall

Hall, George W., 1879, *The Kelly Gang, or The Outlaws of the Wombat Ranges*, Mansfield: G.W. Hall, Transcribed with annotations by Stuart Dawson, 2017, <https://guten-berg.net.au/ebooks19/1900581p.pdf>

Hare, Francis Augustus, 1894, *The Last of the Bushrangers: An account of the capture of the Kelly Gang*, London: Hurst and Blackett

Jones, Ian, 2003, *The Fatal Friendship: Ned Kelly, Aaron Sherritt and Joe Byrne*, Melbourne: Lothian Books

Jones, Ian, 2008, *Ned Kelly: A short life,* Sydney: Hachette

Kennedy, Leo & Looby, Mick, 2018, *Black Snake: The real story of Ned Kelly*, South Melbourne: Affirm Press

Macfarlane, Ian, 2012, *The Kelly Gang Unmasked,* Melbourne: Oxford University Press

McIntyre, Thomas, ca. 1922, *A True Narrative of the Kelly Gang,* unpublished, held by the Victoria Police Museum, VPM 2991

McNicoll, Ronald, 1988, *Number 36 Collins Street: Melbourne Club 1838–1988*, Sydney: Allen & Unwin

McQuilton, John, 1979, *The Kelly Outbreak 1878–1880: The geographical dimension of social banditry*, Carlton: Melbourne University Press

Morrissey, Doug, 2015, *Ned Kelly: A lawless life, with an introduction by John Hirst*, Redland Bay, Qld: Connor Court Publishing

Morrissey, Doug, 2018, *Ned Kelly: Selectors, squatters and stock thieves*, Redland Bay, Qld: Connor Court Publishing

Sadleir, John, 1913, *Recollections of a Victorian Police Officer*, Melbourne: George Robertson & Co.

Terry, Paul, 2012, *The True Story of Ned Kelly's Last Stand: New revelations unearthed about the bloody siege at Glenrowan*, Sydney: Allen & Unwin

The Australian handbook and almanac and shippers' and importers' directory for 1880, 1879, London: Gordon & Gotch

Woods, Carol, 1985, *Beechworth: A titan's field,* North Melbourne: Hargreane

Police Royal Commission

Police Commission, *Minutes of Evidence taken before the Royal Commission into the Police Force in Victoria, together with Appendices*, Melbourne: Government Printer, 1881

Police Commission, *Police Special Report on the Detective Force*, Melbourne: Government Printer, 1881

Police Commission, *Second Progress Report of the Royal Commission of Enquiry into the Circumstances of the Kelly Outbreak*, Melbourne: Government Printer, 1881

Websites

The following independent websites have been helpful:
denheldid.com
ironoutlaw.com
kellygang.asn.au
nedkellyunmasked.com

Index